D0873138

THE
SYNOPTIC
GOSPELS

THE
SYNOPTIC
GOSPELS

With an Introduction by
Scot McKnight

John Riches, William R. Telford
and Christopher M. Tuckett

Sheffield Academic Press
www.SheffieldAcademicPress.com

BS
2555.2
.R49
2001

Part I originally published by Sheffield Academic Press 1996 as John Riches, *Matthew* (New Testament Guides, 1)

Part II originally published by Sheffield Academic Press 1995 as William R. Telford, *Mark* (New Testament Guides, 2)

Part III originally published by Sheffield Academic Press 1996 as Christopher M. Tuckett, *Luke* (New Testament Guides, 3)

New Testament Guides General Editor A.T. Lincoln

Copyright © 2001 Sheffield Academic Press

Published by
Sheffield Academic Press Ltd
Mansion House
19 Kingfield Road
Sheffield S11 9AS
England

www.SheffieldAcademicPress.com

Typeset by Steve Barganski
and
Printed on acid-free paper in Great Britain by
MPG Books Limited,
Bodmin, Cornwall

British Library Cataloguing in Publication Data

A catalogue record for this book is available from the British Library

ISBN 1-84127-210-8

CONTENTS

Abbreviations   7

An Invitation to the Synoptic Gospels   9
    Scot McKnight

Part I

MATTHEW
John Riches

Further Reading on Matthew   42

1. Leading Questions in Matthaean Scholarship   43
2. What Sort of a Book?   53
3. Matthew's World   74
4. Matthew's Christology   109
5. Conclusion   125

Part II

MARK
William R. Telford

Commentaries on Mark   128

1. Introduction   131
2. Mark as History: The Gospel as a Historical Document   151
3. Mark as Literature: The Gospel as a Literary Composition   192
4. Mark as Theology: The Gospel as a Religious Text   221
5. Conclusion   244

138004

Part III

LUKE
Christopher M. Tuckett

Commentaries and General Works on Luke's Gospel   252

1.	Introduction	254
2.	Eschatology	272
3.	Jews, Gentiles and Judaism	286
4.	The Person and Work of Jesus	304
5.	Luke and the Christian Life: Poverty and Possessions	323
6.	Concluding Hermeneutical Reflections	337

Index of References   343
Index of Authors   356

ABBREVIATIONS

AB	Anchor Bible
ABD	David Noel Freedman (ed.), *The Anchor Bible Dictionary* (New York: Doubleday, 1992)
ABRL	Anchor Bible Reference Library
ANRW	Hildegard Temporini and Wolfgang Haase (eds.), *Aufstieg und Niedergang der römischen Welt: Geschichte und Kultur Roms im Spiegel der neueren Forschung* (Berlin: W. de Gruyter, 1972–)
BBB	Bonner biblische Beiträge
BETL	Bibliotheca ephemeridum theologicarum lovaniensium
Bib	*Biblica*
BNTC	Black's New Testament Commentaries
BibRes	*Biblical Research*
BTB	*Biblical Theology Bulletin*
BZ	*Biblische Zeitschrift*
BZNW	Beihefte zur *ZNW*
CBQ	*Catholic Biblical Quarterly*
CBQMS	*Catholic Biblical Quarterly*, Monograph Series
CGTC	Cambridge Greek Testament Commentary
DBI	R.J. Collins, J.L. Houlden (eds.), *The Dictionary of Biblical Interpretation* (London: SCM Press; Philadelphia: Trinity Press International, 1990).
EKKNT	Evangelisch-Katholischer Kommentar zum Neuen Testament
EvT	*Evangelische Theologie*
ExpTim	*Expository Times*
HNT	Handbuch zum Neuen Testament
HTKNT	Herders theologischer Kommentar zum Neuen Testament
HTR	*Harvard Theological Review*
ICC	International Critical Commentary
IDB	George Arthur Buttrick (ed.), *The Interpreter's Dictionary of the Bible* (4 vols.; Nashville: Abingdon Press, 1962)
IDBSup	*IDB*, Supplementary Volume
Int	*Interpretation*
JAAR	*Journal of the American Academy of Religion*
JBL	*Journal of Biblical Literature*

JSNT	*Journal for the Study of the New Testament*
JSNTSup	*Journal for the Study of the New Testament*, Supplement Series
JTS	*Journal of Theological Studies*
MeyerK	H.A.W. Meyer (ed.), Kritisch-exegetischer Kommentar über das Neue
Neot	*Neotestamentica*
NICNT	New International Commentary on the New Testament
NIGTC	The New International Greek Testament Commentary
NovT	*Novum Testamentum*
NovTSup	*Novum Testamentum*, Supplements
NPNF	Nicene and Post-Nicene Fathers
NRSV	New Revised Standard Version
NTS	*New Testament Studies*
Peake	M. Black and H.H. Rowley (eds.), Peake's Commentary on the Bible (London: Thomas Nelson, 1962).
PTMS	Pittsburgh Theological Monograph Series
RNT	Regensburger Neues Testament
SBLDS	SBL Dissertation Series
SBLMS	SBL Monograph Series
SBT	Studies in Biblical Theology
SNTSMS	Society for New Testament Studies Monograph Series
TLZ	*Theologische Literaturzeitung*
TRu	*Theologische Rundschau*
WBC	Word Biblical Commentary
WUNT	Wissenschaftliche Untersuchungen zum Neuen Testament

AN INVITATION TO THE SYNOPTIC GOSPELS

Scot McKnight

An Apology for the Synoptic Gospels

The Gospels should be to the Christian what the Pentateuch is to the orthodox Jew—the foundation of theology and the ground upon which the rest of the (in the Christian case) Christian superstructure stands. I do not thereby demean the rest of the 'canon' and assign to it a secondary status. Instead, the rest of the New Testament gains its clarity, as the Germans might term it, through 're-actualization' (*Vergegenwärtigung*) of that original Jesus tradition. The starting point of Christian practice and theology is Jesus, who is confessed as Lord. Confessing Jesus as Lord certainly involves considering pre-eminent, listening attentively to, and following his message. Sadly, his teachings and his practices have not always been given the prominence a consistent confession might entail. And so, as we begin the twenty-first century, we are compelled to 'apologize' for the prominent place the Jesus traditions ought to play in the faith of the catholic Church. I mention a few points.

First, in a broad sense Christians 'confess' a *salvation-historical climax in God's work in Jesus*, in the real Jesus who wore sandals in Galilee and in the Jesus who died, rose, and intercedes for his people. Again in a broad sense, Christians confess that the Hebrew Scriptures are the 'Old' Testament because it anticipates in time and message its *telos* in the 'New' Testament, that is, in God's revelation in Jesus Christ. But, in fact, if one examines the theological creeds and confessions, if one examines in fact the fundamentals of the faith as articulated by most Christian denominations—even more, if one simply asks most Christians today, one discovers that Christians, especially those of an evangelical persuasion, know precious little about Jesus' teachings, about what he says about God (they do know he urged his disciples to call God 'Father'), about the Kingdom of God as both present and future, and about his radical call to discipleship. Instead, most Christians operate on the basis of watered-down post-Reformation systematic theology in which theology the teachings of Jesus played an alarmingly small role. If Luther shelved the teachings of Jesus in favor of the dialectical relationship of law and grace, Calvin operated with a more balanced appreciation of the teachings of Jesus—though his classic *Institutes* revolve more on a Pauline (read: Romans) foundation. This post-Reformation history is at least one reason why the Synoptics have been neglected by the Church (though I am aware Protestant Liberalism has carried the banner of Jesus' teachings high at times) and why we need to give more attention to them today.

A second reason is this: never in the history of Western society has the foundation of basic morality, virtue, and ethics been more eroded than in the last half of the twentieth century. I am no weather vane when it comes to social behavior but I do hear those who are—and the voice is unanimous that social conventions are at an all-time low. We are talking here, not about big issues like nuclear warfare and world relief and HIV, but instead about the fundamentals of human inter-action, about civility, and about manners—how we speak to and about one another, how we treat one another, and about how we think about one another. Apart from the glorious morals of the Pen-tateuch and the Prophets, I can think of no collection of books more valuable for reconstructing human virtue than the Synoptic Gospels, and one can make the Sermon on the Mount the epicenter. If that watered-down post-Reformation theology decentralizes the impor-tance of 'works' and 'basic morals' as unnecessary for salvation, even a quick reading of the Synoptic Gospels will re-centralize human behavior as the focus of God's will for his people. Let me say this, however: recent attempts by the conservative right in American politi-cal discussions to re-enter morals into the political discussion are, most often, misguided attempts to resurrect a bygone era. I am not speaking of this when I speak of the value of the Jesus traditions for a reconstruction of morals and virtue. I envision, instead, a refashioning of how we do theology, what role ethics plays in our perception of Christian belief, where we begin our theological constructions, what categories we use for Christian theology, and how we appropriate the kerygma for our society. There is not a better place to begin than in the Synoptic Gospels and, in contrast to what often gets attention under the name of 'discipleship', we may well be surprised what the Gospels say about ethics.

Third, *what is the gospel*? Is the gospel about 'going to heaven', about 'escaping punishment', and about 'exclusive privilege for few (espe-cially Western Caucasians)'? Sadly, Christian triumphalism impedes true perceptions here. I confess to being shamed by what the Church allows itself to say about its basic message at times. Let me ask this same question in another way: 'What was the gospel according to Jesus?' And, is the gospel preached today by the Church the same message Jesus preached? Why, then, are there so few references to 'Kingdom of God' and fewer still to the rigors of discipleship in Christian proclamation? The answer: the gospel today is in need of redefinition because it is gospel that has wandered away from its Lord's original definition and articulation. Where might we begin if we wish to return, as Israel did to the Covenant, to the gospel? Answer: the Jesus traditions, the Gospels. The 'gospel according to Jesus' is about the centrality of God's reign in the lives of his people as they live before him in love, in holiness, in righteousness and as they strive for God's full establishment of his kingdom throughout the world.

Finally, there are more *ecumenical and inter-faith discussions today* that can settle into fruitful discussions by simply examining the figure of Jesus and the structures of his teachings. In 1973 Geza Vermes, a man born Jewish who became a Roman Catholic priest and then 'converted' back to Judaism (see his *Providential Accidents*), published a book on Jesus called *Jesus the Jew* which has shaped and guided fundamental discussions about Jesus ever since. His 'discovery' was that Jesus was after all a Jew; today this is a commonplace, but an important one always in danger of slipping from our grip. Jewish scholarship on Jesus has been studied by D.A. Hagner (*The Jewish Reclamation of Jesus*) and he shows that Christians and Jews have entered a new era of discussion of their deeply related faiths. And within the Church itself some old wounds are showing signs of healing: fractures between Lutherans and Roman Catholics, between 'free churches' like the Anabaptists and 'high churches' like the Church of England, between American mainline denominations and the finely splintered evangelical movement. Each of these fractures claims Jesus as Lord and his teachings as foundational. Discussions that divide can become dialogues that draw together if these dialogues will center on Jesus instead of church polity that has little claim to centrality.

Where can we begin? Before I suggest some 'strategies' for reading the Synoptic Gospels, I shall present a fairly comprehensive survey of the schools of thought and the history of Synoptic scholarship that shape the discussions of the following studies by J. Riches, W.R. Telford, and Christopher M. Tuckett. In so detailing these schools of thought we can have before us an agenda that permits 'Synoptic literacy'. In what follows presently the focus will be on the specific aims of various scholars as they read the Synoptic Gospels—some read for information about the real Jesus, others for information about the specific agendas of the Evangelists themselves, while others seek information about the interpreter's world as well as the individual interpreter's influence on the very act of reading the Synoptics.

Windows Twentieth Century and Beyond

If the Reformation and post-Reformation era, with a noteworthy (if also distinct) voice being found in nineteenth and twentieth century's Protestant Liberalism, were characterized by a systematic theological appropriation of the biblical message in terms of the logic of salvation (creation, fall, death of Christ, justification by faith alone, sanctification, glorification), the last half of the twentieth century shifted dramatically to a focus on *story* in terms of the plot of God's work in Jesus. Accordingly, if the systematic emphasis found in such scholars as John Calvin, Martin Luther, F.D.E. Schleiermacher, Karl Barth, and several influential liberation theologians, filtered its concerns through Romans and the Pauline epistles, the shift to story enabled scholars to shape its concerns around the Gospels, especially the Synoptic Gospels (called 'synoptic' because they follow one another closely in events and can therefore be 'seen together'), if also to the narratives of the Hebrew Bible. When N.T. Wright set out to write an extensive study of the development of early Christianity, he began with a prefatory volume in which 'story' played a prominent role and his work merely exhibits the growing trend to explicate Christian 'truth' by means of *story* (see *The New Testament and the People of God*).

Why *story*? While it is not possible to trace the precise reasons a society, and it involves an entire world, finds meaning in a story, the recent brilliant lectures by Andrew Delbanco, Julian Clarence Levi Professor in the Humanities at Columbia University, offer a penetrating glance into how humans find 'story' significant. In sum, he traces American history as it appropriated three stories—God, citizenship in a sacred union (nation), and self—and concludes that *stories provide hope and meaning to a people*. No story, no hope—just melancholy. The presence of a meaningful, life-orienting story, when pregnant in a society, begets culture and tradition; further, it provides perspective and markers for the journey of life. Cicero, perhaps Rome's greatest orator, expressed this sentiment long ago: 'For what is the worth of human life, unless it is woven into the life of our ancestors by the records of history?' (*Orator* 34.120). It is not the purpose here to trace why Christians of the second half of the twentieth century have turned more to story for articulating the Christian message, for surely the systematic emphasis of yesteryear had its own kind of 'story', but to note instead that the emphasis on truth *qua* story today is manifest. Instead, we shall look at how the story of Jesus as recorded by Mark, Matthew, and Luke has been examined by modern scholars because it was one of these 'stories of Jesus' that shaped the consciousness of many early Christians.

Modern Synoptic specialists examine three dimensions of the Synoptic story: they look *through the window* of the story to find what really happened in history, they look *at the window and its frame* to recognize the narrative art of the author/authors in shaping the story, and they *stare at the window* to find the reflection of their own self and world and story. Each of these deserves comments.

Through the Window and the Quest for the Historical Jesus
First, an explosion of interest in the Synoptic Gospels has taken place since the early 1980s because of the discussion of the 'historical Jesus', an expression used by scholars to distinguish the 'real, sandal-wearing Jesus' from the 'Gospel portrait' of Jesus and the 'Church's belief about Jesus'. At the turn of the century it was concluded by critical scholars that one had to choose between the portrait of Jesus in the Gospel of John or in the Synoptic Gospels, with a massive consensus favoring the latter texts because, as we can say in this context, the windows of John's Gospel were little more than 'stained glass'. The real Jesus can be seen more clearly through the Synoptic windows than through the Johannine 'stained glass'—though discordant voices have made their voices known now and again throughout this century. The most trenchant division occurred in distinguishing the 'historical Jesus' from the 'kerygmatic, biblical Christ that is preached in the Church'.

If some have made their appeal to the 'real, discoverable Jesus' on the basis of their theology, whether a doctrine of Scripture or a christological category, others have done so on the basis of external historical factors, like archaeology, verisimilitude, and historical logic. Those who favor the Synoptics have raided its pages and examined its every word and letter, leading to several distinct portraits of Jesus—including Jesus the religious Sage (M. Borg), Jesus the Prophet (N.T. Wright), and Jesus the Cynic (J.D. Crossan). The debate about 'how' to recover the real Jesus has involved a passage through the tunnel of technical criteria, spelled out most clearly by Norman Perrin, but has emerged onto a broader mesa from which scholars look at Jesus in light of a larger portrait of who he was and what he was like—a theory built on exegesis and historical study, and then, in light of that portrait, a more careful examination of the evidence. This has been the procedure of

B.F. Meyer, E.P. Sanders, R.A. Horsley, G.B. Caird, N.T. Wright and in my own smaller contribution to the question.

'Portrait' is the right word here. Some find the 'window' murky, or at least made of stained glass, perhaps even frosted, while others think the window is clear, if not nearly invisible. If the latter have perhaps too much confidence in a one-to-one correlation between the 'real Jesus' and the 'Synoptic Jesus', the former set of scholars think that we can indeed find Jesus by looking through the window of the Synoptics but the window has been altered enough (by the early church traditions and by the Evangelist) to give us but glimpses and glances of the Jesus who inspired the gospel traditions themselves.

Some of those who look through the window think, however, that the task is daunting and the results quite miniscule. Among such scholarship is the North American Jesus Seminar led by R.W. Funk, so well known because of its success in marketing its ideas and views into the larger populace in the USA. The Jesus Seminar meets regularly to vote on sayings and deeds of Jesus and has published its results in two easy-to-read volumes. In summary, the Jesus Seminar thinks the earliest churches and the Evangelists have bowdlerized the 'real Jesus' and framed a portrait of Jesus substantially inconsistent with the 'real Jesus'. The Evangelists, all of them (especially John), stained the glass so heavily the real Jesus is hard to see. What is more, the entire tradition of Christendom needs to be dismantled in light of a more accurate presentation of who Jesus really was. Confidence, of course, sustains such claims.

Not all think the Evangelists completely bowdlerized the 'real Jesus', however. The dominant use, in fact, of the Synoptic Gospels in the last two decades of the twentieth century is for information about the historical Jesus. Books, articles, pamphlets, even national and international magazine articles as well as lengthy television broadcasts, have each given attention in the last two decades to questions surrounding the 'historical Jesus'. If there is a consensus today it is that the 'real Jesus' was Jewish and needs to be understood in the context of contemporary Judaism. The convergence of interest in Jesus as a Jew and of the development of scholarship on Judaism itself happily provides for scholarship today an explosion of insights into Jesus as it corrects and revises some of the older, more orthodox treatments which virtually lifted Jesus from the human plane of activity. If the Bultmann era (roughly 1920 through the 1950s) cast a dark shadow over the quest of the historical Jesus in what was an essentially systematic re-framing of the Christian 'kerygma', that shadow has now been lifted and we are now in a 'sunny day' for Jesus research. The most notable books in this resurgence of Jesus scholarship are those by G. Vermes, B.F. Meyer, E.P. Sanders, R.A. Horsley, M. Borg, J.D. Crossan, J.P. Meier, and N.T. Wright. The last-mentioned of these scholars has dubbed the new trend the 'Third Quest', with a focus on Jesus as prophet and as emerging naturally from his Jewish context. Not without reason, several scholars have traced a decisive impetus of this quest for Jesus (looking through the window of the Synoptics) to the British scholar, G.B. Caird. Since in the three separate studies that follow less interest is shown in the historical Jesus than in the perspective of the individual Evangelists, I shall turn to the perspectives from which these studies arise.

At the Window and the Rise of Classical Synoptic Criticism

If the historians look through the window as framed by the Evangelists in an attempt to find the 'real Jesus', the earliest focus of Synoptic scholarship in the second half of twentieth century has been to look intently *at the window and its framing* to see how the Evangelists have presented the story itself. This approach, as is abundantly clear in the separate studies of W.R. Telford, John Riches, and Christopher M. Tuckett which follow, seeks to understand how the Evangelist drew on ancient Jesus traditions and then collected those traditions into a new portrait so that the Evangelist could use the traditions to speak to his contemporaries. How is this approach of 'looking at the window' done today?

The Synoptic Problem. It begins with what today we call the *Synoptic Problem*. In brief, the Synoptic Problem arises as a result of careful comparison of the three accounts (especially in comparison with the Gospel of John) and it calls attention to two phenomena: *similarities* between the Synoptic Gospels and *dissimilarities*. The similarities are in fact so astounding at times that one suspects copying or the copying of a common source; the dissimilarities are so consistent in one Gospel to suspect the Evangelist's own influential pen dominated the record. These two phenomena gave birth to a question: which of the Synoptics is most likely the first one? For, it was believed (and still is by most), if we know which is first (priority) and which is second and third we have fundamentally objective clues for interpretation. That is, if Matthew and Luke are copying Mark but diverge from Mark in this or that matter, then the 'this or that matter' is a vital clue to what Matthew and Luke are attempting to communicate as they write their Gospels. And a fundamental notion of this approach to the Gospels is that the authors are attempting to communicate, and their intention is manifest in their work (see F. Watson, *Text and Truth*).

In the eighteenth century an old assumption was questioned (it was the age of such questioning, after all). That assumption was not only that the Gospels are historically perfect depictions of the chronological life of Jesus, but that the order of the Synoptics was maybe not what Augustine thought it was. St Augustine, writing for polemical and philosophical reasons, had contended that the Synoptic Gospels were chronologically written in their canonical order: first Matthew, second Mark, and third Luke. (A recent technical study by David Peabody, however, suggests that Augustine may well have changed his view later to Matthew, Luke, and only then Mark. The evidence of Augustine, I believe, is not quite as clear as Peabody thinks.) Augustine's viewpoint, largely because of the authority of his scholarship as well as the lack of interest in genuinely historical questions of this sort, became the traditional position of the ancient church and tradition is hard to budge. Clearly, one of the earliest to question the view of Augustine was J.J. Griesbach who, in his important study, came to the view that Matthew was the earliest Gospel, Luke was derived from Matthew, and then Mark came along to summarize and synthesize these two great Gospel stories of Jesus. This view has come to be called the 'Griesbach Hypothesis' or, in its more modern terms, the 'Two Gospel Hypothesis'. Griesbach's was a bold step to rearrange Mark and Luke.

Notwithstanding this influential piece of research by Griesbach, other Germans and an influential group of scholars at Oxford overturned this view as well as Augustine's view to articulate what is now called the 'Two Document/Source Hypothesis' or, as I prefer to call it, the 'Oxford Hypothesis'. The most influential Germans were G.C. Storr, K. Lachmann, and H.J. Holtzmann, while the notable English scholars include W. Sanday, J.C. Hawkins and most especially B.H. Streeter. Regardless of the impetus given by eighteenth- and nineteenth-century German scholarship, it was the hands of B.H. Streeter and W. Sanday that gave pristine shape to the theory now known as the 'Oxford Hypothesis'. This view contends, in its final form, that Mark was the first Gospel written and that Matthew, adding two sources to Mark (Q and M), and Luke, also adding two sources (Q and L), composed their Gospels to adapt the Markan Gospel to their contexts. In this theory, 'M' means 'material unique to Matthew taken from one source' and 'L' means 'material unique to Luke taken from one source'. Scholarship, however, has backed off considerably from Streeter's confidence in the 'M' and 'L' sources and has instead seen both of these as 'fluent traditions' rather than specific documents.

(Incidentally, Streeter both dated them and assigned them to a geographical location.)

The major arguments used for this theory, as formulated by B.H. Streeter himself, are as follows:

1. that the content of Mark, Matthew, and Luke is substantially the same;
2. that the wording of individual pericopes is similar in the Synoptics;
3. that the order of Mark is followed by Matthew and Luke and when one departs from that order the other follows that order.

An important dimension of this theory, now taking on a life so vital and speculative, is that Matthew and Luke each used independently a collection of the sayings of Jesus we now call 'Q'. If 'Q' is a well-deserved conclusion for best explaining the relationship of Matthew and Luke, the attraction to 'Q' of so many speculative theories is undeserved. The 'Q' hypothesis remains an important element in an overall solution to the Synoptic Problem: Matthew and Luke evidently used a common source but used that source independently.

The 'Oxford Hypothesis' is by far the most widely held theory on the origins of the Synoptic Gospels, though the Griesbach theory has found two thorough defenses in the second half of this century: W.R. Farmer and D.L. Dungan, both of whom have operated a salvage operation of Griesbach's hypothesis with admirable detail and scholarly grace. More importantly, their work on the Synoptic Problem has pointed out the weaknesses of argument, logic, and evidence as fashioned by the proponents of the 'Oxford Hypothesis' and has led to a resurgence of careful work examining and defending that theory, seen especially in the important research of Christopher M. Tuckett. However incisive their criticisms at times, the Griesbach scholars and their students shall remain but an enclave until they can compellingly explain the linguistic data.

Those linguistic data involve a simple observation: if we are given a copy of Mark, Matthew, and Luke where they each record a similar event or saying in the life of Jesus, we are permitted to ask the simple question, derived from the science of textual criticism (the science of attempting to find the most original text when more than one text exists), 'Which is most likely the origin of the others?' It is the answer to this question, a question about objective linguistic data, that tips the balance heavily and quickly in favor of the 'Oxford Hypothesis'. I am not alone in defending the view that the linguistic data alone permit scientific analysis and a true weighing of probabilities on which Gospel is more likely the original. One example shall suffice. I record the texts in separate columns from Mt. 15.29 and Mk 7.31:

Matthew	Mark
Jesus left there and went along the Sea of Galilee.	Then Jesus left the vicinity of Tyre and went through Sidon, down to the Sea of Galilee and into the region of the Decapolis.

This evidence, a verse from Matthew and Mark describing the same relocation by Jesus, can be examined with the following question: 'Which is more likely—that Matthew has altered Mark or that Mark has altered Matthew?' According to the standard canons of textual criticism, it is more likely that Matthew has abbreviated Mark than that Mark has expanded Matthew. Why? Matthew's text is perfectly sensible: Jesus left Tyre and Sidon and then retired to some (unspecified) location near the Sea of Galilee. Mark's text, however, is at best unclear, at worst confusing: Jesus leaves Tyre through Sidon (along the coast of the ultra-chic Med) and retires to the Sea of Galilee in the middle of the Decapolis. A trip southeast begins by going north and then lands in the Sea of Galilee region by going even further southeast. I am not saying the latter trip is impossible—I have seen such things happen by vacationers who perambulate wherever they might wish with no timetable—but what I am saying is this: if we have two texts like this and ask which is most likely the original (assuming that they are related, and Gospels scholars are nearly unanimous on this one) we come to one conclusion: it is more likely that Matthew simplified Mark than that Mark took Matthew's perfectly straightforward route and turned it into a vacation of wandering around!

Redaction Criticism. Once it was agreed that Mark was first and Matthew and Luke secondary but combining Mark with some other traditions and sources, scholarship was keen on looking through Mark, now the earliest Gospel, to the life of Jesus. But it was not just historical Jesus studies that profited from the 'Oxford Hypothesis'. This preoccupation of the Synoptic Problem with the chronological relationship gave birth to a productive step-child: a focus on *what the authors of the individual Gospels were doing to the traditions they inherited, in particular, what Matthew and Luke were doing to Mark.* Thus, research into the Synoptic Problem gave rise to *redaction criticism*, a method of Gospel criticism that examines the window, its frame and its contours as clues to the builder's theories. In short, it examines how the Evangelist 'hung his window' for his church and his audience. It asks not only who is the origin for the other (the Synoptic Problem) but *what the Evangelists Matthew and Luke did to Mark, why they did what they did, and what their changes tell us about their communities.* (Of course, the Griesbach Hypothesis also implies the same redaction-critical method — concrete observations of what later Evangelists did to their sources — but this theory finds Mark as a 'conflator' of Matthew and Luke with all the theological implications that follow from such a conclusion. And it is only recently that Griesbachians have been offering such studies [see Farmer, *The Gospel of Jesus*]. This introduction to the three studies that follow follows the slant of those books: it assumes the general correctness of the 'Oxford Hypothesis' and makes no attempt to balance those treatments by redressing the issue.)

This focus on the Evangelists' distinct crystallizing of the traditions has a long history, harking back to Tatian and Augustine, but owing its particular contributions to the redaction critics of the middle of this century, namely Hans Conzelmann, Günther Bornkamm, and Willi Marxsen. When we speak of an Evangelist 'crystallizing' the tradition at hand we mean that the Evangelist has (1) used other Jesus traditions, say the Gospel of Mark or 'Q', (2) added to those traditions some other traditions no longer available to us apart from higher levels of speculation (say, 'M' or 'L'), and (3) *shaped* the new product in such a way that the 'Gospel' speaks to his particular community about its own specific issues and concerns. The result of this process, called 'redacting', is a Gospel tailored by a single mind (the Evangelist) for a special community (the Evangelist's church community). To be sure, the process was more complex — perhaps stages of redaction, perhaps more than one community, perhaps less than a full community and more by an author for another person, and what not. Nonetheless, the direction of this hypothesis has sustained two or three generations of scholarship.

What are the results? I shall answer this in two ways: first, with general observations and then, second, with an example or two from each of the Synoptics. By way of general observation, *redaction criticism has unmasked the Evangelist and his theology.* (I continue to use 'his' instead of 'her' because presumption and early Church traditions are in favor of a male author in the first century. I should be happy to discover that Matthew was written by a 'Martha'!) Instead of our perception of the Synoptics as 'bald, anonymous histories of Jesus' life', redaction criticism has forced interpreters to take into consideration the 'bias' of the individual Evangelist. Some, in fact, have contended that the shaping was so strong that the life of Jesus was actually obscured in the process. For example, the fierce debates we discover in Mt. 23 between Jesus and the Pharisees (along with the scribes) has been argued, at times, to derive more from Matthew's own day than from Jesus' day. Hence, we learn more about *Matthew's* view of the Pharisees than Jesus'. In short, redaction criticism forces interpreters to take seriously the *author and his text*, a concern that was neglected in the classical studies of form and source criticism, where more attention was focused on the prehistory of the text and the historical Jesus.

Second, *redaction criticism unmasks a period in church history to which we previously had little or no access*. If the redaction critic is able to show, for instance, that Luke's theology is directed much more in the direction of social justice, then we are probably on safe ground arguing that such a concern is part and parcel of Luke's community. Through such an inferential procedure, then, we are able to establish hypotheses and trends and theological concerns of the community behind Luke's Gospel. Learning about the earliest churches, or at least about the three communities behind the Synoptics, fills in information about the development of the early church and enables historians to grasp more concretely the living concerns of earliest Christianity and how it appropriated in different ways the living traditions about Jesus.

Third, *redaction criticism unmasks how early Christians treated the Jesus traditions*. In short, it becomes clear that the earliest Christians were not afraid of adjusting the sayings and deeds of Jesus for a new day; put differently, the traditional sayings of Jesus were not 'red letter words' but a living, evolving, and adapting religious tradition. If Mark can say that Peter said Jesus was 'Messiah', then Matthew can develop that further—no doubt in light of his own christological views—and contend that he was not just 'Messiah', but also 'the Son of the living God' (cf. Mk 8.29 and Mt. 16.16; Lk. 9.20 has a clipped 'the Messiah of God'). A significant implication of unmasking how early Christians treated the Jesus traditions is that we learn more about the *genre* of the Synoptic Gospels. While I am reasonably convinced that the Synoptics remain with the general rubric of 'biographies', that does not mean 'chronological life of Jesus *tout simple*'. In fact, the Synoptics are shown by redaction criticism to be biographical (some kind of life of Jesus), kerygmatic (exhorting Christians), didactic (teaching Christians), polemical (criticizing opponents), and apologetic (defending Christian beliefs). Lots of motives are swirling around in a Synoptic Gospel. If some feel that this approach robs the Gospels of a supernatural dimension, it might be argued that in the place of a simplistic concept of 'inspiration' one finds instead 'the realism of how God worked'. What we surrender in chronology we gain in accuracy. We learn most of all that we need to let the Synoptics be the Synoptics.

Besides these three general observations, we need also to provide *examples* of how redaction criticism shapes our understanding of the Synoptics. Redaction criticism thrives on two kinds of observations: (1) detailed changes to Mark or Q which invite exploration into larger motives and (2) overall compositional patterns of each of the Evangelists. Mark tells us (6.51-52) that, after Jesus had walked on the water, the disciples did not understand the loaves because their hearts had been (divinely) hardened. *In the same location*, Matthew tells us that, after Jesus had walked on the water, those who were in the boat (the disciples, perhaps) worshiped and said, 'Truly, this was God's Son!' (14.33). A detailed observation, true. Capable of harmonious explanation? I suppose one could say that the 'confessional' stance of Matthew is less than adequate (after all, the noun 'son' is anarthrous and not 'the Son'). But, more realistically, we are led to explore Mark's attitude to the disciples versus Matthew's attitude—and the results are not meager. Matthew consistently presents the disciples in more favorable light in contrast to Mark who seems to be incurably harsh on the disciples of Jesus; a clue, perhaps, to Mark's and Matthew's larger strategies? I think so. This is the type of observation that we glean from a redaction-critical approach to the Synoptic Gospels. Mark's 'redactional orientation' will begin our specific examples of redaction criticism.

Here is, in my judgment, a reasonable summary of Mark's purpose: *Jesus Christ is the Son of God but is not, indeed cannot be, understood until he is understood as the suffering, crucified Son of God who will be vindicated by God the Father.* Several implications flow from this general understanding, and many others could be mentioned: (1) the so-called 'secrecy' of Mark's Gospel is best explained on the basis of Mark's larger purpose of postponing a full identity of Jesus until he is seen as one who is crucified; (2) the failure of the disciples, so prominent in Mark's Gospel, is also a correlate of his Christology: since Jesus cannot be understood until the cross, the disciples *could not have* understood Jesus prior to that cross; (3) the prominence of the cross in Mark's Gospel, with that special urgency he shows in getting Jesus to the cross as well as the space he gives to the passion week, reveals dramatically the purpose of the Second Gospel—the whole Gospel is shaped by a Christology of suffering; (4) scholars have long debated where Mark's Gospel originally ended—at 16.8 or did we lose a page?—but the christological focus, shaped as it is by the cross, may well explain why and how Mark's Gospel ended at 16.8—there is no need for a resurrection (even if it is anticipated at several crucial junctures in the Markan journey; e.g., 8.31) if the focus is to show a

crucified Messiah as the secret revelation of God; (5) finally, discipleship in Mark takes its cue from Christology: if Jesus is a suffering
Messiah (8.31), then discipleship, too, must also be a suffering following of Jesus (8.34). It follows, also, that a suffering followed by
vindication for Jesus (8.38–9.1) implies a similar vindication for those
who follow the suffering Messiah (8.34-38). Some have even suggested that, at the polemical level, Mark was battling those who
refused to embrace the logic of a crucified Messiah who, instead, em-
braced nothing but a glorious, miracle-working Jesus. Such a suggestion is as close as we perhaps shall ever be in coming to terms with the
motive of an Evangelist in his context.

It is with this orientation, I suggest, that Mark set out to write his
work. Accordingly, we should not ask questions about historicity or
about historical context or about systematic theology until we have let
the 'story' of Mark shape our understanding of his texts. To be sure,
this is a 'bias' revealed in his pen—he had an angle on telling the
'story of Jesus', but angles are not necessarily distortions. Furthermore, if we are truly honest, all 'stories' are biased, and there is no
way to tell anything about anyone without selecting items to tell—a
selection that emerges from a bias. Redaction criticism is designed to
show us the author's 'bias'. In the mordant words of E.B. White, perhaps America's greatest essayist, 'I have yet to see a piece of writing,
political or non-political, that doesn't have a slant. All writing slants
the way a writer leans, and no man is born perpendicular', and then
laconically, 'although many men are born upright' (*The Essays of E.B.
White* [New York: Harper & Row, 1977], p. 104.). Our Synoptic writers,
so I think, lean and tilt while I think also that they do not fall all over
themselves!

Luke's 'bias' is different and a thematic statement's emphases
reveal the differences between Luke's and Mark's story: *Jesus, the Messiah, is empowered by the Holy Spirit and fulfills the Old Testament Law and
prophets so that he can proclaim salvation to those who repent (especially
those drawn out of the corners and cracks of society) but he is rejected by
Israel and its religious leaders so he pronounces a historical judgment on
Jerusalem prior to his vindication by resurrection.* Since the reigning
hypothesis sees Luke dependent on Mark (and 'Q'), I shall make
observations that highlight what Luke has 'done' to Mark's Gospel.
First, Luke embraces much of Mark's Gospel though he shifts the
emphasis from cross to vindication and glory. Second, Luke washes
into his portrait of Jesus a much greater focus on the power of the
Holy Spirit, and readers of the New Testament will know that the
Acts of the Apostles so carried this theme throughout its pages that it

influenced Luke when he wrote his Gospel. Third, Luke throws special Rembrandt-like light onto the concept of 'salvation', though Luke's perception of that term is less forensic than Paul's and less cruciform than Mark's. Fourth, Luke's Gospel is noteworthy in its concern with social outcasts and, to carry the notion further, he has a penchant for personal anecdotes and stories. Luke is responsible for telling us about Zechariah and Elizabeth, Mary and Joseph, Anna and Simeon, not to forget also the worthy and honorable centurion, the Good Samaritan, the ungrateful (but one!) lepers, Zacchaeus, and the widow who knocked on the judge's door until she got what she wanted. If the author is not a physician (as tradition has it), then he should have been a psychologist for all his observations about personalities. Fifth, though hardly distinctive to Luke, the recording of Jesus' prediction of the destruction of the Temple gains in Luke, no doubt through some hindsight, a realistic clarity not otherwise seen in Mark (or Matthew); cf. Lk. 21.8-31 and pars.

If the theological shape of the Evangelist's perspective is a primary result of redaction criticism, an even further development is the placing of such a perspective into its *historical context*. Recent study of Matthew, for instance, notes the obvious polemic Matthew engages with the Jewish leaders (a rough label for the Pharisees, sometimes involving also the scribes) and asks what period in Jewish history this reflects. Questions like, 'Was the title Rabbi used in the first century — early, middle, late?' and 'Does Matthew's use of that title indicate that he has transposed the words of Jesus for a later occasion?' Even more: is Matthew's Gospel a reflection of a special form of Christianity? Is it a Jewish form of Christianity? Or is it a Christian form of Judaism? Where do we locate Matthew in the gradual emergence of earliest Christianity? Eventually, of course, the two faiths split away from one another, creating the emergence of orthodoxy as well as the foundations of rabbinic Judaism. Does Matthew's Gospel reflect a split, does it anticipate the split, or does it pre-date that split? To use the important category of James D.G. Dunn, does Matthew's Gospel reflect the 'parting of the ways'? Because of the sheer force of Matthew's language, Matthew's Gospel has become a bit of a showcase text for examination of such a historical question in light of his redactional perspective.

The question is wide ranging, involving mastery of both Christian and Jewish history, the ancient Jewish texts, as well as a dollop of sociology. Two recent studies share the front stage, those of G.N. Stanton and A.J. Saldarini. Saldarini argues that Matthew's community is a Jewish-Christian community, not yet separated from Judaism, even though contemporary (non-Christian) Jews label these 'messianic Jews' as 'deviants'. What makes Saldarini's research so commendable is its balancing act: here we find an examination of a critical question (Matthew's relationship to Judaism) that involves historical and theological gravity as well as a sifting of the evidence in light of questions about anti-Semitism, the diversity of Judaism, as well as the development of the early churches. G.N. Stanton's essay, published in the noble *Aufstieg und Niedergang der römischen Welt* series, contends that Matthew's community is in fact separated from Judaism but, in spite of that distance, still defines itself and shapes its identity over against Judaism (rather than, say, over against other Christian groups). Stanton's essay, designed as a *Forschungbericht* of recent studies in the Gospel of Matthew, deserves credit for formulating the question and shaping an answer in the context of the emerging consensus of the most recent scholarship.

Recent scholarship aside, what is the primary evidence used for such a question? In fact, it can be asked rather boldly if it is possible to know *when* the evidence in the Gospel of Matthew is speaking more historically (Jesus argued with the Pharisees) than contemporarily (Matthew is arguing with the Pharisees)? Most scholars today would argue that we can know, even if rather tentatively and only at a level of probability—though many do not hesitate to speak in bolder terms! Once again, redactional features become the key evidence: when Matthew makes detailed changes to his sources (Mark, 'Q', 'M') and when these changes add up to a consistent and significant pattern the scholar concludes we are onto something. For an example, there can be no gainsaying that Matthew consistently edits his sources in the direction of polemics with the Pharisees. In a 'Q' tradition about John the Baptist, we are told (by Lk. 3.7) that it was the 'crowds' who approached John and heard his stinging words about vipers and the need to show repentance in good works. But, in Matthew, it is not the 'crowds' but, instead, 'many of the Pharisees and Sadducees' who approached Jesus (Mt. 3.7). A detailed change; perhaps important, but maybe an innocent change. But, when we examine this change in the context of Matthew's other emphases on the Pharisees we become convinced that we are on sure ground to argue that Matthew has 'colored the crowds' to serve his purpose of criticizing the Pharisees for their false leadership.

And from this observation of emphasizing criticism of the Pharisees, and exegeting all the texts so involved (e.g., 5.20; 6.1-18; 9.9-17; 9.32-34; 12.1-8, etc.), scholarship next asks about the historical context. The question for Matthean scholarship has been narrowed to asking if

Matthew is *intra muros* or *extra muros* (inside the larger parent body of Judaism or outside of it) and it is this kind of evidence that is used to answer the question. In addition, there is the intriguing, but slightly ambiguous, use of 'their' with 'synagogues' in Matthew (e.g., 4.23). Does this 'their' mean 'their synagogues—as opposed to ours', 'their synagogues—as opposed to our churches', or 'their synagogues—as opposed to our not having any place to gather for worship'? And, to top this question off, just when did the synagogue get its real beginning? Was it a functioning place of worship in the Galilee of the first century of the Common Era? The evidence is not yet clear and is currently being discussed. However intriguing, the historical questions emerging from redaction-critical conclusions are frequently messy.

These 'leanings' of Mark, Luke, and Matthew eventually led scholarship in the Synoptics to embrace a composition-critical approach and, in so doing, much less attention was given to the 'through the window' approach as well as to the Synoptic Problem as it shaped the classical redaction-critical approach. Instead of asking 'how Matthew changed Mark', or how 'Luke redacted "Q"', a newer set of questions was being asked, and these questions pertaining to author's strategy, textual plot, and reader appropriations led to a massive explosion of interdisciplinary studies. Questions were much less concerned with what the editors did than with what the Evangelists as authors say in the context of their whole Gospel, regardless of the sources of their various words and lines. It is to these approaches that I now turn.

Aesthetic Criticisms. In this century Synoptic studies have moved from a strictly life-of-Jesus approach, through which method the Synoptics were seen as more-or-less chronological lives of Jesus, through the intense examination of the sources and forms behind the Synoptics, on to a fruitful examination of the Evangelists' reshaping of earlier traditions to speak to their context and now into a phase where 'less is more': where less knowledge of the prehistory of the text is permitted for exegesis and where the 'more' of knowing the text itself and how it is shaped and how it impacts its readers is the desired approach. These approaches, including narrative, rhetorical, genre, and literary methods, take a self-consciously negative stand over against the older 'through the window' and redaction-critical orientations of an 'at the window' approach. Instead, these approaches fundamentally are asking, *What goes on in a text as a reader puts the text to a test in a reading?* Once again, however, there is a spectrum and I shall begin with approaches that, while they are not strictly redaction critical, are still fundamentally concerned with an 'at the window' approach and then

I shall move on to see those studies that are more seriously concerned
with the 'reflecting window' approach.

In my assessment (and I have lived through this stage as a student
and professor), the most significant 'hinge figure' in the development
from a classical redaction-critical approach to a more composition-
critical as well as literary-critical approach is Jack Dean Kingsbury,
erstwhile Professor at Union Theological Seminary in Virginia. Kingsbury's books are models of clarity, argument, and rigorous limitation
of the evidence to what can be known from the text of Matthew itself.
Furthermore, Kingsbury began his work in Basel, under Bo Reicke, on
the Gospel of Matthew in an atmosphere of classical redaction criticism in the early 1960s. (Jack once told me he went for a walk in Basel,
early in his studies with little direction on what topic to choose, and
came back from that walk determined to examine the parable chapter
of Matthew.) That early book on the parables of Mt. 13 (*The Parables of
Jesus in Matthew 13*) led him to further redaction-critical studies, which
climaxed in a monograph on Matthew's structure, Christology, and
salvation-history which shaped Matthean scholarship for nearly two
decades (*Matthew: Structure, Christology, Kingdom*). At this point, however, Kingsbury was not strictly a 'classical redaction critic', largely
(so it seems to me) because he was not as confident in the conclusions
of source critics as others might be when it came to minute redaction-
critical observations, but was moving in the direction of a broader
approach to the Gospel of Matthew: a composition-critical approach
(now connected especially in its origins with Ernst Haenchen). This
approach, finding the redactional reshapings of Matthew useful as a
starting point, delves more deeply into the surface meaning of the text
and so broadens the discussion to more than just minute redactional
changes. Whatever Matthew said was game for theological analysis
rather than just the changes Matthew made.

It was this composition-critical approach that led Kingsbury to his
narrative studies of Matthew that have so influenced the American
scene of Matthean scholarship. In 1986 Kingsbury published *Matthew
as Story* (2nd edn, 1988) and it is here that his narrative approach
revealed itself. The question was no longer 'what has Matthew done
to Mark, "Q", and/or "M"?' but instead, 'what does the text of Matthew say as a text'? Once again, Kingsbury's previous approach was
not purely redaction critical in that he was more of a composition
critic, but the shift he made was noteworthy. Substantively, Kingsbury's theological perception did not change (Matthew's Christology
was still a 'Son of God' Christology, etc.) but his orientation did, and
with that orientation an entirely new set of questions began to be

asked and a new scholarship surrounding Matthew arose, and the chief vehicle for this discussion was the Matthew Section of the Society of Biblical Literature which Kingsbury led admirably into these new questions.

If previous studies necessarily began with questions of how the Evangelists treated their sources, the newer studies eschewed such questions (R.C. Tannehill, for example, said they no longer mattered for the *interpretation* of the text of Luke), and examined such issues as character, plot, and how the community was presented in the text. Furthermore, such studies dropped an interest in the historical context shaping our perceptions of its meaning. If history was 'dropped' at this point in favor of a literary approach to the Synoptic Gospels, it was nearly the same time that an interest in the historical Jesus also emerged, leading some Synoptic scholars to drop out of the literary discussion and pursue questions about the historical Jesus.

Those who did follow the aesthetic line (asking questions about the 'art' of the Synoptic texts — and no longer necessarily about the 'real' historical author) pursued another set of questions: what is the 'story' of Matthew, or Mark, or Luke? Questions about 'story', as developed by Seymour Chatman (who was first used, as far as I can see, by D. Rhoads and D. Michie), involve questions about 'events', 'characters', and 'settings' and these as set forth by a 'narrator' who has a 'style', 'point of view', and 'standards of judgment' all woven together into a 'plot'. It gets more complex: the author, who previously was a real person (sometimes even considered to be identical to the name of the traditional ascription!), was now split into three sorts: 'real', 'implied', or as 'narrator'. Instead of 'community' or 'audience', the intended readership of the text was now examined as 'real' and 'implied' readers.

The obvious advantage of this development in Synoptic studies was that the text *qua* text was given integrity again and rescued from the hands of those who were only concerned with finding their way 'through' the text to Jesus or who were concerned more specifically only with the 'redactional features' of the text. For the aesthetic critics, however, the text was to be left alone and *read as a text*, and for many it was to be read as one is taught to read modern novels. In other words, *art form took precedence in interpretation*. Historical, form-critical, source-critical, and redaction-critical questions were to be bracketed off, shelved for the moment (sometimes permanently), to give the reader the experience of seeing what the text says as a literary phenomenon. There can be no question that the historically and redactionally minded scholars could get lost in a maze of mere possibilities and construct large, non-falsifiable theories on the basis of meager contingencies. The aesthetic critics brought many of these theories to their knees. For instance, whether or not Matthew's community was set in an 'upper class' or 'middle class' or 'lower class' may not be answerable—but that did not stop Matthean specialists from speculating about the issues and to build larger theories on the basis of such a conclusion. Mark's theology, for instance, for more than a decade was discussed within the nest of whether or not Mark was battling a *theios aner* christological rival. Whether there was sufficient evidence ever to establish such a Christology led some, however, to fly from that nest to other trees where the shade and protection might be more promising. The aesthetes simply laid these questions to rest and asked others.

Furthermore, this approach gave even more elbowroom to the question of genre: what is a Synoptic Gospel? The discussion of what a 'Gospel' is got a decisive impetus from C.W. Votaw at the turn of this century but it was not until Charles Talbert asked this question anew, with a thorough perception of classical prototypes, that the question of genre was given a scientific orientation. Since Talbert's work several other studies have delved even more deeply into this question, including those of Shuler, Strecker, and Burridge.

Finally, this approach reminds scholars that the *only* acceptable form of reading an ancient text is, first of all, to accept its assumptions, presuppositions, and orientations, rather than forcing the text to answer questions brought to the reading by the interpreter. If the classical critics asked questions that forced an interpreter to see 'through' the text or, at least, to entertain questions not directly addressed by the text (e.g., what church polity is found in the Lukan Gospel), the aesthetic approach rigorously prohibits such questions from being tossed around the table. Instead, the questions are restricted to textual interpretation.

Readings, however, can be given too much credit. If an aesthetic critic claims to be giving, say, Luke a fair reading by looking only at the text, the cynic in all hermeneutical theories raises its head to suggest every reading as emerging from an interpreter's presuppositions. In particular, the historian claims that any reading that methodologically ignores the historical context, whether it be Jewish, Roman, or Christian history, circumvents an accurate reading. The redaction critic contends that ignoring Matthew's or Luke's intentional changes blunts the reading instrument and leads the reader away from what might be highly useful information for understanding a text. After all, they would argue, if Matthew and Luke did use Mark and 'Q', then ignoring such information ignores what the 'real author' was actually doing as he wrote. If the historical critics have had their day, the aesthetic critics do not have the last word. Furthermore, the history of interpretation has proven that 'every age wears its own blinkers'. The Chicago School, in the early decades of the twentieth century, asked questions of the Gospels that impinged on the massive economic-political questions of the day; Protestant Liberals asked questions about social improvement and cultural critique throughout the heart of the twentieth century; University students of the 1960s asked questions about nuclear war and the Christian response to global conflict; and the last decades of the twentieth century saw a set of questions (and, conveniently, answers that meshed with one's hopes) that emerged from its social agendas and cultural questions (economy, meaning, global relationships). I do not pretend to think such questions are unimportant; but the next school of thought I shall discuss has a knack of finding the 'blinkers of every age'.

Staring at the Window and Wirkungsgeschichte *(History of Effects)*
A subtle shift occurs among the aesthetes of Synoptic studies when the window is no longer 'looked at' but used as a 'reflecting glass' on to one's own time or one's own person. The shift involves an act of reading that is considerably more 'self-conscious' than 'text-conscious'. Which is not to say that this dimension of Synoptic criticism is oblivious to the text, even if some critics are tempted to such an accusation. Instead, what takes place is that the interpreter considers her own self-consciousness, as well as her community and society, *as contributing to textual meaning*.

The best place to begin here is with the brilliant insights of Germany's Matthean specialist, Ulrich Luz, in his interpretive method called *Wirkungsgeschichte*. *Wirkungsgeschichte* is an approach to interpreting the Synoptic Gospels (indeed, the entire Bible) that admits up front that the historical situation of the reader and the Bible involve themselves, over time, in a dialectical process of mutual influence — the Bible influencing the person and the society in which that person lives as well as the person and the society influencing how the Bible is read. Once set loose, the text and the interpreter (involving a concrete situation) seek for meaning, discover meaning, and that meaning influences and shapes the community, which influence in turn influences the Bible as well.

Luz's method originates in modern Europe, and Luz himself is specially tuned to the German Lutheran environment and its 'despair' with the results and tediousness of the historical-critical method —

which as a method is concerned with separating the modern reader from the text, finding the original meaning of that text in its specific historical context, and leaving the text naked in that context. Few can approximate the German capacity to describe despair even if one, like Luz, is thoroughly committed to its (limited) usefulness. I quote Luz's general approval: 'the great era of prominent German New Testament scholarship is over' and he sees a 'certain exhaustion' (Luz, *Matthew in History*, p. 5; cf. his items on p. 12). Truly, most readers of the Bible do not do so in order to reconstruct a redactional history of Luke nor do most historical-critical enterprises find much interest in the millions who have read the Bible with profit. *Wirkungsgeschichte* seeks to include the effective use of the Bible. In fact, some have contended that a text has 'no meaning' until it is particularized in a historical reality; meaning and life are fundamentally related. Historical critics may want to know what the social world of Mark looked like but they have no right to usurp the Gospel for that purpose alone.

However, this exhaustion with the historical-critical method not-withstanding, 'the *principle* of historical interpretation of the biblical texts is as firmly advocated [in Germany] as ever' (p. 6). The historical-critical method, according to Luz (and here, of course, he follows the great line of thinkers that began with G.E. Lessing), however, does not lead to truth for truth cannot be found through historical recon-struction. The historical-critical method, to be sure, had one salient feature: it emancipated the text from ecclesiastical dominance. But it was not able to lead the reader to truth. (I would add, however, that both Judaism and Christianity, however much each is committed to a 'canonical faith', structure their faith around certain 'historical events', apart from which both faiths suffer—for example, God's election of Israel, God's redemptive acts in liberating Israel from Pharaoh, in giving to Israel the Land, in guiding Israel back to the Land, and, from the Christian side, God's election of the Church, God's redemptive acts in atoning through the cross, in raising Jesus from the dead, and in granting the Church the Holy Spirit).

Alongside the historical-critical method, a more holistic model is proposed that takes into consideration a more *realistic* perception of what a text is: 'Biblical texts are always secondary to biblical history and to the life of the people of Israel or the early Christian communi-ties' (p. 13). In other words, *life gives birth to text* and apart from that life the text remains dead. This 'life' works both in shaping the origins of a text so that it 'crystallizes' the symbolic story of the community out of which that story comes and the life shapes meaning so that the text comes to life for the community ever anew. For Luz, texts are *sec-*

ondary to events and interpretation within a community; the community gives rise to the text not the text to the community (though a dialectical relationship obtains once the text has been set in motion). If the aesthetic forms of Gospel criticism tilt in the direction of too much textual emphasis, *Wirkungsgeschichte* redresses this balance by appreciating the human realities behind and in the textual witness. In fact, 'Gospel texts are testimonies of the creative power of the transmitted history of Jesus in new situations' and the aesthetic criticisms 'that do not look 'through the window' into the real world of the author and his readers' will be 'of limited value for understanding the biblical texts' (p. 24).

Furthermore, *texts produce meanings over and over in history*. The Gospel of Mark, according to *Wirkungsgeschichte*, does not have one and only one meaning; instead, that text has *the power to produce meanings for individuals, for communities, and for societies over time and in various ways.* The text is not a reservoir that can be emptied of its stagnating water but a well that continually produces new waters of meaning. In summary, Luz argues, a Synoptic text has two layers of meaning: *a kernel meaning* (roughly equivalent to its historical sense) and *a directional meaning* (its sense in a given location in history for a given community). On another occasion he refers to the 'stable' and 'variable' senses. Both are needed for a text to fulfill its function for a community.

Does this not suggest then that a text has 'no meaning' but only 'meanings'? Is a text without a determinative sense but with only directional senses? Luz counters such questions that raise questions of ambivalence and subjectivity. For the 'truth' to be determined, the derived meaning (by an individual, a community, or a society) must *correspond to the history of Jesus* (understood roughly as the Jesus who has been proclaimed by the New Testament and not just the 'historical Jesus') as well as *bear the fruit of love* (so that its effects in modern society can never be destructive). Texts, then, produce 'truth' for Christians but only when interpreted properly, in line with these two criteria. An older scholarship would see here what the Germans call a form of *Sachkritik* ('substance criticism') or others a 'canon within the canon'.

Thus, 'History of effects brings together the texts and us, their interpreters; or better: the history of effects shows us that we are already together and that it is an illusion to treat the texts in a position of distance and in a merely "objective" way' (p. 25). Never is there an interpretation that is not shaped by the context of the interpreter. If *Wirkungsgeschichte* shows similarities to the Bultmann agenda, the

New Hermeneutic, or even some themes of a Barthian approach, it goes beyond each to achieve a new level of sophistication that shows potential for the interpretation of the Synoptic Gospels.

What might that be? For one, *Wirkungsgeschichte* unmasks the interpreter and, by holding up his interpretation to a mirror, reveals that the questions brought to the reading are the questions of the reader and his context. Even if some historical-critical inquiries operate on the basis of fundamental analogies (worship then, worship now), the interpreter needs candor to admit that his interpretation is only rarely a purely textually derived hypothesis. For example, those who ask about the 'social class' of Matthew's readers, the 'liturgy' of Mark, and the 'social agenda' of Luke are framing such questions in the light of modern interests. Three generations ago and three generations from now those questions were, and will be, irrelevant. An awareness of how the text has produced meanings throughout history makes us critically aware of our context and humbles us in our dogmatic conclusions regarding 'meaning'. 'The history of influence *describes* the ditch between past and present and makes clear that there was never an interpretation of a text that did not bear the mark of the historical situation of its interpreter' (p. 26).

Secondly, *Wirkungsgeschichte* informs us of the interpretive stances of other Christians throughout history and throughout the world — leading us many times not so much to judgment (mine is better than yours) as to *ecumenical awareness and appreciation*. We might try to explain Matthew's harsh language about the Pharisees in a manner that exonerates Matthew from the charge of anti-Semitism — as I have tried to do (McKnight, 'A Loyal Critic'). We might appeal to rhetorical acceptabilities in the ancient world (and so excuse Matthew from what appears to us to be outrageous language in Mt. 23); we might set Matthew's entire polemical and apologetic stances in a broader theological argument (and so see his strategy as similar to the deuteronomist or the prophets); or we might simply say that 'that's the way things were'. And we might be right; and we might find satisfaction. But, until we listen attentively to how modern Jews 'hear' and 'read' Matthew, we will never know the 'power' and 'potential meaning' of a text. A recent study of Amy-Jill Levine permits any modern reader to hear how a modern Jew interprets the text. Professor Levine calls our attempts to exonerate Matthew 'benevolent disculpation' (Levine, 'Anti-Judaism and the Gospel of Matthew', p. 10). She knows the 'effects' of Matthew's Gospel, none being more destructive than the Holocaust. A *wirkungsgeschichtlich* approach makes us aware not only of other meanings derived from a text but also of the indissoluble connection of the text with its interpreter(s). It won't do to say 'that meaning is wrong' for, whatever else one might say, 'that meaning has been set loose in society'. Luz would argue that the modern Holocaustic interpretation does not correspond to the history of Jesus and that it does not bear the fruit of love but that does not undo the 'potential power of meaning' inherent in what for all Christians is an embarrassing chapter in the history of interpretation.

Or, we might learn that what is significant about a text, say the healing of the social outcast Centurion's son (Mt. 8.5-13; Lk. 7.1-10), for Christian life in inner-city Chicago, may bear a different significance for someone fighting injustices in an African context, or an even different meaning for an upper-class American male in a New York high rise—and a *Wirkungsgeschichte* approach would suggest that, as long as each seriously grapples both with the history of Jesus and the fruit of love, each interpretation can be true to the text.

Reading the Synoptic Gospels Today: Strategies

This welter of tools and approaches to reading the Synoptic Gospels is not intended to scare the reader into running for cover (or a different part of the Bible) but, instead, to give to the reader *options* to be shaped by *the intention of the reader*. If the reader wants to be a historian, companions await a new reader; if it is theology, and church contexts and historical development that the readers wants, friends can be found; if the reader simply likes to read for the pleasure of seeing how the text works, many have traveled that path, too; and, if a reader is out to see what happens to her personally or what has happened to other readers, then a fresh start has been taken in that direction as well. Let me suggest then a few ways we can read the Synoptic Gospels today and, if one is an attentive reader of the separate studies that follow, one will find these approaches in each of the authors.

Strategies for Reading the Synoptic Gospels
First, we can read the Synoptic Gospels *historically*. Because of an explosion of scholarship in the field of ancient religions, history, society, and culture, readers of the Synoptic Gospels today can relate what they find to the Jewish world contemporary with Jesus and the Evangelists. One thinks here, of course, of what we have learned about Judaism because of the discoveries in the Judean desert, the Dead Sea Scrolls. We can ask questions like this: how do we compare the 'entry requirements' at Qumran with those of Jesus? How do we relate the eschatology of both movements? What about leadership and laity in

both movements? What about purity concerns for Jesus and for those at Qumran? How does Jesus compare to the 'Teacher of Righteousness'? To pursue such questions (and we have treated only a few questions touching on the Essenes without raising issues about common Jewish practices or other sectarian movements) involves, to be sure, some expertise in both sets of documents but a student can begin the quest by simply reading the Dead Sea Scrolls, which recently have begun to rival the Bible in translated versions, and then the Synoptic Gospels and then compare the information according to the questions being asked. Furthermore, the recent publication of a translation of the Jewish Pseudepigrapha under the able editorship of J.H. Charlesworth makes similar questions 'do-able' for an entirely different set of ancient historical texts. And, along other lines, we can ask questions about the Synoptic Gospels in light of recent archaeological studies, numismatic developments (the study of ancient coins), as well as ancient social customs. Further yet, the explosion of interdisciplinary studies, especially those dealing with anthropology and sociology, invites the reader of the Synoptic Gospels to ask other questions. What is the social make-up of Jesus' world? How did the poor relate to the rich? How was social and political power organized in ancient Galilee? What was family life like in the ancient world? What were the 'core values' of ancient Jews, ancient Romans, or first-century Galileans? Information about such questions, arising as they do from the social sciences, has led Synoptic Gospel scholars to renewed questions about Jesus and the Evangelists (e.g., what was so interesting about the Zacchaeus story of Lk. 19?) as well as to renewed appreciation for what kind of information is actually embedded in these texts.

Second, we can read the Synoptic Gospels *thematically*. We might ask about a theme historically and so ask what, for instance, Jesus taught about prayer. Or, we might ask about a theme in a given Evangelist's perspective (a redactional concern) and ask what Luke says about the death of Jesus. In this approach, care must be taken to ask questions that emerge from the text rather than those that emerge from our society (e.g., what is Mark's view of homosexuality?). More particularly, we need to read the Gospels carefully and with enough of an open mind to catch the concerns of the Evangelists. We need to see how Mark shapes discipleship to dovetail with Christology; to see how Matthew debates the Pharisees over issues of the Law and self-identity; and to see how Luke emphasizes the outcasts of society and includes them in the people of God. And, we need to let their categories and agendas dominate our thinking rather than forcing their texts into our moulds. A few other themes are worthy of mention here: Christology and specific titles for Jesus (e.g., Son of Man, Son of God, Lord, Teacher, Rabbi, servant), discipleship and ethics (e.g., love, demands for righteousness, servanthood, aid for the poor), kingdom of God (e.g., what is present and what is future?, what does 'kingdom' mean?, why sometimes kingdom of 'God' and others 'heaven'?), debates with Jewish leaders and authority figures (e.g., Jesus and the Pharisees, Sadducees, Herodians, Romans, soldiers), as well as concepts of salvation (e.g., what place does the cross play in Jesus' thinking according to each Evangelist?, what does kingdom have to do with unbelieving Israel?). Each of the studies that follow has addressed specific themes from the perspective of a single Evangelist; the reader can follow these up by re-reading the text to 'check on' the author, and can follow up these studies with further themes more tailored to the reader's questions.

Third, we can read the Synoptic Gospels *individually*. Following on from the previous strategy, readers can become attuned to the individual Evangelist's overall theology and perspective, an approach that emerges directly from redaction, composition, and various sorts of aesthetic criticisms. As I have summarized briefly above, the reader can attempt to write out an overall synthetic perspective of each Evangelist's purpose or intention. What is Mark, what is Matthew, what is Luke trying to get across in the broad canvas of his Gospel? In doing this, the reader needs to discipline her synthesis to the specific categories used by that author. For instance, it is unfair to Matthew to neglect in an overall statement his ethical emphasis just as it is unfair to Mark to make anything of the theme of righteousness. We need to let each Evangelist be who he is in order to make sense of his perspective. It might do us good to reconstruct what we would know about Jesus if all we had was one of the Synoptic Gospels—as was probably the case with most of the readers of Mark, Matthew, and Luke. This approach raises questions connected to the 'fourfold' canon of the Gospels (and in this book to the 'threefold' Synoptic tradition) as well as those related to how each Evangelist appropriated the Jesus material for his own setting (an early instance of what Ulrich Luz calls its *Wirkungsgeschichte*). But these questions can only be settled by those who have pursued the questions related to the interpretation of the individual Synoptic Gospel.

Fourth, we can read the Synoptic Gospels *comparatively*. A deeper appreciation both of the Evangelist's perspective as well as how the Gospels were related to their specific contexts can be gleaned by simply comparing them. This can be done at two levels: at the macroscopic level and at the microscopic level. In the first case, we compare Mark's Christology with Matthew's and ask big, general questions: how does Mark depict Jesus and how does Matthew depict Jesus? Readers of what appears to be three books that 'are basically the same' can be surprised, even frustrated, by carefully comparing the Synoptic Gospels. In the second case, the reader will want to have what scholars call a 'Synopsis' (a book that lays out parallel passages in columns so careful comparisons can be observed) in order to compare how each Evangelist records a similar saying or event. For instance, readers of the Beatitudes will observe that Luke has 'blessed are the poor' while Matthew has 'blessed are the poor in spirit'. Apart from the question as to which is original, the comparative reader of the Synoptics will ask 'why' Luke does not have 'in spirit' and 'why' Matthew does. The readers will then ask what difference it makes and whether or not there are specifics in each of the texts that lead the reader to see a pattern. Does, for instance, Matthew do this elsewhere? (The answer is 'No'.) Does Luke emphasize social and economic poverty? (The answer is 'Yes'.) And do answers to these questions lead us to a renewed appreciation of the text and what each Evangelist intends to communicate. If readers arm themselves with a Synopsis when reading specific passages, a host of questions arise that frequently sharpen our understanding of the text.

Finally, we can read the Synoptic Gospels *corporately*. Western society breeds individualism; whether we bemoan this situation is immaterial since it is a fact. Nonetheless, as families best function when they discuss issues together, so scholars and students learn the meanings of texts when they work together. Scholars call this the 'Academy' because it was Socrates and Plato who have been idealized as learners within the context of a community. Churches, denominations, and small-group Bible studies function in a similar manner: individuals gather together to ask questions about a text and, in asking questions of one another and in proposed meanings by separate individuals we gain by listening to one another's perceptions. As the old adage has it, 'two heads are better than one—even if they are sheep heads!' Corporate readings take place in several ways: one reads a text and then consults a commentary (another reader whose interpretation is recorded in a book and is not usually physically present in person), one reads a text and then consults with someone else who reads the text (sometimes a teacher, sometimes a peer), or one reads a text and consults with more than one person (sometimes a classroom, sometimes a church group, etc). As iron sharpens iron, so our separate readings can sharpen one another's perceptions. If we can be delivered from the fear of being wrong, we can find that corporate discussions can enlarge our interpretations and reveal to us the glory of our common humanity.

FOR FURTHER READING

On the 'Apology for the Synoptic Gospels':

D.A. Hagner, *The Jewish Reclamation of Jesus* (Grand Rapids: Zondervan, 1984).

E. Hoskyns and N. Davey, *The Riddle of the New Testament* (London: Faber & Faber, 1941). An older study that remains valuable for emphasizing the historical orientation of early Christian faith.

J. Jeremias, *The Problem of the Historical Jesus* (trans. N. Perrin; Philadelphia: Fortress Press, 1964).

E. Lemcio, *The Past of Jesus in the Gospels* (SNTSMS, 68; Cambridge: Cambridge University Press, 1991).

S. McKnight, 'The Hermeneutics of Confessing Jesus as Lord', *Ex Auditu* 14 (1998), pp. 1-17, with the response by David Cassel, pp. 18-20.

B.F. Meyer, *The Aims of Jesus* (London: SCM Press, 1979).

G.N. Stanton, *Jesus of Nazareth in New Testament Preaching* (SNTSMS, 27; Cambridge: Cambridge University Press, 1974).

G. Vermes, *Jesus the Jew: A Historian's Reading of the Gospels* (London: Fontana/ Collins, 1976).

—*Providential Accidents: An Autobiography* (London: SCM Press; New York: Rowman & Littlefield, 1999).

On the 'Windows Twentieth Century and Beyond':

A. Delbanco, *The Real American Dream: A Meditation on Hope* (Cambridge, MA: Harvard University Press, 1999).

N.T. Wright, *The New Testament and the People of God* (Christian Origins and the Question of God, 1; Minneapolis: Fortress Press, 1992), here pp. 29-80.

On 'Through the Window and the Quest for the Historical Jesus':

M. Borg, *Jesus: A New Vision* (San Francisco: Harper & Row, 1988).

G.B. Caird, with L.D. Hurst, *New Testament Theology* (Oxford: Clarendon Press, 1994).

J.D. Crossan, *The Historical Jesus: The Life of a Mediterranean Jewish Peasant* (San Francisco: HarperSanFrancisco, 1991).

R.W. Funk, *Honest to Jesus* (San Francisco: HarperSanFrancisco, 1996).

R.W. Funk, with R.W. Hoover and the Jesus Seminar, *The Five Gospels: The Search for the Authentic Words of Jesus* (New York: Macmillan, 1993).

—*The Acts of Jesus: The Search for the Authentic Deeds of Jesus* (San Francisco: HarperSanFrancisco, 1998).

R.A. Horsley, *Jesus and the Spiral of Violence: Popular Jewish Resistance in Roman Palestine* (San Francisco: Harper & Row, 1987).

J. Jeremias, *New Testament Theology: The Proclamation of Jesus* (trans. J. Bowden; New York: Charles Scribner's Sons, 1971).

S. McKnight, *A New Vision for Israel: The Teachings of Jesus in National Context* (Studying the Historical Jesus; Grand Rapids: Eerdmans, 1999).

J.P. Meier, *A Marginal Jew: Rethinking the Historical Jesus* (ABRL; 3 vols.; New York: Doubleday, 1991–).

B.F. Meyer, *The Aims of Jesus* (London: SCM Press, 1979).

N. Perrin, *Rediscovering the Teaching of Jesus* (New York: Harper & Row, 1967).

E.P. Sanders, *Jesus and Judaism* (Philadelphia: Fortress Press, 1983).

G. Vermes, *Jesus the Jew: A Historian's Reading of the Gospels* (London: Fontana/Collins, 1976).

N.T. Wright, *Jesus and the Victory of God* (Christian Origins and the Question of God, 2; Minneapolis: Fortress Press, 1996).

On 'At the Window and the Rise of Classical Synoptic Criticism':

On the 'Synoptic Problem', for a brief selection, see:

St Augustine, *The Harmony of the Gospels* (trans. S.D.F. Salmond; NPNF, 6; Grand Rapids: Eerdmans, 1979).

D. Dungan, *A History of the Synoptic Problem: The Canon, the Text, the Composition, and the Interpretation of the Gospels* (ABRL; New York: Doubleday, 1999).

W.R. Farmer, *The Gospel of Jesus: The Pastoral Relevance of the Synoptic Problem* (Louisville: Westminster/John Knox Press, 1994).

—*The Synoptic Problem: A Critical Analysis* (New York: Macmillan, 1964).

J.J. Griesbach, *A Demonstration that Mark Was Written after Matthew and Luke*, in B. Orchard and T.R.W. Longstaff (eds.), *J.J. Griesbach, Synoptic and Text-Critical Studies, 1776–1976* (trans. B. Orchard; Cambridge: Cambridge University Press, 1978), pp. 103-35.

J.C. Hawkins, *Horae Synopticae: Contributions to the Study of the Synoptic Problem* (Oxford: Clarendon Press, 2nd edn, 1909).

J.S. Kloppenborg, *Q Parallels: Synopsis, Critical Notes and Concordance* (Sonoma, CA: Polebridge Press, 1988). This book gives a reader the best access to modern scholarship on Q.

S. McKnight, 'Source Criticism', in D.A. Black and D. Dockery (eds.), *New Testament Criticism and Interpretation* (Grand Rapids: Zondervan, 1991), pp. 137-72 (revised edition forthcoming).

D.B. Peabody, 'Augustine and the Augustinian Hypothesis: A Reexamination of Augustine's Thought in *De consensu evangelistarum*', in W.R. Farmer (ed.), *New Synoptic Studies: The Cambridge Conference and Beyond* (Macon, GA: Mercer University Press, 1983), pp. 37-64.

W. Sanday (ed.), *Oxford Studies in the Synoptic Gospels* (Oxford: Clarendon Press, 1911).

B.H. Streeter, *The Four Gospels: A Study of Origins, Treating of the Manuscript Tradition, Sources, Authorship, and Dates* (London: Macmillan, 1924).

C.M. Tuckett, *The Revival of the Griesbach Hypothesis: An Analysis and Appraisal*

(SNTSMS, 44; Cambridge: Cambridge University Press, 1983).

F. Watson, *Text and Truth: Redefining Biblical Theology* (Grand Rapids: Eerdmans, 1997), here esp. pp. 33-176.

On 'Redaction Criticism', for a brief selection, see:

See the various entries in the standard dictionaries, including *The Anchor Bible Dictionary* and the *Dictionary of Jesus and the Gospels* (ed. J.B. Green, S. McKnight and I.H. Marshall; Downers Grove, IL: IVP, 1992).

G. Bornkamm, *Tradition and Interpretation in Matthew* (with G. Barth and H.J. Held; trans. P. Scott; Philadelphia: Westminster Press, 1974).

H. Conzelmann, *The Theology of St. Luke* (trans. G. Buswell; New York: Harper & Row, 1960).

J.D.G. Dunn, *The Partings of the Ways: Between Christianity and Judaism and their Significance for the Character of Christianity* (London: SCM Press, 1991).

W. Marxsen, *Mark the Evangelist: Studies on the Redaction History of the Gospel* (trans. J. Boyce, D. Juel, W. Poehlmann and R.A. Harrisville; Nashville: Abingdon Press, 1969).

S. McKnight, *Interpreting the Synoptic Gospels* (Guides to New Testament Exegesis; Grand Rapids: Baker Book House, 1988).

N. Perrin, *What is Redaction Criticism?* (Philadelphia: Fortress Press, 1974).

J. Rohde, *Rediscovering the Teaching of the Evangelists* (trans. D.M. Barton; Philadelphia: Westminster Press, 1968).

A.J. Saldarini, *Matthew's Christian-Jewish Community* (Chicago: University of Chicago Press, 1994).

G.N. Stanton, 'The Origin and Purpose of Matthew's Gospel: Matthean Scholarship from 1945 to 1980', in *ANRW*, II.25.3, pp. 1889-1951.

R.H. Stein, *The Synoptic Problem* (Grand Rapids: Baker Book House, 1987).

—'What is Redaktionsgeschichte?', *JBL* 88 (1969), pp. 45-56.

On 'Aesthetic Criticisms', under which category I lump together a vast array of approaches because they are more or less concerned with the text *qua* text rather than as text *qua* history or *qua* the result of a traditional process, see:

R. Alter, *The Art of Biblical Narrative* (New York: Basic Books, 1981).

J.B. Green, *The Gospel of Luke* (NICNT; Grand Rapids: Eerdmans, 1997).

E. Haenchen, *Der Weg Jesu* (Berlin: W. de Gruyter, 2nd edn, 1968).

J.D. Kingsbury, *Matthew as Story* (Philadelphia: Fortress Press, 2nd edn, 1988).

—*Matthew: Structure, Christology, Kingdom* (Philadelphia: Fortress Press, 2nd edn, 1989).

—*The Parables of Jesus in Matthew 13: A Study in Redaction-Criticism* (St Louis: Clayton, 1969).

N.R. Petersen, *Literary Criticism for New Testament Critics* (Philadelphia: Fortress Press, 1978).

D. Rhoads, D. Michie and J. Dewey, *Mark as Story: An Introduction to the Narrative of a Gospel* (Minneapolis: Fortress Press, 1999).

M. Sternberg, *The Poetics of Biblical Narrative: Ideological Literature and the Drama of*

Reading (Indiana Literary Biblical Series; Bloomington, IN: Indiana University Press, 1985).

R.C. Tannehill, *The Narrative Unity of Luke–Acts: A Literary Interpretation*. I. *The Gospel According to Luke* (Philadelphia: Fortress Press, 1986).

On 'genre' questions, see:

R.A. Burridge, *What Are the Gospels? A Comparison with Graeco-Roman Biography* (SNTSMS, 70; Cambridge: Cambridge University Press, 1992).

R.H. Gundry, 'EUAGGELION: How Soon a Book?', *JBL* 115 (1996), pp. 321-25.

L.W. Hurtado, 'Gospel (Genre)', in Green *et al.* (eds.), *Dictionary of Jesus and the Gospels*, pp. 276-82.

H. Koester, *Ancient Christian Gospels: Their History and Development* (London: SCM Press, 1990).

E. Lemcio, *The Past of Jesus in the Gospels.*

P.L. Schuler, *A Genre for the Gospels: The Biographical Character of Matthew* (Philadelphia: Fortress Press, 1982).

G.E. Sterling, *Historiography and Self-Definition: Josephos, Luke–Acts and Apologetic Historiography* (NovTSup, 64; Leiden: E.J. Brill, 1992).

G. Strecker, *History of New Testament Literature* (trans. C. Katter, with H. Mollenhauer; Harrisburg, PA: Trinity Press International, 1997).

C.H. Talbert, *What Is a Gospel? The Genre of the Canonical Gospels* (Philadelphia: Fortress Press, 1977).

C.W. Votaw, *The Gospels and Contemporary Biographies in the Graeco-Roman World* (Facet Books: Biblical Series, 27; Philadelphia: Fortress Press, 1970).

On '*Wirkungsgeschichte*', see:

A.-J. Levine, 'Anti-Judaism and the Gospel of Matthew', in W.R. Farmer (ed.), *Anti-Judaism and the Gospels* (Harrisburg, PA: Trinity Press International, 1999), pp. 9-36 (with responses by P.L. Shuler and W. Carter following).

U. Luz, *Matthew in History: Interpretation, Influence, and Effects* (Minneapolis: Fortress Press, 1994).

—*Matthew 1–7: A Commentary* (trans. W.C. Linss; Minneapolis: Fortress Press, 1989). A three-volume set scheduled to be re-published in the Hermeneia series.

S. McKnight, 'A Loyal Critic: Matthew's Polemic with Judaism in Theological Perspective', in C.A. Evans and D.A. Hagner (eds.), *Anti-Semitism and Early Christianity: Issues of Polemic and Faith* (Minneapolis: Fortress Press, 1993), pp. 55-79.

For further bibliography, see:

S. McKnight and M.C. Williams, *The Synoptic Gospels: An Annotated Bibliography* (IBR Bibliographies, 6; Grand Rapids: Baker Book House, 2000).

Part I

MATTHEW

John Riches

FURTHER READING ON MATTHEW

As will be clear I have been most helped and have drawn most on the works of two scholars.

G.N. Stanton, *A Gospel for a New People: Studies in Matthew* (Edinburgh: T. & T. Clark, 1992). This is an attractively written book which engages with both social-historical and literary-critical questions in a fresh and persuasive way. For those who would like something briefer from the same author, *The Gospels and Jesus* (Oxford: Oxford University Press, 1989) is a useful introduction to Gospel study; *The Interpretation of Matthew* (London: SPCK, 1983) provides a selection of important articles in the field of Matthaean studies, with a helpful introduction.

U. Luz, *Matthew 1–7* (Minneapolis: Fortress Press, 1989 [vols. 2 and 3 presently only available in German]) is in some ways a fairly traditional commentary, paying close attention to Matthew's editing of his sources and basing its findings on a close reconstruction of the traditions behind Matthew. But he is a master of this craft and shows its strengths, not least because he is aware of its difficulties. The real discovery of the commentary is the light it sheds on the Gospel through the history of effects. For those who want to follow this up Luz's *Matthew in History: Interpretation, Influence, and Effects* (Minneapolis: Fortress Press, 1994) contains some valuable essays. For those who want more detailed work on the Jewish background to the Gospel, W.D. Davies and D.C. Allison, Jr, *A Critical and Exegetical Commentary on the Gospel according to Matthew* (Edinburgh: T. & T. Clark, 1988, 1991) provides a rich store. For handier and cheaper commentaries, D. Hill, *The Gospel of Matthew* (London: Oliphants, 1972) and E. Schweizer, *The Good News According to Matthew* (London: SPCK, 1976) are generally reliable and informative. For those who would like to explore literary approaches to the Gospel, there is R.H. Gundry, *Matthew: A Commentary on his Literary and Theological Art* (Grand Rapids: Eerdmans, 1982).

There are, of course, many other works which I have drawn on, some of which are contained in the lists at the end of each chapter. These too can be explored and will lead the reader to more and more books and articles. The important thing is not to be overwhelmed by the flood of literature: it is there for you to use and to guide you in your own lines of enquiry.

Chapter One

LEADING QUESTIONS IN MATTHAEAN SCHOLARSHIP

Introduction

The discipline of New Testament studies has its perennial questions and methods of answering them; it also undergoes changes of mood and interest when the focus of scholars' attention shifts from one set of issues to another, when certain methods and approaches gain favour. A study guide of this kind should, I think, both try to indicate something of the questions and ways of tackling them which have engaged Matthaean scholars over the years and also to give at least a flavour of the current debates which animate scholars working in the field.

When Donald Senior wrote his excellent guide to recent Matthaean scholarship in the early 1980s (*What Are they Saying about Matthew?* [New York: Paulist Press, 1983]), he focused first on questions of the setting, sources and structure of Matthew's Gospel and then turned for the bulk of his survey to questions of Matthew's theology: his views on salvation history, the Old Testament, the Law, Christology, the church. That is to say his book reflects accurately the concern of scholars of the 1960s and 1970s to chart as fully as possible the evangelist's own theological stance. They wanted to discover the view of the Christian faith and practice that Matthew was trying to advocate as he edited his sources and presented them in the form of a Gospel like, but significantly different from, Mark's.

If one were to write the same kind of survey today one would certainly want to focus it rather differently. Of course, there has not been a total sea-change over the last ten years. But, on the one hand, there has been greater interest in the community out of which Matthew came and for which he wrote, on the ways in which his contemporaries might have read and received his Gospel, and indeed on the ways in which it has been received in the churches subsequently. On the other hand, there has also been a change in the ways in which Matthew's own work is viewed. If earlier scholarship focused on the way in which Matthew took up and made detailed modifications to his sources, more recent studies have been interested in the way in which Matthew composed his narrative, in the overall shape which he gave to his work. This kind of interest also goes hand in hand with a renewed discussion about the sort of literature which Gospels are, indeed with a renewed interest in the biblical writings as literature, rather than as historical sources for the views and practice of the early church.

The nature of such shifts in scholarship can be exaggerated. Obviously scholars cannot keep on going over the same ground endlessly and so there are bound to be shifts of emphasis and fashion. However, some claims need to be treated with a little caution, for example, that the new literary approaches to the Bible have broken the mould of biblical studies. On the other hand, it is important to note where there is change in scholarly consensus in a discipline, just as it is important that there should be such changes. A discipline which never changed its mind would be one which was stagnant. Equally a discipline which never entertained new ways of looking at its subject matter or which was never prepared to learn from developments in other cognate areas of study would also be in danger of ossification.

So we shall follow a simple path in this guide. The first chapter will take a look at the major questions which have engaged scholars over the years, and at the ways in which they have tried to answer them. This will at least serve to map out the territory.

Then we shall proceed more selectively under three main heads. First, we shall consider questions of the literary form and nature of the Gospel, its sources, its relation to other literary forms, its structure and composition, and the new literary modes of reading the Gospel. Next we shall look at Matthew's community, its place in the development of the early church, its relation to other forms of religious belief, its internal dynamics and problems, and briefly, its subsequent reception in the church. This will provide a spring-board for considering the evangelist's own theology, specifically his Christology. Here we shall consider how his theology is expressed through his use of a narrative form, as well as through his careful modification of the texts which he has taken over. This choice of topics will make it possible to give an idea of how the discipline has developed over the last ten years or more and to place recent contributions to the debate in the framework of perennial questions which have intrigued scholars in this field of studies.

Obviously what I choose to highlight would not be everyone's choice. This kind of book can make no claim to comprehensiveness. I would hope, however, that it will help most of its readers to read Matthew with more enjoyment and understanding than previously, and that it will encourage many to make good my deficiencies by reading their way more fully into some of the scholarly discussions themselves.

Data Concerning the Gospel of Matthew

What then are the questions which have engaged scholars working on Matthew's Gospel over the years? Perhaps the easiest way to answer this question is to set out some of the raw data concerning the Gospel itself, and then to see how the main questions arise out of the conjunction of certain aims and interests on the part of the interpreters with the matter on which they are working.

The first and most obvious thing to say about Matthew's Gospel is that it is one of three very similar works of literature in the New Testament. That is to say, it is very like Mark and Luke in form, content and indeed phrasing, and rather less like John, particularly as regards content and phrasing.

When the first three Gospels (known as the Synoptic Gospels) are set out side by side certain things become immediately apparent. In the first place they all follow to a considerable degree a common order. Certainly there are significant differences, not least in the way the teaching material is arranged in Matthew and Luke, but the agreement between the three is so significant as to require some kind of explanation. Secondly, it becomes apparent that there are remarkable agreements in the way the stories and sayings are narrated in all three Gospels. This is not just a matter of agreement about what actually happened or about the substance of what was said, such as one might expect from faithful and intelligent eye-witnesses. It is rather a matter of word for word agreement in the way the incidents and sayings are recorded which suggests some dependence on a common source, oral or literary.

Let us consider the nature of these agreements a little further, particularly as they relate to Matthew. Matthew has all but about 50 of Mark's 662 verses. There is also substantial agreement between Matthew and Mark in the order in which stories and sayings are presented, particularly in the second half of Matthew's Gospel. Additionally, Matthew has some 230 verses in common with Luke, most of which contain sayings of Jesus. However, the order in which these sayings occur in Matthew and Luke is for the most part quite different. As well as these two very substantial bodies of material, about a quarter of Matthew is not found in either of the two other Synoptic Gospels. As we shall see, all of this will generate some intriguing discussions about the relationships between the Gospels and about the source of Matthew's material.

This measure of agreement between the first three Gospels makes it possible to see why it is necessary to distinguish the first three Gospels from the fourth. Nothing like the same agreement in order or in content occurs between any of the first three and John. There are, moreover, substantial differences in the accounts they offer of Jesus' ministry and teaching. In the Synoptics, Jesus conducts his ministry in the north of the country before going up to Jerusalem to die. In the Fourth Gospel he moves back and forth between Galilee and Jerusalem. There are interesting disagreements too about the details of the story: in John, the 'cleansing' of the Temple occurs at the beginning of the Gospel; Jesus' ministry starts before John is put in prison; Jesus performs no exorcisms; Jesus' arrest is precipitated by the raising of Lazarus (not recorded in the Synoptics); the date of the crucifixion is different (in John it coincides with the slaughter of the Passover lambs, in the Synoptics it is on the day before). Perhaps more significant than this are two other facts. First, we need to note that where there is common material between the Synoptics and the Fourth Gospel, as for example with the story of the centurion (Mt. 8.5-13; Lk. 7.1-10; Jn 4.46-53), there is often such a difference in the details of the telling of the story that we cannot easily suppose they knew each other's account. Secondly, there is a world of difference between the kind of teaching that is ascribed to Jesus in the Synoptic Gospels and in John. In the Synoptics, Jesus for the most part utters short sayings: proverbs, legal and prophetic sayings, parables, and so on. Sometimes these occur, as in Matthew, in longer discourses, but even here the discourses are composed of a number of shorter sayings. By contrast Jesus' teaching in John is typically given in long discourses which focus significantly on questions about his own person and make explicit claims about his divine mission and nature which it is hard to parallel in the Synoptics. In this respect the saying in Mt. 11.27 is exceptional and is sometimes referred to as the 'Johannine thunderbolt'.

In short, we may say that Matthew's Gospel forms one of a group of three which are marked out by their very close agreements in order and detailed phraseology; that they share a common pattern for Jesus' ministry and agree significantly both in the kinds of activity which they ascribe to him: preaching, teaching, healing and exorcism, and in the kind of teaching which he is portrayed as giving: very broadly of a kind for which it is not difficult to find formal parallels in the contemporary Jewish world.

However, while it is important to begin by emphasizing these shared characteristics, there are, of course, significant differences between Matthew and the other Synoptics which can best be sketched by giving a brief account of the contents of Matthew's Gospel and drawing attention within it to certain specific features of his work.

The content of Matthew's Gospel can conveniently be set out in the following summary:

1–2	Genealogy and infancy narratives
3–4	John the Baptist and the beginnings of Jesus' ministry
5–7	The Sermon on the Mount
8–9	The miracles of Jesus
10	The Mission Discourse
11–12	John the Baptist and controversies over Jesus' miracles
13	Jesus' parables
14–17	Death of John; first feeding and walking on the lake; discussion of purity; Canaanite woman; second feeding miracle; discussion of miracles; Peter's confession; discipleship sayings; Transfiguration; faith and miracles; Temple tax.
18	Community rule
19–22	Teaching on divorce, celibacy; the commandments; wealth; the parable of the Labourers in the Vineyard; greatest in the kingdom; healing of the blindmen; triumphal entry and cleansing of the Temple; fig tree and teaching in Jerusalem
23	Woes on the Pharisees
24–25	Apocalyptic discourse
26–28	Passion and Resurrection

We shall discuss Matthew's way of composing and the relationships between his Gospel and the others more fully in the next chapter. Here we simply need to make a number of preliminary observations. First, unlike Mark but like Luke, Matthew starts his Gospel with stories about the young Jesus. Secondly, there are a number of major discourses positioned fairly regularly through the Gospel. Not all the teaching material is found here but these five blocks are striking features of the Gospel, not found in the same measure in Mark or Luke. Thirdly, from ch. 14 onwards it becomes less easy to give neat summaries of the non-discourse chapters. This is most easily explained by saying that Matthew is here following Mark. Certainly he is closest to Mark in these sections.

So much for the bare outlines of Matthew's Gospel. It will be useful here also to list some of the more specific characteristics of Matthew's material.

1. Matthew has ten quotations from the Old Testament which
    are typically introduced by a formula of the form: 'to fulfil
    what the Lord declared through the prophet': Mt. 1.22-23;
    2.15, 17-18, 23; 4.14ff.; 8.17; 12.17ff.; 13.35; 21.4-5; 27.9-10.
2. Matthew uses a range of titles for Jesus: Lord, Son of David,
    Son of Man, Son of God, Son, Christ, King of the Jews. Some
    of these titles occur more frequently than in Mark.
3. A number of traits in Matthew's story indicate a strong sense
    of separation between Matthew's community and the people
    of Israel: references to 'their synagogues' (12.9, cf. Mk 3.1; Mt.
    13.54, cf. Mk 6.2); statements to the effect that the Kingdom
    has been taken away from the Pharisees and High Priests
    (Mt. 21.43, cf. 22.1-14); the crowd's calling down Jesus' blood
    on themselves and their descendants (Mt. 27.25); Jesus' send-
    ing his disciples to the Gentiles after his resurrection (Mt.
    28.18-20).
4. Nevertheless, Matthew has a strong interest in the Law as is
    evidenced by his grouping of Jesus' teaching into the Sermon
    on the Mount and by the sayings strongly affirmative of the
    Law in that complex (5.17-20, esp. 5.18). At the same time,
    however, Matthew underlines the difference between the tra-
    ditional teaching of Israel and Jesus' teaching by the 'anti-
    theses' in the Sermon on the Mount (statements of the form
    'You have heard it said...but I say unto you': 5.21-22, 27-28,
    31-32, 33-34, 38-39, 43-44).
5. Matthew is the only evangelist who refers to the 'church'
    (*ekklēsia*): 16.18; 18.17.

Clearly, the 'raw data' which I have just set down are themselves
matters to which scholars working on Matthew's Gospel have drawn
attention over the years. How people see and read the Gospel depends
a great deal on their particular viewpoint. Nevertheless, those data do
represent some of the clearly statable facts about the Gospel which are
worth memorizing and which will provide the basis for our coming
discussions.

What sorts of enquiry are raised in scholars' minds by such data?
The answer to that question depends to a considerable degree on the
state of the scholars' minds themselves, more particularly on the beliefs and aims with which they approach the texts. One of the fascinating things about New Testament studies is that scholars who are
engaged in them do indeed represent a great variety of viewpoints
and are often pursuing very different goals and agenda.

Some will see the canonical texts as together constituting divine revelation and will therefore principally be concerned to understand the ways in which Matthew's Gospel contributes to the content or purport of that revelation.

The facts about the relationships between the Gospels which we have noted will raise some quite thorny questions in this regard. The more clearly it is appreciated that Matthew's Gospel was written by taking and *adapting* other written sources, including Mark, the more difficult it will be simply to harmonize the Gospel accounts. Biblical theologians working on the Gospels need to provide a positive explanation of the diversity of Gospel accounts of Jesus' life, teaching, death, passion and resurrection.

One way of providing such an explanation that has been extremely attractive to many theologians over the last 30 years is through what is known as redaction-critical studies. If Matthew's Gospel is the result of his drawing together different literary sources and editing them in such a way that they form a composite whole, then it will be interesting to look in detail at the ways in which he has edited those sources. Careful scrutiny of the fine editorial touches he made to the texts he took over will provide us with clues to the particular perspective from which he views his story. So too will an examination of the overall structure and composition of his Gospel (sometimes referred to as 'composition criticism'). In these ways we may hope to arrive at a theology of Matthew which can be set alongside that of Mark and Luke.

What such studies show above all are the analogies between Matthew's modes of working and those of other literary editors. It shows him, that is to say, as a human author reflecting on the story which he has received. He is not simply a recorder of divine–human history: his reflections on that history are part of the process by which its meaning and message are made known. The theologies of Matthew, Mark and Luke are part of a tradition of biblical theologizing which continues on into the history of biblical interpretation in the church.

Others may be interested more in the history of the ancient world and of the Christian community in particular. They will want to know as much as they can about the development of early Christianity and its relation to other religious movements in the ancient world. Their reasons for this may be various. They may see the hand of divine providence in such movements and wish to understand the way in which they contribute to the 'education of humankind'. They may alternatively recognize that such movements have played and indeed continue to play an important part in the life of human society and wish to contribute to the better understanding of such powerful contemporary forces. They may simply enjoy uncovering the past.

Again the particular character of Matthew's Gospel will raise interesting questions for those of such a historical bent. The placing of Matthew within a particular stratum of Christian history, the Synoptic tradition, is itself an important lead for those trying to write a history of the development of the early Christian communities. At the same time the references within the Gospel to the Jewish community and to the Law draw our attention to the Matthaean community's relation to Judaism, which was itself undergoing major restructuring at this point in the wake of the destruction of the Temple in 70 CE. There are fascinating and extraordinarily complicated questions to be addressed here about the lines of development within the Judaeo-Christian tradition. In what sense does Christianity emerge out of the Jewish tradition? To what extent are post-70 Judaism and Christianity both off-shoots of pre-70 Judaism? And at the same time there are questions to be asked about the development of the human moral and religious consciousness. Should Matthew's digest of Jesus' teaching be described as a 'new law'? Does the teaching of the Sermon on the Mount stand as a major and largely innovative contribution to the development of human moral consciousness? Or indeed, more darkly, what is Matthew's contribution to the growth of anti-Semitism in Europe? What is his contribution to the development of exclusivist understandings of the church?

Yet again others may be interested in the biblical texts as works of literature. It is not so much what their authors once intended to say which intrigues such scholars as the varieties of ways in which such *texts* may convey meaning. Texts, that is to say, are not simply messages sent by an author to a particular destination; they are literary entities which have the power to convey meanings even when they have become divorced in time from their original context. They have the power to shape communities, indeed to create new worlds of meaning which may again lead to new readings of the texts.

Those who approach Matthew from such a broad standpoint are not always interested in the sort of data about literary sources and relationships that were discussed above. They may regard Matthew's relation to the Synoptic tradition and to Mark as being largely irrelevant to questions of the literary character of Matthew's Gospel as such. A 'purely' literary study of Matthew would consider the work as it stands and explore, for example, the Gospel's narrative character, employing a range of concepts drawn from modern literary theory. Others may be interested in the ways in which readers of the Gospel receive it and again may consider the literary history prior to the final form of the text irrelevant to such an undertaking. For them the text is constituted less by its relations to its antecedents than by its relation to those who read and make of it what they, and their interpretative communities, will.

On the other hand, those who wish to know more about the literary character of the text may find much to help them in the presentation of the data above. It will help them in the task of understanding the literary process of production, just as it will be of help in the task of determining the literary character of the New Testament texts in relation to the other literary genres of the time. It will be grist to the mill of those who wish to situate the Gospels in a literary history which stretches from the earliest Gospel to the most recent commentary on Matthew.

Such questions — theological, historical and literary — are not hermetically sealed off from each other. Questions do not put themselves, they are put by real people who have a variety of interests and may each participate in a number of different communities which variously pursue different enquiries and conversations. In what follows we will therefore not simply divide the book up under these three heads of enquiry. Even though each chapter will take up a subject which seems to fit neatly under one of these headings, in practice each chapter will raise historical, literary and theological questions. In Chapter 2 we will consider the literary origins, character and history of the first Gospel. Here the enquiry is principally literary and historical, but theological matters will not be far afield. A literary and historical view of the biblical writings raises sharp enough questions about the way in which truth is conveyed through the Gospels. We shall see how the nature of the enquiry changes from the early interest in literary sources, to a focus on the largely oral tradition behind the Gospels and then on again to the question of their literary form and of the authorial activity of the Evangelists. Finally, we shall look at some more recent contributions which threaten to leave the historical dimension behind altogether and instead focus attention exclusively on the literary, narrative character of the Gospel.

In Chapter 3 we shall turn to matters more strictly historical: the location of Matthew's community in the development of early Christianity and Judaism and the subsequent history of the reception of Matthew's Gospel in the church. But here again literary and theological matters will also play an important part. The question of literary origins and subsequent literary history will help us to get a fix on Matthew's community. And so too will questions of theology. The more we know about the theological positions adopted by Matthew, the easier it will be to situate him among the diverse forms of early Christian and Jewish belief; the more we know about the subsequent theological exploitation of Matthew's text, the more we shall know about its potential for meaning.

Finally, in Chapter 4 we shall look at a specifically theological topic: Matthew's Christology. Interestingly, we shall see here how different views of the literary structure and character of the Gospel affect scholars' views of the content of Matthew's Gospel. We shall see how Matthew's theological ideas are expressed not only in the titles which he gives to Jesus, but also in the way those titles are placed in the Gospel, the way they are elaborated by association with other texts and figures from the Old Testament and by the narrative in which they are found. And of course the more we understand about the setting in which Matthew is writing, the more we shall understand about this process of elaboration.

Chapter Two

WHAT SORT OF A BOOK?

This chapter will deal with literary matters: how was Matthew written, what sort of a book was it, where do we place such literature in the ancient world, what modes of reading are appropriate to this kind of work of literature?

Such questions have often been dealt with in Introductions to the New Testament, almost as a separate branch of the subject. There is something to be said for this: similar questions arise about other books and it is convenient to lump such discussions together. Much of what we say here will be, with suitable modifications, applicable to other Gospels. Nevertheless, too sharp a separation of such questions from detailed interpretation of the text is inadvisable. Views about the literary sources, genre and structure of Matthew will need to be tested against a close reading of the Gospel itself.

These are important preliminary questions. It makes a difference to the way we read something whether it is an anthology, a monograph, a novel, a letter, a set of essays, a dissertation. At least it does if we are aware of its literary nature. It helps us to know how to relate the parts to the whole, how to identify the author's own emphases and comments.

Sources

Discussions about the sources of the Synoptic Gospels are for some people all-absorbing, for others rather arcane crossword puzzles which seem of little importance to the central task of interpreting the Gospels. One may not want to devote one's life to solving the problem, but in order to understand the study of Matthew it is at least essential to see what the problem is.

Put at its simplest the problem is this. If we compare the texts of the first three Gospels in a Synopsis (a book which sets out the first three Gospels in parallel columns) we discover remarkable similarities and agreements among them, such that their accounts are often almost word for word identical. We also discover striking disagreements between them: different versions of Jesus' sayings, different versions of events, and indeed a considerable amount of material which is not shared by all three, or indeed which occurs in only one Gospel. How do we account for these agreements and disagreements?

Writing just over 120 years ago, Bishop Christopher Wordsworth felt he could explain the agreements by appealing to the divine author-ship of the Spirit who used the principle of repetition to inculcate divine truth (as indeed he did in the Old Testament where prophecies and psalms are found in different though largely identical versions). The differences, on the other hand, could be explained partly by the fact that Jesus spoke in 'Syro-Chaldaic' (Aramaic) whereas the Evan-gelists wrote in Greek, partly by the inadequacy of human words to express the full meaning of the divine wisdom, so that the Holy Spirit offered different versions to uncover the fuller meaning of the say-ings.

To be reminded of such arguments is to realize how far opinions have changed in academic circles in a hundred years. His account is remarkable enough in that it solidly refuses to countenance the source-critical studies which had been pursued with such vigour in Germany throughout the nineteenth century. My own copy adds a twist to this. It was given by C.H. Dodgson (Lewis Carroll) to his nephew. It is revealing that such a formidable logician and story-teller should have been satisfied with such explanations.

Wordsworth's account is problematic for at least two main reasons. First, it allows human agency in the writing of the Gospel a very un-certain and partial role. As far as the agreements between them are concerned, the Evangelists are mere mouthpieces of the Spirit. The disagreements, however, are partly accounted for by the human pro-cess of translation from one language to another, partly by the Spirit's agency in providing the kind of variety which will reveal the true meaning of Jesus' words. Secondly, it ignores what are much more evident explanations of such agreements and disagreements, evident, that is, if we regard the Evangelists as authors in their own right: the use of literary sources, of different oral traditions in which the stories and sayings had been modified in the course of transmission. The interesting thing is that it was only after these other kinds of explana-tion had been thoroughly investigated and accepted by most scholars that it was possible to go on and see the Evangelists as just that: authors in their own right.

What sorts of explanations can we then offer of such agreements and disagreements? Consider for a moment a striking example of verbal agreements which made headlines after the Poll tax riots. In the trial of Roy Hanney (a TV production engineer with no previous convictions) the two police witnesses agreed uncannily in the statements which they made, supposedly independently, on the evening of the riot. Here is how *The Observer* of 11 November 1990 presented them:

'The Damning Statements'
The following are the beginnings of the accounts supposedly written independently on 31 March

PC EGAN: 'We were deployed on a short shield cordon attempting to push a violent crowd of 500 plus north in Charing Cross Road, WC 1. All the time we were under prolonged attack of missiles consisting of bricks, bottles, pieces of concrete and coins. The order was given to charge into the extremely violent crowd. As we moved forward I saw a man whom I now know to be Roy Hanney. He was wearing an army-type jacket which was zipped up, and he had closely shaven fair hair. As he came to the front of the crowd I saw him shouting something at us which I could not hear, due to the noise of the crowd. I then saw Hanney pull his right arm back and throw what appeared to be a lump of concrete into the police cordon.'

PC RAMSAY: 'We were deployed as a short shield unit forming a cordon attempting to push a violent crowd of about 500 plus north in Charing Cross Road. We were under constant fire from numerous missiles including brick, bottles, sticks and metal bars. The order was given to charge into a violent crowd, as we moved forward, I noticed a man I now know to be Roy Hanney. He had a close-cropped head and an army combat jacket on. He came to the forefront of the crowd shouting swearing at us. I could not make out what he was saying but he shouted it in an aggressive manner. I then noticed him draw back his right arm and throw what appeared to be a brick into the police cordon. Myself and PC Egan ran forward with other officers towards Hanney.'

Not unreasonably, at the trial, the Defence Counsel questioned the independence of the two accounts. 'PC Ramsay denied emphatically having copied PC Egan's statement. *But the structure of the two statements, and much of their phraseology, was identical, down to a mistake about the day of the incident — both said Sunday, not Saturday*'. In response PC Ramsay said that the similarities were 'coincidence' and pointed to the different descriptions of Hanney's hairstyle: 'close-cropped', as opposed to 'shaven'. Mr. Dias asked him to look at his handwritten original. PC Ramsay had crossed out 'shaven' and substituted 'close-cropped'. Most of the jurors reacted with laughter. Shortly afterwards, in a rare legal move, the jury intervened to stop the trial.

The point here, of course, is not to compare the motives of the Evangelists with those of PCs Egan and Ramsay but rather to compare the modes of production of the two statements and the Synoptic Gospels. It is hard to see how this mixture of agreement and disagreement could have come about other than by someone copying and making minor changes to a written document. They might of course both have been copying from the same document; the point is that they were, or at least one of them was, copying from a *written document. There is, that is to say, a relationship of literary dependence between the two*, without which it would be hard to explain the agreements in structure, syntax, phraseology, detail and mistakes between the two accounts.

Certainly one explanation which the jury ruled out in the Poll tax trial was that the two accounts were the independent work of two eye-witnesses. Nor, quite reasonably, did they consider whether the policemen were simply recounting a popular and well-known story about the riot. That was not being claimed and there clearly had not been time for such stories to become widespread. However, for the Synoptic Gospels, written some 30 or more years after the event, this might be a possible explanation. Perhaps the sources of the Synoptic Gospels were in a measure oral sources, oral traditions which had been circulating in a relatively stable form for some time and which were recorded in their own way (with, that is, minor variations) by the Evangelists. This is a by no means impossible but, in view of the close verbal agreements, still less likely explanation than that what we have in the Synoptic Gospels is the result of some kind of literary dependence.

Of course, it is one thing to come to the conclusion that there is a literary relationship between the Synoptic Gospels, quite another to decide how the relationships ran. Who, in simple terms, was copying whom? Were there other documents involved? What role if any did well-established oral tradition have in shaping the Gospels? We shall not spend long over this question. There is a strong consensus among the majority of scholars as well as a persistent, if small, band of doubters. We shall then simply set out the majority view and look at a few objections.

Since the end of the last century in Germany and at the latest since B.H. Streeter's *Four Gospels* (1924) in this country, the accepted view has been that Mark wrote his Gospel first, drawing on material which came to him largely by word of mouth (whether from Peter or some more widespread fund of stories about and sayings of Jesus is still debated) and a Passion narrative which had already received fairly fixed form in the liturgy of the church; that Matthew and Luke used Mark as the basis and framework of their Gospels but also used a written collection of sayings—generally called Q—together with some material of their own. This is known as the two document hypothesis and can be represented diagrammatically as follows:

One of the simplest ways to see the force of this explanation is to look at Alan Barr's *Diagram of Synoptic Relationships*. What this shows can be summarized as follows:

1. Virtually all of Mark appears in either Matthew or Luke.

Matthew omits:

Mark
1.23-28	Synagogue at Capernaum
1.35-38	Withdrawal of Jesus
9.38-40	Strange Exorcist
12.40-44	Widow's mite

Luke omits:

Mark
6.17-29	Death of the Baptist
6.45–8.21	From the Walking on the Sea to the Leaven of the Pharisees
8.32-33	Prediction of the Passion
9.9b-13	Conversation on Elijah
9.28-29	Power of prayer
10.1-12	Marriage and divorce
10.35-40	Sons of Zebedee
11.12-14, 20-25	Cursing and withering of the fig-tree

Both omit:

Mark
3.20-21	Crowd presses
4.26-29	Seed growing secretly (?//Mt. 13.24-30)
5.4-5	Demoniac's fetters
8.22-26	Blind man of Bethsaida
9.15-16	Exchange between Jesus and crowd
9.21-24	Exchange between Jesus and father
9.49-50	Salt (Mt. 5.13; Lk. 14.34-35)
14.51-52	Young man at arrest

2. The order of the Markan material in Luke is very close to that in Mark itself. Only the following passages occur in different order:

Luke	*Mark*	
6.12-16	3.13-19	Appointment of the Twelve
8.19-21	3.31-35	Jesus' Mother and Brethren
22.56-62	14.66-72	Peter's Denials

3. Matthew follows Mark's order closely though there are a substantial number of displacements in the first half of the Gospel:

Matthew	*Mark*	
4.23	1.39; 3.7-8	Preaching and healing
7.28-29	1.22	Effect of preaching
8.14-17	1.29-34	Healing of Peter's mother-in-law; healings in evening
8.23-24	4.35–5.17(20)	Stilling of Storm; Gadarene Demoniac
9.18-26	5.21-43	Jairus's daughter; woman with issue of blood
10.1-4	6.7; 3.13-19	Appointment of Twelve
10.9-14	6.8-11	Mission of Twelve
21.18-19	11.12-14	Cursing and withering of fig tree

4. Where Matthew and Luke have material in common there is less overall agreement in order than in any of the above cases, but still significant agreement in order.

None of this of course adds up to a simple proof of the two document hypothesis. Arguments based on order are easy to turn round. If Matthew had been written first, there would of course still be very considerable agreement in order between the three. But then we would have to look at alternative views of the relations between the three. Suppose, as some would suggest (e.g. W.R. Farmer, reviving the Griesbach hypothesis), that the relationships went:

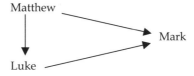

Then we would have a situation where (a) Luke had made much more radical changes to the order of Matthew than on the former hypothesis he had made to Mark (for now we would suppose that he was taking his 'Q' material from Matthew); (b) Mark had largely followed Luke's order but had on occasion (in the Passion narrative) preferred Matthew's; and (c)—most difficult of all—Mark had chosen to omit large parts of Matthew and Luke: the infancy stories, great blocks of teaching material and the resurrection accounts.

Augustine and others have suggested that Mark was an abbreviator, something like a digest writer, which, it is asserted, was not uncommon in the ancient world. But then we have to look at the accounts in rather more detail. The fact is that where all three have the same accounts, Mark's is often longer, containing extra details which an abbreviator would hardly have added. This then presents Mark as a poor literary craftsman, whereas his work is a remarkable piece of natural storytelling.

This is to say that the cumulative effect of the observations above (and of course of a great deal of more detailed observations) is to favour the two document hypothesis based on Markan priority. It might then seem that we can be confident that where Matthew differs from Mark we have evidence of Matthew's modification of Mark. As Graham Stanton has recently argued (*A Gospel for a New People*, pp. 36-41), there are difficulties with this which may make us somewhat cautious about our use of the two document hypothesis in exegesis of the Gospels.

1. The minor agreements. There are a number of cases in the so-called triple tradition, that is, where all three have the same material, where Matthew and Luke agree against Mark, either in offering a slightly differing account or in both omitting part of Mark's account altogether. The differences are not great, more the kind of fine editorial adjustments which an editor would make to the text. Why then did Matthew and Luke both, independently of each other as our hypothesis demands, make the same kind of minor adjustments? This kind of challenge can only be met by detailed argument. In many cases the minor agreements can be shown to be fairly obvious kinds of changes to make. But a look at the omissions which both Luke and Matthew have in common, listed above under (1) may perhaps be better explained by the existence of slightly differing versions of Mark at the time of the writing of Matthew and Luke. This view is supported by the existence of similar different versions of contemporary documents, such as *The Testament of the Twelve Patriarchs, Life of Adam, Testament of Job*.

2. We cannot be confident in every case that we can establish the final form of the text of Matthew. Stanton lists 9.34, 13.14-15, 16.2b-3 and 21.44 as doubtfully original and 21.29-31 as 'in disarray' (p. 37). It may well be that the present form of the Matthaean text has been influenced by the Lukan parallel.

3. It is also not possible to be sure to what extent Matthew's

other sources, Q and his special material and even Mark, had already undergone change and redaction before he came to them.

4. It may also be that Matthew's Gospel as we know it now contains redaction which occurred after the Evangelist had completed his work on it.

5. Some of the differences between Matthew and Mark and Q may be explained by the continuing existence of the oral tradition which lay behind those sources. If Matthew had just heard a story in a variant version, he may have preferred, unconsciously or consciously, some detail which was not in his written source.

What this means cumulatively is not insignificant, perhaps even more significant than Stanton would allow. At the very least it means that in any case where there are minor variations between Matthew and his sources we cannot simply take this as a benchmark of Matthew's own theology. It may be no more than the reflection of a difference in his version of Mark or in the continuing oral tradition. Only if we can build up a consistent pattern in such variations can we be sure that we have evidence for Matthew's own viewpoint. So much Stanton would largely concede. But does it not mean more than this? Does it not mean that there are far fewer cases where we can be sure that we have redactional modifications by the Evangelist? The details of Matthaean redaction may now be less the benchmark of his theology than part of the evidence which has to be carefully weighed alongside the evidence of his arrangement of his sources, of his composition as a whole. I shall return to these thoughts when discussing literary approaches to the Gospel later in the chapter.

There is one other area which exercises some scholars and that is the question of Q. Was it a written document or a relatively discrete oral tradition? Is such a hypothesis necessary at all? Arguments for a written document have to be based principally on evidence of common order between Matthew and Luke. Here the problem is that there is not the same degree of order in the Q material as there is in the Markan material. What there is, however, is by no means unimpressive. This suggests to many that there were different versions of Q circulating and that Matthew and Luke used different versions. This is further supported by the very considerable differences in wording and phraseology between some of the material in Matthew and Luke. The more one becomes aware of these differences, however, the more one might feel inclined to see Q as a relatively coherent body of oral tradition, rather than as a series of documents. This simply reinforces the points made above about the need for caution in judgments about Matthew's editorial work. The less certain we are about the form of Q which Matthew used, the less confident we can be about Matthew's redaction of it, which of course does not stop some scholars from putting forward very detailed reconstructions of different editions of Q.

More radically some scholars would want to dispense with Q altogether (Farrer, Goulder, Drury). The real problems with such proposals, which are in many ways most attractive, lie in the way Luke is then thought to have edited Matthew. As this is not strictly a problem for this guide, we shall merely note the point and pass on.

Literary Characteristics

We have just seen that doubt about our ability to know the precise form of the sources which Matthew was working on means that we have to be cautious when making judgments about his detailed redaction. They need to be set alongside the views we may form about his composition of the Gospel as a whole. Matthew, after all, did not simply work on the small scale, making little changes to his received sources here and there (though he certainly did that); he also put together large blocks of material, drawing on a variety of sources to compose a work we call a Gospel, and which is one of a number of such works.

The questions which flow quite naturally from this are: first, what was it to compose a Gospel? What sort of book did Matthew have it in mind to write? And secondly, how did he set about arranging the sources at his disposal into a book? What principles (if that is the right word) of composition did he employ?

It is important to know what sort of a book one is reading if one wants to grasp its meaning fully. The form is an integral part of the way in which a writer communicates to his readers. It may be more or less simple, more or less fixed and rigid. A sonnet is a complex form with very strict rules; a novel or short story much less fixed and capable of both considerable simplicity and considerable complexity. But in all cases it matters whether or not we realize what the form is. If we think we are reading a traveller's tale and it is really a novel, we may well miss some of the pointers which the writer has given us which are important to the development of the narrative. Our expectations will be different and therefore we may not give attention to aspects of what is being said.

Writers too need to be aware of the rules which govern the literary

forms which they employ. They need to know what their readers'
expectations might be in order to get their attention, to communicate
easily, but also to surprise and puzzle. Creative writers may well re-
model the literary forms or genres with which they work; but they still
need to work broadly within the literary conventions of their day.

Therefore, when we come to consider an ancient literary work like
the Gospel of Matthew we want to know as much as we can about its
form, that is to say about the then existing literary conventions which
governed this kind of writing.

This question is not nearly so abstract as it might seem. Literary
conventions do not (often) exist in some kind of rule book, though
critics may try to tabulate and analyse them. They exist in living
communities of writers and readers; they require, that is to say, a 'literary public'. On occasion, as with some Greek and Roman literature of
the time, such a public would be sophisticated and educated, a wealthy
elite meeting in each other's houses for public readings of the latest
literary works: poetry, memoirs, lives, letters, dialogues. In other cases
the public will have been more extensive, as with the audiences of
plays and comedies in the ancient world. Not all will perhaps have
appreciated the finer points of form, but most will have had at least an
intuitive grasp of the genre and known broadly what to expect in the
development of, respectively, a tragedy and a comedy. Other works
will have been more at home in religious communities of different
kinds: liturgies, psalms, narratives, legal material, and these will have
had their proper context and rules which will have had to be
observed.

So we need to ask: What sort of 'literary public' was Matthew's
Gospel written for? *and* What other models of literary production did
Matthew have before him when he wrote? The questions are interrelated and the first will occupy us considerably in the next chapter,
but still here we need to give some provisional answers. Let us take
the question of literary models first.

Obviously, when Matthew wrote, his principal (one of his principal?) model(s) was Mark but what kind of a book was that? Mark's
book starts: 'The beginning of the gospel of Jesus Christ...' Scholars
are generally agreed that 'gospel' here refers to the Christian message
which Mark's book will relate, not to the type of book—a Gospel—
which Mark was beginning to write. They are rather less in agreement
about what kind of book it was that Mark wrote.

One obvious parallel to Mark's Gospel might be thought to lie in
ancient biography. This view was widely held in the nineteenth century but was questioned earlier this century, notably by German form

critics who argued (1) that the Gospels were folk literature rather than high literature; (2) that the 'literary understanding of the Synoptics begins with the recognition that they are collections of material. The composers are only to the smallest extent authors. They are principally collectors, vehicles of tradition, editors' (M. Dibelius, *From Tradition to Gospel*, p. 3). That is, the Gospels were in form (if not in content) more like collections of Faust legends, for example, than like literary biographies.

However, as interest in the editorial activity of the Evangelists has grown since the end of the war, so this sharp distinction between the literary forms of the Hellenistic world and the Gospels has come to be challenged. Some, notably David E. Aune (*The New Testament in its Literary Environment*), have argued that the Gospels should be seen as examples of Graeco-Roman biography at a popular level. Aune states that such biography tends to be in the form of 'complex or host genres serving as literary frames for a variety of shorter forms' (p. 28) and stresses the great variety of such biographical forms, while indicating many striking analogies in the content, motifs and purposes of ancient biographical literature and the Gospels. Others, like Ernest Best (*Mark: The Gospel as Story*, pp. 140ff.), have suggested that the closest literary parallels to Mark are to be found in Old Testament narrative cycles, like the Elisha–Elijah cycle. This view can find considerable support, not least in the analogies between the particular stories and motifs associated with the central figures: cures of lepers, feeding of crowds, raising of the dead.

This is a difficult debate to summarize or indeed to adjudicate. What the form critics saw rightly (as is stressed again by Best) is that the Evangelists, notably Mark, were 'preservers of the tradition' (*Mark: The Gospel as Story*, pp. 109ff.), that they collected it and treated it with respect and made only relatively modest alterations to it. They saw too, and this is agreed by Aune, that the works they produced were written in popular style and, certainly in Mark's case, could lay no claim to being works of sophisticated literature. Thus they compared them (so especially K.L. Schmidt, *Place*) to later collections of legends and sayings, The Sayings of the Fathers, the Legends of St Francis and the collections of Faust Legends, rather than to the more carefully organized (whether chronologically or topically) lives of ancient biography. But the form critics' interest in the traditions which the Evangelists collected led them to ignore the sense in which they had composed a work which was more than the sum of its parts. Mark's narrative is a powerful and moving piece of writing and this is missed if one simply analyses out the 'framework' which he constructed to contain his collection of stories and sayings and presents it as a rather crude literary expedient.

Thus Aune is right to explore the contemporary literary parallels to the Gospels. Few writers produce powerful works of literature, whether polished or not, without some literary models. Contemporary lives are one obvious source of such models for the Evangelists, particularly if we allow that writers may draw on such models freely and creatively. Of course the freer we allow them to have been, the more difficult it is to decide which model they were following. One does not have to come down on one side or another. Mark may well have been influenced by contemporary lives and have formed the wish to write such a life to justify and commend the way of the Gospel to its followers. But it would be strange if someone so obviously steeped in the Scriptures had not learnt something of his narrative craft from the great stories of the Pentateuch and the books of Samuel and Kings.

But if Mark is Matthew's closest model when he starts to write what other influences shaped his work? Stanton (*Gospel for a New People*, pp. 66ff.) has argued interestingly that Matthew takes up and develops the genre of both Mark and Q. Q (here Stanton follows Kloppenborg, *The Formation of Q*) is a collection of wisdom sayings which is a genre widely found in ancient Near Eastern writing. It is also like the collections of *chreiae* (anecdotes) in Greek. Both these forms may have 'a biographical interest' and so it is possible that Q itself had with the addition of the temptation narrative developed closer to ancient lives. Thus when Matthew takes it up, so Stanton, he does not simply destroy it by incorporating it into Mark. In the first place it is not, as we have just noted, a completely alien form. Secondly, although Matthew reorganizes his Q material more freely than (it is generally accepted) does Luke, he does so in a way which preserves (at least in part) the genre of Q. By creating a series of distinct discourses which are signalled as such at the end of each section by very similar phrases: 'when Jesus had finished these sayings' (7.28; 11.1; 13.53; 19.1; 26.1), Matthew creates smaller versions of Q within his narrative framework. At the same time he extends the Markan genre by incorporating more discourse material which is arranged topically.

One way of bringing these kinds of discussion into focus is to ask, what was the literary structure of the Gospel? The question here is often put but the word structure is one which tends to be overworked. What exactly is meant?

'Structure' is a word which suggests some kind of geometrical or otherwise regular configuration of materials. It is applied readily to building design and other forms of construction, but can be easily used figuratively of arguments, works of music and literature. In all cases one is looking for some kind of patterning which is linked to some purpose or intention: the construction of a strong, elegant, durable building, or the creation of a work of art of beauty and clarity. It is in this fairly broad and obvious figurative sense that it is most obviously used by New Testament scholars. This is quite different from its use among a particular school of 'structuralist' literary critics, who were looking for ways in which texts, rituals and other products of the human mind were thought to betray certain 'deep structures' which are determined by the mind's own inherent patterns of thought. We shall then ask: what evidence is there of some shaping by Matthew of his material and in what sense does this betray any kind of rational purpose?

We have already noticed certain characteristics of Matthew's use of his sources, Mark and Q. We saw that in his use of Mark he sometimes departs from Mark's order in the first part of his Gospel, while following the order very closely from ch. 11 onwards. We also saw that Matthew had constructed a number of discourses: chs. 5–8 the Sermon on the Mount; ch. 10 the mission discourse; ch. 13 parables; ch. 18 advice for the community; chs. (23)24–25 judgment and the End. Much of the material in these sections comes from his other sources, Q and his own special material. Thus we can say very simply that Matthew has followed Mark closely, though he has rearranged some of the material in the earlier chapters, notably to give an extended section on miracles in chs. 8–9, and that he has fitted a series of extended discourses into this largely given narrative framework.

One of the earliest explanations of this pattern was offered by an American scholar, B.S. Bacon (*Studies in Matthew*). He suggested that Matthew had deliberately constructed five books each with a narrative section and a discourse of Jesus by way of comparison with the Pentateuch, so as to suggest that Jesus was the new Moses. That such patterning is deliberate is shown easily by Matthew's use of a recurring phrase: 'when Jesus had finished these sayings' (7.28; 11.1; 13.53; 19.1) culminating in 'when Jesus had finished all these sayings' in 26.1 to mark off the end of each section. Such patterning cannot be accidental. What more obvious purpose should Matthew have here than to compare Jesus' teaching with the Law given by Moses? The contrast is again brought out clearly in the Sermon on the Mount in the antitheses between 'you have heard it said of old' and 'but I say unto you'. In all this, as Graham Stanton has suggested recently, Matthew is using a familiar and favorite rhetorical device of the day, comparison (*sugkrasis*, *Gospel for a New People*, pp. 77ff.).

There are, however, difficulties with Bacon's account. First, there is no place in his scheme for the infancy narratives of chs. 1–2 and the passion and resurrection narratives of chs. 26–28. While it may be not unreasonable to treat the infancy narratives as a kind of prologue, it will hardly do to treat the expanded Markan passion and resurrection account as an epilogue. Secondly, the scheme seems to leave out some of the discourse material, 11.7-30 and 23.1-39, though the latter may, of course, be regarded as part of the fifth discourse. Further, it has been questioned whether the recurring phrase 'when Jesus had finished...' is a *concluding* phrase rather than a transitional one; and lastly it is disputed whether the Gospel gives any evidence for Matthew's thinking of Jesus as a 'new Moses'.

Perhaps the real problem with Bacon's analysis is that it tries to solve too much. It proposes a schema for the whole book, rather than offering an explanation for Matthew's arrangement of his discourse material within the Markan framework. If it is revised, to assert that Matthew's intention in placing these five major blocks of teaching evenly through the Gospel is to stress the importance of Jesus' teaching — and indeed to compare it with the Mosaic Law — then most of the objections will fall. Even the objection that the phrase itself is not strictly a concluding phrase, even to a discourse on its own, is hardly telling. In the first place it clearly does refer to the fact that Jesus had concluded his teaching; secondly, even if it is true that it inaugurates the next section, it is still a clear marker, delineating the start of a new section, and hence the end of another.

Such a revision of Bacon's thesis leaves unexplained the nature of Matthew's narrative scheme and purpose. We have seen that he largely takes over Mark's framework, but also that he makes certain changes in the first half of the Gospel. J.D. Kingsbury (*Matthew: Structure, Christology, Kingdom*) has suggested that we may find a clue to Matthew's narrative purpose in another recurring phrase: 'From then on Jesus began...' True, this phrase only recurs once after its first use in 4.17, namely at 16.21. Nevertheless, the two occurrences mark off, in the first instance, Jesus' ministry from the ministry of John the Baptist, and in the second, the move from Jesus' ministry to his death and resurrection. That is to say, this schema draws the readers' attention to the different stages in salvation history which occur in the Gospel. It demonstrates to Kingsbury that Matthew is primarily concerned with his narrative rather than with the teaching material.

There are considerable problems with this view. Matthew 4.17 is not an entirely obvious division between John the Baptist and Jesus. This seems more readily to occur at 4.12. Nor indeed is 16.21 the most obvious point at which to mark the transition to the Passion; 26.1, one of the occurrences of the other phrase, would be just as suitable.

Lastly, and most seriously, it seems strange to suggest that Matthew is *exalting* narrative over discourse, when he has taken such care in the construction of his major discourse sections and their insertion into his Markan source. Clearly Matthew is unlike his source 'Q' in that he produces a work in which there is a balance of narrative and discourse material but it would be a serious mistake to underestimate the importance of his discourse material, as a comparison with Mark makes clear. In his earlier work, Kingsbury rejected such a comparison. We should allow Matthew to stand for itself. This is puzzling. Why should we ignore some of the most striking evidence that we have, namely that there is a relationship of literary dependence between Mark and Matthew and that in all likelihood it is Matthew that has used Mark? This must affect our view of his literary purposes, particularly where we are concerned with structure. If he has rearranged or modified existing structures, that must tell us something about his intentions.

What we do know is that he has modified his Markan framework somewhat differently at different stages of the Gospel, more at first, only by way of insertion in the latter half. The earlier modifications principally serve the purpose of gathering together much of the miracle material into a section (chs. 8–9). Some have seen in this a presentation of Jesus as the Messiah of deed to complement the presentation of him as Messiah of Word in chs. 5–7. This would fit quite neatly with the suggestion that in modifying Mark's Gospel Matthew has followed patterns of contemporary lives which arranged matters topically. It would of course also say something about Matthew's Christology.

Further, the contrast between his use of Mark in the two halves of the Gospel would suggest that Matthew is less than wholly consistent in his restructuring of Mark and that we should be content to discover what design we can without seeking a total explanation for every aspect of the Gospel. This view is advocated persuasively by Stanton. In particular, Stanton (*Gospel for a New People*, pp. 71-76) has suggested that such an approach to the Gospel does justice to its original mode of delivery. Such texts, so Stanton, would have been primarily read aloud in public. The length of the Gospel would have made it unlikely that it was often read on one occasion in its entirety so that, while people may have picked up detailed points of arrangement within sections, they would have been less able to see overall structures, and Matthew equally would have been less concerned with intricate overall structures.

Against this others have still thought to see very intricate structural patterns in the Gospel. Davies and Allison in their recent commentary have suggested that chiasm (arrangements of material which are patterned in the form A B C B' A' and variants thereof) plays a significant role in its structure and have arranged the whole Gospel chiastically with its centre at ch. 13. This requires too much detailed discussion here. There is always a certain subjectivity in spotting chiasm, though it is not to be ignored. Matthew may well have used it as a device on the small scale, but its use to structure the whole Gospel given its manner of composition by 'pasting together' various sources is unlikely.

Finally, in this section we need to say something briefly about Matthew's audience. Who, in his own view, was he writing for?

We noted in passing that Mark's Gospel was stylistically rough. This is hardly an indication that it was written for a cultivated literary public. Its readers were probably members of house-churches in Graeco-Roman cities who were for the most part less than well educated, though there may have been some for whom Mark's Gospel came across as unpolished. Was Matthew attempting to bring Mark's Gospel more into line with the cultural milieu of the Hellenistic city? Quite possibly. Luke, writing his preface to Theophilus, certainly gave himself the airs of a Hellenistic historian (Lk. 1.1-4). But was Matthew writing primarily for an educated Greek audience?

This is a question we shall explore further in the next chapter but there are some points to be made here. The fact that Matthew is concerned to improve Mark's style, that he writes with conscious literary purpose, is significant. It shows him as wishing to conform to certain literary standards and it is reasonable to infer from this that there were those among his audience who would have been able to appreciate the value of what he was doing. Who were they? Were they Jews or Gentiles? The simple answer is that they might have been either. There are some notable examples of educated Jews writing in Greek: Philo and Josephus. Thus we can make no easy move from the fact that Matthew wrote educated Greek to the religious background of his readers. More significant may well be his use of the Old Testament. Appeal to the fulfilment of Old Testament prophecy as vindication of one's story does not necessarily mean that one assumes that one's readers accept the authority of the Scriptures. Fulfilment of prophecy—any prophecy—might in itself be enough to convince many. Nevertheless, Matthew's appeal to the Old Testament on such a regular basis does suggest, at the least, that it was his natural point of reference and authority and might well also suggest that his community was well able to identify with the religious authority of the Scriptures quoted. Can we go further and suggest that his community was some kind of scholarly community eager to seek out the meaning of the Scriptures, a school of Matthew? We will take up these questions again in the next chapter.

Reading the Gospel of Matthew

The kind of work we have been considering so far has been principally concerned with the sources, composition and literary genre of the Gospels. Recent studies of Matthew have included a good number of literary-critical studies which have claimed to be essentially distinct from such studies. The term 'literary-critical' is itself a little confusing in the context of biblical studies, for it was originally used to refer to such matters as we have discussed above under the heading of source-criticism. It was, that is to say, concerned with the biblical texts from a historical point of view, exploring their genesis, the manner in which they came to be written. More recently, however, such historical concerns have been contrasted with a literary mode of studying texts, which in its extreme form is wholly uninterested in the historical genesis or reception of texts.

This is, I think, unhelpful. Literary studies of Matthew may be written from many different theoretical perspectives: some scholars may attempt a reading of the Gospel which uses the canons of modern narrative theory; others may be much more interested in attempting to trace out the literary conventions of the time and to follow the history of the text's reception. They may both shed light on the text.

Certainly, it seems to me indisputable that biblical scholarship needs to take the Gospels seriously as works of literature. Simply to see them as repositories of Christian doctrine, or worse to see them solely as evidence for the life of the early Christian communities would be to ignore their character as stories, just as it would be to ignore the very different quality of their telling. In this respect studies like those of J.D. Kingsbury (*Matthew as Story*), R.A. Edwards (*Matthew's Story of Jesus*) and D.B. Howell (*Matthew's Inclusive Story*) have been valuable in reminding us of the narrative character of the Gospel.

The question which such studies raise is: what kinds of narratives are Gospels? Do we see them as somehow timeless works which can yield up their secrets to modern understandings of narrative? Do we see them as works which are indebted to the literary canons of their own time and which therefore can fully be understood only when we appreciate the rhetoric and indeed the manner of their production?

It may not be inappropriate at this point to invoke a Matthaean maxim: 'By their fruits you shall know them'. Reading Gospels from the point of view of modern narrative theory alerts us to features of the text we might well otherwise miss. Thus in Howell's book we are invited to consider the way in which the Evangelist organizes his material according to a certain 'point of view'; to explore the way in which certain key themes such as promise/fulfilment or acceptance/rejection are emplotted in the narrative; above all to consider the way in which the reader is drawn into the story, not so much by identifying with any particular character in the narrative as, for example, the disciples, but by coming to see Jesus himself as the model for discipleship. We are encouraged, that is to say, not simply to see the Gospel as propounding a particular view of history, a particular Christology, but as a complex rhetorical strategy for winning over its readers.

There is a great deal of detailed discussion in Howell's book and it is possible here only to look at one instance of the application of these notions to the Gospel. Howell sees the opening section of the Gospel as serving to produce certain competencies in the reader by introducing the major characters, adumbrating the conflict between Jesus and his opponents and establishing the plotting devices which are used throughout the narrative (p. 115). Thus the genealogy is used to place Jesus firmly in the history of Abraham and David and in ch. 2 the theme of Abraham is taken up again as Jesus is shown as 'heir to the promise of blessing to the Gentiles'. Above all, the genealogy and its summary point to the providential purposes of God which are being fulfilled in Jesus and so introduce us to one of the two main plotting devices, which, along with the notion of acceptance/fulfilment, controls the development of the narrative.

We need not follow all the detail of Howell's exposition of Mt. 1.1–4.16 but an example or two of how he sees these motifs operating may be useful. In the stories relating the birth and naming of Jesus, 'Joseph is confronted with the choice of either accepting or rejecting the angel's instructions' (p. 117). Because of Joseph's obedience the 'will of God is fulfilled in the predictive sense in that his pre-determined plan is carried out—but is also fulfilled in the volitional sense, in that divine instructions are accepted and executed by Joseph' (p. 117). There is, that is to say, a neat intertwining of the two motifs which can also be observed elsewhere.

As the story develops, so the contrast between those who accept, like Joseph and the Magi, and those who reject, like Herod, is played out and interwoven with the motif of fulfilment which is provided largely, but not entirely, by the fulfilment citations which occur freely in this section. So too with John the Baptist, whose conflict with the Pharisees and Sadducees is initiated by his denunciation of them in 3.8, which Howell says 'contains the suggestion about what called forth the condemnation: their actions were incongruous with true repentance' (p. 122). By contrast Matthew does not use the theme of rejection but rather 'uses the theme of acceptance to plot Jesus' baptism. Jesus' response to John in 3.15a, which for the evangelist provides the answer to the question of how Jesus could submit to John for baptism, highlights the theme of acceptance' (p. 123).

And so Howell's treatment of the 'narrative temporal ordering and emplotment' proceeds. The last remark may help to focus some of the reservations which I feel about this kind of discussion. To say that the discussion between Jesus and John at the baptism 'highlights the theme of acceptance' is clearly not false—but is it sufficient? The exchange clearly highlights a good deal more: on the one hand it contrasts Jesus and John, on the other it unites them in their mutual acceptance of God's will whereby they 'fulfil all righteousness'. As Luz points out, the reference to *all* righteousness transcends the situation of the baptism: it now refers to the total will of God which all are commanded to do (*Matthew 1–7*, p. 178). By accepting, Jesus becomes the example to Christians. At the same time, John's acquiescence also points to the way in which Jesus is to be emulated. Now clearly this is entirely consistent with what Howell says. He explicitly supports an exemplary reading of the passage against a salvation historical one: Jesus' baptism marks a key point in the divine plan. My concern is that Howell's rather timeless mode of proceeding, by invoking generalized notions of emplotment, overlooks contemporary literary conventions which might have drawn out other important aspects of the texts. Graham Stanton has drawn attention to Matthew's use of comparison which was a widely used rhetorical device (*Gospel for a New People*, pp. 77-84). By the same token, there is no doubt that his exemplary reading gains much support from contemporary linguistic evidence which shows that 'righteousness' undergoes a change in meaning from its biblical sense of 'God's saving and righteous order' to 'righteousness' understood as an ethical norm to be fulfilled by men and women.

What this raises then is a wider set of questions as to whether there is not more to be learnt from at least a combination of modes of interpretation based on modern literary theory with those which pay greater attention to the literary conventions which were in force at the time when the Gospels were written. More, we should also consider what we know about the mode of production of the Gospel: the way in which Matthew worked with his sources, the extent to which he was free and/or constrained by the community for which he wrote. And finally, none of this should distract us from the solid philological task of determining the lingusitic conventions which were in force when Matthew wrote.

Conclusion

The conclusions of this chapter may be briefly drawn together. Matthew's Gospel is a complex variant of Mark's. He has taken an existing work and reworked it. Stylistically he has improved Mark's rather rough Greek. Structurally he has woven into it a substantial amount of discourse material, creating five blocks of teaching material reminiscent of the five books of the Law. He has also reordered some of Mark's original Gospel to give a certain grouping of Jesus' deeds in chs. 8–9. In this Matthew has not substantially altered the form of Mark's work: it remains a book that, like the ancient Hellenistic biographies, is a 'host genre': a broad narrative capable of accommodating many different forms. Like Mark it draws on the Old Testament. But there is a slackening of Mark's narrative tension and pace which shows Matthew as perhaps more interested in the discourse material drawn from his other main source 'Q'. In this, he is of course also less close to the Old Testament and closer to the Jewish writers who would compile the Mishnah at the end of the century. Thus already this consideration of the literary character of the Gospel suggests its proximity to contemporary Jewish concerns about the interpretation and teaching of the Law.

FURTHER READING

D.E. Aune, *The New Testament in its Literary Environment* (Philadelphia: Westminster Press, 1987).

B.S. Bacon, *Studies in Matthew* (London: Constable, 1930).

A. Barr, *Diagram of Synoptic Relationships* (Edinburgh: T. & T. Clark, 1938).

E. Best, *Mark: The Gospel as Story* (Edinburgh: T. & T. Clark, 1983).

M. Dibelius, *From Tradition to Gospel* (London: Ivor Nicholson & Watson, 1934).

J.H. Drury, *Tradition and Design in Luke's Gospel* (London: Darton, Longman & Todd, 1976).

R.A. Edwards, *Matthew's Story of Jesus* (Philadelphia: Fortress Press, 1985).

W.R. Farmer, *The Synoptic Problem* (New York: Macmillan, 1976).

A.M. Farrer, 'On Dispensing with Q', in D. Nineham (ed.), *Studies in the Gospels* (Oxford: Basil Blackwell, 1955), pp. 55-86.

M.D. Goulder, *Midrash and Lection in Matthew* (London: SPCK, 1974).

D.B. Howell, *Matthew's Inclusive Story* (Sheffield: JSOT Press, 1990).

J.D. Kingsbury, *Matthew: Structure, Christology, Kingdom* (Philadelphia: Fortress Press, 1975).

—*Matthew as Story* (Philadelphia: Fortress Press, 1986).

J. Kloppenborg, The Formation of Q (Philadelphia: Fortress Press, 1987).

K.L. Schmidt, *The Place of the Gospels in the General History of Literature* (trans. B.R. McCane, with an introduction by J. Riches; Columbia: University of South Carolina Press, 2001).

G.N. Stanton, *A Gospel for a New People* (Edinburgh: T. & T. Clark, 1992).

B.H. Streeter, *The Four Gospels* (London: Macmillan, 1924).

The New Testament of our Lord and Saviour Jesus Christ, in the Original Greek, with Notes and Introductions, by Chr. Wordsworth, D.D. Bp. of Lincoln (London: Rivingtons, 7th edn, 1870).

Chapter Three

MATTHEW'S WORLD

Where do we place Matthew in the world of the first-century Mediterranean? The question is not simply a geographical one. It is also, and more answerably, a cultural-historical one. Matthew's Gospel is without question a book of enormous significance in the development of the cultures of Europe. It stands at the parting of the ways between church and synagogue. It also marks a significant point in the development of the church into an institution with rules and formal organization. It would then be good to know as much as possible about its location and the subsequent history of its reception in the church. How much can we know?

Let us start with its origins. The difficulty, as with so many New Testament writings, is that we have very little, other than the Gospel itself, to go on. We need to pick up what clues we can in the Gospel itself. That is by general acknowledgment a difficult task even when one is dealing with the Epistles. They are at least mostly addressed to particular situations; but then one hears only one side of the question. The Gospels by contrast are stories ostensibly, at least, telling about events which precede the Evangelist's situation by some 50 years. How much then can we learn from Matthew's Gospel about the situation of his church?

J.L. Martyn, in a book which has been highly influential in Johannine studies, suggested that the stories of the Fourth Gospel have to be read on two levels: as referring both to particular events in Jesus' life and to Jesus' 'presence in actual events experienced by the Johannine church'. This is a useful proposal which works well in Martyn's case because he can find some clear pointers to the situation in the life of his community. A reference to 'being put out of the synagogue', such as we find in Jn 9.22, 12.42 and 16.2, may start off a whole train of inference which will cast light on the original setting of the Gospel. It is probably mostly true that good story-tellers shape their story in such a way as to resonate with their hearers' situation, but that does not mean that it is always easy to infer from the story what precisely that situation was.

There are in fact some clues, references in the telling of the story, which clearly reflect Matthew's situation rather than that of the stated situation in the life of Jesus.

Thus when Jesus refers to the church in 16.18 and 18.17 (the only two occurrences of the word in all the Gospels) we are clearly being transported from the world of Jesus' Galilean ministry to the life of the early Christian community.

Again, there are some tell-tale features associated with Matthew's presentation of Jesus' opponents. Matthew portrays the Pharisees as Jesus' main opponents. He often adds them into Mark's account (12.24, 38; 21.45; 22.34-35, 41). They are specifically targeted in 5.20 and 15.12-14 and they are the subject of a particularly fierce attack in ch. 23.

Furthermore, the Pharisees are often paired with the Scribes (5.20; 12.38; 15.1; 23.2, 13, 14, 15, 23, 27, 29). This linking is specific to Matthew and may reflect a situation after 70 CE when there were only Pharisaic scribes.

Another interesting feature of Matthew's narrative is the coupling of the Pharisees and the chief priests in Mt. 21.45 (whereas Mark has previously referred to the chief priest and scribes and elders) and in 27.62 (the narrative, peculiar to Matthew, of the sealing of the tomb). This puts the Pharisees in a position of authority which they did not hold during Jesus' lifetime but did after 70. We have here a kind of double reference, on the one hand to the situation at the time of Jesus and on the other to that of Matthew's church.

Finally, we might notice the way in which Matthew refers to 'their synagogues' on a number of occasions: 4.23; 9.35; 10.17; 12.9; 13.54. These references are peculiar to Matthew where they occur, although the expression also occurs in Mk 1.23 and some textual traditions have a similar expression in Mk 1.21. Clearly such an expression reflects a separation between the narrator and the 'synagogue' which must tell us something about his stance. The same is also true of expressions like 'their scribes' (7.29), 'their cities' (11.1) and 'their country' (13.54).

Thus there are at least some indications that Matthew's Gospel was written in a situation where the church was in process of developing its structures and where there was a sense of both antagonism and separation between the Christian community and the Jewish community.

Matthew in the History of the Early Church

With these brief but not insignificant clues in mind let us turn first to consider Matthew's situation in the development of the early Christian community.

It has been said that the earliest history of the Christian church is almost impossible to reconstruct. What we have in the New Testament are merely fragments of a much larger canvas most of which we shall never be able to recover. The danger, if this is right, is that we then try to piece together the fragments which we have into a complete picture, with inevitable distortions. There is obviously truth in this, although we cannot of course know how much is missing. We should proceed with caution when constructing the larger picture.

What then can we say with some measure of confidence?

Christian Mission and the Hellenists

We know from Acts 6 that quite early on the church in Jerusalem, which played a very important role in the first generations of Christianity, experienced some kind of a division. The immediate cause was the difficulties experienced by the Hellenists in relation to the daily distribution of food to widows. The 'Hellenists', as opposed to the 'Hebrews', clearly felt that their widows were disadvantaged in the daily distribution. The upshot, according to Acts, is that there were appointed Seven to oversee the daily distribution.

So much we can read in Acts. We need to do some reading between the lines to pick out its meaning. First, who were the 'Hellenists' and 'Hebrews'? Martin Hengel ('Between Jesus and Paul') has suggested that the terms refer to different language groups within the early community, those who spoke Greek and those who spoke Hebrew or Aramaic. Among the former will have been those who had come to live in Jerusalem in their old age, and who may have felt excluded not only from the distribution of food but also, for linguistic reasons, at the meetings of the church for worship and prayer. It is also noticeable in Acts 6 that although the Seven are appointed to serve tables, their leader, Stephen, immediately appears as a powerful preacher who causes great anxiety among the Jewish leaders in Jerusalem because, they say, he speaks 'words against the holy place and the law' (Acts 6.13). Thus it appears that the Seven were not merely 'deacons' with limited administrative tasks. Hengel believes that they were in fact the appointed leaders of a new Greek-speaking group with its own meetings for worship and prayer. Once the group gains a measure of autonomy, they preach openly and publish their understanding of Jesus' teaching which is said to be critical of the Law and the Temple. The immediate result is that this group of Christians is persecuted, Stephen is martyred and they flee to Antioch from where they continue to proclaim their version of Christianity. By contrast the 'Hebrews' remain in Jerusalem and continue to worship in the Temple.

Wandering Charismatics and Urban Communities
This provides us with one early account of the way in which Christianity spread. The persecution of Christians in Jerusalem led to their scattering 'throughout the region of Judaea and Samaria' (Acts 8.1). Acts adds 'except for the apostles'. This suggests a picture of the apostles ruling over the Jerusalem church while Christianity spread through the agency of those who had been persecuted. As G. Theissen has argued in *The First Followers of Jesus*, this picture is oversimplified. We have evidence from Paul's letters that not all the apostles were always to be found in Jerusalem. At his visit recorded in Gal. 1.18-19 he sees only Peter and James, the Lord's brother. Galatians 2.11 tells us of Peter's visit to Antioch and of course there are many traditions of Peter's visit to and martyrdom in Rome. Rather than seeing Christianity as almost an accidentally missionary movement (though of course Luke records the mission charge to the disciples in Acts 1), Theissen has argued that we should see it as, in its early stages at least, a movement which is driven by 'wandering charismatics', those who are actively seeking a new mode of existence driven by a sense of the breakdown of the old order (social anomie). It is such people who are idealized by stories like the mission charge in Mark 6 and by passages like Mt. 6.25ff., 8.18ff. and 10.1ff. Prophetic figures occur in Mt. 7.15, 10.41 and 23.34, were still to be found in the church of the second century (*Did.* 11.4), and required the support of the local communities, something, as the *Didache* suggests, which could easily become a problem. There is, that is to say, room for tension here between those who are driven by the Spirit to a wandering, mendicant existence, proclaiming the Gospel, and those who seek to realize their Christian discipleship in small Christian communities, living a relatively stable existence. The latter group will soon begin to develop goals of its own, to seek ways of surviving as a community, of dealing with disputes, of distributing power and of working out its relationship with the surrounding society.

Of course we have vivid evidence in Paul's letters of the tensions that could arise between such itinerant figures and the local churches.

Paul is certainly someone caught up in the Spirit, driven to preach the Gospel to the Gentiles in the vivid expectation of the coming of the new age. Nevertheless his missionary activity may well originally have started at the behest of the church at Antioch (Acts 13.1ff.). When, however, he loses the support of that church he can portray himself as a free apostle (1 Cor. 9.1-2), a claim based on his 'seeing the Lord' (1 Cor. 9.1; cf. Gal. 1.12). He has the right to food and support, but rarely makes use of it (1 Cor. 9), though this may cause his churches to question his trust in them. He proclaims a gospel free from the Law and finds himself sometimes in controversy with those of his converts who wish to give shape to their lives by appeal to the Law (Galatians). Nevertheless his letters are testimony to the need of his churches for advice and guidance on practical matters which threaten to divide the community. His authority, which is based solely on his churches' recognition of him, is challenged by other itinerant prophets who come with letters of recommendation from elsewhere (2 Cor. 3). His churches can all too easily be swayed by other itinerant preachers, just as he himself once swayed them. Paul, however, is deeply uneasy with any form of external authority, whether it be some form of official recognition or status, or some 'written code' (2 Cor. 3.6) of law, even, it might seem, of an appeal to the words and life of Jesus (2 Cor. 5.16). Nevertheless, he too seeks recognition from Jerusalem and is anxious that the collection from his churches will be received by Jerusalem as a mark of such recognition (Rom. 15.30-31). And of course he appeals to the written 'Scriptures' and writes authoritative letters himself.

Thus we can see here clearly enough some of the issues which will increasingly engage the early Christian communities and their leaders, their prophets, teachers and evangelists. What claims to recognition and support do wandering prophets properly have? If they are not to be allowed to disturb the peace of the local community and if the community is to form its own judgment between their sometimes conflicting messages, then it must develop some canons of judgment of its own. But what sort of canons? Is the church which is led by the Spirit to return to the letter? Is the freedom of the Spirit which empowers prophets to preach the gospel to be restricted by the development of a local church leadership which is officially appointed and maintained? Does the church not need to develop appropriate codes of conduct in order to avoid suspicion and persecution? How far should it deviate from existing norms and patterns of behaviour? Some may have argued that in the light of the imminence of the end, such codes were now out of place, but as time went on the need to order the church's affairs grew. In all this the church is necessarily beginning to construct for itself a 'social world' which will enable it to live more or less at peace with its surrounding society. Such questions run through the writings of the New Testament. They have already left their mark on the writings and traditions which Matthew inherited.

Evidence of the Issues of Community Norms in Matthew's Sources
1. *Mark*. We have of course to be careful when we attempt to describe the way in which Matthew's sources were already addressing such questions. We should not simply assume that their authors or compilers are always addressing such issues directly. Mark may have had many reasons for compiling his Gospel, not the least of which may have been the simple desire to preserve the church's traditions about Jesus. Ernest Best (*Mark: The Gospel as Story*, pp. 51-54) has suggested that Mark writes primarily as a pastor, trying to reassure his congregation in the face of doubts and difficulties, by presenting to them a picture of Jesus as a caring pastor and shepherd of the church.

But of course the very fact of wanting to preserve the tradition indicates that Mark no longer expects the *imminent* end of the world (see Mk 13.10) and one may certainly ask whether his intention in recording the tradition is not also in a broad sense apologetic. Time and again, Mark refers to Jesus as a teacher, while recording relatively little of his teaching. Here is a new teaching 'with authority' (1.27). He certainly does on occasion speak very dismissively of the Law (7.19; 10.5), but for the most part, such issues are not directly engaged. The overall picture, however, is of a 'teacher' who is itinerant and whose closest associates are called to follow him in an itinerant ministry. In the end, it is the narrative itself which is Mark's great achievement. Is not the act of recording this life and death also a way of staking out a claim that this Jesus is the Son of God, that what is recorded here shall form the basis of a new view of the world? That is to say, the process of forging authoritative writings which can anchor the community, give it direction and stamp out a place for it in the ancient world has begun. We should, however, be wary of seeing too much direct engagement with the specific issues of itinerant prophets, of community norms and discipline.

2. *Q*. The collection of sayings on which Matthew and Luke drew, 'Q', is, of course, a more shadowy document, if document at all. One striking feature is the number of sayings which exalt a life of radical discipleship: 6.25-33; 8.18-22; 10.7-16, 26-40. Here one feels that the life of the itinerant preacher is being commended and upheld, a radical new

way of life is being commended which breaks sharply with old rules
and ways ('leave the dead to bury their dead'). Yet at the same time
the collection contains sayings which strongly affirm the law and the
teaching of Jesus as transcending the Law: 5.18, 39-42, 44-48; 7.12.
Moreover, as a collection of Jesus' sayings and parables, it is, as we have
seen, analogous to other collections in the ancient world of the sayings
of philosophers and wise men. So, again, there is a step being taken
here, particularly if it is a written document, towards establishing the
position and authority of Jesus the teacher. The emphasis on Jesus'
teachings is, of course, all the more striking in Q, because of the
absence of any miracle stories or passion narrative. However, it would
be a mistake to think that Q simply presents Jesus as a philosopher-
teacher; there is a strong sense of his imminent return as the Son of
Man in power (24.26-28, 37-41), which one assumes is closely related
to the ethos of radical discipleship we have already noticed. Jesus'
teaching is the announcement of the wisdom of God which presages
the final revelation of his glory. The miracle of it is that it has been
revealed to 'babes' (11.25-27). (There are some scholars who argue that
there were different versions of Q, and that the predictions of the return
of the Son of Man belong to the later editions. As we do not have any
separate version of Q, it seems to me impossibly bold to speculate about
different recensions.)

3. *Matthew's Special Traditions, M.* Finally, there is Matthew's own special material, which may or may not have been in written form. This
contains material of different kinds: a genealogy, infancy narratives,
parables, miracles and other narratives, sayings of Jesus. Strikingly, it
contains much material about community affairs (16.17-19; 18.15-22;
23.8-11) which reflects a concern with order and discipline. It contains
sayings which are strongly affirmative of the Law (5.17, 19-20) as well
as sayings which affirm Jesus' transcendence of the Law (5.21-24, 27-
32, 33-37, 38-42). It also contains a number of parables which deal with
the subject of judgment: 13.24-30, 36-43 (wheat and the tares); 13.47-50
(the dragnet); 25.1-13 (wise and foolish virgins); 25.31-46 (sheep and
goats).

All of this is Matthew's immediate tradition. We know that he was
familiar with it, that he took it over and dealt with the problems which
it raised in his own way. We are on pretty firm ground here; not
simply fitting pieces together because they are the only bits which we
have. Summarizing, one might say that in Matthew's immediate tradition we can discern: (1) differing attitudes to the Law: some strongly
affirmative, some critical, some dismissive; (2) differing attitudes to

the *eschaton*, ranging from urgent expectation (Q), to the dimming of such expectations (Mark) and their parabolic reworking in Matthew's special material; (3) different presentations of Jesus, as miracle worker, teacher, as crucified and risen Lord; (4) some evidence that questions of institutional structures were becoming problematical.

Matthew's Community

Before we can ask how Matthew uses these given materials to provide a sense of direction to his community, a further question arises. In order to know how Matthew attempted to give direction to his community, we need to have some idea about the kind of community he was writing for and the situation in which it found itself. Where was it located geographically? Where is it to be placed in relation to developments in the early Church? Where did it stand in relation to Judaism?

The Geographical Location of Matthew's Community

Scholars are divided as to where to locate Matthew geographically. There is general agreement that it comes from Syria: its Jewish character and its relation to Q would speak for this. Some favour Antioch, for the reasons that a large town like Antioch would make possible the rapid distribution of the Gospel that occurred, that there was a substantial settlement of Jews there, and that the Gospel is mentioned by Ignatius of Antioch shortly after the turn of the century. The first two points would be true of other Syrian cities, the third has some force.

There is also a good, indeed a prior question, raised by Stanton (*Gospel for a New People*, pp. 50-51), about whether we should speak of Matthew's 'community' at all. Was he undertaking such a major work only for the sake of one 'house-church' or did he not from the start envisage a much wider circulation and therefore write with general aims rather than in order to meet quite specific needs of a particular group? It is probably right to say that the average Christian group meeting for worship in a house in a Hellenistic city would not have numbered more than 50 or so. But then the Christian community in Antioch or some other Syrian city might well have been made up of a number of such groups who would presumably have had contacts among each other, though quite possibly they had varied backgrounds and may have seen things rather differently. Hellenistic Christians in Antioch from the first persecution of Stephen may subsequently have been joined by Jewish Christians from Jerusalem after its fall. Other groups may have been related to the communities which preserved the Q traditions. Moreover, this situation may well have been repeated in a number of cities in the area, making Matthew's community not untypical of his day. Any Gospel, that is to say, which was written for a particular cluster of house-churches in a Syrian city will have been likely to have appeal outside its immediate milieu, even though (or indeed, precisely because) it could be related to pressing issues of the community to which it was originally addressed. Nor should we assume too uncritically that Matthew was writing only with his own community in mind. The different groups within it may well have alerted him to the diversity of views within the wider church and he may have intended that his Gospel should speak to this wider grouping.

Place of Matthew's Community within Earliest Christianity
What can we say about the nature of this community and of its placing in the development of early Christianity which we sketched out briefly above? U. Luz has suggested persuasively that Matthew's community has a particular closeness to the Q tradition (*Matthew 1-7*, pp. 65-66) and argues that this can be seen from his treatment of the offices of prophet and scribe in the community. References to prophets (23.34: the exalted Lord sends prophets, sages and scribes to Israel; 10.41: on the reception of prophets in the community; cf. also 5.12; 23.37) and to false prophets (7.15-23; 24.10-12) suggest strongly that such prophets were known in Matthew's community and that, moreover, these were wandering prophets of the kind referred to in Q. It is true that, as Luz acknowledges, nearly all these references are taken from Q; but their number and distribution makes it reasonable to suppose that the topic was of concern to Matthew himself.

Matthew also inserts references into his traditional material about Christian scribes (13.52, cf. 8.19; 23.34 where Q had only prophets and wise men; cf. also 'their' scribes, 7.29). In neither case is it Matthew's intention to emphasize the position of the office within the community: 'one is your teacher' (23.8); the whole community has the power of loosing and binding (18.18). The intention is to see scribes as part of the community and equally to relativize the importance of the wandering charismatics. 'Matthew writes from the perspective of a sedentary community' (*Matthew 1-7*, p. 66). In a similar vein, one might add that the radical ethos of Mt. 6.25ff., with its call for freedom from preoccupation with possessions, is somewhat tempered in its closing verses: 'Seek first the kingdom of God and its righteousness and all these things will be added to you'. This is a call for the subordination of concern for daily needs to the demands of the gospel, rather than for radical freedom from them: the ethos of the itinerant mendicant is exchanged for the ethos of the urban Christian community.

One of the questions which this discussion raises is to what extent Matthew's church could be seen as a scribal community, some kind of 'school of Matthew', as K. Stendahl suggested. Evidence for this comes from the extensive use of the Old Testament in the Gospel and from the 'fulfilment quotations'. We shall consider these more fully below. Here we need only say that the point made above, namely that Matthew's intention is to integrate the scribes into his community, without however giving them a position of prominence, tells against Stendahl's view.

In sum: Matthew's community seems to be growing away from the earlier stage of Christianity where wandering, prophetic figures exercised power and influence over small gathered groups. It may never have been wholly dependent on such figures and may, with its close links to Judaism, have had members who exercised a teaching role within the community, not least in their attempts to relate the faith to the Hebrew Scriptures. For all that, Matthew does not wish to elevate such figures into a central position of power and authority. It is still the presence of Emmanuel with the community (1.23; cf. 28.20) which is the ultimate authority

The Relation of Matthew's Community to Judaism
At least since the major work of W.D. Davies on rabbinic Judaism and the Gospel of Matthew scholars have had to confront the question: how far did Matthew's community still see itself as part of the Jewish community, how far had it already parted company? That is to say, we may need to see Matthew and his community not only as part of the developing world of earliest Christianity but also as part of the Jewish world which was undergoing a process of re-formation after the catastrophe of the destruction of the Temple in 70 CE.

This is, of course, not a simple matter. The difficulties of constructing a picture of first-century Judaism are formidable. The Dead Sea Scrolls have shed light on some aspects of it, but the community which produced them was eccentric to mainstream Judaism. The main sources for our knowledge of the Pharisees were not compiled till the end of the second century. The Jewish historian Josephus (*Ant.* 18.11-25, cf. 13.171-73; *War* 2.119-66), who has to be read with care, speaks of different 'philosophies': Pharisees, Sadducees, Essenes and a 'fourth philosophy' the followers of Judas the Galilean, who were the forerunners of the Jewish freedom fighters at the time of the Jewish War.

How sharply such groups were divided is, of course, a matter of debate. E.P. Sanders has strongly argued that we need to be more conscious of the broad base of 'common Judaism' before 70, with its central focus in the Temple cult. It was this which the majority of the people, both in Palestine and in the Diaspora, supported and which they were in the end prepared to die for and which in all likelihood held the various groups together. By the same token, once the Temple was gone there was need for a radical reconstruction of the Jewish community and its religion. After the disastrous first Jewish War, a coalition of those groups which had survived, associated with the town of Jamnia and the Pharisee Johanan ben Zakkai, was gradually put together and took responsibility for the construction of a new form of Judaism without the Temple. Within this coalition the Pharisees, who had already been actively concerned with developing forms of purity laws outside the Temple, were increasingly influential.

Again there are significant debates among historians about the nature of this development. (A convenient discussion of these is given by J. Andrew Overman in *Matthew's Gospel and Formative Judaism*.) The rabbinic accounts of the events after the Fall of Jerusalem suggest that the Roman authorities empowered the Pharisees under Johanan ben Zakkai to establish an academy at Jamnia, which regulated Jewish life and worship. In practice the emergence of the Pharisees as the dominant force in Judaism may have been more gradual, a process accompanied by conflict and struggle.

Thus the development of Christianity as a distinct religious grouping with its own self-definition begins crucially at a time when major changes are taking place within Judaism. Moreover, the picture is further complicated by the fact that these two movements, which will in time become sharply distinct despite their common roots, for a time see themselves as rival contenders for the future of Israel. In retrospect one can also see that the Christian movement itself divides: there is a form of Jewish Christianity which is both separate from the main body of the Church and from Judaism itself and which eventually quietly disappears from view. There is Catholic Christianity which admits Gentiles to full membership of the church without requiring them to submit to the Jewish Law and which becomes dominant. The question scholars have to consider is: where in all this does Matthew stand?

Does Matthew's community still essentially see itself as part of Israel, indeed the 'true Israel'? Was it written before or after the Fall of Jerusalem? If after, did the community see itself as in competition with the leaders of the Jewish people around the coalition of Jamnia? Or does it already stand on the other side of the parting of Christianity and Judaism, regarding itself as part of a new community which is separate and distinct from the Jewish people (as, for instance, Paul sees his churches as distinct from Israel)? Or was Matthew not a Jew at all, as some have suggested, nor particularly interested in the controversies which troubled Jewish-Christian communities at their inception?

It is important here to realize that the answers to such questions depend on careful and detailed work on the text of the Gospel. We have no independent, external evidence: there are no other first-century documents which would give us the answers to such questions. We have to look at the way Matthew works with his traditional material, reworking Mark's narrative and incorporating large amounts of teaching material, all the time modifying and putting his own particular interpretation upon it. However, in a short study guide I shall be able to do no more than give the outline of such arguments.

First, U. Luz in his commentary (*Matthew 1–7*, pp. 79-82) has made a strong case for the Jewishness of Matthew, based on the Jewishness of Matthew's language and style of composition. Against this need to be set the claims that the anti-Jewishness of Matthew is so strong that it could not have been written by a Jew, that he supported the Gentile mission and that he avoids Aramaic words. I think Luz's case is the more telling. People may have all sorts of views, though, being of the same ethnic origin, it is almost, though not quite, impossible to shake off inherited linguistic characteristics. Avoiding the use of words in another language is of course a matter over which one does have control.

Secondly, I think that it is wholly unlikely that Matthew was written before 70. Mark's Gospel cannot be any earlier than the later part of the 60s and if, as is highly probable, Matthew used Mark, then this simply would not allow enough time for the dissemination of Mark's work and for Matthew's redaction of it.

It is much more difficult to know on which side of the parting of the ways between Judaism and Christianity to place Matthew's Gospel. There are elements in the Gospel which seem to indicate a living connection with Judaism. The disciples who are sent out in ch. 10 are told to go only 'to the lost sheep of the house of Israel'. Matthew includes the story about the Temple tax (17.24-27) which would seem to be of doubtful interest to those who have parted company with Judaism altogether. Perhaps most tellingly in Mt. 23.2-3 we read: 'the scribes and Pharisees sit on Moses' seat; so practise and observe whatever they tell you, but not what they do; for they preach but do not practise'. This certainly seems to read much more convincingly as a recognition by people within Israel of the *de facto* position of power which the scribes and Pharisees hold in their community, *which power is therefore to be acknowledged*, than as an outsider's statement. It is hard to see how Matthew could have let something like this stand if his community had just parted company with the Jewish community precisely over questions which included important matters of interpretation of the Law.

There are, on the other hand, powerful arguments which suggest that the community stands on the other side of the parting of the ways. G.N. Stanton (*Gospel for a New People*, pp. 124ff.) has put these clearly and argued for this position extensively throughout his book. He gives five main reasons:

1. the sustained attack, often in passages which are clearly Matthew's redactional work, against scribes and Pharisees;
2. the association of the scribes and Pharisees with the synagogue (often referred to in redactional phrases, 'you' or 'their' synagogues);
3. the clear distinction Matthew makes between church and synagogue, where the church has its own entrance rite and liturgical practice and where the presence of Jesus with the church supersedes the presence of God in the Temple;
4. passages which speak about the 'transference' of the kingdom to a new people who will include Gentiles: 8.5-13, 15.13 and Stanton's prime witness, 21.41 and 43: 'Therefore I tell you, the kingdom of God will be taken away from you and given to a people who will produce the proper fruit';
5. in 28.15 Matthew addresses his readers directly and refers to the 'Jews' with their rival account of the resurrection as a group separate from the church.

Needless to say there are counters which can be made to some of these points.

1. Stanton himself has said that conflicts tend to be fiercest between those who are closely linked together, and one could find sufficient parallels in the literature of Jewish sectarianism for Matthew's attacks on the scribes and Pharisees.
2. Matthew's references to 'their' synagogues may be distinguishing different assemblies within Judaism.
3. The development of a church with its own forms of organization and structures, in some sense parallel to those of the

other forms of Judaism, could be a development located either in or outside of Judaism. Nevertheless, Stanton's point about the presence of Jesus in the church remains a powerful one.

4. Nor are the passages about the 'transference' of the kingdom easily dismissed. One might, however, ask when this transference is to occur. The parable of the vineyard in 21.33-41 might suggest that the removal of the kingdom is the direct result of the crucifixion of Jesus and therefore takes place immediately. On the other hand, Luz (*Matthew 1–7*, pp. 84-85) has suggested that Matthew's community saw the destruction of Jerusalem as the judgment of God on the Jewish people for their rejection of the Christian mission. Even this is presumably a retrospective judgment. Passages like Matthew 23 suggest dialogue and conflict with the leaders of Judaism for some time after the destruction of the Temple.

The issue here is, I think, delicately balanced, though Stanton finds the view that the Gospel was written before the parting of the ways 'implausible' (*Gospel for a New People*, p. 124). Perhaps part of the problem lies in defining the parting of the ways. When Qumran vilified the Temple hierarchy and decreed that only those who had taken the oath of the community were sons of the covenant, they had obviously parted company with the Temple priesthood in a significant sense. Yet in another sense they still saw themselves as the faithful remnant of Israel. In this sense they can be properly described as a sect, living within the wider community, yet vilifying its leadership. Did Matthew's community go through such a stage before it eventually ceased to see itself as part of the wider community at all, and instead attached itself to the (majority?) church which had broken with the Law over the non-circumcision of Gentiles? It is interesting that Stanton can compare Matthew's polemic against the Pharisees with the similar polemic against them in the Damascus Document of the Qumran community as both instances of a minority community distancing itself from the parent body (see esp. p. 96). But that is of course precisely a move made by those who have not yet fully *parted company* with the parent body.

Luz has suggested that the Gospel is written at a 'turning point' (*Matthew 1–7*, p. 84) in the life of the community which is constituted by the decision whether or not to engage in the Gentile mission. He sees Matthew as an advocate of the Gentile mission, but recognizes that there are still vital issues which will not have been clarified by his Gospel, namely the extent to which those engaged on the mission would then be free to modify the Law. Thus for him too it seems that the vital step is being proposed which will lead to the separation of the two communities, but that, even so, not all the ties have yet been cut. The process of parting, whether more or less painful (Stendahl speaks of 'a far smoother transition from Judaism to Christianity than we usually suppose', *School of Matthew*, pp. xiii-xiv), was certainly not such that it is easy to say exactly when the transition occurred. I think, however, that there is no reasonable doubt but that by the time of the composition of Matthew's Gospel the writing was, in a manner of speaking, on the wall.

Matthew's Formation of his Community
At this point we can now ask what part Matthew intended his Gospel to have in the development of his community. What contribution did he expect it to make to the internal problems that the community was facing: the interaction between different styles of leadership, the need for clearer definition of roles within the group, the need for some form of disciplinary procedures? And what contribution to the crisis which was precipitated by the imminent or actual parting of the ways with Judaism: the need for redefining the boundaries and markers of the community once it had left the matrix of Judaism, indeed for defining the beliefs and rituals of the new community? It is unlikely that Matthew would have posed the questions in that sort of way; or that he would have separated the tasks out as neatly as that. He would have been aware, presumably, of the community's needs at different levels and must have had some overall strategy in writing his Gospel, but he would have also, to some extent, been forced by the nature of his work in redacting traditional material to respond *ad hoc* to themes and issues as they were raised by the material with which he was working. We should not, moreover, assume that his only purpose in writing the Gospel was to deal with issues of community building: he may, as Luz has suggested, have been equally interested in rekindling the flame of Christian faith and devotion. But again such matters are not wholly unrelated. Lastly, we need to remind ourselves that Matthew's community, in seeking to give clearer definition to its organization and world-view, is engaged in the same task as other forms of post-70 Judaism. It may not just have been in conflict with Judaism but it may also have been taking a few leaves from its book about how to achieve such ends.

These kinds of questions gain added sharpness when they are seen through the lens of sociological studies of the development of religious groups. They have only fairly recently been raised in such form

in New Testament studies and work is therefore at a fairly preliminary stage. One useful book which has drawn together a lot of the
relevant material is J. Andrew Overman's *Matthew's Gospel and Formative Judaism*. This, along with the discussion in Stanton's *Gospel for a
New People*, ch. 4, gives a fuller introduction to the theoretical issues
which such study raises.

1. *Scripture and Law.* For Jews, God's purposes and will for his people
had been revealed in Torah, in Scripture. Any new or reconstructed
community which wanted to claim continuity with Israel would have
to show where it stood in relation to Scripture. This would mean on
the one hand providing scriptural, that is traditional, support for what
one was actually doing, and also showing how the new elements that
one wanted to introduce, or had introduced, related to the Law.

The first thing to notice is that there is a considerable difference
between the way in which Matthew went about providing scriptural
legitimation for his community and that in which 'Jamnian' Judaism
did. Whereas Matthew principally tells a story, though one which
includes a substantial amount of discourse material, Johanan ben
Zakkai and his group set about collecting together the sayings of the
scribes and the Wise men, which would provide the substance of the
new interpretation of the Law and eventually find their way into the
Mishnah and Talmud. This is not to say that the followers of Johanan
ben Zakkai stopped telling stories but that the principal product of their
efforts to reshape Judaism was comprised predominantly of sayings.

One of the important features of Matthew's use of narrative is to set
the story of Christ and the church within a wider historical context
going back to Abraham and revealing the continuing purposes of God
for his people. In the telling of that story, however, there is room for
showing how it is anchored to Scripture, for showing Jesus as interpreting the Law and expounding his own authoritative teachings as
its fulfilment. In both of these contexts the notion of 'fulfilment' is
central.

a. *Scriptural quotations.* Matthew's concern to show how the Christian story is rooted in Scripture is evidenced by the frequency of its
citation and of the allusions to it in his Gospel. He has all of Mark's
quotations and allusions and all the Q references, as well as a substantial number of references of his own. One of the features of the
Gospel that has attracted particular attention is the 'fulfilment quotations', quotations which are introduced by a formula including the
words: 'in order that what was spoken by the prophet…might be fulfilled': 1.22-23; 2.15, 17-18, 23; 4.14-16; 8.17; 12.17-21; 13.35; 21.4-5;

27.9-10. There are some difficult issues raised by these quotations. What text is being used: the Hebrew Bible or the Greek translation, the Septuagint? There is certainly a marked divergence in many cases from the Greek translation which Matthew otherwise seems to favour when citing Scripture. Were these 'fulfilment' quotations sought out by Matthew himself, or was he using a collection put together by a group of scribes within his own church?

These are technical questions. A number of points can be made. There is no agreement between scholars as to whether or not Matthew was responsible for the choice of scriptural quotations. Many, including Luz (*Matthew 1–7*, pp. 156-63), favour the view that the fulfilment quotations, which have a rather distinctive form of text as opposed to the rest of Matthew's quotations, come from some kind of scribal activity within his community. Stanton (*Gospel for a New People*, pp. 358-59), who questions Matthew's dependence on the Septuagint for his biblical text outside the 'fulfilment quotations', suggests that he may well have been responsible for at least some of them. Certainly the formula itself can be seen as arising out of Matthew's redaction of Mk 14.49 and if Matthew has composed the formula may he not be responsible for the quotations too?

The form of the quotations is important, too. They are not words of Scripture put into any of the characters' mouths (though Matthew can do this, cf. Mt. 9.13) but rather words addressed by the narrator to his readers. As such they may give us an important indication of Matthew's purpose. R.E. Brown has written: 'these citations emphasize that the whole of Jesus' life, down to the last detail, lay within God's foreordained plan' (cited by Overman, *Matthew's Gospel*, p. 74). Their purpose is not simply to anchor the events of Jesus' life in history (to prove that it happened), but to show that it was part of God's saving purpose for his people. However, the quotations, which are unevenly distributed through the Gospel, seem to do more than just that. They underline central themes of Matthew's work: Jesus is God with us, the presence of God in the world (1.23); he is the shepherd of his people (2.6); God's Son (2.15).

Matthew's use of Scripture here has sometimes been compared to the form of scriptural interpretation found at Qumran, known as pesher. In the Qumran pesher on Habakkuk, for instance, the reader is taken through the text verse by verse, each verse being shown to refer to some event of significance in the life of the community. Matthew's procedure is in one sense clearly different. He does not follow the text of a particular book, but rather chooses his quotations widely. Nevertheless, the comparison is interesting. Just as Qumran was a community seeking reassurance that its chosen path was in continuity with God's will, so too was Matthew's. Overman has suggested that what is going on here is part of a struggle *within Judaism* for legitimacy; Matthew's church had yet to part from Judaism. Possibly, but even if Matthew's community had already left the Jewish fold, it would still need powerful traditional forms of legitimation, indeed arguably would need them even more. The point is that both Judaism and Matthew's community orientate themselves by 'Scripture' and will continue to struggle over the interpretation of Scripture whatever their relationship to each other.

b. *Interpretation of the Law.* The question of the correct interpretation of the Law is raised sharply in a number of stories in the Gospel which scholars define as 'conflict stories', stories, that is, where Jesus is engaged in dispute by opponents, often enough the scribes and the Pharisees. Matthew shows his interest in such conflicts by creating three more conflict stories additional to the ones he has found in that form in his sources: Mt. 12.38-42; 22.34-40; 22.41-46 (so Overman, *Matthew's Gospel*, pp. 78-86). Not all of these stories are directly concerned with law in the sense of rules of conduct; some are, some address broader matters of theology and faith.

I shall discuss one which Matthew already found as a conflict story, the dispute about purity in Mt. 15.1-20, taken from Mark 7. Matthew has made a number of significant changes to his source. In the first place he has reshaped the first part of the story. In Mark 'the Pharisees and some of the scribes' ask Jesus why his disciples eat with unwashed hands, thus breaking the tradition of the elders. Jesus responds by quoting Isa. 29.13 which accuses them of teaching 'as doctrines the human precepts'. There then follows a section in which Jesus in turn accuses them of breaking the Law in the practice of Corban (declaring something owed to one's parents a sacrificial gift and therefore withholding it). Matthew has changed the order; he has Jesus challenge the Pharisees over the tradition of the elders by confronting them immediately with the practice of Corban, and then deliver the saying from Isaiah as a conclusion to the encounter.

This section is followed in Mark immediately by a further saying by Jesus on the subject of purity, addressed first to the crowd and then explained to his disciples by Jesus. Matthew interposes between the saying to the crowd and the explanation to the disciples a section in which Jesus attacks the Pharisees as blind guides and a 'planting' not from his Father, which will be torn out (vv. 12-14). Three other changes to this section need to be noticed: first Matthew reformulates Jesus' saying to the crowds about purity. Whereas Mark's form: 'there is nothing outside a person that by going in can defile; but the things that come out are what defile' makes a general distinction between what is outside and what is inside, Matthew's version: 'it is not what goes into the mouth that defiles a man, but it is what comes out of the mouth that defiles', omits this distinction and focuses strictly on what goes into the mouth. Secondly, Matthew omits Mark's editorial comment in 7.19 'thus he declared all foods clean'. Thirdly, he discusses impurity in terms of what comes out of the mouth, meaning from the heart, and changes Mark's list of such terms to bring it much closer into line with the Ten Commandments.

Two things are striking here: one is the way in which Matthew has heightened the polemic against the Pharisees. He refers to them in terms which, as Stanton has pointed out are reminiscent of Qumran's polemic against the Pharisees (*Gospel for a New People*, p. 96: 'blind guides', CD 1.9). The second is the way he has withdrawn from Mark's wholesale rejection of food laws and instead emphasized the commitment of his community to the weightier matters of the Law. I think Overman is mistaken here to think that Matthew is attempting to argue that 'Jesus and the disciples do not play fast and loose with the law *or the Pharisaic paradosis*' (*Gospel for a New People*, p. 83, my italics). On the contrary he is arguing that the Pharisaic traditions break the Law (possibly identifying the whole people of Israel with this practice: this *people* honours me with their lips...teaching', whereas the practice of eating with unwashed hands (*not*, as Mark would have it, eating unclean foods) is properly in accordance with the Law, so at least Matthew's summary at the end of the section.

What precisely is going on here? Is Matthew simply conducting a battle against the Pharisees *at a distance*, now that the separation has occurred between the two communities? Or is this part of Matthew's struggle, albeit from outside the synagogue, against the Pharisees' attempt to make their understanding of Torah normative for the whole of Judaism? But then we might ask whether Matthew would have been interested in conducting such a struggle if he had already parted company with Judaism and was arguing instead for the Gentile mission. Again we need perhaps to say that the process of parting is not a sudden one and that the battles being fought out here are still ones which matter to Matthew, whether because he still hopes to bring Judaism round to his way of thinking, against the Pharisees; or whether because he is here using the Pharisees as a foil by which to bring home to his community — and the wider Gentile church which he is correcting here — that there is no conflict between the Law as such and Jesus' and the Church's teaching. In the latter case his position would be not unlike that of Paul's Galatian congregation who turn to the Law (as John Barclay has suggested in *Obeying the Truth*, pp. 68-72), because they need some such strong ethical tradition to anchor themselves and to enable them to consolidate their community once they have broken away from their former paganism. Here Matthew, of course, is not looking for a new source of authority but rather fighting both against Pharisaic counter-charges and against anti-Torah elements in his own tradition.

2. *Community Norms and Discipline.* Whether or not Matthew was writing from inside or outside the Jewish community, he was engaged in consolidating and legitimizing his community. There were inherited problems arising out of the development of forms of Christian ministry in the earliest days; there were problems which came with the growth of sedentary communities; there were problems which arose out of the heightened tension and conflict between his community and the Jewish leadership. How Matthew set about dealing with all this was, as I have said, partly by detailed editing of his traditional material (as we saw when looking at the section on purity in Mt. 15.1-20), partly by constructing large blocks of material, which would give shape and sense to the Gospel as a whole. In particular he constructed five large discourses, and a subordinate one (ch. 23), in which the majority of Jesus' teaching is contained. In these sections the foundations are laid for a new community: a new social world is being created. Whether Matthew specifically intended his readers to draw a connection between his five major discourses and the five books of the Pentateuch may be disputed; but he was claiming that his community had a substantial body of teaching which had been revealed by God. In a somewhat similar way the Rabbis would at the end of the next century produce the Mishnah, their compilation of teaching which too was claimed to have its origins in divine revelation. We shall not be able to deal with all these discourses. Instead we shall look at the Sermon on the Mount, which is the fullest exposition of community norms, and ch. 18 which deals explicitly with matters of community discipline.

a. *The Sermon on the Mount.* Matthew's Sermon on the Mount is based on a collection of sayings which existed in Q and of which we find a much shorter form in Lk. 6.20-49. Matthew has largely followed the order of Q but has considerably expanded it by the addition of sayings from elsewhere in Q and from his own special material.

Its structure is not easy to identify clearly. There are certain patterns which appear to emerge obviously. Matthew 5.17, which forms the opening of the main section of teaching after the beatitudes is picked up again in 7.12 and so brackets the main section, which is preceded by an introduction and followed by a concluding passage which principally sets out the two ways between which a disciple has to choose. The form of the first half of the central section is clear too: there are six 'antitheses' (about murder, adultery, divorce, oaths, retaliation, love of enemies), that is, passages where Jesus' understanding of the Law is related to and contrasted with the teaching of, largely at least, the Scriptures. Thereafter things are less clear, though one thing is obvious, namely the importance in what follows of the Lord's prayer in 6.9-13. Bornkamm ('Der Aufbau der Bergpredigt') has suggested that what follows the prayer is a commentary on it. This may be too specific a proposal but what it shows is the extent to which the values in the prayer correspond to the injunctions which are then subsequently given to the disciples. Luz (*Matthew 1–7*, pp. 211-13) sees the prayer as the central pivot of the Sermon as a whole.

Two points emerge from this: that Matthew has taken great care over his construction of this passage, and that there is not just ethical instruction in the Sermon but instruction in worship and prayer. What we have here is not just a set of rules, but the foundation document of a new religious community which sees itself as children of a heavenly father who will forgive and reward the 'righteous' (5.6, 10, 20, 45; 6.1, 33), those who are faithful to him and his Son's commands.

This interweaving of religious imagery with ethical instruction is of vital importance in the construction of a new community. It is not enough to lay down rules. As Peter Berger has argued, a religious community needs to know itself protected under a 'sacred canopy', living in a world which is as it were shaped and held together by the source of all reality. It is therefore striking that Matthew has almost certainly himself added the phrase 'as in heaven so on earth' in 6.10 and that the same motif is to be found in 6.45 where love of enemies is enjoined so that you may be sons of your father in heaven, and in 5.48 where the disciples are told to 'be perfect as your heavenly father is perfect'.

What then are the values which Matthew commends to his community? The term which occurs throughout the Gospel and at significant stages in the Sermon itself is 'righteousness' (7 times in the Gospel; the adjective 'righteous' occurs 17 times). Those who hunger and thirst after righteousness will be filled (5.6); to those who are persecuted for righteousness' sake belongs the kingdom of heaven (5.10); the disciples' righteousness is to exceed that of the scribes and Pharisees (5.20); the disciples are not to 'do their righteousness' ostentatiously (6.1);

they are to seek first the kingdom of God and his righteousness (6.33). It is important to realize how different this use is from that of Paul who contrasts righteousness by 'works of the law' with righteousness which comes from faith. Here Matthew is quite clear about the connection between righteousness and works, as the saying in the context of warnings against false prophets makes clear: 'By their fruits you shall know them'. It is 'not everyone who says 'Lord, Lord' who will enter into the kingdom of heaven but the one who does the will of my Father who is in heaven' (7.20-21). Such an emphasis means that Matthew remains firmly in the tradition of the Hebrew Scriptures which sees the Law as being there to provide guidance for God's people in the practical affairs of life. It is God's gift of guidance to his people and it is there to be done. Blessedness results from its performance, as well as from its study and from mediation on it. The righteous person is the one who sets his or her heart on doing the law and who indeed does it, as opposed to the sinner who does not.

But then what exactly is Matthew's community being enjoined to do? Is it simply to keep the Law? Is it to keep a new Law promulgated by Jesus on the Mountain to replace the Mosaic Law? Or is it to keep the Law as definitively interpreted by Jesus? The difficulty here is this: if Matthew was suggesting that Jesus was proclaiming the definitive understanding of the Law, then one would expect him to be much more concerned to show how Jesus' interpretation differed from that of his contemporaries, notably of course the Pharisees (in 23.3 the disciples are even commanded to observe the teaching of the Pharisees!). If he was wanting to suggest that Jesus replaced the Law with a new Law then we would expect a much sharper distinction between the provisions of the old and of the new. We would not expect such strong affirmations of the continuing validity of the Law and the prophets.

The point can be made most clearly in relation to the antitheses which form the larger part of ch. 5. Here Jesus contrasts his teaching with what has been 'said of old'. This, of course, is not a bad thing. What is 'of old' is hallowed by tradition; the passive form 'is said' is probably a *passivum divinum*, that is to say a passive form which avoids the use of the divine name but which implies that it is God who has acted. Such 'contrasts' do not necessarily imply a contradiction between what was said in Scripture and what is now said by the teacher. Similar forms can be found in rabbinic traditions to introduce the teaching of the sages on disputed verses of Scripture (Luz, *Matthew 1–7*, p. 276).

What contrast is then implied between that which was said of old and Jesus' teaching? There seem to be a number of different kinds of comparisons being made. In the case of the sayings about murder and adultery (5.21-26, 27-30), there seems to be a simple extension of the Law to embrace thoughts and desires as well as specific actions. Here one might say that the Law is being deepened, though it is true that it is also being made a lot less enforceable. In the case of the sayings about oaths and retaliation (5.33-37, 38-42) we might say that there is a similar extension of the intention of the old law. Here the old laws had been intended to limit swearing and the taking of vengeance. Jesus proposes that it should stop altogether. What is interesting by contrast with the previous cases is that here something which was permitted in the old law is now being forbidden. The intensification of the Law leads to its replacement by a new, more radical law. The saying about divorce (5.31-32) is altogether more difficult. Were it not for the exception for adultery we might have a case very similar to that of oaths and retaliation. The Law limits the freedom of men simply to cast their wives out: there must be a 'cause of offence' and he must give her a bill of divorce. Jesus extends this by forbidding divorce and declaring divorce to be another form of adultery. If Matthew had used the form of the saying as we have it in Lk. 16.18, then that is what we should have. But he, or his community before him, added the 'exception'. Now the saying reads like a contribution to the contemporary Pharisaic debates about what might constitute a 'cause of offence'. One school, the school of Hillel, ruled that anything that displeased the husband could constitute grounds for divorce; the other, that of Shammai, that only adultery could count (*m. Giṭ.* 9.10). In this sense Jesus is here presented as entering into contemporary debate and taking sides, rather than distancing himself from Pharisaic positions altogether.

Finally, Jesus commands love of enemies rather than love of neighbour and hatred of enemies (5.43-48). There is, however, no scriptural base for hatred of enemies, at least not in the form of an explicit command. There are plenty of examples of it, a good number of which have divine sanction (e.g. Ps. 137.9; Josh. 10.12-14). Such explicit commands can be found in the Qumran literature (1QS 1.10-11; 9.21-22; cf. 10.17-18) though even here it is fairly clear that hatred for enemies is not to be converted into action.

The Qumran community had disappeared by Matthew's time but its influence will not have vanished altogether. So this may be another example where Jesus is confronting contemporary interpretations of the Law. In that case here he is rejecting such interpretations: at the same time he is proposing his own interpretation which goes beyond the sense of the Levitical command (Lev. 19.18). For what he now proposes is not the intensification of love for one's neighbour, as in loving him or her not merely in explicitly commanded deeds, but in one's thoughts and motives. In fact, interestingly, Matthew omits here the Levitical phrase 'as yourself'. Rather what is commanded is the extension of the same love to another group, namely those who are antagonistic to the group itself. This is a radicalization of tendencies which are to be found certainly in the older Scriptures but which are nowhere so explicitly or boldly stated. What is being commanded here is, moreover, an imitation of God, such that the disciples may become his children. It is in such open generosity that divine and therefore human perfection lies (Mt. 5.48; cf. 19.21). Is there a deliberate contrasting here with the Levitical command to be holy as I am holy (Lev. 19.2) with its implications of separation from all that is alien to God (cf. Lev. 20.26)?

What this discussion suggests is that there is a studied ambiguity about the way that Matthew is presenting the relation of Jesus' teaching to the Law. Alternatively one might say that there are reflected in the Sermon on the Mount some of the different attitudes to the Law which the community had evinced over the period in which it had moved ever closer to a complete break with Judaism. What his readers would have taken from it is clear, I think. They would have seen it as a clear legitimization of the community's way of life, over against the direction in which the Pharisees and their allies were trying to take Judaism.

b. *Matthew 18 and community discipline.* We need to say something more briefly about the way in which Matthew dealt with specific problems of discipline in his community. We have already noticed that there were tensions which might arise from the existence within the community of scribes and prophets with different claims to a hearing, particularly if the prophets saw themselves as having special authority which required them to answer to no one but God. We have already seen above how Matthew integrates the scribes into his own community. Where prophets are concerned, he is quick to warn against false prophets, and sets out clear criteria by which they are to be judged. They are to be judged by their conformity to the community norms (7.15-23). The language is admittedly graphic rather than specific. What are the 'ravenous wolves' doing? Presumably not making peace as children of God should (5.9). But Matthew may have had to face other problems which came partly from the simple fact of trying to institute some kind of internal disciplinary procedures in a community which had none, partly from the fact that his community

was a very non-hierarchical one, which treated all members as brothers and was opposed to ranks and titles within it (23.8-12 which may
well indicate that there were people in the community, perhaps not
uninfluenced by the Pharisees, who saw this as the way to develop
some system of authority). There is also a further problem which is
clearly indicated by ch. 18. The community was not only an egalitar-
ian community; it was a community based on a principle of forgiveness which made it difficult to discipline people.

Matthew 18 is a chapter which provides some guidance in such a
situation, though by no means all of it is simply practical guidance. A
good deal of it is moral or theological exhortation. Thus it is probably
a mistake to see it as a community rule, distinct in that respect from
the other discourses in the Gospel. It certainly includes specific rulings
on discipline (vv. 15ff.), but it is also, like the Sermon on the Mount, a
source of general ethical guidance.

The chapter starts with a section on the notion of greatness in the
kingdom of heaven (vv. 1-5). True greatness consists in humility. Here
Matthew takes a section from Mk 9.33-37 and reworks it. In Mark the
disciples argue among themselves about which of them is greatest. In
Matthew the question has been widened into a general question about
status and position within the community: 'Who is the greatest in the
kingdom of heaven?' Again Matthew adds his own interpretation to
Jesus' action with the child by underscoring the child's lowliness. The
Greek word has two meanings, either the virtue of humility or the
humility of affliction (Ambrose). Commentators are divided over
whether what is meant here is the virtue or simply the lowliness or
powerlessness of the child. This is a slightly odd debate: the point of
the injunction is that those in the Kingdom should acknowledge their
smallness in the face of God: and such acknowledgment—theological
or religious humility—can properly be seen as underpinning moral
humility: not thinking of ourselves more highly than we ought to
think. The whole section provides an interesting reworking of the
opening of the Sermon on the Mount. The question of greatness is not
unrelated to the question of the enjoyment of the blessings of the
Kingdom. The exhortation to humility is close to the beatitudes to the
poor in spirit and the meek. It sets out, as Trilling suggests (*Das wahre
Israel*, p. 113), the broad theological perspective which informs the
sayings about the little ones, about community discipline and about
forgiveness in the rest of the chapter.

The chapter moves on in vv. 6-10 to consider the question of 'little
ones'. The identity of the little ones is not clear but one possibility is
that they were the poorer members of urban churches. Precisely who

is causing them to stumble is also not clear. The principle invoked is, however, evident: it is better that those who cause such people to stumble should be cut out of the community, than that the community should suffer. Here again Matthew is following Mark (9.42-48), but he changes Mark's section which talks metaphorically about the need for self-discipline into a section about the need for community discipline and exclusion.

This is, however, balanced by the particular slant which Matthew gives to the parable of the shepherd and the sheep (vv. 11-14). Here he is using a story from the common tradition he shares with Luke. Whereas Luke refers to the 'lost' sheep (Lk. 15.4) and explains the parable in terms of repentance (v. 7), Matthew speaks about the sheep 'going astray' (Mt. 18.12) and explains the parable in terms of 'not being lost' (v. 14). Luke's parable is about bringing those outside the group in; Matthew's about the need to do all in one's power to ensure that the erring member is not finally lost to the group. Matthew's concern here is clearly that of the pastor who is seeking all means in his power to hold his congregation together.

What we have had so far, however, has been in the nature of general injunctions, using and modifying material which already existed in the community's traditions. What comes next, 18.15-20, is both more specific and also more original. Matthew 18.15-17 proposes procedures for dealing with recalcitrant members of the community. If there is a dispute this should be settled, if possible, between the two persons concerned. Beyond that a small group should attempt to mediate; if that fails, then the congregation as a whole should be brought in and, if necessary, the offending party should be excluded. The section probably bears some relation to the similar section in Lk. 17.3-4, but has been substantially developed, possibly in Matthew's own tradition. The meeting with one or two others probably is intended first as a means of winning the brother back, but it may also function as a form of legal procedure, insuring that there are adequate witnesses if it should come to more formal proceedings in front of the congregation. The model here is clearly an Old Testament one, as the reference to Deut. 19.15 makes clear. The climax of the procedure is the congregation's decision which may lead to the exclusion: 'let him be to you as a Gentile and a tax-collector'. In the context of a chapter which stresses the need to search for the one stray sheep and contains the injunction to forgive seventy times seven times, this can only be a painful acknowledgment of the realities of community life and of the need to have some way of drawing the line. Matthew invokes the authority which is given to the congregation of 'loosing and binding'

(Mt. 16.19). This is a phrase which occurs regularly in later rabbinic writings where it may refer to the teaching authority of the rabbinate. Here it is more likely to be taken in a strictly disciplinary sense. Overman (*Matthew's Gospel*, p. 105) has drawn attention to parallel usage in the contemporary Jewish writer Josephus who talks about the Pharisees in the reign of Alexander Jannaeus having power 'to banish and recall, to loose and bind whomever they would' (*War* 1.5.111-16).

This exercise of the congregation's authority is then linked to the power of the congregation in prayer, itself linked to the presence of Jesus with them (18.19-20). The power to exclude, terrible though it is, should not be seen as the sole or indeed the principal power given to the congregation. Its principal function is to pray for the needs of the community. Moreover, in so doing it will be reminded that its authority is not simply devolved to it, so that it, as it were, exercises it independently, it is rather power which comes from the living presence of the Lord with them.

Two final points may be made about this section. As Overman has pointed out, the congregation's action in loosing and binding will be confirmed in heaven. 'The actions and decisions of the community carry the force and authority of heaven' (*Matthew's Gospel*, p. 104). The same can be seen elsewhere in Matthew's Gospel (5.48; 6.10; 12.32; 16.19). The community reflects the order and values of the heavenly kingdom. 'In their power to bind and to loose, the Matthean community represents a "mimetic reiteration" of the power and authority of the kingdom of heaven... In sociological terms the social nomos and the universal cosmos appear as coextensive' (*Matthew's Gospel*, p. 104).

The other point to notice is the emphasis placed throughout the chapter on forgiveness. In a sense the problems of community discipline and control are exacerbated by the community's focus on forgiveness as a fundamental value. How can you take tough decisions and discipline people if you teach that it is one's duty to go on and on forgiving? The two parables in the chapter both attempt to elucidate the point. The first, the parable of the straying sheep, as we have seen, stresses the importance of making every effort to bring back into the community those who have strayed. The second, the unjust steward in 18.23-35, makes a rather different point. Just as the highest virtue is forgiveness, so too those who have experienced forgiveness and refuse themselves to forgive have the greatest fault. In such circumstances, we are told, they deserve to be excluded: 'the lord delivered him to the jailers until he should pay all his debt' (18.34).

Matthew's Sectarianism

What can one say about the type of community which Matthew was helping to build? Both Luz (*Matthew 1–7*, p. 219) and Overman (*Matthew's Gospel*, p. 154) have suggested that it is helpful to characterize Matthew's community as a sect. This is, of course, a very elastic term and might seem to some to suggest a group which is simply obscurantist. It certainly suggests a sense of opposition to the prevailing forces in society. As a term it was used by Ernst Troeltsch in contradistinction to 'church'. A church, as an institution which dispenses salvation, is marked by a religion of grace and a piety of redemption. A sect, by contrast, as a free association of strict and conscious Christians has a religion of law and makes more vigorous efforts to establish a Christian way of life based on love. In such a group Christ is lord, example and lawgiver, rather than first and foremost a redeemer figure. Achieving holiness is what is of primary importance for the group; redemption is expected in the future.

Luz acknowledges his debt to Troeltsch and his conviction that in these terms Matthew's *theology* offers a classic example of sectarian theology. It is the theology of a minority group which takes Jesus as its leader in its quest to establish its own way of life based on obedience and love. It is perfectionist, a religion centred on law, where grace is essentially practical assistance. As we shall very shortly see, in the course of church history Matthew's Gospel has often provided marginalized groups with theological support, just as it has been such groups who have attempted to live out its demands most strictly.

Overman draws his definition of sect from the British sociologist Bryan Wilson. Here sects are defined in terms of their 'response to the world', that is, to the dominant groupings within their environment who determine the social and cultural norms. Characteristically sects develop strategies for enforcing their own norms against those of the wider society by setting tight boundaries around their group, by polemic against the dominant group and its leaders, and by consolidating and legitimizing their own structures and norms. Much of Overman's book is given over to showing patterns of sectarian behaviour within Judaism of the first century. These patterns of behaviour have, he believes, had a considerable influence on Matthew's community which was 'clearly sectarian' (p. 154). It was a minority over against the parent group, formative Judaism out of which rabbinic Judaism emerged. The harsh language of the Gospel against the Jewish leadership betrays its sense of marginalization. It was, relatively speaking, 'more concerned with world-maintenance than being open to the world...interested in community formation, and not primarily world transformation' (p. 154).

The term 'sectarian', as used by Wilson, covers a variety of social groups, all of which are more or less sharply distinguished from the dominant society within which they live. Among the different types of sects, however, it is important to distinguish different responses to the world outside. It is one of the weaknesses of both Luz's and Overman's analyses that they do not address this question sufficiently clearly. Luz is more concerned to identify certain typical theological features of the sect, while Overman assumes too easily that the identification of certain features—polemics against the leaders of the majority society, the search for legitimation, community building—speaks for a particular type of sect, namely one that is interested in maintaining its own life rather than in transforming the wider society. This is strange in view of the missionary emphasis of the conclusion of the Gospel. There is of course, as we have seen, clear evidence that Matthew was interested in providing norms for his community, in dealing with matters of community discipline and with sharply distinguishing his church from the synagogue. One might add that there is also a shift in the way in which motifs concerning the end of the world are employed. If for Mark the foretelling of an end to the world as it is presently known (ch. 13) is a way of underscoring the need to part company with the ways of this world, in Matthew the depiction of the last judgment in the parable of the sheep and the goats in ch. 25 is designed to reinforce the norms of the new community. So there is undoubtedly a sense in which Matthew's community is setting itself up as an alternative society with its own norms contrasted with those of its Jewish neighbour, if of course claiming common roots in the Torah. But this does not mean to say that it is not interested in world-transformation: it claims authority over the whole world for the Son and sends its members out into the world to make disciples of all. It may have turned its back on Judaism but this was only to take up the task of the Jewish nation to proclaim God's rule in all the world and to bring all the peoples to acknowledge it.

The Gospel in Later Communities

We have been considering Matthew's contribution to the formation of the early church communities for whom he wrote. Of course we can only speculate about the actual effect which the Gospel may have had on those communities. To be quite clear, we cannot make more than informed guesses about their actual situation. It is, however, interesting to ask what the continuing role of the Gospel was in the development of the church. How was it read by later communities and how did it contribute to the particular form which those communities took?

This takes us into the realm of what is sometimes called 'history of effects'. This is a somewhat awkward translation of the German *Wirkungsgeschichte*. It is a study of the way in which certain texts have a history in terms of the literary traditions, social communities, attitudes, political consequences which they engender. It is usually distinguished from the history of interpretation in that it is not just concerned with cataloguing the different ways in which commentators have read the texts, but is also interested in the wider implications and impact which texts have had in the course of time. For Matthew we are particularly well served by Luz's commentary which has made study of the history of effects into a valuable tool for understanding the 'potential for meaning' (*Sinnpotential*) of texts. His claim is that we fully understand the meaning of texts only when we have seen their potential for generating a wider set of meanings which can be embodied in different communities.

We can here give only a sample of what this approach contributes to the understanding of Matthew's Gospel and will do so in relation to the beatitudes and the antitheses of the Sermon on the Mount. These are clearly central texts and ones which Luz has discussed not only in his commentary but in other places as well.

The Beatitudes
We first need to situate Matthew's own redaction of the beatitudes within a continuum of development from Jesus. According to Luz (*Matthew 1–7*, pp. 227-29), whose views I am summarizing throughout this section, it is likely that three beatitudes go back to Jesus: those addressed to the poor, the hungry and those that weep. Here Jesus is proclaiming the unrestricted grace of God to the disadvantaged, regardless of anything that they may have done to earn it. And the blessings that he announces are already to be experienced in the dawning of the Kingdom in Jesus' activity, 'in his turning to the poor, in the love which he lived and called for' ('Die Bergpredigt', p. 40).

Other beatitudes were added in the course of time. Q probably added a fourth to Jesus' original three: 5.11-12 which announces blessing to those in the congregation who are persecuted. That is to say the blessings are being interpreted as addressed to the congregation and not simply to the disadvantaged in the world. A further four were added before Matthew came to write: vv. 5, 7-9, all of which are addressed to those who possess certain ethical characteristics, among which are those which tend towards a certain 'inwardness': humility, purity of heart. Finally Matthew added v. 10: 'Blessed are those who are persecuted for righteousness' sake, for theirs is the kingdom of heaven' and added the reference to righteousness in v. 6. The effect of this is again to emphasize the particular concrete action which denotes the blessed, rather than simply to point to the situation in which they happen to find themselves.

That is to say, there is a major change in the use of the beatitudes between Jesus and Matthew. Whereas Jesus preached salvation to the poor and suffering, Matthew holds up a 'mirror of virtues' to his congregation. So striking is this reworking of the tradition that we have to question its legitimacy. Luz wants to affirm it. The situation of those who first heard Jesus' proclamation of radical grace is altogether different from that of Matthew's hearers who had grown too accustomed to it and now needed to be reminded of its demands. 'The problem of Matthew's congregations seems to be how properly to remain within grace' ('Die Bergpredigt', p. 42). Matthew uses his creative fantasy to address such problems. He does not merely change the mode of the beatitudes from indicative to imperative; he embeds the demands of the beatitudes in the story of God's gracious dealings with his people in his Son Jesus.

The history of the appropriation of this text by later generations is one which divides into three. Some interpreters stress the imparting of grace to those who are unworthy. In the classical interpretation of the early church the ethical aspects of the texts are stressed. For Gregory of Nyssa the beatitudes constitute a royal stairway which leads from the first movement of repentance to the Christian's final perfection. The individual beatitudes are interpreted ethically, so that 'poor in spirit' is taken to refer to the humble (*Matthew 1–7*, p. 234). Alongside this, in certain monastic and clerical traditions, where the way of the perfect is distinguished from that of the normal Christians, it is taken to refer to voluntary (taking 'in spirit' to mean 'by decision of the human spirit') material poverty. This tradition of ethical interpretation, which contrasts with Jesus' announcing the radical grace of God, continues down to the first Reformers. Luther speaks of the commandments which the Gospel contains (p. 234).

However, in the second generation of the Reformation a more Pauline interpretation begins to be developed. 'Poor in spirit' is understood as 'being conscious of sin' and taken to refer to those who 'seized by the experience of their sins, far from all pride, subject themselves to God' (Theodore of Beza). Similarly 'thirsting for justice' is understood as longing for the divine grace of imputed righteousness (A. Calov) and Hengel stresses that it precisely does not say 'blessed are the righteous'. Thus read from a different (Pauline) perspective the texts are largely purged of their strong ethical note ('Die Bergpredigt', p. 44; cf. *Matthew 1–7*, p. 237). While this clearly overlooks significant elements in the text, such interpretations do bring out the tendency towards inwardness we noticed in Matthew's tradition.

At the risk of great simplification we may say that the early church interpretations with their strong emphasis on the ethical demands of the Gospel provide the basis for an embodiment of Christian norms in a Christian community, whether this was conceived as an alternative to the dominant society, as with Matthew and as in the first three centuries, or whether it was conceived as coterminous with society as a whole, as in the period of imperial recognition of Christianity. By contrast, the Protestant interpretations, notably those from a Lutheran tradition, show the way in which Christianity can develop into a religion of inwardness which then allows the state gradually to assume control of the moral regulation of society. On the other hand it has to be said that the later Protestant readings are faithful to one aspect of Matthew's handling of the beatitudes, namely his tendency to interiorize the beatitudes.

The Antitheses
As Luz shows, such tendencies become even more striking when we come to look at the antitheses, the sayings which employ some such formula as 'you have heard that it was said to those of old...but I say to you'. Again there has been development in the tradition between Jesus and Matthew. Jesus probably only uttered two sayings in this form: those about murder and adultery (*Matthew 1–7*, pp. 274-76). Moreover, he probably understood the passive 'it was said' as a divine passive (an indirect way of referring to God, i.e. with the meaning 'God said') and 'those of old' to refer to the generation of Sinai. Thus Jesus is contrasting his authority with the authority of the divine revelation on Sinai. This is an amazing contrast, particularly in light of the fact that what he actually asserts is in many ways no more than 'rabbinic commonsense'. Nevertheless, Jesus is not interested in legislation, in working out the practical details of the interpretation and application of the Law. His sayings offer exhortation, often with an element of the impractical. What would it be for a Galilean to leave his gift and go back home to settle a dispute while on his way to Jerusalem? Such extravagance has its location within Jesus' expectation of a dramatic inbreaking of the Kingdom of God ('Die Bergpredigt', p. 51).

Matthew's treatment of the antitheses is characterized by two striking features: (1) that he chooses as the first and the last antitheses sayings which deal with love and hatred (cf. too the summary of the Law in 7.12), thus there is a strong suggestion that it is the love command which provides the key to all Jesus' sayings about the Law and indeed to the understanding of the Law in general; (2) that he prefaces the whole sermon with the strongest possible affirmation of the continuing significance of the Law. Thus sayings of Jesus which originally contrasted the authority of the Law with his own now become sayings which at most intensify the meaning of the Law. This creates a tension where there is serious conflict between Jesus' sayings and the Law, as with the sayings about non-retaliation.

The history of effects shows quite clearly how these tensions can generate very different readings of the Matthaean antitheses (see the detailed discussions in Luz's commentary, and also 'Die Bergpredigt', pp. 53-62). Luz focuses attention particularly on the differences at the time of the Reformation between mainline Reformers and the Anabaptists. The Anabaptists, who quickly became the subject of brutal repression, took and applied the antitheses literally. They saw them as contrasted with the Old Testament Law and therefore understood the New Testament as the proclamation of a new and better law. (Unlike Matthew they had no need to show the continuity between their ethic and the Law, for the Jews were by now in a very different position of influence.) This in turn led them to apply the commands of the Sermon on the Mount very seriously. Thus they refused to take oaths or to carry arms. In part, this may have been the result of a rather biblicist approach; in part, the outcome of a lay approach to theology, which did not have sophisticated theological schemata at its disposal to enable them to finesse the sharper demands of the Sermon. More importantly there is a recognition here of the character of the Gospel as Law. The Swiss Anabaptist, Hans Denck wrote:

> Whoever finds God's command difficult, does not love God and does not know him, how good he is...God's covenant and the yoke of his Son is heavy only to those who have not carried it...The more the elect works in God's vineyard, the less he tires; even the work is rest for him in God (quoted in 'Die Bergpredigt', p. 55).

By contrast, the mainline Reformers saw the antitheses as correctives to Jewish misinterpretation of the Law. Particularly for Calvin, there could be nothing wrong with the Law that Jesus would have needed to modify. This in turn led him to play down the force of Jesus' commands in the antitheses, not least his injunction to shun the use of violence.

Further, the Reformers tended to read Jesus' commandments in the light of the love command and thus to soften their demands. Christians were enjoined to consider the effects of their actions on their dependents. In general this led to an ethic of motive (it's the intention which counts), whereas the Anabaptists argued that the commandments gave concrete expression to the love command.

What is noticeable too is the lack of real conviction on the part of the Reformers that Jesus' commandments could be lived out either by individuals or by the church as a whole. People were permanently sinful, *simul justus et peccator*, and therefore the best one could do was to preach repentance and grace to the individual. By contrast the Anabaptists sought to create a holy community, faithful to Jesus' teaching.

As Luz points out there is much in common between the Anabaptists and Matthew. In their emphasis on the gracious character of Jesus' commandments, in their understanding of discipleship as the keeping of the commandments, as a way of righteousness which Christ helps the believers to follow so that they may enter life (Mt. 7.13), in their attempts to forge a community which would live out the life of discipleship, they were close to Matthew's intentions and to the situation of his communities. Like him, they were a closed, somewhat sectarian group, at odds with the world around them but trying to live out their ideals with some intensity in the fellowship of the group. The Reformers, by contrast, were attempting to create a new society in which the church would be an important institution. They were much more cautious about the application of the radical ethic of the Gospel to their societies, which had to defend themselves and administer a legal system with binding oaths. For this reason, they gladly seized upon those elements in Matthew which could allow them to soften the demands of Jesus' kingdom ethic and which would make it more serviceable as a civil code. They would also enthusiastically develop the tendencies already present in Matthew, and indeed in his tradition, towards an interiorization of the Gospel.

The story of the appropriation of the Sermon on the Mount in Christian history brings out very clearly the contrary tendencies within the text itself. As Luz shows, these are themselves the result of a complex history in which the early Christian community has attempted to live out Jesus' teaching and preaching. As circumstances changed, and indeed as theological emphases shifted, so the tradition developed and was moulded until it was written down in the form of Matthew's Gospel. Subsequent generations, from their own standpoints, have also contributed to the development of this tradition by the way they have emphasized different aspects of the text and indeed by the way that they have interpreted and given imaginative life to them. Those who wish to engage creatively in this continuing process of appropriation of Matthew's Gospel will do well to be aware both of the diversity of interpretations there have been and also of the way in which such interpretations are rooted in the text. This will both encourage fresh and open readings of these texts, as readers bring their own perspectives to bear on them and also close readings, as they allow their readings to be challenged and informed by the complex meanings of Matthew's composition.

FURTHER READING

J. Barclay, *Obeying the Truth* (Edinburgh: T. & T. Clark, 1988).

G. Bornkamm, 'Der Aufbau der Bergpredigt', *NTS* 24 (1977–78), pp. 419-32.

P. Berger, *The Sacred Canopy: Elements of a Sociological Theory of Religion* (Garden City, NY: Doubleday, 1969).

W.D. Davies, *The Setting of the Sermon on the Mount* (Cambridge: Cambridge University Press, 1966).

M. Hengel, 'Between Jesus and Paul', in *Between Jesus and Paul* (London: SCM Press, 1983), pp. 1-29.

U. Luz, 'Die Bergpredigt im Spiegel ihrer Wirkungsgeschichte', in J. Moltmann (ed.), *Nachfolge und Bergpredigt* (Munich: Chr. Kaiser Verlag, 1981).

J.L. Martyn, *History and Theology in the Fourth Gospel* (New York: Harper and Row, 1968).

J.A. Overman, *Matthew's Gospel and Formative Judaism* (Minneapolis: Fortress Press, 1990).

A.J. Saldarini, *Matthew's Christian-Jewish Community* (Chicago: The University of Chicago Press, 1994).

E.P. Sanders, *Judaism: Practice and Belief* (London: SCM Press, 1992).

D.C. Sim, *The Gospel of Matthew and Christian Judaism: The History and Social Setting of the Matthean Community* (Studies of the New Testament and its World; Edinburgh: T. & T. Clark, 1998).

K. Stendahl, *The School of Matthew and its Use of the Old Testament* (Philadelphia: Fortress Press, 2nd edn, 1968).

G. Theissen, *The First Followers of Jesus* (London: SCM Press, 1978).

W. Trilling, *Das wahre Israel: Studien zur Theologie des Matthäusevangeliums* (Munich: Kösel, 1964).

Chapter Four

MATTHEW'S CHRISTOLOGY

So far we have been looking at the kind of book that Matthew's
Gospel is, at the ways in which it was written and at the broader context in the life of the church and of Judaism in which it was set. But
what was Matthew trying to say to his readers? What specifically did
he want to say about Jesus and about God? It is reasonable to suppose
that a first-century writer close to the Jewish tradition who writes a
book in which the central figure is acclaimed by God at his baptism
and transfiguration as his son is making theological claims.

But how are we to get at the central theological import of the
Gospel? Part of the problem is connected with the way in which New
Testament scholars have approached theological questions; part is
related to divergences of approach to Matthew's Gospel. Let me
explain.

1. When scholars first started to look at the New Testament historically and critically in the eighteenth century, the more radical spirits,
like H.S. Reimarus, questioned how far the New Testament could
support the views of Jesus' divinity that were set out in the creeds. It
could be fairly convincingly shown that the title 'son of God', for
instance, in its Old Testament usage did not mean anything like 'the
second person of the Trinity'. A fully fledged doctrine of the Trinity is
indeed a product of some centuries of Christian reflection. The question is then how far such developments are already prefigured in the
New Testament writings themselves. When biblical terms like 'son of
God' were used by the New Testament writers were they being filled
with new meaning? What other terms were employed to express early
Christian beliefs about Jesus' theological status? What other means
were used to express nascent Christian beliefs in Jesus' divinity? Did
Jesus himself claim some kind of special relationship to God? Did
such beliefs originate in early Christianity itself and, if so, at what
point?

Such questions are clearly of major importance to Christian

theologians and of considerable interest to others too. It is not, however, our task to tell the story of their scholarly investigation. Two
points are pertinent here. First, perhaps rather unsurprisingly, much
of the debate has been conducted in terms of christological titles. This
is obviously important as such titles represent an important part of
first-century linguistic resources for making theological statements.
But there are other linguistic resources. Imagery and metaphor, such
as that deployed in the Fourth Gospel, typology and scriptural allusion may also tell us much about the Evangelists' views of Jesus'
theological status. The way the Evangelists narrated Jesus' story, the
range of literary techniques which they employed, may tell us a great
deal about who they thought he was.

The second point is related. Until some 30 years ago scholars had
tended to focus attention either on the theological titles in the epistles
and the long discourses of the Fourth Gospel or on the development
of such titles in the tradition which lay behind the Synoptic Gospels.
They had paid little attention to the way in which the Synoptic Evangelists set out their views about Jesus' status. The most notable exception to this was William Wrede's discussion of the Messianic secret.
Jesus' commands to silence, his parable theory and the disciples' lack
of understanding were identified by Wrede as motifs in the Gospels
which were making a theological point about Jesus. He was, however,
less certain about whether such motifs were to be attributed to the
early Christian communities or to the Evangelists, above all Mark,
themselves. With the rise of redaction criticism in the late 50s attention
at last turned to the Evangelists. Even so, initially it was the titles
which formed the centre of discussion. Interest in the Evangelist's
'narrative Christology' is a relatively recent phenomenon.

2. The other part of the problem is related to the approach taken to
the Gospels. Do we see the Gospels as the outcome of a complex literary process of production, which process can give us the clue to the
intended senses of their editors? Or do we see them as literary works
in themselves, which can yield up their secrets to an eye trained to
recognize the complex relationships between the various parts, motifs,
plots, characters, authorial devices etc. which go to make up the
whole? The former view will take very seriously the literary *history* of
which Matthew's Gospel is a part; the latter will treat it as an isolated
phenomenon which can stand on its own. It is fashionable to characterize such views as on the one hand historical, on the other literary-
critical. This seems to me to be dangerously misleading: both are
interested in literary texts which are part of the culture of a particular
age; the question at issue is whether one believes that the appreciation

of such texts is assisted or hindered by attending to the historical circumstances of their production and reception. Interestingly, as we
shall see, more attention to the narrative or literary character of Matthew's Christology is paid by those who would often be characterized
as working in a purely historical-critical mode.

Kingsbury's Account of Matthaean Christology

Kingsbury, whom we have already met in conjunction with literary
discussions of the Gospel, has raised questions about Matthew's
Christology which have prompted vigorous debate. In his first major
contribution to this area, *Matthew: Structure, Christology, Kingdom,*
Kingsbury argued that 'Son of God' is the 'central christological category of Matthew's Gospel' (p. 82) and that it is in the light of this title
that all the others are to be interpreted. 'Son of God' is the one title
that is found distributed across all the major parts of the Gospel; it is
found at the major events of Jesus' baptism (3.17), temptation (4.3, 6),
after the walking on the water (14.33), at Peter's confession at
Caesarea Philippi (16.16), at the transfiguration (17.5), at the trial
(26.63) and crucifixion (27.40, 54). But this is not all. Kingsbury
believes that the title lies behind much of the other material in the
Gospel (the references to the Son and Jesus' address to God as 'my
Father' — many Matthew's own) and that it is presupposed in the
account of the resurrection. Thus, for instance, when Jesus goes up on
to the mountain at 5.1 to deliver the Sermon on the Mount, this is an
indirect allusion to his Sonship. This might be surprising, but Kingsbury asserts that 'the mountain is the place of eschatological revelation' (pp. 56-57), listing 4.8, 5.1, 15.29, 17.1 and 28.16 (of which he
notes all but 17.1 as Matthew's own addition or creation). He sees the
reference to Emmanuel ('God with us') in 1.23 and echoed in 18.20
and 28.20 (and, he argues, 14.27) as containing '*in nuce* everything that
Matthew otherwise says in 1.1–4.16 of Jesus Son of God' (p. 53). The
title is distinguished by being a 'confessional' one (hence its relative
scarcity in the long section on Jesus' public ministry, 4.17–10.42 — the
demon in 8.29 knows who Jesus is even if he does not confess him);
where it is used by non-believers, it is blasphemous. It is revealed to
those who make the confession. This distinguishes it from one of the
other major titles in the Gospel, Son of Man, which Kingsbury sees as
a public title, addressed only to those outside the group of disciples. It
does not occur until 8.20 and 'except for the "righteous" in the scene
of the Last Judgment, it marks the people in view of whom it is used
as being unbelievers or opponents of Jesus' (p. 115). Its principal

interest for Matthew is in its reference to Jesus as the eschatological judge; in this respect it 'coalesces' with the title Son of God (p. 121).

Later in *Matthew as Story* Kingsbury argued the same case on rather different grounds. If in his first book he was working as a redaction critic, looking to see what changes Matthew had made in his sources, attending to patterns of usage and emphasis throughout the book, here he dons the robe of the *ahistorical* literary critic. Historical consid- erations of setting, sources, mode of composition are set aside and we are invited to attend to the composition itself and to the literary con- ventions by which writers can make themselves heard. Two points are crucial to Kingsbury's argument in this book. First, he now pays greater attention to the placing of the titles within the Gospel itself. Son of God is seen to occur as the culmination of each of the three major sections which Kingsbury has identified: 1.1–4.17; 4.18–16.20; 16.21–end. Secondly, he distinguishes the various 'points of view' which are presented in the Gospel. In simple terms we need to distin- guish between the point of view of the author, of Jesus and of God. It is clear that in the Gospel Jesus' point of view and that of the author coincide. What is interesting is that these receive ultimate accredita- tion from the entry of God as 'actor' in the divine voice in 3.17 and 17.5 where God declares Jesus to be his beloved son. Thus the ulti- mately authoritative point of view in the Gospel accredits the title 'Son of God' as the one truly authoritative title in the light of which all others have to be read.

There is a further aspect to this literary approach to the question of Matthew's Christology which concerns his use of the Son of Man title. Kingsbury has argued that it is 'Son of God' as opposed to 'Son of Man' which represents God's point of view in the Gospel, and this is reinforced for him by the fact that in the first section, 1.1–4.16 which sets out who Jesus is, the title 'Son of Man' does not occur. Further- more, he argues, its use in Matthew is quite distinct from that of other titles, which are used to say 'who Jesus is', whereas the phrase 'Son of Man' occurs only on Jesus' lips and is never used predicatively (i.e. in the form 'I am the Son of Man'). '"The Son of Man" is not meant to clarify for the reader who Jesus is but must itself be clarified' ('Figure', p. 23).

Rather strangely, he finds confirmation of this view in his discus- sion of the trial scene before the High Priest. Jesus' reply to the High Priest's demand: 'tell us if you are the Christ, the Son of God' is 'You have said so'. Kingsbury takes this as a straight affirmative and reads Jesus' subsequent remark 'But I tell you hereafter you will see the Son of Man seated at the right hand of power...' as merely a 'tacit reference to himself as "the Son of Man"' ('Figure', p. 23). The reason for this is twofold: one that he rightly observes that the title is nowhere picked up by those to whom it is uttered. In this case the priests in mocking him refer to him as Christ. The other is that he wants to translate the phrase not as a special title, carrying certain sense contents, but as a mode of self-reference, 'this man'.

What then is the purpose, according to Kingsbury, of Matthew's use of the phrase? '"The Son of Man" may be defined as the title by means of which Jesus refers to himself "in public" or in view of the "public" (or "world")…as "the man", or "the human being" (earthly, suffering, vindicated), and to assert his divine authority in the face of opposition' ('Figure', p. 27). By speaking of 'Son of Man' as a public title, Kingsbury means two things: first, that it is principally addressed to the world; secondly, that it can be used openly without any of those who are addressed actually picking it up and using it. How is it to be understood? The key is in the exchange between Jesus and Peter at Caesarea Philippi: Jesus (not Peter, as Kingsbury rather oddly suggests) asks who is the Son of Man and Peter replies, You are the Son of God.

It might seem then that Kingsbury is saying that the term has no content at all. Nevertheless, he does suggest that it is 'associated' with Jesus' assertion of his divine authority ('Figure', p. 29) and that it is a phrase used specifically in situations of opposition. It signifies the opposition which Jesus encounters as well as pointing to his ultimate vindication, themes which Kingsbury shows, without too much difficulty, run through the Gospel.

Thus Kingsbury's literary-critical analysis neatly confirms his earlier findings about Matthew's Christology. While there has been general agreement among scholars that Kingsbury has been right to highlight the importance of Son of God in Matthew's Gospel, there is much less agreement that it should be seen as the central title. One of Kingsbury's most persistent critics, David Hill, has suggested that overvaluing the Son of God title leads to a lack of sensitivity to the many other rich allusions which are to be found in the text. Hill himself has drawn attention to the importance for Matthew of the Servant of Yahweh imagery of Isaiah which is presented in the long quotation of Isa. 42.1-4 in Mt. 12.17-21, alluded to by the divine voice in 3.16-17 and 17.5 and the citation of Isaiah 53 at 8.17. Hill's point is not that the image of Servant is more important than the title Son of God, but rather that the image gives *content* to the title which otherwise in Kingsbury's treatment seems only to refer to Jesus' authority, whereas the Servant image would associate it with notions of healing and

atonement. Hill's own work shows the value of exploring the intertextual relationships between Matthew and the Old Testament. He
suggests that the quotation of Isaiah 42 at 12.18-21 is substantially
modified by Matthew himself in the light of the divine voice in 3.17 at
the same time as the quotation itself shapes ch. 12, emphasizing Jesus'
empowerment by the Spirit and his humility and his saving concern
for 'the weak, the lost and the broken' ('Son and Servant', p. 12)

Hill is equally critical of Kingsbury's treatment of Son of Man in
Matthew. Of *Matthew: Structure, Christology, Kingship* Hill says that its
treatment of the evidence is 'Procrustean' ('Son and Servant', p. 2),
forcing it to conform to his own preconceived ideas. Why should the
scribe in ch. 8 be regarded as in opposition to Jesus? Again, is it credible that 'Matthew can use "Son of Man" at 20.28 only because it is the
mother of James and John (i.e. an unbeliever or opponent?) whose
request provokes the utterance?' ('Son and Servant', p. 3). And he
rightly turns to Kingsbury's treatment of the trial before the High
Priest to ask why there is no discussion there (or anywhere else) of
Daniel 7 to which there is clear allusion in Jesus' reply.

Similar suggestions have been made by Dale Allison, the co-author
with W.D. Davies of the new ICC commentary on Matthew. In an
early article ('Son of God as Israel', pp. 74-81), Allison suggests that
Kingsbury's concentration on the text alone, irrespective of its roots in
and allusions to the Old Testament denies to him insights which
would have enriched his work. Not only are there clear allusions to
the Servant of Yahweh from Isaiah, as Hill has pointed out, there is
also a strong typological interplay between the notion of Jesus as Son
of God and that of Israel as God's Son (something that R.E. Brown has
also argued in *The Birth of the Messiah*). This is seen most clearly in the
quotation of Hos. 11.1 at 2.15: 'Out of Egypt have I called my son',
which in Hosea clearly refers to Israel and in Matthew points to the
close parallels between Jesus' story and Israel's. Thus when Jesus is
addressed by the divine voice in 3.17 as 'my beloved Son' is he not
'also here identified in some sense with Israel?' (p. 76; note that the
page numbers need renumbering: read in the following order: 74, 75,
78, 79, 76, 77, 80, 81). Israel's history of exodus, wanderings in the
desert and revelation on the mountain is mirrored in Jesus' story in
Matthew.

Recently Allison has developed this kind of approach in an excellent study of Moses typology in ancient literature and in Matthew, *The
New Moses*. The value of this book is that it both sets out clear criteria
for identifying typological allusions, and that it provides a full survey
of the use of Moses as a typological figure in a wide range of ancient

texts prior to Matthew's Gospel. This certainly helps to give an element of precision and control to this kind of discussion which is needed.

Allison identifies six kinds of textual allusion to figures or events from the past:

1. Explicit statement: Jn 3.14 refers directly to the incident with Moses and the serpent.
2. Inexplicit citation or borrowing: Mk 1.7 in referring to John's leather girdle actually cites words from the Greek translation of 2 Kgs 1.8 about Elijah.
3. Similar circumstances: Joshua's crossing of the Jordan may be intended to recall Moses' crossing of the Red Sea.
4. Key words or phrases: the Gospel accounts of the miraculous feedings pick up the barley loaves which are mentioned in the miraculous feeding in 2 Kgs 4.42-44.
5. Similar narrative structure: Mark's account of the calling of the disciples in 1.16-20 is structurally close to that in 1 Kings 19.
6. Word order, syllabic sequence, poetic resonance. In Jn 1.1 there are clear echoes of Gen. 1.1, not only in its identical 'in the beginning' but also in the rhythmic and syllabic structure in the Greek (pp. 19-21).

Given this variety, we need some guide as to where we can be confident of intended allusions. Allison lays down three conditions, which if satisfied make it likely that the author intended an allusion:

1. Priority in time: the work alluded to must precede that in which the allusion is made and intended.
2. The tradition or book referred to must have been known to the author making the allusion.
3. Unless there is explicit allusion, a *combination* of features 3-6 above is required if we are to be confident that there has been an intentional allusion on the part of the author.
4. The type referred to should be prominent.
5. The alleged typology is more likely if frequently used.
6. The more unusual the shared imagery, motifs, etc. the more likely there is an intended connection (pp. 21-23).

The strength of Allison's argument depends very much on his careful demonstration of the richness of typological allusion that is to be found in Jewish literature prior to Matthew. He demonstrates, that is to say, that this was a widespread cultural phenomenon which was employed to link key figures in Israel's history, Moses with Joshua, Gideon, David, Jeremiah, the promised Messiah, to show the continuity of God's dealings with his people. In this Moses may function as type in various capacities: as leader/king (Joshua, Josiah), as saviour/ deliverer (Gideon, Messiah), as lawgiver/teacher (Ezra, Ezekiel, Hillel), and as intercessor/suffering prophet (Jeremiah and the Servant in Deutero-Isaiah). What is noteworthy is that in most cases the connection is *not* made explicit and that therefore the readers are required to pick up the allusions for themselves. Such comparisons (and comparison/*sugkrasis* was a widespread phenomenon in the ancient world) clearly served to exalt the figure who was being compared to, for example, Moses. They were not, however, by any means the only points which were being made; rather they occur alongside any number of differences in the accounts. Finally, Allison notes that all the extensive literature covered in his survey was known to Matthew (*New Moses*, part I).

How then does Matthew himself deploy such Moses typology in relation to Jesus? There is not room to discuss Allison's treatment of the whole Gospel but only to look at one section: the infancy narratives (pp. 140-65). Allison finds evidence of textual linking under all the heads mentioned above except the last. The treatment is full but a selection of the points may indicate its persuasiveness.

1. Explicit citation of the Exodus story occurs in 2.11 where Matthew cites Hos. 11.1. Noting that this is in the first place a reference to Israel rather than Moses, Allison avers that they are correlative conceptions.

2. Inexplicit citation: Allison notes a number of close similarities in the accounts of Mt. 2.19-21 and Exod. 4.19-20, some of which look like verbal echoes of the Exodus account. Both Moses and Jesus go into exile until the king who is pursuing them dies (Matthew's account 'those seeking the life of the child have died' echoes closely that of Exodus 'all those seeking your life have died'). This intelligence is communicated supernaturally and the two protagonists return with their family.

3. Similar circumstances: comparing Matthew's narrative with the Moses' story in later Jewish tradition (Josephus and the targums — Aramaic translations of the Hebrew Bible), Allison notes that in both the fathers are worried about the mother's pregnancy (see Josephus, *Ant.* 2.210-16); both figures are known as saviours (2.228); in both cases the order is given for

the slaughter of all the male children because the king learns of the birth of a future liberator of the people (2.205-209), from scribes (2.205, 234) and magi (Jerusalem targum on Exod. 1.15); both kings are disturbed when they hear the prophecy (*Ant.* 2.206).

4.   Key-words and phrases: see above under 3.
5.   Similar narrative structure: Allison believes that he can discern a similar tri-partite structure containing two dreams experienced by the father and the persecutor and then the birth and deliverance of the saviour.

While individual details of this might be disputed, and while there is obviously a problem about the reliance on Josephus who is at best a contemporary of Matthew, the evidence accumulated here and in Allison's continuing discussion of the rest of the Gospel is undeniably impressive. At the end of his treatment, Allison summarizes his findings as follows (*New Moses*, pp. 267-70).

The Moses typology is one theme among many, a main branch rather than the trunk itself. It is especially strong in the Infancy narratives and the Sermon on the Mount and generally shapes chs. 1–7 with the infancy, crossing of the water at baptism, temptation in the wilderness, and law-giving. Subsequently there are important further allusions in the sayings about the reciprocal knowledge of Father and Son, in the transfiguration where Moses himself appears and in the commissioning of Jesus' successors in 28.16-20. In all this Matthew is following established conventions of typology. The typology is, moreover, for the most part hidden: Moses is named only seven times.

What implications does this have for our understanding of Matthew's Christology? Fundamentally, Matthew, by developing the comparison between Jesus and Moses, is attempting to root the new dispensation in the old, 'to pour new wine into old wineskins'. Matthew draws freely on the typological resources of the tradition: Jesus, by dint of the comparison with Moses, is seen as the prophet-king, as the Messiah, the miracle worker, the giver of Torah, the mediator for Israel and the suffering servant. What is interesting in all this is that there is no polemic against Moses. Moses is the typological herald and foreshadower of Jesus as the law-giver, not his rival. However, in developing such a broad comparison, one theme is of particular importance: that of Jesus' *exousia*, authority (cf. 7.29; 8.27; 9.6; 10.1; 21.27; 28.18). Just as Moses is the incorporation of authority for the Jews, so too is Jesus for the church. The Sermon on the Mount culminates in the crowd's exclamation that Jesus teaches as having author-

ity; 11.25-30 declares that all things have been revealed to Jesus; at the
transfiguration the voice from heaven declares that they are to 'listen
to him'; and in the final commissioning Jesus declares that all authority has been given to him. According to Allison, Matthew 'draped the
Messiah in the familiar mantle of Moses, by which dress he made
Jesus the full bearer of God's authority' (p. 277).

It will be clear that I regard this as an important and instructive
book. The question of Jesus' relation to Moses is of course not new. It
was raised, as we have seen, by B.S. Bacon with his suggestion of a
fivefold structure to the Gospel, mirroring the five books of the Law.
Others, including W.D. Davies and R.E. Brown, have explored the use
of this kind of typology in Matthew's Gospel. The merits of Allison's
treatment lie in his careful portrayal of the ways in which ancient
Hebrew texts develop the Moses typology and then in his use of this
knowledge to track down Matthew's intention through the Gospel.
The question which it raises most acutely, precisely because of its
careful and thorough documentation of the Moses typology in Jewish
(and Christian) tradition, concerns the extent to which Jesus is seen, as
is Joshua, as like but essentially subordinate to Moses; to what extent
he is seen as replacing Moses as a figure of authority in Judaism. Allison is very keen to stress the continuity which is implied in such
typological treatment. According to him, the purpose of such a
comparison is precisely to remind the church of its roots in Judaism as
it is casting or being cast loose from its parent body. Yet on any reading it should be clear that what is occurring is in many respects different from what occurs in Jewish tradition.

Clearly there are intended similarities. Jesus, like Moses, instructs
the people, imparts to them the will of God. What he teaches is consistent with, 'fulfils', the Law and the prophets (5.17; 7.12). In 23.2-3,
the crowds and the disciples are told to obey the scribes and Pharisees
because 'they sit on Moses' seat'. These are texts which are only found
as such in Matthew. There are others which Matthew has taken over
from Mark which also stress the continuity. Jesus commands the leper
to show himself to the priest and to offer the gift as Moses commanded (Mt. 8.4). In 17.3-4 he is transfigured with Moses and Elijah
(here Matthew has changed Mark's 'Elijah with Moses' to 'Moses and
Elijah' — orders of precedence were important in the ancient world).
But while Matthew thus asserts that what Jesus does is consistent with
the work of Moses, that is to say that God is acting through him in a
manner which is in accord with the way he acted through Moses,
there are distinctions to be made. What Jesus teaches is contrasted
with Moses' teaching. In the antitheses in the Sermon on the Mount (a

feature Matthew has developed, contrast Luke's three occurrences with Matthew's six), Jesus contrasts his teaching with what they have heard of old. In the controversy over divorce, Jesus indicates that Moses' teaching is given for the hardness of their hearts and is to be replaced by his own re-emphasis of the creator's purposes in creating male and female. Again, in the transfiguration, while Jesus is associated with Moses and Elijah, he is also singled out by the divine voice as the beloved Son, as the one to whom the disciples must listen (17.5). Similarly, but with greater clarity and emphasis, Jesus at the end of the Gospel is accredited as the one to whom 'all authority in heaven and earth' has been given and whose commands are therefore to be taught and obeyed among all nations (28.16-20).

The claims to authority made for Moses and Jesus are in one sense analogous, inviting us to see them as comparable figures; in another sense they are rivalrous, precisely because of their scope. To say that 'all authority is given to me' is by implication to deny that others possess authority. Matthew wants to preserve his lines with the Jewish tradition; but he wants to be the judge of the nature of that continuity.

Perhaps this contrast between Jesus and Moses is most clearly indicated in the final clause of the Gospel: 'and lo, I am with you always, to the close of the age'. There are clear echoes here of two very important verses in the Gospel, 1.23 and 18.20. Whereas Moses was brought into the presence of God at significant points of his life, see, for example, Exodus 3 and 18 and the people of Israel are accompanied by the pillar of fire, Jesus is himself the presence of God with his people. Moreover, he will be with them wherever they gather to pray. Matthew's retention of the incident of the tearing of the veil of the Temple strongly suggests that the presence of God which was previously associated with the Temple has now passed to Jesus himself, however paradoxical this may appear in view of Jesus' death.

Thus in the end Matthew is pointing clearly enough to the way in which Jesus transcends Moses and the old dispensation. It is evidently important to him to stress the continuity between God's purposes in the old dispensation and what is now taking place, as the 'fulfilment quotations' show. Similarly, it is important for him to show that there is consistency between God's revelation of his will in the Mosaic legislation and Jesus' own teaching. But here there is an equally strong concern to assert that Jesus' teaching transcends that of the old legislation; that true authority now lies with the Christian community which has indeed received the divine commission to propagate Jesus' commandments throughout the world.

Matthew's Christology as Narrative Christology

Allison's study is principally a study of allusion, of the rhetorical device of comparison, though of course it attends, within this overall aim, to narrative structures and circumstance. Fuller attention to the christological import of Matthew's *narrative* is given by Ulrich Luz in an important article: 'A Sketch of Matthew's Christology in the Form of Theses'.

Ulrich Luz has certainly produced some of the most elegant and carefully researched work on Matthew in the last fifteen years. As yet he has not produced a full statement of his views on Matthew's Christology in his commentary, but in a number of articles he has begun to set them out. In the article just mentioned he is principally concerned with Matthew's use of three titles: Son of David, Son of Man and Son of God. He considers them, however, within the narrative of the Gospel, which he believes determines their meaning. For whereas before the Gospels it was the titles which served to say who Jesus was (which, as he puts it, were used 'predicatively'), in Matthew it is the other way round: 'the Matthean story of Jesus functions as the predicate and redefines the meaning of the traditional titles' ('Sketch', p. 223). In this sense the meaning of the traditional titles becomes fluid.

Matthew's story is an inclusive story: it tells the story of Jesus' life in such a way that the whole history of his mission to Israel, of the divisions which it provokes, his judgment by the leaders of the Jewish people and his sending of the disciples to the nations, mirrors that of the church. 'It is the story of the "Emmanuel" (1.23, cf. 28.20), Jesus, which tells how in Jesus "God is with us", that is to say how Jesus accompanies his community along their way through obedience, experience of faith and suffering' (p. 223). The Emmanuel formula with its deep Old Testament roots shows how far the Christology of the Gospel is theology. 'Jesus in Matthew's Gospel is the new and definitive form of God's presence with his people' (p. 223).

What then of the three titles? 'Son of David' indicates that Jesus comes as the expected Messiah—but in practice he acts very differently to what is expected of him. Above all he heals, something not traditionally associated with the Son of David; Luz thinks that Matthew's inspiration for the interpretation of the title comes from Mark, esp. 10.46-52. In particular he heals the blind (9.27; 12.23; 20.30-31, cf. 21.14-16). 'The Messiah Jesus heals (metaphorically) the blindness of Israel, while the leaders remain blind (cf. 23.16-26)' (p. 225). However,

22.1-46 shows that the Son of David is more than Messiah, he is the Lord of the world and in the main christological sections of the last chapters the title no longer appears. Its purpose was to 'characterize Jesus' coming as the fulfilment and transformation of Israel's hopes and so to help overcome the shock of the separation of Christian congregation and synagogue' (p. 226).

More significant in the end are the two other titles. 'Son of Man' is again a title which Matthew takes over from the tradition. Matthew assumes that his readers know that the Son of Man is homeless and rejected, that he must suffer and die and that he will come to judge the world. It is a title, that is to say, which reminds the reader of the whole course of Jesus' story and which Matthew uses carefully. Luz differs, however, from Kingsbury in his assessment of the way Matthew uses it. He agrees that before 16.13 the majority of the Son of Man sayings are directed to the public. But thereafter Jesus speaks only to the disciples of the Son of Man with the exception of 26.64. In fact with two exceptions Jesus never speaks publicly about the Son of Man as coming judge or as the one who will suffer and rise again. It is only the sayings about the present Son of Man that are addressed to the public and these occur predominantly in the first half of the Gospel. Luz agrees with Kingsbury that the phrase is not used predicatively; it is not, that is to say, 'used to say who Jesus is, but to narrate what he does or suffers' (p. 227). In his reworking of the traditional material which he has taken over, Matthew has emphasized above all the sayings about the future coming of the Son of Man as judge (new sayings at 13.41; 16.28; 19.28?; 24.30a; 25.31).

How then does Matthew use the term in his Gospel? It is above all a phrase which draws a line between those who understand who Jesus is and those who do not, between the disciples and the 'ignorant and evil intentioned opponents on whom the judgment of the Son of Man will suddenly and unexpectedly fall' (p. 228). Thus Luz can speak of a 'Son of Man secret' in Matthew's Gospel. Just as the disciples in Mark are not to reveal the secret of Jesus' identity as the Messiah, so in Matthew the secret of his identity as Son of Man is hidden from those outside the community of the church, though in this case it is only rarely reinforced by a command to silence (16.20; 17.9). Above all, the title functions to hold together the various aspects of Jesus' life, including his future coming as judge. It is 'a horizontal title', which by contrast with the 'Son of David' title has a universal and future perspective.

Luz is fully aware of the questions about the origins of Christology with which we started. His treatment is designed to address such questions. For him Matthew's 'horizontal' Son of Man Christology forms a bridge between Jewish apocalyptic expectation of a heavenly cosmic judge and the later two-natures Christology which used the expression Son of Man for the humanity of Jesus. In such developments Matthew is taking up tendencies already present in Mark, particularly in his second part (8.31–14.62) which, as we noted, he follows more closely than the first. But he also 'deepens and reinforces Mark's horizontal understanding of the Son of Man with the help of the paradoxical use of the expression in Q (e.g. Q 9.58 the homeless Jesus as judge of the world)' (p. 231). From here the lines lead on to the use of the term in Ignatius of Antioch (early second century)

How then does this relate to the 'Son of God' title in Matthew? Matthew takes over the title from Mark where it has a strongly vertical sense (and where it also has a confessional sense) and adds to it a horizontal dimension which stresses Jesus' obedience to the Father. Here he is developing elements already to be found in Mark (willing acceptance of suffering) and Q (temptation stories) but is also drawing importantly on the Jewish notion of the righteous man who suffers unjustly (Ps. 22; Wis. 2.18).

Luz agrees with Kingsbury that Matthew places important Son of God passages at the climaxes of the main sections of his Gospel (though he disagrees with Kingsbury's threefold division, seeing 11.25-30 as forming the climax of the second section of the Gospel which runs from 4.23–11.30) and he shows how in practically all important Son of God texts the vertical and horizontal dimensions are combined. Matthew 11.25-30 in particular shows how Matthew combines an interest in the ethical dimension (not least through his addition of a Wisdom saying, vv. 28-30 with its emphasis on Jesus' obedience: 'gentle and lowly in heart') of Jesus' existence with a high Christology which stresses 'the mutual "mystical" knowledge' of the Father and the Son (p. 233). The central fulfilment quotation of 12.18-21 speaks not of the Servant of God, as David Hill argues, but 'uses the biblical language of Isaiah to speak of the *child* of God, that is, the Son of God who is known to the readers from 3.17' (p. 233). But while the Son of God title marks out major junctures of the Gospel, it does not appear in the final section 28.16-20 (except in the triadic baptismal formula), though there are echoes of other important christological passages. 'In this way it shows the way in which Matthew's narrated Christology is greater than the titles which he uses. Matthaean Christology is more than a semantic field which is determined by titles which define different aspects of the field; it is the story of a man in whom God is and was "with us"' (p. 234).

Conclusion

Matthew, we have seen, develops his views about Jesus' person and relationship to God by weaving titles and motifs from his tradition into a rich narrative. Focusing on the titles is one way to see what Matthew is attempting, but it needs at the least to be supplemented by a consideration of the narrative setting of the titles and their interaction with other motifs. This means, I think, that we cannot expect to extract a neatly formulable Christology from the Gospel. We can see how certain emphases are being set: clearly on the close relation of Jesus to his Father and his purposes. He is the one declared by the Father as his Son who is obedient to him and to whom all authority will be entrusted. He is the one who fulfils, but strangely, the hopes of Israel and thus can be seen in a sense as Son of David, as a new Moses, as mirroring in his own history the key moments of the history of Israel, above all as announcing the will of God to his people. But the fact is that Matthew sets all this in the context of a story which relates Jesus' humiliation and death as well as his resurrection from the dead. In simple terms Jesus touches depths and heights which are not attained by the figures from the past with whom Jesus is most closely associated—David, Elijah, Moses. And the claim is that God does not simply use this strange figure as his messenger and instrument, but that he is in his very lowliness, obedience and suffering, as well as in his exaltation, God with us.

As Luz has suggested it is possible to see a line of development between Matthew's Christology with its equal emphases on Jesus' Sonship and his earthly fate as Son of Man and the later thought of the church which used the terminology of Son of God and Son of Man to develop a doctrine of the two natures, the divinity and the humanity of Christ. If one of the features of earliest Christian belief in Christ was belief in his coming as the heavenly judge at the end of time, then here the narration of his life and death is the means whereby reflection can begin to encompass the meaning of his earthly life and suffering. It too shares, more or less evidently, in the authority which will be manifested in the final judgment.

Thus Matthew has created a rich subject for subsequent Christian thought and reflection. The two natures Christology of the early Church is of course only one way in which it could be developed. Christian theology will constantly have to struggle to find ways of expressing the mystery of the presence of God in the figure of the suffering, crucified and risen Christ to which Matthew has given such powerful expression.

FURTHER READING

D.C. Allison, Jr, 'The Son of God as Israel: A Note on Matthean Christology', *Irish Biblical Studies* 9 (1987), pp. 74-81.

—*The New Moses: A Matthean Typology* (Minneapolis: Fortress Press, 1993).

R.E. Brown, *The Birth of the Messiah* (New York: Doubleday, 1977).

D. Hill, 'Son and Servant: An Essay on Matthean Christology', *JSNT* 6 (1980), pp. 2-16.

J.D. Kingsbury, *Matthew: Structure, Christology, Kingdom* (Minneapolis: Fortress Press, 2nd edn, 1989 [1975]).

—*Matthew as Story* (Philadelphia: Fortress Press, 1986).

—'The Figure of Jesus in Matthew's Story: A Literary-Critical Probe', *JSNT* 21 (1984), pp. 3-36.

—'The Figure of Jesus in Matthew's Story: A Rejoinder to David Hill', *JSNT* 25 (1985), pp. 61-81.

U. Luz, 'A Sketch of Matthew's Christology in the Form of Theses', available only in German as 'Eine thetische Skizze der matthäischen Christologie', in C. Breytenbach and H. Paulsen (eds.), *Anfänge der Christologie* (Göttingen: Vandenhoeck & Ruprecht, 1991), pp. 221-35.

—*The Theology of the Gospel of Matthew* (Cambridge: Cambridge University Press, 1995).

W. Wrede, *The Messianic Secret* (Cambridge: James Clarke, 1971) (first published in German in 1901).

Chapter Five

CONCLUSION

Matthew's Gospel is a work of contrasts: it takes Mark's rough and dramatic narrative and inserts into it large blocks of teaching material which might well seem to threaten its narrative force, turning it into a mere teaching manual for the church. But this does not happen: the narrative, though undoubtedly flattened in some places, continues to draw the reader into the story of Jesus and his disciples. As it does so, it provides further grounds for reflection on the complex figure of this teacher, healer, Lord and redeemer, reflection focused partly on the titles given to him, partly on the rich allusions to Israel's past which his story contains and partly by the conjunction of all this with the narrative of his life, death and resurrection.

It is then scarcely surprising that this diverse and complex book has provided a steady source of inspiration for church leaders, theologians, legislators, preachers and believers through the centuries, so much so that for long it largely overshadowed its darker and more dramatic forebear, Mark. That is to say, it is in an important sense a perennial Gospel. It is a primary source of theological reflection on the nature of Jesus' Sonship; it embeds the Christian story firmly into the traditions of Israel and the Hebrew Scriptures; it sets out the teaching of Jesus in its fullest and most systematic form.

All of this might seem to argue for a treatment of Matthew's Gospel which is less rather than more historical: the circumstances of its genesis might well be thought to be less significant than its perennially fruitful contents, however achieved. And yet we have spent—and scholarly studies of Matthew still spend—much time on relating the Gospel to the community in and for which it was written. Is this simple academic perversity, the habits of the guild, which should have been long since abandoned? I think not: for the history can help to shed light on the strange and fruitful contrasts which typify the book.

Matthew's Gospel, it has been argued, is in important senses, sectarian: it is the work of a writer seeking to strengthen his community, to enable it to assert its own distinctive identity over against the more powerful (if traumatized) Jewish community in which it has its roots. But it does not just see itself as a 'new people' to whom the Kingdom has now been entrusted (21.43); it also sees itself as living out the fulfilment of all that has been promised of old. Just at the moment of the sharpest sense of rupture with the past Matthew vigorously asserts his community's continuity with that past. It is Matthew (and to a lesser extent Luke) more than Mark, John or indeed Paul (Galatians!) who ties Christianity to the traditions of Israel and ensures that the Christian Bible is composed of two 'testaments'; just as it is Matthew who ensures that this relationship will be a stormy and indeed tragic one.

The Matthaean community's separation from Judaism leaves its marks in other ways. In his sense of separateness from the mainstream of society, Matthew sets out, foremost in the Sermon on the Mount, the guidelines for a new way of life. It is an alternative community ethic, in significant ways sharply contrasted with the dominant ethos of the surrounding culture (antitheses; ch. 23!). This radical ethic has posed problems for the church when it has itself entered into the mainstream of political and cultural life and found it increasingly difficult *not* to compromise the bright ('utopian'?) ideals of the Sermon on the Mount. By the same token it can provide a source of inspiration for those who find themselves out of sorts with their contemporary culture and who seek renewal and reinvigoration.

One thing is sure: interest in Matthew is unlikely to diminish. Where Matthaean studies will be in ten years time, I will not speculate. Let me finally suggest two areas where it would be timely for there to be further work. First, Luz's work on the history of interpretation whets the appetite for more, this is surely one area where much illumination is to be gained; and secondly, there is room for more thought to be given to the place of Matthew's theology within the theologies of early Christianity. How does Matthew's theology relate to Paul's—and also to Mark's and John's and Luke's? Comparative studies would help to throw all those compared into a sharper light.

Part II

MARK

William R. Telford

COMMENTARIES ON MARK

The first commentary on the Gospel of Mark was written by Victor of Antioch in the fifth century, and it was a matter of complaint to him that he could find nothing in it which compared with treatments given to Matthew and John. Victor would have less reason for complaint today, since Mark is relatively well served for commentaries, or at least those on the English text. Among these, the following should be noted:

H. Anderson, *The Gospel of Mark* (New Century Bible; London: Marshall, Morgan & Scott, 1976). A very good popular commentary based on the RSV, which is well informed (up to its date of publication) by modern scholarship. It has in particular an excellent sixty-page introduction to the Gospel. Published in paperback in 1981.

R.A. Guelich, *Mark 1–8.26* (WBC, 34A; Dallas: Word Books, 1989). Careful, cautious, conservative scholarship with a well-balanced discussion of the problems. Guelich's untimely death unfortunately deprived us of a second volume from his own hand.

M.D. Hooker, *The Gospel According to St Mark* (BNTC; London: A. & C. Black, 1991). Though taking account of modern scholarship on the Gospel, this excellent 'middle of the road' commentary, in running style, does not, in the tradition of the series, 'overburden the reader with names and theories'.

W.L. Lane, *The Gospel According to Mark* (The New London Commentary on the New Testament; London: Marshall, Morgan & Scott; NICNT, 2; Grand Rapids: Eerdmans, 1974). Detailed, conservative scholarship based on the American Standard Version of 1901.

C.S. Mann, *Mark: A New Translation with Introduction and Commentary* (AB, 27; Garden City, NY: Doubleday, 1986). A substantial seven hundred-page commentary in a series aimed at the general reader with no special formal training in Biblical Studies. The only major modern commentary to be based on 'the Griesbach hypothesis', namely that Mark is a simple conflation of Matthew and Luke. Mann's 'Mark' for that reason is at odds with the more sophisticated author revealed by modern literary-critical study of the Gospel.

J. Marcus, *Mark 1–8: A New Translation with Introduction and Commentary* (AB; New York: Doubleday, 1999). The first of two volumes in the renowned Anchor Bible series. Interprets Mark against the backdrop of the Romano–Jewish War of 66–73 CE and the apocalyptic fervour it occasioned.

D.E. Nineham, *The Gospel of Mark* (The Pelican Gospel Commentaries; London: A. & C. Black, 2nd edn, 1968). The classic commentary on the English text and still worth buying. Though first published in 1963, its scholarly insights and forward-looking approach have anticipated later developments.

E. Schweizer, *The Good News According to Mark* (trans. D.H. Madvig; London: SPCK, 1971). Translated from the German, this commentary is by a major scholar on Mark's Gospel who has contributed much to our understanding of the evangelist's theological achievement.

B.M.F. van Iersel, *Mark: A Reader-Response Commentary* (JSNTSup, 164; Sheffield: Sheffield Academic Press, 1998). Adopting a reader-response approach to the Gospel, this commentary explores the effect of Mark's narrative on both ancient and contemporary readers. The first readers of the Gospel are taken to be Gentile Christians in Rome shortly after the Neronian persecution.

Commentaries on the Greek text of Mark:

Sadly, most are now, for the most part, out of date although some new ones are about to be published or are in preparation, for example: R. Barbour (ICC) and A.Y. Collins (Hermeneia). Recently published and offering an exposition of each pericope which engages scholarly views and pays special attention to Mark's grammar and style is R.H. Gundry's hefty *Mark: A Commentary on his Apology for the Cross* (Grand Rapids, MI: Eerdmans, 1992). See also J. Marcus, *Mark 1–8* above. Provided that they are used with discretion and in combination with more recent commentaries such as the above, the following can also be found useful, especially for linguistic purposes:

C.E.B. Cranfield, *The Gospel According to St Mark* (CGTC; Cambridge: Cambridge University Press, 1959). Reprinted frequently with revised additional supplementary notes, but essentially predating contemporary approaches and understandings of the Gospel.

V. Taylor, *The Gospel According to St Mark* (London: Macmillan; New York: St Martin's Press, 2nd edn, 1966). The classic commentary on the Greek text. Preserves much of value but its emphasis on the historicity of the Gospel has been long overtaken by modern preoccupation with the Gospel's literary and theological aspects.

Helpful condensed treatments are to be found in the following one-volume commentaries or dictionaries:

N. Perrin, 'Mark, Gospel of', *IDBSup*. A succinct discussion of more recent approaches and issues by an American scholar who dominated Markan studies in the seventies.

D.J. Harrington, 'The Gospel According to Mark', in R.E. Brown, J.A. Fitzmyer and R.E. Murphy (eds.), *The New Jerome Biblical Commentary* (London: G. Chapman, 1989), pp. 596-629. Introduction rather brief but the most recent condensed commentary there is.

W.R. Telford, 'Mark, Gospel of', *DBI*. Reviews the history of interpretation of Mark and the variety of critical approaches to it.

The major foreign-language commentaries include:

J. Ernst, *Das Evangelium nach Markus* (RNT; Regensburg: Pustet, 1981). Draws on recent Markan research to accent literary and theological questions.

J. Gnilka, *Das Evangelium nach Markus* (2 vols.; EKKNT, 2/2; Zürich: Benzinger Verlag; Neukirchen–Vluyn: Neukirchener Verlag, 1978/1979). A major work of German scholarship which in its moderate assessment of the Gospel perhaps comes closest to representing the consensus (if such exists) on matters which divide the scholars. Includes discussion on the history of interpretation.

R. Pesch, *Das Markusevangelium* (2 vols.; HTKNT, 2; Freiburg: Herder, I, 4th edn, 1984; II, 3rd edn, 1983). A magisterial commentary of meticulous conservative scholarship which views Mark as a relatively unoriginal collection of historically reliable traditions which determined, along with his own minimal editing, the structure of his Gospel.

W. Schmithals, *Das Evangelium nach Markus* (2 vols.; Ökumenischer Taschen-buchkommentar zum Neuen Testament, 2; Gütersloh: Mohn, 1979). Represents two extremes of interpretation by seeing Mark as the ultra-conservative editor of an extensive underlying source written by someone with great originality.

D. Lührmann, *Das Markusevangelium* (HNT, 3; Tübingen: Mohr-Siebeck, 1987). A major German commentary which, while still in the German mainstream, comes closest to incorporating insights from the newer literary studies.

Among other classic foreign-language commentaries which still repay consulta-tion are:

M.-J. Lagrange, *Evangile selon Saint Marc* (Etudes Bibliques; Paris: Gabalda, 5th edn, 1929).

E. Lohmeyer, *Das Evangelium des Markus* (MeyerK; Göttingen: Vandenhoeck & Ruprecht, 10th edn, 1963 [1937]).

J. Wellhausen, *Das Evangelium Marci* (Berlin: Georg Reimer, 2nd edn, 1909 [1903]).

Chapter One

INTRODUCTION

The Traditional View of Mark

Contents
No other text has arguably made as great a contribution to the history of Christianity and to the development of a Christian literary tradition as has the Gospel of Mark. From a traditio-historical perspective, it represents the earliest connected literary account of the teaching and activity of Jesus as interpreted by a Christian community in the Mediterranean world some forty or so years after his death. Viewed as literature, it presents within the relatively brief compass of the 16 chapters into which it is now divided a deceptively simple but nonetheless vivid narrative world into which the reader is drawn right from the start. The narrative has a 'unit structure' and is 'episodic', that is, it presents itself to the reader in a series of discrete or self-contained scenes which are linked by summary passages (e.g. 3.7-12; 6.53-56). After a prologue (1.1-13) depicting John the Baptist's mission in the wilderness and Jesus' baptism and temptation, a series of such scenes describes the appearance of Jesus in Galilee as an eschatological (or end-time) preacher of the gospel (1.14-15), his appointment and commissioning of disciples (1.16-20; 2.14; 3.13-19; 6.7-13), his activity as a miracle worker, healer and exorcist (e.g. 1.21-45; 4.35–5.43; 6.30-52; 7.24–8.26) and his fame, inside and outside of Galilee, as a popular and charismatic teacher 'with authority'. His words and deeds produce conflict as well as liberation. Related sequences of episodes show him not only healing (as, for example, 1.21-45; 4.35–6.54) but also in controversy with Jewish religious authorities over matters of the Law (cf., e.g., 2.1–3.6; 7.1-23). Using parables as a characteristic teaching device, the Markan Jesus proclaims the coming of the Kingdom of God (4.1-34) but provokes consternation (and even rejection) on the part of his Jewish kinsfolk, opponents and disciples concerning the nature of the authority (*exousia*) which all these activities reveal (cf. 2.1–3.6; 3.20-35; 4.41; 6.1-6; 7.1-23; 8.14-21). For the author of the

Gospel (and for the implied reader), this authority is that of the concealed Son of God (cf. 1.1, 11; 3.11-12) whose true significance, to the
eyes of faith, is linked with the divine necessity of his redemptive suffering and death.

This motif of concealment and revelation which runs throughout
Mark is dramatized in the ambiguous confession of Peter (8.27-33)
which marks a turning point in the narrative. Where Jesus' activity
has centred until now upon Galilee and the surrounding regions, the
focus now turns increasingly towards Jerusalem. The central section
of the Gospel (8.27-10.52) is set within the context of Jesus' journey to
the Jewish capital, and ultimately to the cross. While remaining episodic, this section is carefully constructed, with its disparate units
revolving around the twin themes of discipleship and the fate of the
'Son of Man'. In these three chapters, the disciples are further invited
(unsuccessfully) to recognize the secret of Jesus' identity and mission
(cf. 8.27-33; 9.2-8, 9-13, 30-32; 10.32-34) and instructed on the nature
and cost of the discipleship springing from it (cf. 8.34–9.1; 9.33-50;
10.1-31, 35-45).

With ch. 11, the story now turns directly to the passion and
resurrection of the 'Son of Man' which has been predicted no less than
three times in the central section (8.31; 9.31; 10.33-34). Jesus arrives in
Jerusalem where he is fêted (11.1-10), dramatically 'cleanses' the
Temple (11.15-19), confronts and bests in argument the Jewish leaders
who challenge him (11.27–12.40) and withdraws after predicting the
apocalyptic signs leading both to the Temple's future destruction and
the Son of Man's triumphal appearance and vindication (13.1-37). In
this final part of the Gospel, the story is from a literary point of view
more coherent. In a relatively continuous narrative, with episodes
linked chronologically, the reader is given the now familiar account of
Jesus' last meal with his disciples, the betrayal by Judas, Jesus'
anguish in Gethsemane, his arrest, trial and crucifixion (14.1-15.47).
The closing section of the book (16.1-8), which represents the first
extant narrative account in the developing Christian literary tradition
of the empty tomb story, ends curiously (but with dramatic appropriateness) with the silence of the women before the announcement of a
young man. No post-resurrection appearances are recounted. Instead
the women are told that Jesus has risen and goes before his disciples
to Galilee where they will see him. Thus the author redirects his readers back to the opening scenes of the Gospel where Jesus' first appearance in Galilee was announced.

Authorship

But who was the author of the Gospel? The term 'author' as applied to a literary text and as used nowadays by literary critics can be taken to mean a number of things (the narrator, the 'ideal' or 'implied' author, the 'real' or 'actual' or 'historical' author) as we shall see in Chapter 3. In biblical studies it has traditionally meant the historical author whose actual identity has often been sought by reference not only to the internal evidence of the text but also to the external evidence supplied by church tradition (such as the testimony of the Church Fathers). The anonymity (or even pseudonymity) of most biblical texts, combined with the ambiguity of the internal evidence and the unreliability of the external evidence has led most of the biblical scholars nowadays who pursue a historical-critical method to abandon as fruitless the search for the named individual responsible for the text and instead to construct a more general profile of the historical author in terms of his (or her) cultural background, socio-political situation and religious concerns. Such factors, if recovered, can help in the interpretation of the text. Obviously such a profile can only be constructed after the text itself has been comprehensively analysed using the various critical tools at our disposal, and it is for this reason that we shall leave this aspect until Chapter 5.

It should be noted in the interim, however, that the Gospel according to Mark has not always been regarded as the complex text which modern scholars now view it as. Hitherto it has been seen as an unsophisticated and untheological piece of historical reportage, a faithful and relatively unadorned transmission of the reminiscences of the apostle Peter by the John Mark of the New Testament. Since this traditional view can be traced back to the early second century, it is worth stopping for a moment to consider it. The tradition is given in Eusebius, *Ecclesiastical History* 3.39.14-16, which quotes its ascription by Papias, bishop of Hierapolis (c. 140 CE?) to an unknown contemporary, 'the Elder' (Presbyter):

> And the Presbyter used to say this, 'Mark became Peter's interpreter [*hermeneutes*] and wrote accurately all that he remembered, not, indeed, in order, of the things said and done by the Lord. For he had not heard the Lord, nor had he followed him, but later on, as I said, followed Peter, who used to give teaching as necessity demanded but not making, as it were, an arrangement of the Lord's oracles so that Mark did nothing wrong in thus writing down single points as he [Mark? Peter?] remembered them. For to one thing he gave attention, to leave out nothing of what he had heard and to make no false statement in them (Loeb Classical Library, p. 297).

This piece of ancient testimony is not without its difficulties, not the least of which are the ambiguities inherent in what is actually being claimed. The 'Mark' referred to is not actually identified. The word *hermeneutes*, here translated 'interpreter' (and hence expounder of Peter's teaching), can also mean 'stenographer' (is dictation of Peter's reminiscences in view?) or even 'translator' (of Aramaic into Greek?). The Gospel does not, however, appear to be a translation. What does the phrase 'not in order' imply? Notwithstanding such ambiguities, there have been those who regard this tradition as historically reliable. From the second to the fifth century, church tradition (e.g. the anti-Marcionite Prologue, Justin, the Muratorian Canon, Clement of Alexandria, Origen, Jerome) was virtually unanimous in claiming 'Mark' as the author and although the specific identification of Papias's 'Mark' with the 'John Mark' of the New Testament was not actively made until Jerome, it is probable that the latter was meant by Papias. Arguing also for its authenticity is what might from one point of view be regarded as the 'understated' nature of the testimony, namely its ascription to a non-apostle (and hence not a direct eye-witness) and the disclaimer regarding its 'order'. That this Gospel was also used as a source by the authors of at least two of the three later canonical Gospels (Matthew and Luke) may also attest to the strength of the tradition lying behind it.

There are, however, serious objections to be raised to Papias's testimony, even apart from its ambiguities or the question of the identification of the 'Mark' whose name was early attached to the Gospel (the name Mark was after all a common one in the Graeco-Roman world and the text itself, apart from its later superscription, makes no mention of its author). If the 'John Mark' of the New Testament is meant, then we have to reckon with the fact that the New Testament traditions about him (if indeed they are all referring to the one person) all connect him with Paul, and not with Peter (cf. Acts 12.12, 25; 13.5, 13; 15.37, 39; Col. 4.10; 2 Tim. 4.11; Phlm. 24). The one exception is 1 Pet. 5.13 where a connection between 'Mark' and the apostle Peter is posited ('my son Mark'). Since this epistle is widely regarded as pseudonymous, the most that can be said is that it is witnessing to a late first-century or early second-century tradition that associated the apostle with a 'Mark' (even *the* John Mark) and this could even have been the source of the Papias tradition.

The claim that Mark was Peter's *hermeneutes*, whatever precisely is meant by this, and hence that its author has access to immediate historical reminiscence, also goes against the findings of form criticism which we shall be considering in Chapter 2. While the vivid details within the Gospel indicate the author's closeness to the oral tradition, the nature and variety of the 'forms' in Mark (apophthegms, prophetic or apocalyptic sayings, legal sayings, wisdom sayings, parables, miracle stories, etc.), their stereotypical character, and the loose connections between them all point to the fact that the Gospel is a product of a long process of 'community tradition' and not of direct eye-witness testimony. Ironically, one of form criticism's findings is that the Gospel material was not, for the most part, arranged, as Papias stated, 'in (chronological) order'. Nevertheless, whatever Papias himself (or his informant) meant precisely by this, the claim was probably related to the desire to defend the Gospel against charges that it differed in its arrangement from that of the other Gospels (especially John).

The Papias tradition has indeed a defensive or apologetic air and this may be the clue to its origin. In emphasizing the accuracy of its contents (though not of its order of words) and its link (in the persons of Mark and Peter) with the first generation of disciples, it may have been seeking to champion this Gospel's version of the Christian tradition against the competing claims of other Gospels (including Gnostic ones) which were likewise vying for the allegiance of Christians. That early church tradition was virtually unanimous in supporting the claim is not surprising since the later church fathers were almost certainly dependent upon Papias, and hence offer no independent attestation. At the beginning of the fifth century, however, Augustine did speculate, contrary to the tradition, that Mark was an abbreviation of Matthew, and this view was to prevail for centuries. Nevertheless, the theory now commonly held that Matthew and Luke used Mark as their source cannot be used in support of the Papias tradition since neither of the evangelists precisely identify their sources far less capitalize on the alleged Petrine authority of Mark.

If the external evidence then is unreliable where authorship is concerned, what about the internal evidence? Attempts have been made to correlate Papias's testimony with clues offered by the text itself. Some have seen John Mark's artistic signature in the curious datum of 14.51-52 which describes a young man in Gethsemane who fled away naked leaving his garment behind. Others have pointed to the prominence of Peter in the Gospel, in the so-called Petrine passages (the extent of these, according to T.W. Manson, is as follows: 1.16-39; 2.1-14; 3.13-19; 4.35–5.43; 6.7-13, 30-56; 8.14–9.48; 10.32-52; 11.1-33; 13.3-4, 32-37; 14.17-50, 53-54, 66-72). Two observations are particularly important. On numerous occasions, Peter plays the role of a spokesman for the twelve (cf., e.g., 1.36; 5.37; 8.29; 9.2; 11.21; 13.3; 14.54; 16.7) but one also notes that an unflattering picture is often painted of him (cf., e.g.,

8.33; 9.5-6; 14.30-31, 66ff.). Peter, it is therefore argued, could only have been the source for such stories since, in the first place, only he or a few others are described in certain instances as having been present, and in the second the early church itself would not otherwise have preserved such a discreditable portrait. This last point touches upon the more general character of the Gospel which is noteworthy (in comparison with Matthew and Luke) for its harsher, more 'human' presentation of Jesus and his disciples. Its so-called 'primitiveness' in this respect has often been taken as a mark of historical authenticity.

Against this rather naive historicism, a number of points can be made. First, while the naked young man of 14.51-52 is intriguing, it is pure romantic fiction to suppose that John Mark is here signing his name to his work. The youth is quite anonymous and his presence in the narration—which does demand explanation—has been variously attributed to literary artifice, the influence of the Old Testament (e.g. Amos 2.16) or bad editing of the underlying source(s). Internal clues as to the historical author provide little correlation with the New Testament traditions about John Mark. John Mark, we are told, was a cousin of Barnabas, Paul's travelling companion, a Jewish Christian of Palestine and someone who lived in Jerusalem. The author of our text, however, shows unfamiliarity with the geography of Palestine (cf., e.g., 5.1; 6.45; 7.31; 8.22; 10.1; 11.1), Jewish customs (7.2-4; 10.2; 14.1; 14.64) and even the Jewish leadership groups (cf., e.g., 3.6; 6.17; 8.15; 12.13 and in all the preceding examples the commentaries *ad loc.*). The Gospel was written in Greek with Gentiles in mind (cf., e.g., the Aramaic translation in 3.17; 5.41; 7.11; 7.34; 14.36; 15.22, 34) and has a strong anti-Jewish bias, as we shall see in Chapter 4.

Secondly, Peter is not significantly more prominent in Mark than he is in the other Gospels for which Petrine authority is not claimed. Mark, for example, mentions him 25 times, Matthew 25 times and Luke 30 times. Since Mark's Gospel is shorter than the other two, the frequency is statistically greater in the case of Mark but this is partially explained by the incorporation into the later Gospels of a special source, Q, which does not mention him. The so-called 'Petrine' material can as easily be attributed to the tradition taken over by Mark as to direct dependence upon Peter. It is naive indeed to assume that if an account indicates that only one person witnessed an alleged event, that person must have been the source. Ancient texts like the Gospels do not operate like this. They are rather the product of a complex interplay between received tradition, literary artifice and religious imagination (cf., e.g., 15.39, where the Roman centurion almost certainly functions as a mouthpiece for the author's Son of God Christology and where it would be inappropriate to assume he was the source for Jesus' dying words on the cross).

Mark's harsh treatment of Peter and the disciples can also be explained otherwise, as will be demonstrated in Chapter 4. The portrayal may serve an edificatory or parenetic function, to illustrate and develop the author's theme of discipleship, with all its demands, limitations and risks. Alternatively, it may point to a historical author who was critical of early Jewish Christianity and its leaders.

Finally, we must reiterate that Mark's Gospel is not primitive or theologically unsophisticated, even though it represents a developing Christian tradition at an earlier stage than Matthew, Luke or John. To be earlier, furthermore, does not necessarily mean that it is more reliable historically nor can the criterion be used obviously to support specific authorship by John Mark of Jerusalem. In sum, therefore, we shall have to say that it is only the external evidence of the Papias tradition which supports this hypothesis and that this evidence is problematic. The internal evidence of the text, which is ultimately decisive, tilts strongly against it, and indeed without Papias's testimony would hardly have suggested it. The historical author must therefore remain anonymous, although we shall continue to call him Mark, following convention.

Date

If the authorship of the Gospel is unknown, what about its date? On the assumption that Matthew and Luke used Mark as their source, a date no later than 75 CE is normally accepted as the *terminus ad quem* or upper limit. This would allow time for its copying, distribution and general acceptance. The *terminus a quo* or lower limit is more difficult to determine. A very early date (e.g. in Caligula's reign, c. 40 CE; cf. 13.14 and Josephus, *War* 2.184-87, 192-203) is normally dismissed since it runs counter to the signs of development to be discerned in the traditions taken over by the evangelist as well as the internal evidence which points to events in the 60s as the backdrop for the final form of the text. The external evidence is contradictory. Clement of Alexandria claimed that Mark was written during Peter's lifetime while Irenaeus asserted that the evangelist wrote after the death (or *exodos*) of Peter and Paul. Although the term *exodos* literally means 'departure' (and so interpreted would avoid the contradiction with Clement), its use as a euphemism for 'death' (cf., e.g., Lk. 9.31; 2 Pet. 1.15) is usually taken to imply that Irenaeus was referring to the tradition that these two apostles died in Rome at Nero's hands c. 62–64 CE. The Anti-Marcionite Prologue also supports the tradition of composition after Peter's death, and therefore in the period from c. 65 onwards.

As before, however, it is the internal evidence to which we must turn and here the interpretation of ch. 13 is decisive. Most scholars are agreed that although this discourse is expressed in the conventional language of the Old Testament and Jewish apocalyptic, it points to events which occurred within the experience of Mark's community, particularly in the 60s. This was a decade which not only saw the Neronian persecution of churches in Rome in 64 (Tacitus, *Ann.* 15.44) but also serious earthquakes in 60 and 63 (*Ann.* 14.27; cf. Mk 13.8) defeat of the Romans by the Parthians in 62 (*Ann.* 15.13-17), civil war throughout the Empire after the defeat of Nero in 68 and a succession of imperial contenders (Galbo, Otto, Vitellius, Vespasian) in 68–69. It also saw the disastrous Roman–Jewish War in 66–70 CE which led to the siege of Jerusalem by Vespasian and his son Titus. The Jewish historian Josephus recounts the suffering of the Jews as a result of the war, the flight of Jews from their doomed city, the severe famine within (cf., e.g., Josephus, *War* 6.392-408). He mentions too the advent of hireling prophets who promised deliverance (*War* 6.285-87; cf. also 2.258-65). Christian tradition also claims that the Jerusalem church fled to Pella as a result of an oracle during this period (Eusebius, *Eccl. Hist.* 3.5.3) prior to the eventual destruction of the city and its Temple. Before the end finally came, Josephus records (*War* 6.316), Titus's troops, in an act of desecration, sacrificed to their standards in the Temple premises and hailed Titus as their Emperor.

Difficulties exist in fixing a more specific date within this period for the Gospel's composition. Where scholars have ventured to be more precise, three main suggestions have arisen. The first of these is the mid-60s, that is, during the Neronian persecution (cf., e.g., Taylor), and hence the Gospel's interest in suffering, persecution and martyr-dom (in respect of John the Baptist, Jesus and his disciples) is held to be significant (cf., e.g., 1.14; 6.17-29; 8.31–9.1; 9.11-13, 30-32; 10.30, 32-34, 45; 13.9, 11-13; 14.41). A second proposal is the second half of the 60s during the period of unrest and apocalyptic fervour occasioned by the Roman–Jewish War and the civil war but before the actual destruction of Jerusalem (cf., e.g., Marxsen). Here various echoes in the so-called 'little apocalypse' are deemed to be suggestive (cf., e.g., 13.6-8, 17-23, 24-31). A third view is that it was written shortly after the Fall of Jerusalem and the destruction of the Temple in 70 CE (cf., e.g., Brandon) when end-time expectation had perhaps begun to be tempered by the delay in Jesus' second return or parousia (cf., e.g., 13.10, 32-37). A crucial question, therefore, is whether ch. 13 does or does not presuppose the destruction of Jerusalem and whether 13.1-2, which relates to the Temple's destruction, is a prediction after the event (*vaticinium ex eventu*). Some would argue that it is not and that the details of ch. 13 do not correlate specifically enough with the events surrounding the siege of Jerusalem as we have them, for example, in Josephus. For others, and this is my own view, 13.1-2 (together with 12.9; 13.14 'set up where *he* [Titus?] ought not to be'; 13.24 '*after* that tribulation'; 13.30 '*all* these things'; 15.38) is specific enough to indicate that the author was writing in knowledge of that event and that it is unnecessary to require of him a more detailed knowledge of the war such as Josephus, who was a participant, reveals. In sum, then, however we assess the internal evidence of the text, a general dating of between 65 and 75 CE seems highly probable, and this is now widely agreed.

Audience and Provenance

But for whom was the Gospel written and in what part of the Mediterranean world? It is clear, on the one hand, that our author was writing for Greek-speaking Christians of Gentile origin. We have seen already that he takes care to translate Aramaic expressions into Greek and that he mentions and at points seeks to explain, albeit at times inaccurately, Jewish customs (e.g. 7.2-4; 14.12; 15.42). Numerous examples of Latin words translated into Greek are found throughout the text, usually of a military (e.g. 5.9 legion; 15.16 *praetorium*; 15.39 centurion), legal (e.g. 6.27 speculator or military executioner; 15.15 flagellate) or commercial nature (e.g. Roman coins such as the *denarius* 6.37 or *quadrans* 12.42). On the other hand, the presence of Aramaic expressions themselves, together with what some scholars have detected as Aramaic or Semitic forms of speech or thought, and the numerous references to places in Palestine (albeit again at times with some inexactness) indicate the author's access to Palestinian traditions. Where were our author and his community located?

Five main places of origin have been suggested:

Alexandria. This suggestion was first made by John Chrysostom but can easily be dismissed. It derives from a later tradition given by Eusebius that associated Mark and Egypt.

Rome. Though not stated explicitly by Papias, this has been the traditional place of origin for Mark's Gospel. It is suggested by the Anti-Marcionite Prologue ('after the departure of Peter himself, he [Mark] wrote down this same Gospel in the regions of Italy') and was claimed expressly by Irenaeus and Clement. While it may have been deduced from the connection of Mark and Peter with Rome (cf. 1 Pet. 5.13 where 'Babylon' is an early Christian pseudonym for Rome) it is consistent with the evidence which links the Gospel with the Neronian persecution, with a Gentile readership and with the numerous Latinisms. Were the Gospel written after the Roman–Jewish War and, in particular, shortly after 70, it would also explain the anti-Jewish element in the text since feelings were then running strongly against the Jews, and the Christian community may have wished to disassociate itself from them. The fact that Mark came to be used by Matthew and Luke within a relatively short time after its composition may suggest that it emanated from an important church centre.

Scholars have also sought support from small details within the text. The Roman *quadrans*, for example, did not circulate, it is said, in the east. In referring to four watches in the night (6.48; 13.35), Mark is in agreement with a Roman rather than a Jewish method of reckoning time. It has also been suggested, somewhat speculatively, that the Rufus mentioned without explanation in 15.21 is the same Rufus mentioned in Paul's letter to the Romans (16.13). It has even been observed (Martin) that the use of Mark's Gospel is first attested in two texts which are both associated with Rome, and that one of these, *1 Clement* (15.2) quotes Isa. 29.3 in the same form as it is used in Mk 7.6 (but then, as Martin also observes, Isa. 61.24b is quoted in *2 Clem.* 7.6 in the same form as Mk 9.48 and *2 Clement* has an Alexandrian provenance!).

Galilee. Against the traditional view of Rome, however, is the fact that the external evidence is relatively late and may be based, as I have said, on 1 Pet. 5.13 and the Papias testimony already discussed. The Latin loan words, which may even belong to Mark's tradition, do not point specifically to the capital and were used throughout the Empire. Luke–Acts has equally as many Latinisms and a Roman provenance is not suggested for the Lukan writings. The influence of any major church centre would account for its rapid circulation and general acceptance, although the fact of Mark's later neglect in favour of the other Gospels should warn us against pressing this argument too far. While a non-Palestinian origin helps explain the author's explanation of Palestinian-Jewish customs, language, coinage and even, it is suggested, climate (11.13), it fails to account for his very clear dependence on Palestinian traditions and his use, for example, of Galilean and Judaean place-names throughout without explanation. One prominent feature of the Gospel, indeed (as will be discussed in Chapter 4) is its special interest in Galilee (cf., e.g., 1.14, 16, 28, 39; 3.7; 7.31; 14.28; 16.7), the principal sphere of Jesus' preaching, teaching and healing and the place where he is to be seen after his resurrection (or parousia?). Galilee has therefore been suggested as the place of origin (e.g. Lohmeyer, Marxsen) and such a geographical location would cohere believably with the chronological context of the Romano–Jewish war and the circumstances of a Palestinian-Christian community experiencing the situation underlying ch. 13, and expecting Jesus' near return.

Antioch. The emphasis on Galilee need not, however, be taken to imply a literal connection between the Markan community and Galilee, especially given the author's geographical inaccuracies in respect of the region. Such an interest has also been interpreted symbolically, with Galilee (with its mixed Jewish and pagan population) operating in the text as a paradigm for the Gentile mission. Some scholars have therefore looked slightly further afield and have opted for Antioch in Syria as an appropriate eastern centre of Roman and Jewish culture (e.g. Fuller). Ranking as a city alongside Rome and Alexandria, Antioch was an early mission centre for Christian expansion into the wider Gentile world (cf. Acts 11.19-30). Here our author would easily have had access to Palestinian Jesus traditions and here in turn Matthew (and possibly Luke), the provenance of whose Gospel is widely accepted as Syrian, might have found and used as source material his resultant Gospel composition. For those who adhere to the traditional view of Markan authorship, Antioch too has connections not only with Peter (cf., e.g., Gal. 2.11) and Mark's uncle Barnabas (cf. Acts 11.22-26) but also with Cyrene (cf. Acts 11.20) from where the (unexplained) Simon of Mark's text is said to have come (Mk 15.21).

Rural and small-town southern Syria. More recently, in *Community of the New Age* (1977), H.C. Kee has argued that the cultural and linguistic links of the Gospel are with eastern Mediterranean village life, and suggests rural and small-town southern Syria as the base for the Markan community. According to Josephus, those suspected of Jewish sympathies in Antioch were not subjected to persecution by the Gentiles in the years before the fall of Jerusalem. There is furthermore a clear antipathy towards the city in Mark and a consonant portrayal of Jesus' ministry and that of his disciples as an itinerant rural one. This is a sophisticated analysis based on the whole text and its underlying traditions and one employing a more modern sociological perspective. The legitimacy, however, of drawing conclusions about the social and economic situation of Mark's audience from traditions about Jesus and his disciples has been questioned.

Where then does this leave us? Rome is still the most commonly accepted provenance, but if the link with Peter and John Mark is discounted, the question remains an open one. I shall return to it, therefore, in Chapter 5, after the Gospel has been examined in greater detail.

The New Look on Mark

Mark in History

So far we have discussed the traditional view of Mark that it was a Gospel written in Rome in the 60s after the death of Peter and that it represents a relatively faithful and unadorned transmission of the reminiscences of the apostle by the John Mark of the New Testament. Despite Papias's (ambiguous) testimony to this effect and the fact that Matthew and Luke found it an invaluable source, the history of Mark thereafter can be characterized as one of longstanding neglect and recent rediscovery. Irenaeus regarded Mark as one of the four pillars of the church, deriving one of its symbols (the eagle) from the description of the four cherubim of Ezekiel 1 and the living creatures of Revelation 4. Notwithstanding this positive evaluation, Mark appears to have received little attention in succeeding centuries. It almost never appeared first in canonical lists, had relatively few commentaries or expositions devoted to it (that of the Venerable Bede in the eighth century is a prominent exception) and took a decided second place to the other Gospels, especially Matthew. A major factor in this neglect was the view of Augustine (already referred to) that Mark was merely an abbreviation of Matthew, or what is still called 'the first Gospel'. It was not until the latter half of the eighteenth century when this Augustinian view was challenged that Mark began to emerge from its relative obscurity. With the establishment of the priority of Mark, the evidence for which will be considered in Chapter 2, the Gospel took on a new lease of life and its allegedly 'primitive' or 'human' portrayal of the founder of Christianity was used as the basis for the many so-called 'Liberal Lives of Jesus' which prevailed in the nineteenth century. It is at this point indeed that the history of modern scholarship on the Gospel might be said to have commenced, and it is to the hermeneutical approaches in this period, or the ways and methods by which it has been interpreted, that we now turn.

The History of Scholarship

Biblical scholarship has always been interested in hermeneutics (the art or science of interpretation and from the same Greek root—'I understand' or 'I interpret' — as the word *hermeneutes* used of Mark by Papias), although it is perhaps fair to say that its major concern over the last two centuries has been to establish as objectively as possible the meaning of the text in its original historical context rather than to examine or expose the interpretative predispositions of its modern readers, however important this is now seen to be. Broadly speaking, three main types of approaches to Mark, as to the Gospels in general, can be distinguished.

Perhaps the most influential and persistent approach has been what we might call the 'historico-psychological' or 'historical rationalist' approach. It is an approach already touched upon which has long dominated English-speaking scholarship (the nineteenth-century 'Liberal Lives of Jesus' in particular) and one which, despite the problems it involves, is even today perhaps the most common and the most instinctive approach taken by most people who read the Gospels. A merciless criticism of its presuppositions at the turn of the century by scholars such as A. Schweitzer and W. Wrede has meant, however, that it has ceased to be popular in academic treatments of the Gospel. A major presupposition of the approach is that a Gospel text like Mark represents a reasonably accurate account of the events and chronology of Jesus' ministry. The colourful and vivid details which are to be found in the Gospel are taken as a sign of eye-witness testimony rather than the product of creative story-telling or theological embellishment on the part of the evangelist or early church. What is there recorded in the Gospel accounts is faithful in the main to the historical situation of Jesus' lifetime. Ambiguities within and differences between Mark and the other Gospel accounts have often posed problems for this approach but they are frequently explained as the differences in emphasis, or even, to more liberal minds, the distortion which is the inevitable consequence of independent eye-witness report. Some who approach the text in this way are happy, for example, to accept the accounts of Jesus' miracles at face value. Others, more sceptical, but with an implicit trust in the basic historicity of the Gospel, may well entertain *a priori* assumptions about what *must* have happened, even though the tradition may have come in time to distort it. In each case, interest lies in what the text conveys about events in the life of Jesus himself, in what he said and did. Mark is to be regarded as a historian, in other words, and his text as a direct window into history.

A second less common approach which came nevertheless to eclipse the nineteenth-century 'historical rationalist' tendency is what has been called the 'history of religions' approach. The name comes from a translation of the German word *Religionsgeschichte* and describes a method pioneered by a group of German scholars, the *religionsgeschichtliche Schule* in the late nineteenth and early twentieth centuries. Among these are R. Reitzenstein (1861–1931), H. Gunkel (1862–1932) and W. Bousset (1865–1926). The 'history of religions' method does not interpret texts like Mark and the other Christian Gospels in isolation. Rather than focusing on the narrower relation of the Gospel to history (and especially the history of Jesus), it seeks to place the content of what it describes within a broader social, cultural, philosophical and particularly religious context. The Markan Gospel is less a window into history and more a mirror reflecting the religious ideology of the community which produced it. It is less the product of objective reporting and more the product of that universal form of consciousness known as religion, a consciousness which expresses itself in a variety of forms such as myth and legend. This approach places emphasis upon the comparative study and analysis of religions. It sees the Gospel as a text which provides information about the beliefs and practices of early Christianity and it seeks to place the Christianity therein revealed within the general stream of the history of religion itself. In particular, it explores links between early Christianity and its social and cultural environment. It gives special attention to the influences upon early Christian communities of other philosophies and religious movements within Judaism and Hellenism. The nature and extent of such influences are often very difficult to establish and opponents of a comparative method such as this have often criticized it for failing to recognize the distinctive and innovative elements which were a feature of early Christianity. Nevertheless, the strength of the approach is obvious. It has brought to bear upon a first-century Christian text like Mark a considerable wealth of background knowledge about the Hellenistic and Jewish worlds within which it was written and has helped thereby to overcome its strangeness. It has also helped to inspire different types of questions and particularly questions about the religious community whose beliefs and practices are reflected in the Gospel. One of its legacies indeed is the part it played in the development of the view that Mark is the product of the fusion of a Hellenistic Christ myth promulgated by Paul with Palestinian Jesus traditions.

A third method of interpreting the Gospel is that represented by the literary-critical approaches which came to dominate biblical studies as a whole increasingly in the twentieth century. These approaches in broad terms take the text itself seriously both as a literary creation and as the end-product of a complex process in which traditions about

Jesus, initially transmitted orally and influenced by the religious communities which revered him, came eventually in the course of a generation to written expression at the hands of the gifted writer now unknown to us. In its final form, this literary text presents us with a synthesis of the Jesus tradition known to the writer which in turn has had the generative capacity to create fresh formulations of tradition inspired by faith. Some newer literary-critical approaches, as we shall see, concentrate on the text in its final form and ask questions relating, for example, to the work's literary type (genre criticism) or the author's style, point of view or ways of achieving a literary effect (rhetorical criticism). For the major part of the last century, however, the emphasis has focused on the text's component parts and on the complex traditio-historical process which brought it into being in its final form. Tradition-criticism, for example, is interested in the history of development of one or more of the text's constituent traditions before, during and after its incorporation within the Gospel.

Chief among the now established literary-critical approaches which remain historical-critical in orientation are the interrelated methods of source, form and redaction criticism. These methods, which will be discussed more fully in Chapter 2, start with the recognition that, archaeological evidence aside, written texts like the Gospel of Mark are our major route to historical knowledge about Jesus, the early Christian communities and the world of early Christianity. As major champions of an 'excavative' approach, source, form and redaction criticism have taught us to start with the evidence before us and to work back from the text (or behind it) to uncover the historical information it is capable of revealing. Learning to make observations on the text, to pose critical questions to the text and to think backwards or deductively from the text to produce convincing answers is a difficult skill but it can be mastered. These three methods in particular attempt to explain, for example, the discrepancies, ambiguities and awkwardness (which a keen observer will frequently note are a feature of Gospel accounts) in terms of the sources, forms and redaction (editing) of the literary and oral material drawn upon by the evangelist.

Source criticism, or *Quellenkritik*, which was developed largely in the nineteenth century (and practised on Mark's Gospel by pioneers such as E. Wendling or J. Wellhausen) explores the evidence for the use of written sources in the text. Form criticism, or *Formgeschichte*, a method associated with the names of K.L. Schmidt (1891–1956), M. Dibelius (1883–1947) and R. Bultmann (1884–1976) investigates the structured form taken by the traditional material found in the

Gospels, a form related to its function within the life and worship of the communities who transmitted it. Redaction criticism, or *Redaktions-geschichte*, a discipline pioneered by W. Marxsen, G. Bornkamm and H. Conzelmann and developed by N. Perrin and others, analyses the use made by the Gospel writers of their sources, whether written or oral, and seeks to ascertain their contribution to the developing Jesus tradition. It was the application of the redaction-critical method in particular which contributed to the 'new look' on the Gospel which emerged in Markan studies from the 1960s onwards. From this period, the history of scholarship on Mark has tended to de-emphasize the evangelist as historian and to point up his creative role as a theologian, indeed one of the first and major theologians of early Christianity. The focus has not been on the Jesus of history in Mark's Gospel but on the evangelist himself and the nature of his contribution to the tradition about Jesus. The aim has been to ascertain Mark's special purpose in writing, and to determine the theological or 'kerygmatic' (from the Greek word meaning 'proclamation') perspective which gives coherence to the many isolated features of his Gospel.

Some More Recent Methods and Approaches
Scholarship does not, however, stand still and the final decades of the twentieth century have seen the emergence of a bewildering array of new methods, approaches and perspectives in respect of the Gospel. A number of these are related to disciplines outside of the biblical field such as literature or sociology; some have arisen from and developed the established disciplines; others have directly challenged them. The Gospel has been increasingly treated as literature, particularly by American scholars whose contributions have dominated these last decades, and has been analysed using the methods and criteria of modern secular literature criticism. I shall be referring in Chapter 3 to a number of these methods (genre criticism, reader-response criticism, structuralism). The traditio-historical approach is still prevalent, especially in European scholarship, but the influence of secular literary studies has led scholars to distinguish between those methods which treat the Gospel 'atomistically' (which 'disintegrate' or 'fragment' the text) and those which treat it 'holistically' (as a whole). Analysis of the text may be 'diachronic' (from the Greek 'through time'), that is, attuned to the pre-history of its component parts, or 'synchronic' (at the same point in time), that is, directed to its final form, interrelationships and effects without regard to the process which brought it into being in the first place. The distinction may also be expressed in terms of those approaches which are literary-historical

in nature (like source, form and redaction criticism) and those which are literary-aesthetic, that is, which explore the ways the author and/or text achieve their effects.

Many of the literary-aesthetic approaches have strengthened a conclusion that was already becoming apparent in redaction-critical work on the Gospel, namely, that Mark is to be regarded as more than a mere collector and editor of traditions. He should be seen, they have argued, as a genuine author in his own right. Other literary studies have de-emphasized the author, however, claiming that authorial intention is not ultimately significant for the interpretation of the Gospel. Structuralism, for example, has examined more abstractly the ways in which the text itself comes to express its meaning, and has little or no interest in the original historical context or author. Reader-response criticism has focused on the reader of the text (whether ancient, modern or 'ideal') and has explored the nature of its reception.

The modern tendency to bypass the author in favour of the text itself has also been a feature of the more recent sociological approaches to Mark, of which H.C. Kee's aforementioned *Community of the New Age* is a distinguished exemplar, and H.C. Waetjen's *A Reordering of Power* (1989) a more recent one. Applying social theory as well as social description, such studies have attempted to illumine the social location of the Markan text and to investigate the socio-political and economic circumstances of the community from which it arose. Related studies have explored the contemporary relevance of the text not only from a traditional Christian devotional point of view but from a Marxist, liberation theology or feminist standpoint.

Mark as a Historical Document, Literary Composition and Religious Text
In this chapter, after summarizing the contents of the Gospel, I have examined the traditional view of its authorship, a view based on the dubious external evidence of Papias and on certain supplementary but uncompelling indications in the text. The authorship therefore remains for us anonymous. In addition, scholarly views on the date (65–75 CE), audience and provenance (possibly Roman but the evidence suggests, at least for now, an open verdict) were discussed. Thereafter we turned to the history of the Gospel's reception in the church and its interpretation over the last two centuries at the hands of scholars. I drew attention to three basic approaches in particular, namely, that which treats the Gospel primarily as a simple biographical document directly recounting the history of Jesus; secondly, that which sees the text as an expression of first-century religious faith (or

mythology); and thirdly, that which recognizes the historical, literary and theological complexity of the Gospel and seeks the history of Jesus and the early church only through an analysis of the history of the text and its constituent traditions. Furthermore, the progressive emphasis in Markan scholarship on the historical, kerygmatic and literary aspects of the text were observed, and in particular the 'new look' on the Gospel which since the 1960s has laid greater stress on the latter two aspects. Three estimates of Mark have emerged: Mark as historian, Mark as theologian, Mark as author. It has also been noted that the more recent tendency is to distinguish between literary-historical (diachronic) and literary-aesthetic (synchronic) approaches and to view the text either as a window into (tradition-)history or as a mirror reflecting the faith (or ideology) of the author (and/or his community) or the vivid but artificial story-world he has created.

It has therefore become apparent that Mark is no ordinary text but one of considerable complexity. No one approach can therefore do full justice to it. Viewed from different perspectives, the Gospel is a historical document, a literary composition and a religious (or sacred) text, and the degree to which each of these is true can only be determined by close analysis using the appropriate tools. Religions have developed many ways in which to express their relation to what is perceived as the divine, and literary self-expression is but one. When we ask questions about the origins of Christianity, however, then we must begin at the point at which this religion began to develop a literary tradition since it is in documentary form that the major evidence of its beliefs and practices have come down to us. The first Gospel text, that of Mark, gives us information about Jesus, the early church and the evangelist himself, but as a historical source it must be approached cautiously and critically. Being at the same time a literary composition it is subject to all the possibilities and limitations that written self-expression involves. Being also a religious text, it is a mixture of fact and fiction, a blend of history and theology, a product of literary artifice and faith-inspired imagination.

With these things in mind, the next three chapters will go on to examine each of these aspects in turn, before returning in the final chapter to the general questions of the Gospel's purpose and setting. Strictly speaking, this study should begin with the purely literary analysis reserved for Chapter 3, but since most people tend to start with historical questions and since the history of scholarship also proceeded from such questions, we shall first evaluate Mark as a historical document.

FURTHER READING

For a comprehensive coverage of bibliographical resources (classified) on Mark, see:

H.M. Humphrey, *A Bibliography for the Gospel of Mark 1954-1980* (Studies in the Bible and Early Christianity, 1; New York: Edwin Mellen Press, 1981).

F. Neirynck, *The Gospel of Mark: A Cumulative Bibliography 1950-1990* (BETL, 102; Leuven: Leuven University Press/Peeters, 1992).

In addition to the commentaries already referred to (those by Anderson, Lane and Nineham are particularly helpful), the following Introductions have useful sections on the areas covered in this chapter:

R.H. Fuller, *Introduction to the New Testament* (London: Duckworth, 1966).

W.G. Kümmel, *Introduction to the New Testament* (trans. H.C. Kee; London: SCM Press, rev. edn, 1979).

W. Marxsen, *Introduction to the New Testament* (trans. G. Buswell; Oxford: Basil Blackwell, 1968).

D.C. Duling and N. Perrin, *The New Testament: Proclamation and Parenesis, Myth and History* (New York: Harcourt Brace College, 3rd edn, 1994).

The following general works cover various aspects of the Gospel and should also be consulted:

J.C. Anderson and S.D. Moore (eds.), *Mark and Method* (Philadelphia: Fortress Press, 1992).

E. Best, *Mark: The Gospel as Story* (Studies of the New Testament and its World; Edinburgh: T. & T. Clark, 1983).

M. Hengel, *Studies in the Gospel of Mark* (trans. J. Bowden; Philadelphia: Fortress Press, 1985).

H.C. Kee, *Community of the New Age: Studies in Mark's Gospel* (Philadelphia: Fortress Press, 1977).

R.P. Martin, *Mark – Evangelist and Theologian* (Exeter: Paternoster Press, 1979).

W.R. Telford (ed.), *The Interpretation of Mark* (Studies in New Testament Interpretation; Edinburgh: T. & T. Clark, 1995). After a 61-page introduction to Markan studies, this volume presents thirteen articles in English by prominent Markan scholars. A twenty-page select bibliography is also included.

Special Studies: On authorship, though somewhat dated, see:

W. Barclay, *The Gospels and Acts*. I. *The First Three Gospels* (London: SCM Press, 1976), pp. 111-31. A classic statement of the view that 'in Mark we have the simple and straightforward story of an eye-witness'.

T.W. Manson, 'The Foundation of the Synoptic Tradition: the Gospel of Mark', in M. Black (ed.), *Studies in the Gospels and Epistles* (Manchester: Manchester University Press, 1962), pp. 28-45.

D.E. Nineham, 'Eye-Witness Testimony and the Gospel Tradition', *JTS* 9 (1958), pp, 13-25, 243-52 and 11 (1960), pp. 253-64.

P. Parker, 'The Authorship of the Second Gospel', *Perspectives in Religious Studies* 5 (1978), pp. 4-9.

H.E.W. Turner, 'The Tradition of Mark's Dependence upon Peter', *ExpTim* 71 (1959–60), pp. 260-63.

On date, see:

B.W. Bacon, *The Gospel of Mark: Its Composition and Date* (New Haven: Yale University Press; London: Humphrey Milford/Oxford University Press, 1925). The classic treatment but now dated.

S.G.F. Brandon, 'The Date of the Markan Gospel', *NTS* 7 (1960–61), pp. 126-41.

— *The Fall of Jerusalem and the Christian Church* (London: SPCK, 1951), ch. 10.

— *Jesus and the Zealots* (Manchester: Manchester University Press, 1967), ch. 5.

J.A.T. Robinson, *Redating the New Testament* (London: SCM Press, 1976), chs. 1, 2 and 4. Robinson's early dating is not accepted by most New Testament scholars but his assembling of the evidence is valuable.

On sociological and other social-scientific approaches, see:

J.H. Elliott (ed.), *Social-Scientific Criticism of the New Testament and its Social World* (Semeia, 35; Decatur, GA: Scholars Press, 1986). Note especially Elliott's own article with this title, pp. 1-33, and that by J.H. Neyrey, 'The Idea of Purity in Mark's Gospel', pp. 91-128, as well as accompanying bibliography.

Kee, *Community*.

B.J. Malina, *The New Testament World: Insights from Cultural Anthropology* (Atlanta, GA: John Knox Press, 1981).

G. Theissen, *The First Followers of Jesus: A Sociological Analysis of the Earliest Christianity* (trans. J. Bowden; London: SCM Press, 1978) (published as *The Sociology of Early Palestinian Christianity* by Fortress Press, Philadelphia).

On Marxist interpretation, see:

F. Belo, *A Materialist Reading of the Gospel of Mark* (trans. M.J. O'Connell; Maryknoll, NY: Orbis Books, 1981).

On liberation theology see:

M.A. Corner and C.R. Rowland, *Liberating Exegesis* (Biblical Foundations in Theology; London: SCM Press, 1990), pp. 93-114.

C. Myers, *Binding the Strong Man: A Political Reading of Mark's Story of Jesus* (Maryknoll, NY: Orbis Books, 1988).

On feminist interpretation, see Chapter 3 below, but note:

E.S. Fiorenza, *In Memory of Her* (London: SCM Press, 1995), pp. 316-23 (women as paradigm of true discipleship in Mark).

Chapter Two

MARK AS HISTORY: THE GOSPEL AS A HISTORICAL DOCUMENT

History or Myth: The Problem of History in Mark

'The Beginning of the Gospel of Jesus Christ, the Son of God' (1.1)

The problem of history in Mark is encountered right from the start. Despite the ambiguous meaning of its opening verse for modern commentators, and the scholarly debate over the actual extent of the opening section (1.1-8? 1.1-13? 1.1-15?), Mark's narrative opens dramatically and could not have failed to catch the attention of the first-century reader (or hearer) for whom it was intended. By means of an inaccurately cited quotation from Isa. 40.3 (actually a mixed quotation from Exod. 23.20, Mal. 3.1 and Isa. 40.3), the reader is immediately led to connect the preaching of the Jewish prophet John 'the Baptizer' not only with 'the beginning of the gospel of Jesus Christ, Son of God' but also with the fulfilment of Jewish Scripture. The appearance of John in the Judaean wilderness sets the stage for the dramatic arrival of Jesus who, as the reader has been told at the outset (if we discount some textual authorities) is God's Son. John baptizes Jesus in the River Jordan but does so clearly as a subordinate. There is emphasis on his unworthiness over against the majesty of his successor. His baptism is purely for repentance while that of the Coming One will be with the Holy Spirit. At the baptism itself he fades from the scene upstaged by the events that follow.

It is here that the modern critic notes a sudden change from apparent 'history' to 'mythology'. At one moment we are in the Judaean wilderness, by the river Jordan, with crowds from Judaea and Jerusalem coming out to see a figure dressed to fit the part of an Old Testament prophet (and not coincidentally Elijah, cf. Zech. 13.4; 2 Kgs 1.8). The next, the reader is presented with an account of split heavens, the divine Spirit descending like a dove, a supernatural voice from heaven, a force that propels the Son of God into the self-same wilderness, a confrontation with that personalized embodiment of evil itself,

Satan, wild beasts, angels. After his testing, Jesus appears in Galilee preaching 'the gospel of God'.

The Hermeneutical Question

So much for the mood, pace and sense of expectancy created right at the start for the first-century reader, but what are we to make of such a story? The lessons drawn from any religious text depend, among other things, on the nature of the questions that are asked in relation to it. Biblical scholarship has proceeded through time by asking a different set of questions and by taking a different set of approaches to the text. In Chapter 1 I reviewed a number of ways in which Mark's Gospel has been interpreted over the last two centuries. We noted the 'historico-psychological' or 'historical rationalist' approach which would presuppose that this narrative prologue reflects actual experiences in the life of Jesus, with perhaps some allowance being made for a degree of distortion in the course of its transmission. The question that would be posed to the text would be: 'What does this passage tell us about actual events not only in Jesus' life but also in his very consciousness?' Seeing Jesus himself perhaps as the source for the so-called temptation account, this story might be seen as psycho-history or psycho-drama and, taken with the longer accounts given by Matthew and Luke, viewed as the record of Jesus' own intense moral struggle with evil and the style, direction and implications of his future mission.

The history of religions approach, on the other hand, would turn its attention away from the posing of immediately historical or psychological questions and instead would refer to the parallel literature of the ancient world, to the myths and legends of the period, to accounts and motifs in these accounts which are similar to what we encounter here. It sets the story in a wider religious context. The similarities noted would suggest for this school the influence on the story not of historical fact but of mythological and legendary conventions, of folklore and of religious imagination. The terms 'myth' and 'legend', of course, when employed by scholars of religion in a technical sense, do not necessarily carry the negative and dismissive connotations which they have in popular usage. Myth is often viewed as an ancient pictorial way of representing the kind of communal truths or realities which the modern mind might express differently or more abstractly but not necessarily as easily or as forcibly. Legend can often be a valuable pointer to a religious community's view of the importance or significance of its cult founder, holy man or prophet. The question posed to the text by this approach therefore might be: 'What does this passage tell us about early Christianity's world-view (or *Weltanschauung*) and what does it tell us of the way it perceived Jesus' significance *vis-à-vis* other religious agents or heroes?'

Here the immediate answer is clear. The founder of Christianity is greater than John, the charismatic prophet of a Jewish apocalyptic sect. The latter functioned merely as a precursor to Jesus. When we note, however, that apart from John and the Jewish crowds, the chief actors are God, God's Son, the Holy Spirit, Satan, the wild beasts and the angels, and that the places mentioned include the wilderness, the river Jordan, Judaea and Jerusalem—which positively resonate with significance to the Jewish tradition—the mythic elements may lie even deeper. Jesus' experiences and 'the beginning of the gospel' may be seen to recapitulate the origins of Judaism (the exodus, the wilderness experience, testing for forty days/forty years, the waters of Jordan, Jerusalem), Christian discipleship (baptism, confession of sins, the Holy Spirit, testing, the preaching of the gospel) or even the creation itself (the hovering Spirit/dove cf. Gen. 1.1-2, temptation by Satan, Jesus as primal Man/Adam enjoying conditions before the Fall, the wild beasts, the ministering angels).

Seeing the Gospel text as a mythic narrative, a construction of the Christian imagination formed and informed by the Old Testament, is a perspective which owes much to nineteenth-century scholars such as D.F. Strauss. It has undergone a recovery, however, in the past decade (cf., e.g., B.L. Mack, *A Myth of Innocence: Mark and Christian Origins*, 1988), and particularly as a result of the literary-aesthetic approaches (which were also reviewed in Chapter 1). One scholar, John Drury, has recently argued along these particular lines, claiming that the author of Mark begins his story of Jesus, the founder of the new Israel or Christian church, by recalling the foundation events of the old Israel. Mark's Gospel also begins where the Christian reader's experience began—with baptism. Literary-aesthetic approaches such as this ask the question: 'What does this passage tell us about the narrative strategy of Mark as author, the implied reader and the surface rhetoric, narrative coherence and deep structures of the text?'

Viewing the prologue in this light, such an approach would note how the implied reader (whose familiarity with the Old Testament is assumed) is given three pieces of privileged information by the narrator which are not revealed to the human characters in his story, namely the identity of Jesus as Son of God, his superiority to John and his authority over Satan. Introduced at the very start, this information guides the reader's understanding throughout and is to be trusted since it is given by a *bona fide* narrator whose ideological point of view is identical with that of God himself (cf. 1.1 and 1.11) and who appears to have been present in every scene, even those which describe the private thoughts and experiences of Jesus (cf. 1.10-13). Seeing the prologue together with the Gospel as a narrative whole, this approach would look for words, phrases or motifs in the passage which are to recur (the gospel, Jesus as Son of God, the role of John the Baptist, the use of the Old Testament, the wilderness, Galilee, Jerusalem, and the Kingdom of God) or press the significance of formal and thematic parallels and similarities within the Gospel, even, for example, those between the end of the Gospel (16.1-8) and its beginning (God's action in the wilderness/tomb, the supposed places of the dead; a messenger's proclamation about Jesus; Jesus' [re-]appearance in Galilee).

The literary-aesthetic approaches usually remain within the literary world of the text itself, and do not normally venture into making judgments on its alleged historical context. In some cases, they have been content to remain neutral on questions of historicity but in other cases they have been antagonistic to diachronic approaches and have posed, therefore, the major present-day threat to any historical view of the Gospel, as we shall see. Very different in this respect are the three literary-historical methods already singled out: source criticism, form criticism and redaction criticism. Starting from the observation that the content of the Markan prologue is more or less reproduced (with additions, alterations and omissions) by Matthew and Luke, but that, in the case of the temptation story, the two evangelists agree in preserving a fuller version recounting (in almost identical wording but in a different order) three stereotypically structured temptations of Jesus (Mt. 4.1-11 = Lk. 4.1-13), these approaches seek to investigate the traditio-historical process(es) which account for the textual evidence. Source criticism would ask: 'Where did such a story come from? What source or sources did the evangelists use and how reliable might they have been? How many versions of the story do the three accounts actually point to?' A common answer to these questions would be that two principal and independent versions are to be reckoned with, that given by Mark (which, one notes, uses the more Semitic term 'Satan' for the Evil One) and that derived from the other common source used by Matthew and Luke which scholars call Q (which uses, on the other hand, the Greek term *diabolos* for the Evil One).

The second method, form criticism, would search for clues regarding the pre-history of the account(s) in the oral tradition, and would seek to determine the oral or literary status of the unit(s) of tradition in terms of its form and function. Why was the story preserved by the early Christian communities in the form(s) in which it appears and what function did it play within the community's life? How was the account of Jesus' temptation in the wilderness shaped and transformed in the course of transmission by the doctrinal, apologetic, pastoral and liturgical needs of the early church? A key question for form criticism therefore is: 'What does this passage tell us not so much about Jesus but about the beliefs, experiences and practical concerns of the early Christian communities who were the bearers of the tradition about him?' Important in this respect would be the three highly stylized temptations in the Q version followed by three scriptural references from the Greek version (Septuagint) of the book of Deuteronomy, observations which point to the use of the story by a Greek-speaking community, perhaps as a reflective dramatization of the Scripture-oriented obedience of Jesus and the nature of his messianic mission.

The third method, redaction criticism, concentrates on what the evangelists themselves have done with their sources, how they have presented them, modified them, set their own creative stamp upon them. In response to the similarities that exist between the accounts, the question posed by a redaction-critical method would be: 'What does this passage tell us about the literary activity and more importantly, therefore, the theological perspective of the individual evangelists themselves? How, in this instance, do they picture evil and what did they intend to say about Jesus' confrontation with it?' Consideration of the use made by the evangelists of their sources, and in particular of the special features of their narratives, thus provides a window into the mind of each.

Mark's View of History

In the case of Mark's shorter version of the temptation story, certain exclusive features can indeed be commented upon: the stronger, more violent verb used of the Spirit when it 'casts' (*ekballei*) Jesus out into the wilderness, the use of the verb *peirazein* here (1.13) in the sense of 'test' rather than 'tempt', the absence of reference to Jesus' fasting and hunger (as in Matthew and Luke) or of the series of particular temptations, the presence of the wild beasts. What is important in Mark's version is the fact that it stresses the cosmological or even eschatological dimension of Jesus' experience and not the ethical, that is, it conceives of Jesus' encounter with evil not as a matter of (interior) moral temptation but as a crucial trial of strength with a supernatural adversary, Satan. The point of the story, therefore, as some scholars have suggested (e.g. J.M. Robinson, D.E. Nineham), is to help the reader to see the true nature of Jesus' ministry as a decisive engagement with the powers of evil, a cosmic struggle in which the divine Son of God pits himself against Satan and becomes the inaugurator of a new age. The eschatological battle so joined continues both in the exorcisms which follow (cf., e.g., 1.23-27, 34; 3.11-12; etc.) and in the disputes with human opponents (cf., e.g., 2.6-12; 3.1-6, 22-30). It carries the Son of God eventually to the cross where the seeming tragedy of his death is reversed by a supernatural act of resurrection. The contest also continues in the experience of the Markan community, in its sufferings and persecution, but it will shortly be consummated when the Son of Man returns in glory to reclaim his own (ch. 13). Running through Mark's seemingly historical presentation is a particular philosophy of history, therefore, a consistently mythological world-view which separates him in many respects from our modern era and which should be given some weight in any historical assessment of his Gospel.

The Question of Historicity in Mark

What then of the question of historicity in Mark? The issue has not been addressed very much in studies of the Gospel from the 1960s onwards. It is now widely recognized even among conservative scholars that Mark is not a biography in any modern sense, lacking as it does information about Jesus' birth, infancy and physical and intellectual development or details about his age, marital status or length of career. Many of the traditional arguments supporting its historicity have now lost their force. The New Testament writings, it was once argued, are prominent in making claims for the eyewitness status of their contents (cf., e.g., 1 Cor. 15.1ff.; Acts 1.21-22; 10.39-41; Jn 19.35; 21.24; 1 Jn 1.1-3; 1 Pet. 5.1; 2 Pet. 1.12) and although Mark itself does not do this overtly, the tradition of the Gospel's link with John Mark and Peter, its many vivid details (see Taylor) and the *a priori* assumption that eyewitness testimony in the early church would have curbed inventiveness, all conspire to make it a reliable historical document. Through the medium of its preaching, argued the influential British scholar, C.H. Dodd, the early church would even have preserved in its collective memory an outline of the main events of Jesus' ministry.

Against this, it has been said, is the undeniable fact that most of the claims to eyewitness testimony are found in the later New Testament writings and are without much doubt tendentious. I have myself already commented on the doubts expressed against the Papias tradition. As D.E. Nineham pointed out, the early church had a selective memory, preserving for the most part only that which was of practical rather than merely historical interest. Jesus' imminent return and the urgency of the eschatological situation left Christians 'little leisure, even if they had the aptitude, for antiquarian research into Christ's earthly life' (Nineham, *Mark*, p. 18). Nineham also decisively rebutted Dodd's hypothesis of a traditional outline, showing convincingly, as K.L. Schmidt had done before him, that the Markan framework was artificial and that the individual units which it linked together were arranged for the most part topically and for literary and theological reasons.

Since the 1960s the pendulum has swung decisively in favour of the view that Mark's kerygmatic purpose and his theological concerns and achievements are to be regarded as paramount. Most conservative scholars nowadays would not deny, therefore, that apologetic, liturgical, catechetical or doctrinal motivations have played their part in the formation of the Gospel and the traditions it contains, but they would question the extent to which these have affected the historical value of the Gospel. The more modest arguments for the historical reliability of the Gospel today tend to emphasize the fact that Mark used sources and that these were close to the Palestinian tradition (as the many Semitisms indicate). It is also claimed that the form of Jesus' teaching in particular was easy to memorize and that such teaching was transmitted with reasonable accuracy, as was the teaching of prominent Rabbis. One school of thought maintains that Mark was a conservative redactor and that he handled his sources with restraint, taking reasonable care to present the distinction between his own post-resurrection viewpoint and that of the historical Jesus. One example cited is the prologue where Mark presents Jesus as preaching the gospel of *God* (1.14), in order possibly to avoid what might appear (by the use of the word 'gospel' alone) to be an anachronism.

The tension between the two viewpoints (historical and kerygmatic) can be observed indeed in the prologue with which we began. That it is a thematic overture for the Gospel itself can scarcely be doubted given the theological motifs and resonances which we have already observed. On the other hand, the passage appears to be based on a genuine historical tradition that connected Jesus with the Jewish prophet John. While John's role as a messianic precursor to Jesus is likely to be a Christian fiction, that Jesus was baptized by John (a claim later to prove a theological embarrassment given that John's baptism was for the remission of sins; cf. Mt. 3.13-15), that he was therefore a disciple of John, and that he himself went on to conduct a prophetic mission announcing the coming Kingdom of God, all these are without much doubt historical facts.

The Gospel then, to reiterate, is a mixture of fact and fiction, a blend of history and theology, a product of literary artifice and faith-inspired imagination. If it is historical information that we seek from it, then we must learn to ask questions that are appropriate to the nature of this text and find ways of testing the answers which we think we are receiving from it. The Gospel itself supplies clues which enable us to form judgments about what might reasonably be ascribed to Jesus, what might derive from the early church's faith or practice, and what might be the product of the evangelist's own literary artifice or theology. Separating the various layers or levels which make up a complex text like Mark's Gospel is a bit like archaeology and it involves a great deal of careful detective work. Since so much of our modern perspective on the Gospel is based on the application of the three literary-historical tools—source criticism, form criticism and redaction criticism—it is to these tools, to their aims, method and results on Mark, that we shall now turn.

Source Criticism and Mark's Sources

The Method and Criteria of Source Criticism

Source criticism operates from the assumption that if an ancient writer has used sources, certain indications in the text will point to this unless the writer has so reworked his sources as to destroy all traces of these. The incorporation of sources will often produce unevenness or even incoherence in the text. There may be signs of interruption of the context where the sources have been inserted, commented upon or altered, or where the writer has resumed the narrative after employing his source material. Where multiple overlapping sources have been used, there may be frequent repetition or duplication in content, such as two versions of a saying or story (which scholars term a 'doublet'). Another proof that sources have been used and that the writer has not been merely inventive is the independent attestation of parallel material in one or more other texts for which no direct literary interrelationships can be claimed. A major pointer to the use of sources is the presence of inconsistencies or discrepancies. These may be historical in character (such as the aforementioned doublets or tradition variants), leading us to question the details of what we are told actually happened. They may be literary, presenting breaks or disruptions (scholars call these 'aporias') in the sequence or flow of the writer's presentation, or sections of the narrative written in a different literary style or vocabulary. They can also be ideological or more specifically theological, revealing opposing or contradictory ideas or perspectives in the text. To qualify as source-critical indicators, however, such inconsistencies must be of a kind that would not naturally be ascribed to the writer himself or, in other words, to genuinely literary or psychological factors. The line between these, of course, is often a fine one, making the exercise of source criticism a delicate operation.

The Evidence of Sources in Mark

A close reading of the text of Mark would seem to indicate that sources have been used and that the evangelist was not entirely the master of them. There is considerable disjunction in the narrative especially when we read it in the original language. Obvious insertions have been made (cf., e.g., 7.3-4) and there are frequent parentheses, a number of which are puzzling (cf., e.g., 11.13c). The lack of logical coherence in certain passages, such as in the discourses attributed to Jesus, suggest that they may be a compilation of originally separate sayings in the tradition or else extracts from a sayings source or sources (cf., e.g., 4.1-34; 8.34–9.1; 9.33-50, esp. 49-50; 11.22-25; 13.3-37). The Gospel's style is characterized by repetition and there are a number of possible doublets (e.g. the two feeding accounts of 6.30-44 and 8.1-10; the two sea miracles of 4.35-41 and 6.45-52; the two reports concerning Jesus of 6.14-16 and 8.28; the two stories of his receiving children 9.36-37 and 10.13-16) or even triplets (e.g. the three strands of parable material recognized by many scholars in 4.1-34; the three passion predictions of 8.31, 9.31, 10.33-34; cf. also the three repeated references to Judas as one of the twelve in 14.10, 20, 43, or to Mary, the mother of James/Jesus in 15.40, 47 and 16.1).

Much of Mark's material is clustered in common groupings within his Gospel (e.g. miracle stories, controversy stories, parables) and with a degree of patterning which has suggested to some the use of underlying sources. The repetitions referred to apply not only to single motifs, sayings or narratives but even, for example, to extended sequences such as the repetition of the sea miracle, three healing miracles and one feeding miracle pattern which some scholars have observed in 4.35–5.43/6.30-44 and 6.45-53/7.24–8.26 (the latter section 6.45–8.26 being lacking in Luke) or the feeding miracle–crossing of the lake–dispute with Pharisees–discourse on bread pattern which others have seen repeated in 6.30–7.23 and 8.1-21 (and found also in Jn 6). Some of the individual sayings attributed to Jesus in Mark also overlap with those in Q (cf., e.g., Mk 8.35 and Mt. 10.39 = Lk. 17.33) and some of his narratives with those in John (cf., e.g., Mk 1.1-11 and Jn 1.19-34; Mk 11.15-18 and Jn 2.13-22).

Inconsistencies and discrepancies abound at every level. The Levi called to be a follower of Jesus in 2.14 is not mentioned in the disciples list in 3.13-19. For the parable discourse in ch. 4, Jesus is in a boat continuously, it appears (cf. 4.1, 35-36), yet 4.10ff. implies a change of scene. Jesus directs the boat to Bethsaida (6.45) but it lands mysteriously at Gennesaret (6.53). In 10.46, Jesus and his disciples come to Jericho, we are told, and just as quickly depart! As mysterious as the itinerary of the boat or that of Jesus is the sudden unexplained appearance of the 'house' (cf., e.g., 7.17, 24; 9.33; 10.10) or the 'young man' (14.51-52; 16.5).

Literary and theological aspects of the plot are often likewise puzzling. The Pharisees and the Herodians who plot to kill Jesus in 3.6 (cf. 12.13ff.) are not mentioned as named groups responsible for his death in the passion narrative (chs. 14–16). The parables (cf. 4.11-12) are meant to mystify outsiders, yet Jesus' opponents perceive the significance of a parable uttered against them (12.12). Jesus urges that his messianic identity be kept secret (8.30-33), yet he refers to himself openly as the Son of Man (2.10, 28) and stages a public messianic action (11.1-10). Discrepancies in the Markan presentation of the so-called 'messianic secret' are also matched by different attitudes to the timing of Jesus' triumphal return as Son of Man (compare and contrast 9.1 and 13.30 with 13.10 and 13.32ff.).

That Mark used sources, therefore, seems certain, although some of this evidence may possibly be accounted for (as we shall see in Chapter 3) other than as a product of the awkward manipulation of sources. But can the sources themselves be isolated? A variety of options are possible and many have been suggested in the course of Markan scholarship. It is possible that behind Mark lies an extensive written source or *Grundschrift* (to use the German word) and that the so-called Second Gospel is an abridgement of this primitive Gospel or *Ur-Gospel*. Conversely, the Gospel of Mark may be an expansion of an earlier less extensive *Grundschrift*. There may have been, in other words, a *proto-Markus* which has been subsequently edited to produce our canonical Mark. Our Mark may even have been further edited (to produce a *deutero-Markus*) before it came into the hands of the later evangelists. While textual comparisons with Matthew and Luke and certain internal features of Mark itself may point in this direction, the diversity of the Gospel's contents suggest, on the other hand, that Mark is the compilation of a multiplicity of sources rather than an edited version of a single one. But were these sources written, oral or a combination of both?

To prove the existence of any extensive written source, the source critic would have to demonstrate that the Gospel incorporates an extensive sequence of passages which has its own positive and negative distinguishing features, its own characteristic language, vocabulary and style, its own distinctive ideas or theology — in short, its own underlying unity and function prior to its incorporation in the Gospel. To demonstrate further that Mark, or indeed any of the Gospels, is dependent upon prior written documents, to show literary dependency, in other words, the source critic looks for extensive agreement between the Gospel and any other documentary source upon which it is purported to be based. The criteria for literary relationship are fourfold and consist of extensive agreement in content, form, order and wording. When these criteria for literary relationship are considered, a surprising observation emerges, one which was made as early as Augustine in the fourth century but not critically examined until the eighteenth. The fact emerges that on these grounds, three of our four canonical Gospels (viz. Mark, Matthew and Luke) would appear to have a literary relationship with each other. One or more of these three Gospels has used one or more of the others as its source. It is the nature of this literary relationship that constitutes the Synoptic Problem. If Mark is related to these other Gospels and yet was neither the earliest Gospel (as we have previously assumed) nor used by them, then the case for an Ur-Gospel or even for Matthew (or Luke) as Mark's major source is strengthened. The question of the priority of Mark, therefore, is one that we shall consider before resuming our quest for the evangelist's sources.

Markan Priority and the Synoptic Problem

As is now well known, if the three so-called Synoptic Gospels are viewed together (hence their name), certain similarities and differences emerge. All three share a common content. Many of the same sayings or stories occur throughout, an observation all the more significant when one compares the content of John's Gospel which has far fewer of these common passages. Matthew has some 90 per cent and Luke more than 50 per cent of Mark's actual subject matter. The form taken by each Gospel and its common subject matter is likewise similar. In its overall arrangement, Mark's Gospel is episodic, or anecdotal, as we have seen. Matthew and Mark share the same unit structure, presenting, with the exception of the passion narrative, a series of short, discrete stories and sayings loosely linked together and in sharp contrast to the longer, more coherent narratives and discourses of the Fourth Gospel. The individual units themselves are identical in structure, comprising miracle stories, parables and sayings in the same stereotyped form. The order in which they occur is also largely the same, the sequence running roughly in parallel from the appearance of John the Baptist and Jesus' baptism through the Galilean ministry to his journey to Jerusalem, trial, crucifixion and resurrection. Where the order is different, Mark is almost never the odd man out. A similar pattern occurs in the wording of individual units, which is frequently almost identical (cf., e.g., Mk 1.40-45; 2.1-10; 11.27-33 and parallels) and where the pattern of major agreement is such that one or other of Matthew or Luke will agree with Mark's wording and only in a minority of cases (the minor agreements) do they agree together against Mark.

So much for the similarities. The differences between all three Gospels are likewise striking. Two of the three, namely Matthew and Luke, have a body of common material (the double tradition), consisting largely of sayings and discourse, which is not shared by Mark. This material, while arranged differently, comprises almost 25 per cent of each Gospel and also at points shows a remarkable degree of verbal agreement (cf., e.g., Mt. 3.7b-10 = Lk. 3.7b-9). All three, moreover, have special material not shared by any of the others. In the case of Mark, it is less than half a per cent, but in Matthew it is almost 30 per cent and in Luke some 50 per cent.

The difficulty of explaining both these similarities and differences constitutes the Synoptic Problem, as I have said, and in the vigorous quest for the solution from the eighteenth century onwards a variety of hypotheses have been suggested. Their complicated history cannot adequately be summarized here but in general, derivation of all three Gospels independently from a common oral tradition or parent Gospel (possibly in Aramaic) gave way, in light of the literary evidence, to the theory that they were interdependent. In view of the pattern of literary agreements and given that Mark appears to be the common ground between the other two, two main competing solutions have come in time to suggest themselves. The first is that Matthew is the prior Gospel and hence that Mark is an abridgement of Matthew, as Augustine held, or even a conflation of both Matthew and Luke, the view first expounded by J.J. Griesbach (1789). The second is that Mark is prior, and it was this latter view which developed into the now standard two-document hypothesis (2DH) whereby Mark is considered to be the basis of the two later Gospels together with their further common source, Q (the double tradition). Emerging from a wide field of alternative synoptic source theories, the 2DH is associated with the name of K. Lachmann (1835) who, among others, laid the groundwork for it, and with such scholars as C.G. Wilke, C.H. Weisse and (supremely), later in the nineteenth century, H.-J. Holtzmann.

The 2DH is still accepted, even with qualifications, by the majority of New Testament scholars. Its main rival, the Griesbach hypothesis, has experienced something of a revival, however, in recent years. Its protagonists point to the weaknesses of the 2DH, claiming that it inadequately explains the not inconsiderable minor agreements between Matthew and Luke over against Mark and requires acceptance of a hypothetical and ill-defined source, Q, which is no longer extant. Such a hypothesis is unnecessary if Luke used Matthew. Conversely, the Griesbach hypothesis offers a credible explanation for the order of the episodes in the Synoptic Gospels. Mark, it is alleged, shows the characteristics of literary conflation (cf., e.g., 1.32 and parallels) and the harmonizing tendency which produced it fits in well with the cultural context in which the Gospels were produced. The theological and other motivations of the nineteenth-century liberal scholars who first formulated the 2DH (particularly their desire to use the Gospel's 'primitiveness' as support for its historical worth) have also recently been impugned.

Notwithstanding these attacks, the priority of Mark and the associated 2DH still provide the most satisfactory answer to the Synoptic Problem, especially when qualifications are made in the light of our growing appreciation of the continuing influence of oral tradition upon the formation of the written Gospels. While Markan priority itself is not dependent upon the Q hypothesis, belief in the existence of Q is also firmly held today, given the improbability of Lukan dependence on Matthew (or vice versa) as an explanation of the double tradition. The minor agreements may indeed be explained by a number of factors. They may be due, for example, to the influence of both the oral tradition and Q, to later textual corruption (especially scribal harmonization of Luke to Matthew) or to a common redaction policy on the part of Matthew and Luke. Although the arguments from common content, order and wording theoretically fit both the 2DH and the Griesbach hypothesis, the arguments from 'primitiveness' and from 'brevity' tilt the balance strongly in favour of Markan priority. Both in literary style (cf., e.g., the roughness of Mark's grammar and style and its preservation of Aramaic expressions) and in theological development (cf. the harsh treatment of Jesus' disciples and the so-called 'human' portrait of Jesus) Mark appears to be the earliest of the three Gospels. When this is combined with the fact that it is also the shortest then its priority seems more assured.

Matthaean priority and the Griesbach hypothesis, on the other hand, while gaining in respectability, still remains a minority position in view of its inherent weaknesses. Supporters of Matthaean priority have failed to date to offer a convincing redaction-critical theory for a Markan abridgement of the other two Gospels. What would account for his puzzling omissions (e.g. the birth/infancy narratives of Mt. 1–2 and Lk. 1–2; the preaching of John the Baptist, cf. Mt 3.7-10 = Lk. 3.7-9; the Sermon the Mount of Mt. 5–7; so much of Jesus' teaching and especially the double tradition; the specific Old Testament references to prophecy fulfilment, cf. Mt. 21.4-5 par.; the post-resurrection appearances and, by way of a specific example, the reference to the mountain in Galilee in Mt. 28.16)? Even more seriously, how can one explain, if abbreviation were his aim, his curious expansions (e.g. his longer narratives, cf. Mk 9.14-29 par., or his special material, e.g. 4.26-29; 7.32-37; 8.22-26)? Why should he have adulterated the good Greek vocabulary, grammar and style of his sources and why should he have altered negatively their reverential portrait of Jesus and his original disciples? The growing evidence of redaction criticism and literary criticism, as we shall see, has also highlighted the fact that Mark was more than a mere collector and editor of traditions and, by that very token, far less likely to have been a mechanical conflator of two already sophisticated sources. Many of the arguments indeed can still be summed up in the classic words of G.M. Styler: 'Given Mark, it is easy to see why Matthew was written; given Matthew it is hard to see why Mark was needed' (Bellinzoni *et al.*, *The Two-Source Hypothesis*, p. 73).

Mark's Sources

If Mark was prior and not dependent upon one or both of the other Synoptic Gospels, then the question of his sources still remains an open one and to it we return. The search for a single extensive *Grundschrift* underlying the Gospel is not as popular as it once was, although W. Schmithals has recently argued for it in his commentary. To explain the Synoptic evidence, the existence of an older Aramaic Gospel behind all three Synoptic Gospels is still sometimes mooted or even of various Greek translations of the *Ur-Gospel* which were used separately by each evangelist. The theory is occasionally even extended to the Fourth Gospel, given its affinities in some cases with Mark. Proto-Mark or *Ur-Markus* theories have not commanded widespread support since the advent of form and redaction criticism. Linguistic and stylistic considerations do not allow us to isolate a substantial earlier version of the Gospel. The continuing problem of the minor agreements and the overlap existing between Mark and Q have led some scholars, however, still to suggest a second edition of canonical Mark (*Deutero-Markus*) which may have incorporated parts of Q and other material and which may have been used by Matthew and Luke.

The most recent attempts to revive extensive *Grundschrift* theories have come from the comparative analysis of the extra-canonical Gospels or the fragments of such which we possess. Among these are Egerton Papyrus 2 (Mk 1.40-49), the Secret Gospel of Mark (referred to by Clement of Alexandria), the *Gospel of Peter* (a passion narrative only) and the *Gospel of Thomas* (a collection of sayings, some of which are paralleled in Mark). J.D. Crossan and H. Koester have argued, for example, for canonical Mark's dependence on the Secret Gospel of Mark but, intriguing as such suggestions are, most scholars hold that, as with Matthew and Luke, the dependency operates the other way round, and that Apocryphal Gospel literature, while important in other respects, does not provide us with sources for the Second Gospel.

If Mark is not based on a single underlying written source, is it similar to Matthew and Luke in being a compilation of more than one secondary source, or even of a multiplicity of literary sources? In terms of a model, is it to be considered a Christian 'scrapbook' produced by a 'scissors-and-paste' compiler? This view was certainly entertained in an earlier era of scholarship when the unevenness, insertions, discrepancies, repetitions and suggestive patterning revealed in the text prompted a number of different source-theories. For some scholars, the evidence pointed to the combination of three separate Gospels (e.g. A.T. Cadoux), for others to a variety of short individual 'tracts' or 'pamphlets' on such subjects or themes as Jesus' sayings, conflict, the parables, the miracles, the twelve disciples, the apocalypse or the passion story (W.L. Knox). The problem with such theories is that although the Gospel material does evince topical and thematic arrangement, the source critics have never been able to demonstrate convincingly that the alleged sources had enough positive and negative distinguishing features or sufficient unity of thought, language and style to stand out from other sections of the Gospel. Nor have they been able to agree on the precise parameters of such sources. As a result, Markan scholars today have tended to talk in more general terms of the pre-Markan 'traditions', 'collections' or 'cycles' employed by the evangelist or even of the sources underlying sections of the Gospel, without claiming to be able specifically to isolate these.

The underlying sources or collections which have, to varying degrees, been proposed and the sections of the Gospel where they have been detected are as follows:

1.   a John the Baptist-Jesus tradition (1.1-15);

2.   the day in Capernaum (1.21-39);
3.   a controversy collection (2.1-3.6; 7.1-23; 11-12);
4.   a parable collection (4.1-34);
5.   a collection of miracle stories (1.21-2.12; a single cycle in 3.7-12; 4.35-5.43; 6.31-52; 6.53-56 or a double cycle comprising a sea miracle, three healing miracles and a feeding miracle in 4.35-5.43 with 6.34-44, 53, paralleled again in 6.45-51; 8.22-26; 7.24b-30, 32-37; 8.1-10; a double cycle comprising feeding miracle–crossing of the lake–dispute with Pharisees–discussion on bread, repeated in 6.30-7.23 and 8.1-21 as well as in Jn 6);
6.   sayings collections (8.34-9.1; 9.33-50; 10; 11.22-25) including Q (cf., e.g., 3.22-30 par.);
7.   an apocalypse (ch. 13);
8.   a passion narrative (chs. 14–15).

Given the nature of the evidence, the debate over such collections is understandably intense, with some scholars (R. Pesch) claiming that Mark's debt to these is extensive, and others believing it to be limited (e.g. D. Lührmann). Similarities exist, for example, between some Markan sayings and those attributed to Q (cf. esp. Mk 8.12 with Mt. 12.39 = Lk. 11.29; Mk 8.38 and Mt. 10.33 = Lk. 12.9; or Mk 11.23 with Mt. 17.20 = Lk. 17.6) but not such as to make literary dependency a certainty. Scholarly assessments of 'the little apocalypse' range from the theory that it is an edited version of an earlier literary apocalypse to the view that it is composite, a pastiche of traditional apocalyptic sayings. The pre-Markan literary integrity of the passion narrative has also been challenged especially by American scholars, in view of the number of Markan themes which converge in these two chapters.

Were we to sum up the current debate, then, where pre-Markan collections are concerned, it would be fair to say that there is still a general agreement in favour of Mark's use of a collection of controversies (in 2.1-3.6 but not in 7.1-23 or chs. 11–12), parables (in ch. 4), sayings (in ch. 10) and a passion narrative. The issue is more divided in the case of miracles (4.35ff.) and the apocalypse (ch. 13), and generally against in the case of 1.1-15 and 1.29-39. The eclipse or recession of classical source criticism and of specific literary source theories has in fact been in evidence for more than half a century and (with the qualified exception of the passion narrative) many scholars would endorse the judgment of W.G. Kümmel:

We cannot go beyond declaring that Mk is probably based on no extensive written sources, but that more likely the evangelist has woven

together small collections of individual traditions and detailed bits of
tradition into a more or less coherent presentation (*Introduction*, p. 85).

The Gospel of Mark, it has been increasingly recognized, is a text
standing on the borderline between oral and written literature and no
significant stages of literary activity (as with Matthew and Luke) preceded its composition. This conclusion in itself owes much to the
advent and influence of form criticism and it is to this second literary-
historical method on Mark that we shall now turn.

Form Criticism and the Forms in Mark

Form Criticism in History and Scholarship
The essential thrust of classical source criticism of the Gospels was
historical, that is, by arguing for the priority of Mark and in turn
seeking to establish the written sources on which it was based it
sought to produce a reliable picture of the essential features of Jesus'
life, teaching and career. Source criticism's failure to isolate such
sources led, therefore, by the time of the First World War, to an
impasse in historical-critical investigation of the Gospel. Form criticism, in this respect, seemed to promise a way out. As a literary-
historical method dealing with folk material which had at some point
in its existence been orally transmitted, it offered a way to get behind
the literary text to the shadowy period prior to its composition when
traditions about Jesus had formed and circulated.

Form criticism or form history (*Formgeschichte*, to give it its German
title) had been applied in other places before being applied to the
Bible. The analysis and interpretation of secular folklore had its scientific pioneers in the brothers Grimm (Jakob and Wilhelm) in the early
nineteenth century and the insights of such analysis were first applied
to the Old Testament by H. Gunkel (1862–1932) who identified and
classified the smaller orally transmitted narrative, didactic and liturgical units lying behind the Old Testament text. The application of the
method to the New Testament is associated with the names of the
three German scholars K.L. Schmidt, M. Dibelius and R. Bultmann, to
whom reference has already been made. All three published their
results almost simultaneously between 1919 and 1921. It was Schmidt
who drew attention to the 'unit-structure' or 'pearls and string' pattern of the Gospel, pointing out that Mark consisted (with the exception of the passion narrative) of a whole series of separate and
independent units (pericopes) which were joined together by an artificially created chronological and geographical framework. Dibelius
isolated and classified the main units in terms of their literary form

(paradigms or short illustrative stories, *Novellen* or tales of the miraculous, parenesis or exhortations, legends and myths). He also searched for the influences in the oral tradition which had produced these characteristic forms and concluded that preaching had been a paramount one. Bultmann is distinguished for his more elaborate classification of the forms and their creative milieu, as well as for his more radical judgments on the historicity of the tradition. Less sceptical in this respect was the British scholar V. Taylor who helped to make the method known within the world of English-speaking scholarship, but was also critical of certain of its presuppositions and results.

Classical form criticism harboured certain assumptions about the nature of the Synoptic Gospels, the Jesus traditions they embodied, and the forms in which such traditions came to be expressed. The Synoptic Gospels were popular or folk literature (*Kleinliteratur*), unliterary writings which were essentially the product of an anonymous community tradition. They had arisen by an almost inevitable process of aggregate growth, the literary culmination of a collective desire on the part of the early church to preserve and develop its oral traditions in the service of its kerygma or proclamation. Dibelius's judgment on the Gospels in this regard is often quoted: 'The literary understanding of the Synoptics begins with the recognition that they are collections of material. The composers are only to the smallest extent authors. They are principally collectors, vehicles of tradition, editors' (*Tradition*, p. 3).

The traditions about Jesus which the evangelists collected had originally circulated orally, and not in written form, in the 40 or so years after his death. The sayings and stories attributed to him had been taken over in small, individual, self-contained units with little indication as to their time, place or specific context within Jesus' original ministry. Such contextual features had mainly to be supplied by the Gospel writers themselves. The framework linking the pericopes, as Schmidt had shown, was unreliable as a guide to historical developments in Jesus' career. Some collections of pericopes were made prior to the written Gospels (e.g. controversy stories, parables or sayings, as we have seen with Mark) but these were for the most part linked topically, thus making for easier memorization.

The role of memory was itself a limiting factor in the formation of the Gospel tradition. There is a limit, for example, to what the memory can retain and transmit. The early church had, moreover, a selective memory. A particular saying or story was remembered and transmitted if it served the needs and purposes of the early church; in other words, if it had a *function*, be it kerygmatic (promoting the faith), apologetic (defending the faith), polemical (attacking opponents), regulative (disciplining the community), didactic (teaching church members), catechetical (instructing neophytes) or liturgical (aiding worship). The distinct forms in which the Jesus tradition came to expression, therefore, were not an accident but a product of the function played by this material within its particular sociological context, life-setting or *Sitz im Leben* (preaching, worship, exhortation, instruction, etc.). The form critics also pointed to the variety of forms which existed within the Gospel traditions (proverbs, aphorisms, parables, miracle stories, legends, etc.) and drew attention to their universal and stereotyped nature. Each of the forms had certain standard or conventional features which could be recognized in other forms of the same type, not only in the Synoptic (or triple) tradition but in Jewish, Hellenistic and other folk traditions as well.

Form critics like Bultmann made further assumptions about the nature of oral transmission itself. Orality and textuality were not clearly differentiated. Literary tendencies operating within the Synoptic and later Christian texts and illuminated by comparative study were taken as clues to what had also happened in oral transmission. In his discussion of the story in Christian tradition, for example, Bultmann pointed to the 'laws' governing the transmission of popular tradition which such critical comparison could uncover. Primitive stories were characterized by a love of repetition (twos and threes were in numerical terms especially prominent) and by 'scenic duality', that is, despite the presence of others (usually anonymous) in the story, the significant action is almost always centred on Jesus and one other actor or interlocutor (an individual or a group). The motives and feelings of the participants are very seldom referred to. As the story is passed on it becomes subject to imaginative embellishment (cf. Mk 15.38 and Mt. 27.51-53 or Mk 16.2-8 par.) and to an increasing tendency to differentiation and individualization. More specific details are introduced (cf., e.g., Mk 3.1 with Lk. 6.6 *right* hand; Mk 9.17 with Lk. 9.38 *only* son; Mk 14.47 with Lk. 22.50 *right* ear). Personal names are supplied (cf., e.g., Mk 7.17 with Mt. 15.15 *Peter*; Mk 14.47 with Jn 18.10 *Simon Peter...Malchus*) or definite categories of opponents (cf., e.g., Lk. 11.16 [Q] *others* with Mk 8.11 *Pharisees*, Mt. 16.1 *Pharisees and Sadducees*). Speeches are placed on the lips of characters in the story (cf., e.g., Mk 15.32 with Lk. 23.39-43) and indirect speech expressed in more vivid direct speech (cf., e.g., Mk 8.32 with Mt. 16.22). If the story has a parallel in the Old Testament, it may become conformed to the parallel (cf., e.g., Mk 11.2ff. with Mt. 21.2ff. in light of Zech. 9.9 *ass* and colt). Traditions circulating in independent streams may produce different versions, variants or doublets of the same story (cf., e.g., Mk 6.34ff. and 8.1-9 with Jn 6.1-14 or Mk 1.16-20 with Lk. 5.1-11 and Jn 21.1-14). As a story originally conceived or transmitted in a Palestinian tradition is retold within the wider Hellenistic world there may be evidence of diminishing Semitism in its vocabulary, syntax or style.

The Aims, Methods and Results of Form Criticism on Mark
In the words of Dibelius, form criticism had a twofold function:

> In the first place, by reconstruction and analysis, it seeks to explain the origin of the tradition about Jesus, and thus to penetrate into a period previous to that in which our Gospels and their written sources were recorded. But it has a further purpose. It seeks to make clear the intention and real interest of the earliest tradition (*Tradition*, p. v).

The method, therefore, is a literary-historical or tradition-critical one and it has three distinct operations which correspond with its literary, sociological and historical orientations. The first of these operations is the recovery of the traditional units from the editorial work of the evangelist and the classification of these units according to their literary form. The second is the establishment of the sociological function or *Sitz im Leben* of each unit and the determination, therefore, of the particular interest, activity or concern of the community which led to their preservation or even creation. The third and trickiest operation is the tracing of the history of the tradition itself and the assessment, consequently, of its historical value in throwing light either upon Jesus' teaching and activity or upon those of the early church. By comparative analysis (especially of the triple tradition), by knowledge of the 'laws' (or, better, tendencies) of oral transmission and by familiarity with the theological and other interests of the early church, the form critic seeks to evaluate the extent of development that a particular unit of tradition has undergone and hence its basis in history.

In coming to judgments about the historicity of Gospel traditions about Jesus, the form critics have been aided in their task by a number of criteria of authenticity, as they are called. Though neither definitive in themselves nor foolproof, used cautiously and in conjunction with each other, these criteria can help to establish degrees of probability in respect of material that may go back to Jesus himself. The first is the criterion of dissimilarity or distinctiveness which states that a saying or story attributed to Jesus has a higher probability of being authentic if it is uncharacteristic of either contemporary Judaism or the early church (and hence is unlikely to have been derived from or subsequently influenced by each of these environments). Since this criterion may eliminate aspects of continuity between Jesus and Judaism (and between the early church and its founder) it has come to be increasingly qualified in light of considerations of authentic context or appropriate background, that is, whether the Jesus it produces fits believably into a first-century Palestinian context.

The second criterion is multiple attestation or the cross-section method. This holds as more likely to be reliable any tradition about Jesus which is found in two or more independent sources or any aspect or emphasis of his life and teaching which is reflected in two or more literary forms (e.g. in parables, sayings and controversy stories). Again the criterion is a useful one and although, strictly speaking, it proves only the antiquity (or 'embeddedness') of the tradition rather than its authenticity. A third criterion already touched upon is that constituted by considerations of language and environment. If a tradition reflects Aramaic traits or early first-century Palestinian conditions, then it is more likely to go back to Jesus or the Palestinian Jewish-Christian community. Conversely, if it is incompatible with such a context then it is more likely to be a later secondary development. A final criterion is that of coherence or consistency which holds that other traditions about Jesus preserved in the Gospel are likely to be authentic if they harmonize with the minimal core of authentic material stringently established by the other criteria.

Using such criteria, the form-critical method, as practised on the Gospel tradition and especially on Mark, has produced a number of very important, if not revolutionary, results. The main forms of the Gospel tradition have been classified, with suggestions made as to their *Sitz im Leben* and historical worth (i.e. in relation to the primary level of the tradition). Since Bultmann's classification has been more far-reaching and influential than that of other form critics, it is worth summarizing the main lines of his analysis. Bultmann recognized two broad divisions within the Synoptic tradition: the tradition of the sayings of Jesus and the tradition of the narrative material. The division is not a rigid one, however, for sayings attributed to Jesus are often introduced within a brief narrative framework and form a climax thereby to the resultant story. Using a term which comes from Greek literature, Bultmann called these *apophthegms*, further subdividing them into controversy dialogues which focus on some disputed action or attitude and enshrine conflict sayings (cf., e.g., Mk 2.23-28; 7.1-8), closely related scholastic dialogues which present a response to an observation, request or question and enshrine didactic sayings (cf., e.g., Lk. 13.1-5; 12.13-14; Mt. 11.2-6) and the more general and varied biographical apophthegms (cf., e.g., Mt. 17.24-27; Mk 10.13-16). Citing numerous Jewish and Hellenistic parallels, Bultmann noted, for example, how Jewish apophthegms frequently used the question/counter-question format (cf., e.g., Mk 11.27-33) or Hellenistic apophthegms introductory formulae like 'when he was asked by' or 'once when he observed how' (cf., e.g., Lk. 17.20-21). For Bultmann the *Sitz im Leben* of the apophthegms was to be found in preaching, apologetic and polemic and while the sayings which apophthegms embody might be authentic, their imprecise, ideal and often variable narrative framework was hardly likely to derive from historical reminiscence.

Dibelius (who called this form the 'paradigm') and Taylor (who termed it the 'pronouncement story') were less sceptical in this aspect, Dibelius restricting the *Sitz im Leben* to preaching and, in the light of the public control exercised by such activity, claiming 'the nearer a narrative stands to the sermon the less it is questionable, or likely to have been changed by romantic, legendary or literary influences' (*Tradition*, p. 61). Dibelius also drew attention to analogies between these Gospel 'paradigms' and the form taken by sayings attributed to famous men (especially popular philosophers) in the Hellenistic world, in particular the *chreia*, a short pointed saying of general significance, originating in a definite person and arising out of a definite situation.

In addition to sayings with a framework, Bultmann also identified and classified three categories of sayings which appear in the Gospel tradition without a framework. In the first category, there were the *logia* (sayings in the narrower sense), *gnomic* or *wisdom sayings* in the form of proverbs or aphorisms which embodied conventional secular wisdom or general religious truth (cf., e.g., Mt. 6.34b; 12.34b; Lk. 6.31). Collections of such sayings were made by early Christian communities for use in teaching and exhortation and, given their close parallels in the Jewish Wisdom literature and (in respect of Jesus' teaching) their lack of distinctiveness, the question of their authenticity is hard to settle. While Bultmann could ascribe very few of the logia with any certainty, therefore, to Jesus, modern scholarship has, on the other hand, been increasingly less averse to the possibility of Jesus' historical role as a teacher of wisdom.

A second category was *the prophetic and apocalyptic sayings*, with their emphasis on the future. These consist of predictions, admonitions, warnings of impending crisis, summonses to repentance, promises of future reward and so forth (cf., e.g., Mk 10.29-30; Mt. 8.11-12 = Lk. 13.28-29; Mt. 10.17-23). Used in preaching, parenesis (exhortation) and polemic and 'distinguished by their brevity and vigour' (Bultmann), they often employ a blessing or woe formula (cf., e.g., Mt. 5.3-12 = Lk. 6.20-26; Mt. 13.16-17 = Lk. 10.23-24; Lk. 14.15) or possess an easily memorized antithetical structure (cf., e.g., Mt. 10.32-33 = Lk. 12.8-9; Lk. 13.30 par.). While some of these sayings may be the creation of Christian prophets (cf., e.g., Rev. 1.17-18; 3.20; 16.15) and a product therefore of the early church's prophetic activity, their distinctive eschatological flavour argues for the strong possibility that a majority go back to Jesus whose own role as a prophet is now indeed a major emphasis of modern scholarship.

A third category were the *legal sayings* to which have been attached a number of *church* (or community) *rules*. The former consisted of sayings expressing Jesus' attitude to the Jewish Law (e.g. the food laws, almsgiving, prayer, fasting, etc.; cf. Mk 7.15; Mt. 6.2-4, 5-13, 16-18) and the latter sayings which set forth the regulations of the community in respect of its internal organization and discipline as well as its mission (cf., e.g., Mt. 16.18-19; 18.15-22; 23.8-10). Formal characteristics include antithetical construction, the use of conditional clauses (when/if…) followed by a command, or the introductory 'whoever…' formula (cf., e.g., Mt. 5.19, 21-22, 23-24, 27-28, 29-30, 31-32, 33-37). Employed both for apologetic and polemical purposes, and especially for parenesis, the authenticity of such sayings is disputed. In Bultmann's view, the legal sayings, which had a parallel in the preaching of the Old Testament prophets against external piety, might go back to Jesus but the church rules were almost certainly *Gemeindebildungen* or 'community-formations', that is, they originated in the early church.

Included within all three of the distinct groups in terms of their content, but treated separately by Bultmann because of their form, were two further types of saying, namely *christological* (or 'I-sayings') and *parables*. In the former, Jesus speaks about the purpose of his coming, his special relationship with God, his passion and resurrection (cf., e.g., Mt. 10.34-36 = Lk. 12.51-53; Lk. 19.10; Mt. 11.25-27 = Lk. 10.21-22; Mk 8.31). Since they project an understanding or interpretation of his person and work and frequently reflect a retrospective point of view, it is highly probable that they too are *Gemeindebildungen*, an expression of the believing community's own Christology or soteriology (especially that of the Hellenistic churches). Different in this respect are the parables much used by the early church in preaching, apologetic, polemic and parenesis, especially teaching and catechesis. There is a high probability that most of these go back to Jesus although the applications frequently attached to them (e.g. Mk 4.10-20; Mt. 22.11-13; Lk. 18.6-8) are usually secondary, and abundant signs of allegorization (cf. Mk 12.1-12) indicate much overlay from later tradition.

Within his second main division, the narrative tradition, Bultmann identified and classified miracle stories (*Wundergeschichten*, or, in

Dibelius's terminology, *Novellen*) and historical stories and legends. In the various types of miracle story (exorcisms, other healings, raisings from the dead, nature miracles), the main point of interest lies in the display of miraculous power. Here narrative details are more important (in contrast to the apophthegm) and certain formal characteristics such as a basic threefold structure (the condition of the patient recounted; the healing narrated; the cure described) as well as a number of common motifs or emphases (e.g. the gravity of the illness; the magical manipulations of the miracle-worker; the visible demonstration of the cure and the astonished reaction of the onlookers) help define the category. For Bultmann, these stories were of doubtful historicity given their resemblance to other Jewish and Hellenistic miracle-stories (where the miracle worker is shown to be an epiphany or manifestation of a god). Most originated in a Hellenistic milieu, and were designed to prove Jesus' superiority over rival miracle-workers, divine-men and gods. Palestinian elements in the tradition, however, its multiple attestation and ostensibly genuine sayings such as Mt. 12.28 (= Lk. 11.20) have led modern scholarship to revise this estimate and to reckon with the probability that, despite subsequent embellishment, a core tradition depicting Jesus as an exorcist and healer is historical.

Distinguishable, though only to a degree, from miracle stories (and from biographical apophthegms) was the second narrative category of *historical stories and legends*, with their personal (biographical) or cultic orientation and their folkloric conventions (the youthful precocity, clairvoyance, oratory, miracle-working, etc., predicated of holy men, saints or martyrs; the signs and portents attending their birth, life or death and so on). These were used in preaching, worship and parenesis and were intended to edify believers by, for example, elevating virtues or castigating vices (cf., e.g., Mt. 14.28-33; Mt. 27.3-10 = Acts 1.15-20). Since their character was determined by their purpose and content rather than by their form, tradition criticism, which explores the consecutive stages of the transmission of traditions, has proved in fact a better tool than form criticism in evaluating the degree of historicity adhering to them. A similar difficulty in respect of formal definition adheres to the category of *myths*, which Dibelius, though not Bultmann, defined separately as stories 'which in some fashion tell of many-sided doings of the gods' (*Tradition*, p. 266) and which, though rare in the Gospels, are to be recognized as such in the narratives of Jesus' baptism, temptation and transfiguration.

Also included within the historical stories and legends was the *passion narrative*, which, despite differences as to its pre-Gospel extent and coherence, was acknowledged by earlier form critics as the only type of narrative material issuing from the oral period to have existed in a longer, more continuous narrative form. More recent studies have questioned this view, as we have seen, but have also highlighted the kerygmatic or theological motivations which have coloured the presentation, namely the desire to show that Jesus died as messiah or 'suffering righteous man', that his death had salvific significance and that his passion and resurrection were the fulfilment of Old Testament prophecies.

From a classical form-critical perspective, therefore, the Gospel of Mark consists, in addition to the passion narrative, of an edited collection of a number of these forms, drawn from the oral tradition. In Mark, from the sayings tradition, we have apophthegms (cf., e.g., 2.18-19a; 3.31-35; 12.14-17), wisdom sayings (cf., e.g., 2.21-22; 4.21-22; 8.35-37; 10.31), prophetic and apocalyptic sayings (cf., e.g., 8.38; 9.1; 12.38-40; 13 *passim*), legal sayings and community rules (cf., e.g., 2.27; 9.42; 10.11-12; 10.42-44; 11.25; 12.29-30), christological sayings (cf., e.g., 2.17b, 19b, 20, 28; 10.45) and parables (cf., e.g., 4.1-34; 13.28-29, 34-37). From the narrative tradition, we have miracle stories (cf., e.g., 1.29-31; 7.31-37; 8.22-26; 9.14-27), historical stories and legends (cf., e.g., 11.1-10; 14.12-16) and myths (1.9-11; 1.12-13; 9.2-8).

Form Criticism under Criticism
Form criticism has been of great value in throwing light upon the complex process that brought into being the Gospels and their constituent traditions and it has highlighted the role played by the practical needs of the community in the formation of these traditions. It has helped to establish the now common view that the Gospels are not biographies but kerygmatic works, religious texts written 'out of faith, for faith'. As historical documents they have therefore to be treated with caution. Historical data about Jesus, as I have said, cannot be 'assumed' directly from a Gospel like Mark but has to be 'gleaned' after careful literary and tradition-critical analysis. Despite the apparent scepticism displayed by critics like Bultmann, however, such analysis has yielded fruitful results such as the now common consensus that the historical Jesus underlying the 'sayings' and 'narrative traditions' was essentially a Jewish teacher, prophet and exorcist.

Form criticism itself, however, has been under criticism. While Bultmann's analysis is still influential, critics have pointed to the lack of overall consensus among the form critics themselves as to the classification and *Sitz im Leben* of the forms. The forms as they come to us in the written Gospel are seldom 'pure'. Would we classify Mk 2.1-12 or 3.1-6, for example, as controversy dialogues or miracle stories? The relation of form to *Sitz im Leben* is also more complex than we once thought and the two are not necessarily integrally linked. A particular form may have been transmitted in a specific social setting, and indeed have been affected by its use in such a setting, but the setting itself may not necessarily have generated the form. Form and *Sitz im Leben* may not therefore be an altogether reliable guide to historicity.

Uncertainty has also been registered in respect of the oral transmissional process as understood by classical form criticism, whether in terms of its specific operation, or in terms of its actual operators (or tradents) and their degree of fidelity to what was being transmitted. These doubts have led in some cases to radical criticism of the method, in other cases to further form-critical developments. Form criticism pointed, as we have seen, to the operation of certain 'laws' of oral transmission (e.g. increasing differentiation and individualization) although in fact a number of these tendencies have been shown to have acted in reverse (E.P. Sanders). Form criticism further assumed that the transmissional tendencies at work in our literary texts (e.g. indirect to direct speech) were also true of oral transmission. More recent work has challenged this assumption (E. Güttgemanns, W.H. Kelber) and has highlighted some significant differences between orality and textuality.

Recent form-critical developments have also tended to draw sharper distinctions than classical form critics did between forms having a sociological function within pre-Gospel communities (and therefore a putative *Sitz im Leben*) and those having a purely literary function within the text (and hence no *Sitz im Leben*). Investigation of the latter, upon forms as literary devices, as means of persuasion, has focused on the writer and has led to the development of rhetorical criticism which will be considered in Chapter 3. Research into the forms as sociological entities has focused, on the other hand, on the community and has sought to develop a concrete picture of the technical aspects of oral transmission, especially in respect of its tradents (apostles, disciples, teachers, prophets, story-tellers, etc.) and medium (oral/ aural performance etc.). This has led to the newer discipline of media criticism.

These newer developments are responses to what some would see as the failure of classical form criticism to reconstruct precisely the socio-cultural context in which early Christian tradition was transmitted. Scholarly debate has centred, for example, upon the question whether pre-Gospel traditions as found in Mark were transmitted in a controlled or fluid environment. Some, as we have already noted, would press for a reliable transmissional process, holding that the brevity, relatively speaking, of the oral period and the influence of eye-witnesses would have provided a check upon undue embellishment. Drawing on rabbinic analogies B. Gerhardsson and others have posited the controlled context of the master–disciple relationship (in effect Jesus trained his disciples to memorize his teaching) as the appropriate socio-cultural matrix. Others (e.g. W.H. Kelber), drawing on modern oral studies, have taken an opposing point of view and, in the light of the fluidity of oral transmission revealed by such studies, have questioned whether form criticism's quest for an original or even earlier form of the tradition is a legitimate one.

Kelber indeed has radically questioned the notion that the process that led from oral tradition to Mark's Gospel was an inevitable, collective and evolutionary one, the 'aggregate growth model' assumed by form critics, and has argued that the non-linear and multi-directional nature of oral tradition requires us to posit the composition of Mark as the consequence of an individual act of literary creativity, the result of authorial decision adopting a specific genre. Kelber's critique thus highlights, albeit in a highly sophisticated form, a major weakness of form criticism, namely, that in assigning too creative a role to the anonymous community it has thereby underestimated the contribution of the Gospel writer to the developing Jesus tradition. That the role of the evangelist himself in this process is now widely recognized is due to the impact of redaction criticism, the third literary-historical method and the one to which we shall now turn.

Redaction Criticism and the Editorial Process in Mark

Redaction Criticism in History and Scholarship

Form criticism's estimation of the evangelist as a mere compiler of the tradition and of the Gospel framework as an artificial construction had a number of important effects. It led to scholarly preoccupation with the single units of the Gospel tradition and their prehistory and to consequent neglect of the larger literary context in which they were set. The 'pearls' were of value but the 'string' supplied by the evangelist was of very little worth. Increasing acceptance of the secondary nature of this framework had legitimately underscored the futility of attempts to reconstruct in any detail the course of Jesus' career, but it had also hindered consideration of the extent to which the editorial process could throw light not only on the literary but also on the theological achievement of the Gospel writer. It was the evangelist after all who was responsible for selecting the traditions for inclusion (or for omission) and for arranging them in the order we find them in the Gospel. It was he who had to varying degrees modified, altered, reshaped or even expanded them, and it was he who had given them a chronological, topographical or geographical context (where the tradition had lacked such indications of time or place). A form critic like Bultmann did acknowledge this contribution but his classic and oft-repeated judgment on Markan creativity was that Mark was 'not sufficiently master of his material to be able to venture on a systematic construction himself' (*History*, p. 350). It was therefore, in his words,

> a misconception to infer from Mark's ordering of his material, any con-
> clusions about the chronology and development of the life of Jesus,
> but...for the same reason also false to point out, with very few excep-
> tions, what Mark's leading ideas were (p. 349).

The advent of redaction criticism after the Second World War, however, provided a corrective to this position and led to a gradual re-evaluation of the evangelist's role. The Gospel editor came to be seen increasingly not as a mere transmitter of the tradition to which he was heir, but as one of its first exegetes or interpreters—in other words, as a theologian. By the end of the 1960s, indeed, Gospel composition had come generally to be recognized as more than a 'scissors-and-paste' exercise. 'On the contrary'—to cite one prominent redaction critic— 'the "scissors" were manipulated by a theological hand, and the "paste" was impregnated with a particular theology' (R.H. Stein, 'What is Redaktionsgeschichte', p. 46).

In essence it was this awareness which led to the development of the new discipline. The insight itself was not new, for a creative role for the evangelists' theology in the formulation of the Gospels had been postulated by a number of distinguished scholars before this, among them M. Kähler, W. Wrede, E. Lohmeyer and R.H. Lightfoot. The search for a critical method which might more accurately determine the nature and extent of this theological influence was significantly advanced, however, by the work of the three German scholars referred to in Chapter 1, each of whom worked independently of one another on the Synoptic Gospels: W. Marxsen (on Mark), G. Bornkamm (on Matthew) and H. Conzelmann (on Luke).

In seeking to separate pre-Synoptic tradition from the redaction conducted upon it, all three accepted the method and to a degree the conclusions of form criticism, and to this extent regarded their work as a continuation or extension of that of the form critics. Under form criticism, however, the Gospel tradition was seen as having two possible settings: one in the life of the early church and (if it could be traced back to the primary level) one in the life of the historical Jesus. It was Marxsen's major contribution to suggest that each Gospel saying or narrative had a third setting—one in the thought of each evangelist and, by extension, in the life-situation of that particular Christian community to which or for which he speaks. For Marxsen, the writing of the first Gospel was a unique event, an individualistic act of great significance in which a diverse, fragmented communal tradition was for the first time brought into a creative synthesis by the skill of the Markan redactor. In thus focusing on the evangelist's manipulation of his sources and on the theology which motivated the process, Marxsen opened the way for the flood of literature on the Gospel which appeared from the 1960s onwards, and which has not hitherto abated.

The Aims, Methods and Results of Redaction Criticism on Mark

Although it has tended to broaden out in the last decades into a more general literary criticism, redaction criticism is fundamentally a critical method whose primary aim is to investigate the use made of the sources incorporated into the Gospel. Redaction criticism focuses on the way the evangelist has deliberately adapted (or redacted) these sources to his own theological ends, and is thus concerned with the uniqueness of the evangelist's contribution to the developing tradition. The word 'Redaktor' means 'editor' in German, although the term redaction has come to mean editorial work that is to some degree creative in that it represents 'the conscious reworking of older materials in such a way as to meet new needs' (R.T. Fortna, 'Redaction Criticism', *IDBSup*, p. 733).

Like form criticism, the method is a literary-historical one, as its German equivalent, *Redaktionsgeschichte* or 'redaction history' (first coined by Marxsen) implies. Where form criticism deals with the origin of the Gospel tradition, however, redaction criticism deals with it at the final stage of the Gospel's composition. Where form criticism looks at the oral tradition in all its fragmentation, redaction criticism looks at the process of synthesis conducted by the individual editor upon that tradition. In so doing, it seeks to determine the distinctive theological intention that governed that process and hence ultimately the evangelist's purpose in writing.

In relation to form criticism, redaction criticism can be considered a more holistic method. It seeks to view the Gospel as a literary whole and to discern the overall literary and theological conception which underlies the disposition of its various parts. It is for this reason that it encroaches upon general literary criticism by which indeed it has tended to become increasingly absorbed. N. Perrin defined redaction

criticism as a discipline 'concerned with studying the theological motivation of an author as this is revealed in the collection, arrangement,
editing, and modification of traditional material, and in the composition of new material or the creation of new forms within the traditions of early Christianity' (*Redaction Criticism*, p. 1). By allowing
within his definition the composition (and arrangement) of new material or forms as well as the manipulation and emendation of older
source material, Perrin anticipated the direction in which the discipline was subsequently to move in the 1970s and 1980s, that is, from a
strict 'emendation' or 'editorial criticism' to one that was prepared to
look for and evaluate the evangelist's literary activity more comprehensively.

Were we to confine ourselves, however, to the narrower definition
of redaction criticism (as the investigation of the distinctiveness of the
evangelists in relation to their sources), then it is apparent that Mark
presents special problems, given that his sources have not been identified as precisely as they have in the case of Matthew and Luke. Nevertheless, since Mark has manifestly drawn on oral tradition, the
application of form criticism has served to mitigate this difficulty,
even although the precise form of the pre-Markan tradition cannot be
ascertained with any certainty. The first step in the redaction-critical
method indeed is the same as that already described for form criticism: the separation of traditional material from editorial material, of
source from redaction. Once this is done (as far as is possible), the
redaction critic concentrates on those aspects of the data which throw
light on the editorial process and which provide clues leading to the
evangelist's underlying theological motivations.

A first clue to redactional intentions is offered when account is
taken of the material the evangelist selected for his Gospel (and hence
deliberately chose to include) and a second when account is take of
the way(s) the material selected has been arranged. Further clues
emerge when an analysis is conducted of the specific ways that the
various units of tradition have been linked together to form a connected presentation, for example, by the use of 'seams' (linking sections—words, phrases or sentences—at the beginning or end of
individual pericopes), 'summaries' (general statements summarizing
Jesus' message, activity or popular reactions to it, and linking sections
of the narrative) and even of the introduction and conclusion framing
the entire work. Investigation of the seams and summaries or other
aspects of the editorial framework help in turn to isolate typical features of Markan language, vocabulary, syntax and style, as well as
recurrent motifs, themes, ideas or emphases (e.g. the use of christo-

logical titles). Results gained in this way can then inform or reinforce those gained from observing the internal modifications made in individual pericopes by the evangelist, for example, the additions or insertions made, the settings supplied and so on. Thus by consideration of the selection, arrangement, linkage and internal modification of the units, as well as of other factors (e.g. by comparison with the parallel Matthaean or Lukan text or with what is frankly believable as historical tradition), a profile of the evangelist's editorial activity can be constructed and his theological perspective thereby determined.

Redaction criticism of this narrower kind, with its close links to the form criticism which preceded it, has had some clear if limited results, and these were already anticipated and, in large part, described by Bultmann. His analysis of the editorial process, if not of its significance, in large measure still stands today. The raw material used by the evangelist, as we have seen, comprised the isolated, self-contained pericopes (or small clusters of pericopes) of the oral tradition (both 'sayings' and 'narrative'). These have been selected, arranged and linked together—for the most part artificially—to form, in combination with the passion narrative, the first connected Gospel. The individual materials appear in certain main groupings and give evidence therefore of a topical arrangement (created either by Mark or the tradition before him). Miracle stories appear mostly in the first half of the Gospel in the sections 1.21–2.12, 4.35–5.43, 6.35-52 and 7.24–8.10, 22-26 (though note also the single stories in 3.1-6, 9.16-27 and 11.12-14, 20ff.). Controversy stories are found in the sections 2.1–3.6, 3.20-35, 7.1-23 and 11.27–12.40 (though compare also single pericopes such as 10.2-9) and parables in 4.1-34 (though note, for example, the isolated parable in 12.1-11). Teaching on discipleship is concentrated in 8.27–10.45 and that on the future in ch. 13. The various dominical sayings and stories are moreover presented within a loose overall geographical framework, the first five chapters (1.14–5.43) being set in Galilee, the next four (6.1–9.50) in Galilee and the surrounding Galilean area (the northern journey), the tenth on a journey to Judaea and Jerusalem (10.1-52) and the remaining chapters (11–16) in Jerusalem and its environs.

While it is not always entirely clear which editorial links were supplied by Mark rather than the tradition before him, coherence at a narrative level can be seen to be achieved by a number of simple connecting devices (especially in the seams). Individual pericopes are frequently linked by the conjunction *and* or *and immediately* (cf., e.g., 1.16, 21, 23, 29, 35, 40; 2.1, 15; etc.) or by the adverb *again* (cf., e.g., 2.13;

3.1; 4.1; etc.). Narrative progression is also achieved by the use of certain regular verbs of motion (he or they *came/went* into, out, up, away,
etc.; *entered/left, withdrew, returned* and so on as in 1.14, 16, 21, 29, 35,
40; 2.1, 13; 3.1, 7, 13, 19b; etc.). While precise geographical references
(some possibly traditional) are often given (cf. 6.53; 7.24, 31; 8.10, 22,
27; 10.46), the tradition's silence on numerous occasions has led the
editor to supply various loose and indefinite temporal or spatial references (e.g. *in those days* or *from there*; cf. 1.9; 2.1; 6.1; 7.24; 8.1; 9.30; 10.1).
Originally unconnected sayings likewise are found linked by the
simple conjunction *for* (e.g. 8.35, 36, 37, 38; 9.40, 41, 49) by catchword
connection (cf., e.g., the catchword *life* linking 8.35, 36, 37; *salt* linking
9.49, 50 or *prayer* linking 11.23, 24, 25) or, where larger sayings com-
plexes are in view, by such simple formulae as *and he said to them* (cf.,
e.g., 4.2, 11, 21, 24). Groups of pericopes are linked by (previously
described) summary passages (cf., e.g., 1.21-22; 1.39; 2.13; 4.1; 6.6b, 30-
34; etc.) which as well as summarizing Jesus' typical behaviour as a
teacher and exorcist serve to create a bridge between one section of
the narrative and the next. The evangelist is also fond of dovetailing
or interlacing one pericope with another (cf., e.g., 5.21-24, 25-34, 35-
43), a 'sandwiching' device (*intercalation*) which I shall consider further in Chapter 3 when discussing his literary technique.

Considerable research has been done in recent years into Markan
language, vocabulary, syntax and style, although a firm consensus in
respect of these has still not been reached. Some scholars have argued,
on the basis of syntactical and stylistic Semitisms, that the Gospel was
originally composed in a Semitic language (most likely Hebrew) and
then translated into Greek. This is not, however, a necessary hypothesis since Semitisms, which are not always clearly identifiable as such
(similar locutions may be possible in non-biblical Hellenistic Greek),
may simply reflect an author who thought in Hebrew or Aramaic (but
who wrote in Greek) or the use of a tradition (especially of Jesus'
sayings) which was only in its primary stage transmitted in a Semitic
linguistic medium. Two recent studies on Markan Semitisms indeed
have come to apparently contradictory conclusions on this question.
Maloney, using contemporaneous control documents, identifies several types of Semitisms in Mark and is of the opinion that syntactical
Semitic interference permeates every page of the Gospel. Reiser, on
the other hand, using somewhat later Greek parallels, concludes that
Mark is largely free of Semitisms.

Pursuit of a reasonably definite profile of the evangelist's characteristic vocabulary, syntax and style, one that would in turn enable
scholars to establish the redactional text of Mark (a text highlighting

the editorial elements), has been hampered by the difficulty of determining in every case whether particular linguistic usages are in fact
editorial or whether they belong to the source employed. On the basis
of such criteria as their frequency, their presence in seams, insertions
or summary passages or their avoidance by Matthew or Luke, a number of words or phrases have been taken to be characteristic of Mark.
Such words or phrases include, for example: and (*kai* instead of *de*),
immediately (*euthus*), again (*palin*), house (*oikos/oikia*), synagogue (*sun-
agoge*), mountain (*oros*), crowd (*ochlos*), disciple (*mathetes*), he called
(*proskaleisthai*) them to him, and he said to them (*kai elegen autois*), to
begin to (*archesthai*), to teach (*didaskein*), to see (*blepein*), to hear (*akouein*),
to follow (*akolouthein*), to look around (*periblepesthai*), secretly (*kat' idian*).

Similarly, among Mark's characteristic syntactical and stylist features (although often disguised in English translation) may be counted
parataxis (simple consecutive linkage of clauses and sentences by the
use of 'and'; cf., e.g., 1.21 [2×], 22, 23, 24, 25 [2×], 26, 27 [2×], 28), *asyn-
deta* (a lack of connecting links such as particles or conjunctions: so,
therefore, but, etc.) and *anacoloutha* (broken or incomplete constructions, e.g. 11.32). Also typical is the use of the historic present (e.g.
'and they come [came] to Bethsaida', 8.22), two or more participles,
before or after the main verb (e.g. 'Jesus came…preaching…and saying', 1.14-15; 'turning and seeing…he rebuked', 8.33), the verb to be
(*einai*) with a participle for the imperfect ('were fasting', 2.18), impersonal plurals (the use of a plural verb with no definite subject, e.g.
'and they came bringing to him a paralytic', 2.3), double negatives
('say nothing to nobody', 1.44) as well as frequent repetitions, duplications or *pleonasms* (redundant expressions, e.g. 'was silent and made
no answer', 14.61).

One particularly prominent editorial feature is the evangelist's internal modification of pericopes through the use of parenthetical statements which interrupt the Greek in various ways whether as an
afterthought (e.g. 2.15b; 6.14b-15; 16.4b), to provide explanation for
the reader (e.g. 3.21b, 30; 7.3-4, 19c; 13.14b; 16.8c), to supply an Old
Testament quotation (e.g. 1.2-3; 7.6-7; 14.27) or to offer translations of
foreign words (esp. Aramaic; e.g. 3.17c; 5.41b; 7.11, 34; 12.42b; 14.36;
15.16b, 34).

Reference has already been made to recent work on Markan Semitisms. Comparative linguistic analysis of the kind which has under-
girded such studies has also led to some reappraisal of certain of
Mark's so-called syntactical or stylistic 'idiosyncrasies' or 'peculiari-
ties'. According to one study (C.D. Osburn), for example, Mark's use
of the historic present, usually considered a vernacularism, may not

differ from that of Plato, Xenophon or the Septuagint, namely, to denote a semantic shift from one type of material to another, to set the stage for an event narrated entirely with past tense verbs, and to mark the main features of an account.

One convergent result of recent research into Markan language, vocabulary, syntax and style has been a strong impression of the linguistic unity or homogeneity of the Gospel text. Mark's linguistic fingerprints are to be found everywhere in the Gospel, and Neirynck has argued that duality (a collective term incorporating such features as repetitions, duplications and pleonasms) is a homogeneous feature of Mark's style and cannot therefore be relied upon necessarily as a pointer to his incorporation of sources. Once again the difficulty of separating source from redaction in the Gospel and hence of establishing a redactional text of Mark is highlighted.

If the linguistic nature of the Gospel has cast some methodological doubts on the redaction critic's ability to apply a strict 'emendation' criticism to the text, then the broader application of the method which seeks to identify recurrent motifs, themes and interests of concern to the evangelist has proved in the end more popular and, in many respects, more rewarding. A gathering scholarly consensus would now probably identify the following as of prime importance, therefore, in determining Mark's theological purpose insofar as it can be garnered from his redactional activity (it is worth listing these now, but we shall be taking them up later in Chapters 4 and 5, when we examine the evangelist's theology and the *Sitz im Leben* of the Gospel):

1. the secrecy motif and the writer's interest in the true but hidden identity of Jesus;
2. an interest in the passion of Jesus (his suffering, death and resurrection) and its significance for Christology;
3. an interest in the nature and coming of the Kingdom of God and in the question of Jesus' return as Son of Man;
4. an interest in Galilee;
5. his use of the term 'gospel' (*euangelion*);
6. an interest in Gentiles and the Gentile mission;
7. an interest in persecution, suffering and martyrdom and the true nature of discipleship;
8. his harsh treatment of the Jewish leadership groups, Jesus' family and especially his original disciples.

Redaction Criticism under Criticism
The primary aim of redaction criticism, as we have seen, has been to

apply a scalpel to the individual components of the tradition in order to expose the editorial process which brought these into an overall literary and theological synthesis. The importance of redaction criticism as a literary-historical tool has therefore been considerable. Building essentially on the work of source and form criticism, it has highlighted the use made by the evangelist of his sources and has illuminated our understanding of his contribution to the developing tradition. In particular it has focused attention on the evangelist as the author of a literary product and has emphasized further the theological character of his Gospel. It has also sought to contribute to our understanding of the socio-historical context of the Gospel writer and that of his community. Given also its holistic treatment of the text, it can therefore be seen as a comprehensive method with multiple concerns (historical, theological, literary, sociological).

The application of the method, however, is based on certain assumptions which have, to varying degrees, been challenged. At least in its narrower definition (emendation-criticism), redaction criticism is based strictly on assumptions made about the sources used by Mark, and proceeds by attempting to correlate the changes introduced into these sources with an emerging profile of the evangelist's outlook or theology. Some opponents have claimed, therefore, that redaction criticism is not possible on Mark because his sources cannot be definitively isolated. Linguistic studies of the Gospel, for example, have proved an uncertain guide to date in isolating these, given the text's stylistic homogeneity. Others have argued that continuity with the tradition is as important as discontinuity, since what the evangelist decided to include, and may even have included unaltered, may be just as significant a pointer to his concerns as the changes that he introduced. Others still have criticized redaction criticism for overemphasis on the theological character of the Markan redaction with consequent downplaying of other factors or motives governing the editorial process (such as clumsiness, artlessness or sheer lack of skill!). A major criticism of the discipline concerns its dependence on presuppositions regarding the history of the traditions underlying Mark and hence its appeal to extrinsic factors lying outwith the text for its interpretation. Some critics have decried the speculative nature of its reconstructions, therefore, and the lack of consensus in its results.

The inability of scholars to delineate the precise sources (written or oral) on which to establish their understanding of the Markan redaction has led to the widening of the criteria for determining his religious outlook. It has become increasingly agreed, indeed, that summary passages, seams, insertions or modifications or pericopes are an inadequate base for developing a full picture of Mark's style or theology. For this reason a source-editing approach has come to be amplified, if not eclipsed, by analysis of recurrent motifs, themes or interests in the Gospel.

Such broadening of the redaction-critical method, however, has brought it into the field of general literary criticism and hence within the range of dehistoricizing methods and approaches which undermine its validity as a literary-historical method. Mark's theology is to be reached, some have argued, not by seeking to document his modifications of tradition but by studying the Gospel in its entirety. As a result, the borderline between redaction criticism as a tradition-critical method (with a diachronic perspective) and redaction-criticism as a literary-aesthetic discipline (with a synchronic perspective) has become increasingly blurred. Much that passes for redaction criticism, some critics claim, is actually literary criticism. The identification of the Markan motifs, themes and interests listed in the previous section owes as much, if not more, to the application of general literary criticism as it does to a strict 'emendation criticism'.

A series of objections has therefore been raised against the method from a literary-aesthetic perspective. Literary critics have taken it to task for its persistent misplacement of the author (and not the text) at the centre of textual interpretation despite the acknowledged difficulty of establishing the writer's purpose in writing (or 'authorial intention'). The meaning of a text is not given, it is argued, by the author's intention (the intentional fallacy). Mark is a narrative first and foremost and (at least in the first instance) should be treated as such. Another charge laid against it recently has been that of 'methodological imperialism', its detractors (e.g. C.C. Black) accusing it of seeking to hold within its ambit a plethora of historical, theological, literary and sociological issues and concerns which its limited apparatus is not designed to handle.

Redaction criticism is a discipline in tension with itself, seeking to remain a historical method but struggling in particular to come to terms with the literary aspects of its source material. It has tried to reconcile both dimensions and that is its strength as well as its weakness. The differing perspectives of the historical and literary approaches with which it operates have increasingly sought to pull it in radically opposite directions. Insofar as it has remained close to form criticism (and hence treated the text strictly as a redaction) it has come into conflict with the newer literary criticism which has sought to understand the text in its own (undivided) right and as the literary and theological achievement of an individual. Insofar as it has moved closer to literary criticism (and hence treated the text as a narration) it has been drawn into ever greater conflict with form criticism which understands the text as an edited collection of socially conditioned community traditions.

The differences in these perspectives centre upon the question of creativity, the extent to which Mark is believed to have been a master of his material, as well as upon the particular model that is envisaged for the process of Gospel composition. Some, following Bultmann (e.g. R. Pesch, E. Best), would not wish to credit the evangelist with too much masterful control, preferring to see the tradition exerting a stronger influence in the Gospel than the conservative editor who compiled it. Best, for example, asks us to consider Mark not so much as an author but as 'an artist creating a collage' and warns us against looking for a consistent or coherent theology, or theologies, from the evangelist 'since he laid his theology over an existing theology, or the-ologies, in the tradition he received' ('Mark's Preservation', in Telford, *Interpretation of Mark*, pp. 163-64). Others following the newer criticism (e.g. N. Perrin, R.C. Tannehill, W.H. Kelber, J.D. Crossan, F. Kermode, R.M. Fowler) would point to the literary evidence in the text which appears to contradict this impression and argue for Mark as a *bona fide* narrator, exercising a considerable literary and theological creativity.

The issue has not in the end been satisfactorily resolved as is dem-onstrated by the different attitudes to Markan creativity exemplified in three of the major German commentaries (Gnilka, Pesch, Schmit-hals) noted at the end of Chapter 1. The debate has raised the question, for example, whether Mark himself composed entire peri-copes. Some (like Best) would reject this possibility, others (like Cros-san) would accept it, others (like Fowler) would claim that Mark used some stories in the tradition as a model for creating others (e.g. 8.1-10 for 6.30-44 or 10.13-16 for 9.36-37). The issue has also expressed itself in terms of the question whether the Gospel of Mark is to be consid-ered an evolutionary document (i.e. a text organically related to and in continuity with the oral formulations of the Jesus tradition which pre-ceded it) or as a revolutionary one (i.e. in its innovative adoption of 'textuality' a radical departure from the pre-Markan tradition with significant consequences for the development of Christianity).

Modern debate upon the Gospel highlights, therefore, the compli-cated interrelationship that exists between the historical, literary and theological dimensions of this fascinating first-century text. In this chapter, I have raised questions about how the Gospel is to be under-stood and reviewed a number of the ways in which it has been interpreted over the last two centuries. We have focused in particular on the Gospel as a historical document, the end-point of a complex process in which the oral traditions about Jesus which were transmitted by early Christian communities have come to literary expression at the hands of the evangelists. While the Gospel can no longer be considered the product of direct and reliable eyewitness report, it can nevertheless yield valuable historical information when used in conjunction with certain of the tools of modern biblical criticism. Three of the most prominent and productive of the traditio-historical methods used on Mark have been examined—source, form and redaction criticism— and their aims, methods and results as well as their limitations have been highlighted. Each in its own way has helped to build up a picture of the pre-history of the text, in terms of the sources employed, the forms taken by the pre-Markan tradition and the editing conducted upon them. By enabling us to form some assessment of the contribution of both the evangelist and the early church to the developing Jesus tradition, they have permitted us, to some extent, to make a journey back in time, 'behind' or 'beyond' the text to the historical Jesus whose mark has been left upon the tradition itself and whose teaching and activity have inspired it. They have also supplied criteria by which we might judge the authenticity of the various components of that tradition.

Noted also, however, has been the point of view of those who would call for a more holistic approach to the Gospel and who would resist pulling the text apart in the way that such diachronic methods do. A number of voices have cast doubt indeed on the very possibility of reconstructing the pre-history of the Gospel or at least of practising such methods without a knowledge of how texts operate as literary texts and without recourse, therefore, to general linguistics or literary criticism. Interest has shifted significantly, therefore, in recent years from seeing the Gospel of Mark as a window into history to examining its own inner narrative world irrespective of the process that brought it into being or the socio-political or other historical factors that gave it birth. It is to the second of these aspects of the Gospel, then, that we shall now turn, namely to the Gospel of Mark as a literary composition.

FURTHER READING

On the Markan Prologue, see:

J. Drury, 'Mark 1.1-15: an Interpretation', in A.E. Harvey (ed.), *Alternative Approaches to New Testament Study* (London: SPCK, 1985), pp. 25-36.
R.A. Guelich, '"The Beginning of the Gospel". Mark 1.1-15', *BibRes* 27 (1982), pp. 5-15.
F.J. Matera, 'The Prologue as the Interpretative Key to Mark's Gospel', in Telford (ed.) *Interpretation of Mark*, pp. 289-306.

Among classic discussions of the problem of history in Mark may be counted the following:

C.H. Dodd, 'The Framework of the Gospel Narrative', *ExpTim* 43 (1931–32), pp. 396-400.
D.E. Nineham, 'The Order of Events in St. Mark's Gospel — An Examination of Dr. Dodd's Hypothesis', in D.E. Nineham (ed.), *Studies in the Gospels* (Festschrift R.H. Lightfoot; Oxford: Basil Blackwell, 1957), pp. 223-39.
—'Eye-witness Testimony and the Gospel Tradition', *JTS* 9 (1958), pp. 13-25, 243-52 and 11 (1960), pp. 253-64.
J.M. Robinson, *The Problem of History in Mark* (SBT, 21; London: SCM Press, 1957); reprinted in *The Problem of History in Mark and other Marcan Studies* (Philadelphia: Fortress Press, 1982).
E. Schweizer, 'Mark's Contribution to the Quest of the Historical Jesus', *NTS* 10 (1963–64), pp. 421-32 (highlights the kerygmatic purpose of the Gospel).

On source criticism and Mark's sources, see:

Classic but now dated treatments of the subject area found in

A.T. Cadoux, *The Sources of the Synoptic Gospel* (London: James Clarke, 1935).
W.L. Knox, *The Sources of the Synoptic Gospels*, I (Cambridge: Cambridge University Press, 1963).

Taylor's commentary gives a review of these and other older source critics and theories. Helpful and more recent discussion is available in the newer commentaries, especially Anderson, as well as in special studies such as

A.J. Bellinzoni *et al.* (eds.), *The Two-Source Hypothesis: A Critical Approach* (Macon, GA: Mercer University Press, 1985).
P.M. Casey, *Aramaic Sources of Mark's Gospel* (SNTSMS, 102; Cambridge, UK: Cambridge University Press, 1998).
H.C. Kee, *Community of the New Age* (Philadelphia: Westminster Press, 1977), pp. 30-49.
E. Trocmé, *The Formation of the Gospel According to Mark* (London: SPCK, 1975), ch. 1.

On Mark and the extra-canonical Gospels, see:

J.D. Crossan, *Four Other Gospels, Shadows on the Contours of Canon* (Minneapolis: Winston Press, 1985).

H. Koester, 'History and the Development of Mark's Gospel (From Mark to Secret Mark and "Canonical" Mark)', in B. Corley (ed.), *Colloquy on New Testament Studies: A Time for Reappraisal and Fresh Approaches* (Macon, GA: Mercer University Press, 1983), pp. 35-57.

F. Neirynck, 'The Apocryphal Gospels and the Gospel of Mark', *BETL* 86 (1989), pp. 123-75; repr. *Evangelica II* (ed. F. van Segbroeck; Leuven: Leuven University Press/Peeters, 1991), pp. 715-72.

M. Smith, *Clement of Alexandria and a Secret Gospel of Mark* (Cambridge, MA: Harvard University Press, 1973).

—*The Secret Gospel: The Discovery and Interpretation of the Secret Gospel According to Mark* (New York: Harper & Row, 1973; repr. Wellingborough: Aquarius Press, 1985).

—'Clement of Alexandria and Secret Mark: The Score at the End of the First Decade', *HTR* 75 (1982), pp. 449-61.

On form criticism and the forms in Mark see the seminal works of classical form criticism:

R. Bultmann, *The History of the Synoptic Tradition* (trans. J. Marsh; Oxford: Basil Blackwell, 1968).

M. Dibelius, *From Tradition to Gospel* (trans. B.I. Woolf; London: Ivor Nicholson & Watson, 1934).

K.L. Schmidt, *Der Rahmen der Geschichte Jesu* (Berlin: Trowitzsch & Sohn, 1919).

Helpful treatments can also be found as before in the commentaries (especially Nineham and Anderson), dictionaries and New Testament introductions (especially Fuller, and Duling and Perrin).

For a critique of form criticism, see:

E. Güttgemanns, *Candid Questions concerning Gospel Form Criticism* (trans. W.G. Doty; PTMS, 26; Pittsburgh, PA: Pickwick Press, 1979).

W.H. Kelber, *The Oral and Written Gospel: The Hermeneutics of Speaking and Writing in the Synoptic Tradition, Mark, Paul and Q* (Voices in Performance and Text; Bloomington: Indiana University Press, 1997).

J.C. Meagher, *Clumsy Construction in Mark's Gospel: A Critique of Form- and Redaktionsgeschichte* (Toronto Studies in Theology, 3; New York/Toronto: Edwin Mellen Press, 1979).

E.P. Sanders, *The Tendencies of the Synoptic Tradition* (SNTSMS, 9; Cambridge: Cambridge University Press, 1969).

On redaction criticism and the editorial process in Mark, see:

W. Marxsen, *Mark the Evangelist: Studies on the Redaction History of the Gospel* (trans. J. Boyce *et al.*; Nashville: Abingdon Press, 1969). The classic redaction-critical treatment of the Synoptic Gospels.

In addition, helpful introductions to the method are given by:

N. Perrin, *What is Redaction Criticism?* (London: SPCK, 1970).
R.H. Stein, 'What is Redaktionsgeschichte?', *JBL* 88 (1969), pp. 45-56.
—'The Proper Methodology for Ascertaining a Markan Redaction History', *NovT* 13 (1971), pp. 181-98.

On Markan language and redactional style, see:

E. Best, 'Mark's Presentation of the Tradition', in Telford (ed.), *Interpretation of Mark*, pp. 153-68.
J.C. Doudna, *The Greek of the Gospel of Mark* (JBL Monograph Series, 1.2; Philadelphia: SBL, 1961).
J.C. Hawkins, *Horae Synopticae* (Oxford: Clarendon Press, 2nd edn, 1909 [1899]).
E.C. Maloney, *Semitic Interference in Marcan Syntax* (SBLDS, 41; Chico, CA: Scholars Press, 1981).
F. Neirynck, *Duality in Mark: Contributions to the Study of the Marcan Redaction* (BETL, 31; Leuven: Leuven University Press/Peeters, 1988).
C.D. Osburn, 'The Historical Present in Mark as a Text-Critical Indicator', *Bib* 64 (1983), pp. 486-500.
D.B. Peabody, *Mark as Composer* (New Gospel Studies, 1; Macon, GA: Mercer University Press, 1987).
E.J. Pryke, *Redactional Style in the Marcan Gospel* (SNTSMS, 33; Cambridge: Cambridge University Press, 1978).
M. Reiser, *Syntax und Stil der Markusevangeliums im Licht der hellenistischen Volksliteratur* (WUNT, 2.2; Tübingen: Mohr [Paul Siebeck], 1984).
E. Schweizer, 'Mark's Theological Achievement', in Telford (ed.), *Interpretation of Mark*, pp. 63-87.
C.H. Turner, 'Marcan Usage: Notes, Critical and Exegetical, on the Second Gospel', *JTS* 25 (1923–24), pp. 378-86; 26 (1924–25), pp. 12-20, 145-56, 225-40, 337-46; 27 (1925–26), pp. 58-62; 28 (1926–27), pp. 9-30, 349-62; 29 (1927–28), pp. 275-89, 346-61.

On Mark as an oral narrative, see, for example:

E. Best, 'Mark's Narrative Technique', *JSNT* 37 (1989), pp. 43-58.
J. Dewey, 'Oral Methods of Structuring Narrative in Mark', *Int* 43 (1989), pp. 38-44.

For a critique of redaction criticism, see:

C.C. Black, *The Disciples According to Mark: Markan Redaction in Current Debate* (JSNTSup, 27; Sheffield: JSOT Press, 1989).

Chapter Three

MARK AS LITERATURE:
THE GOSPEL AS A LITERARY COMPOSITION

Literary Approaches to Mark

Genre Criticism

To view Mark as literature and not as history or theology means that we must adopt a different perspective from that which sees the Gospel primarily as a historical document or a religious text. To regard it as a literary composition requires us to take it seriously both as the product of a literary process and, in turn, as the producer of a literary effect. It means that we must consider Mark's achievement as an author rather than confine ourselves solely to his value as a historian or a theologian, and it means that we must consider his text in relation to the reader rather than of necessity to the historical or theological situation from which it emerged. The hallmarks of a purely literary approach of this kind have been commented upon already. Literary approaches tend to treat the text holistically rather than atomistically (ways which disintegrate or fragment the text). A number have a synchronic emphasis, that is, one directed to the text's final form, interrelationships and effects without regard to the (diachronic) process which brought it into being in the first place. They explore issues and questions relating, for example, to the text's literary type, the author's style or point of view or the reader's construction of meaning. Some indication of their general approach to the text has already been given in Chapters 1 and 2 as well as some distinctions between them (e.g. literary-historical versus literary-aesthetic emphases). Since there is considerable variety and complexity in these newer approaches, I shall select six (genre criticism, composition criticism, rhetorical criticism, narrative criticism, reader-response criticism, structuralism) and say a little briefly about each before going on to indicate what they have revealed about the Gospel of Mark.

Genre criticism, or *Gattungsgeschichte*, the term often employed in German scholarship, is a discipline which investigates texts in relation to their literary type, category or genre. The term genre is applied to a particular text as a whole (e.g. history, biography, tragedy, comedy, or to give biblical examples, epistle, apocalypse or gospel) and with reference to other texts which share the same traits. The genre of a text is determined by factors such as content, form, style and function, although, given their fluid nature, any instance of a particular genre may depart in certain respects from its ideal or universal type. Insofar as literary genres are usually, though not exclusively, rooted in a particular socio-cultural milieu, genre criticism can be considered a literary-historical method and this is confirmed by the fact that it makes its appeal to extrinsic factors (other texts of a similar type) in interpreting its subject matter. One aim of genre criticism on the Gospel of Mark, for example, is to identify its literary environment as well as literary type and to place it within the history of ancient literature. On the other hand, genre criticism can be seen as a holistic and synchronic exercise when compared with a diachronic one such as form criticism. In dealing with a larger unit (the Gospel) and in asking after the literary antecedents or models for the Gospel text in its entirety, it can be contrasted with form criticism which examines the pre-literary antecedents of the Gospel in respect of its component parts (e.g. apophthegms, proverbs, parables, miracle-stories) and seeks to determine their independent pre-history, social setting and function. Since whole texts as well as their component parts need to be understood in light of their context, the identification of genre is a vital preliminary guide to interpretation. Each genre has its own conventions which influence (though do not bind) authors as they write and, by creating expectations, direct readers in their construction of the text's meaning. As we shall see below, a variety of genres have been suggested for Mark, each of which alters our overall understanding of it.

Composition Criticism
Although it has not achieved the status of a precisely defined discipline within New Testament studies, composition criticism (or *Kompositionsgeschichte*) is a literary-historical method on the borderline between redaction criticism and the other literary approaches described in this section. While some would use it as a general category encompassing all or most of these approaches, others would consider it as one of three categories of redaction criticism (of which the other two would be editorial or emendation criticism and literary criticism). By embracing indicators of the evangelist's literary and theological concerns other than the narrower criteria of source editing, composition criticism represents a broadening of redaction criticism in the

direction of a more general literary criticism. Because of the part played by the evangelist in constructing or composing his Gospel, the term *Kompositionsgeschichte* was preferred by E. Haenchen over *Redaktionsgeschichte* and his terminology has been accepted by students of Perrin (e.g. J.R. Donahue) as well as others (e.g. S.E. Dowd). Where redaction criticism, narrowly conceived, focuses on the editing of the sources, composition criticism focuses on the way the evangelist has assembled diverse materials into a meaningful structure whose form reflects his theology. Like redaction criticism, it is a holistic method which examines the text as a whole to ascertain what concerns motivated its composition and what compositional procedures were employed by the evangelist.

Certain elements make it distinctive. It takes due account of the evangelist's traditional material as well as the changes he has made to his sources. It recognizes his compositional activity in composing both from tradition and *de novo*. It pays particular attention to the structure of the Gospel, seeking to identify its constituent units and to determine how they are arranged and what significance they have in their literary context. It examines the author's compositional techniques, looking for evidence of linear and concentric ('sandwich') patterning (e.g. triadism, the grouping of units in sequences of three, or montage, the juxtaposition of units to suggest meaning by association or chiasmus, inclusio or intercalation which I shall comment on below). The composition critic is also on the lookout for recurrent themes or motifs or other such factors which give coherence to the Markan text (prospective and retrospective devices, narrative interlockings, thematic cross-references, topographical and geographical settings etc.). One area of investigation which has thrown light (and provided checks) on these processes has been ancient Greek rhetoric, and especially what it reveals about how writers of Mark's day were educated and taught to compose as well as persuade. Such study overlaps with rhetorical criticism, our next literary method.

Rhetorical Criticism
Rhetoric is defined by G.A. Kennedy in his *New Testament Interpretation through Rhetorical Criticism* (1984) as 'that quality in discourse by which a speaker or writer seeks to accomplish his purposes' (p. 3). Kennedy describes three of the traditional forms of ancient rhetoric which were designed to elicit certain responses or create certain effects: judicial (with judgment in view), deliberative (with action in view) and epideictic (with praise or blame, or with assent or dissent in view). Rhetorical criticism, therefore, when applied to texts, is a

method which examines the literary strategies employed by an author to guide, persuade or manipulate his readers. Like composition criticism, it also attempts to clarify our understanding of a text as a whole through a study of its literary techniques and structure. Unlike composition criticism, it is less interested in the ways the text has been assembled and more interested in how it achieves its effect. Texts are seen as instruments of persuasion and rhetorical criticism, in J.I.H. McDonald's words, 'provides access to the purposive and persuasive nature of the author's utterance' ('Rhetorical Criticism', *DBI*, p. 600). The method is literary-aesthetic insofar as it explores the ways the author and/or text achieve their effects and literary-historical insofar as it seeks to relate these effects to ancient rhetorical techniques (compare the socio-rhetorical criticism of B.L. Mack and V.K. Robbins). It has obvious links too with the other methods we have discussed. Indeed, in many ways it bridges the gap between the older literary-historical methods and the newer literary criticism. Rhetorical criticism 'reaches beyond form criticism to the individual text as rhetorical unit and examines both its structure and the configuration of its component parts' (McDonald, p. 599, citing J. Muilenburg).

Rhetorical criticism then is a holistic method which, unlike form and redaction criticism, does not seek to separate the text into tradition and redaction.

> Rhetorical criticism takes the text as we have it, whether the work of a simple author or the product of editing, and looks at it from the point of view of the author's or editor's intent, the unified results, and how it would be perceived by an audience of near contemporaries (Kennedy, *New Testament Interpretation*, p. 4).

Kennedy's methodology, as summarized by McDonald, consists of five interrelated stages: determining the rhetorical unit, examining the rhetorical situation and problem, considering the rhetorical arrangement of the text, analysing the devices of style, and reviewing the whole unit as a response to the rhetorical situation. One key proponent of rhetorical analysis has been J. Dewey who defines it as 'the study of the literary techniques and rhetorical structure of a text to see what light such analysis sheds on the interrelationships of the parts of the text and the meaning of the text as a whole' (*Markan Public Debate*, p. 1). Dewey's work on Mk 2.1–3.6, which is akin to composition criticism, has been valuable in providing objective criteria by which we may draw inferences from rhetorical patterns.

Narrative Criticism

Also concerned with literary structure and techniques and their influence upon the reader is another literary approach which is gaining ground in biblical studies, namely, narrative criticism. Narrative is a form of discourse which involves characters, a plot (a chronological sequence of episodes causally connected), a 'narrative world' (a space-time continuum in which the characters engage one another), a narrator (who relates the story), an implied author (a textual construct who may not be the same as either the narrator or the actual author) and an implied reader (the equivalent textual construct to whom the account is ostensibly given). Narrative figures prominently within the Bible and has its own special features (e.g. characterization is usually subordinated to action and there is paucity of description, comment, analysis or psychologizing). According to R.C. Tannehill,

> Narrative criticism is a method of interpreting biblical narratives with the help of modern and ancient literary theory. It approaches the biblical narrative not as a historical source for what lies behind the text but as a literary text which may be analysed in literary terms (plot, characterization, point of view in narration etc.) like other works of literature. Narrative criticism tends to view the narrative as an interactive whole, with harmonies and tensions that develop in the course of narration…Therefore, the significance of a narrative scene cannot be judged without understanding its function within the narrative development as a whole ('Narrative Criticism', *DBI*, p. 488).

The method is a holistic and literary-aesthetic one, therefore, with an 'ahistorical' emphasis. It avoids the fragmentation of the text as well as the use of extrinsic factors in interpreting it, namely hypothetical constructions derived from data outside of the text.

Narrative critics see the Gospel of Mark as a unified narrative within a 'closed and self-sufficient world with its own integrity' (Rhoads and Michie, *Mark as Story*, p. 4).

> At the levels of narrator, plot, characterisation, theology and literary style one can discover a unity and integrity in the gospel that makes it both appropriate and necessary to study the work as a genuine narrative, as a single, coherent, intelligible story (C.D. Marshall, *Faith*, p. 26).

Where source criticism tends to see gaps, ambiguities, repetitions and discrepancies in the text as 'aporias' pointing to sources, narrative criticism is inclined to regard these as literary strategies to excite the reader's interest or imagination. Where form criticism sees Mark as a collector, and redaction criticism as a redactor, narrative criticism sees Mark as a genuine author. While composition criticism preserves redaction criticism's interest in the theology of the evangelist, moreover, narrative criticism focuses much more on the general narrative properties of the text. Its interest in the rhetoric of the text, as with rhetorical criticism, is only part, however, of a wider enterprise. Narrative criticism differentiates two aspects of the text: the 'story' and the 'discourse', or the 'what' and the 'how' of narrative.

> The 'what' is the *story*, apart from how it is told, including: the chain of story events (stated or implied by the narrator in chronological order), the characters, and the details of setting. The 'how' of the narrative is the *discourse*, the particular way in which a given story is told, including: the arrangement of events in the plot, the type of narrator, point of view, style and rhetorical devices (Rhoads, 'Narrative Criticism', p. 412, citing S. Chatman).

Such ways of looking at Mark are very helpful, although critics of this approach (as well as the other holistic literary approaches discussed) tend to fault it for too easily dismissing the evidence of incoherence in the text and for exaggerating the evangelist's narrative and rhetorical skills.

Reader-Response Criticism

Literary communication is an act which involves an author, a text and a reader. Where narrative criticism focuses on the text, its sister discipline, reader-response criticism (audience criticism) or reception theory centres on the reader and the reading process. Reader-response criticism accords the reader a creative role in the interpretative process. Texts do not make meaning, some of its proponents claim, readers do. It provides a language or models in and through which the reading experience can be critically analysed. It analyses the text the way the reader reads the text, that is, as a continuous whole and not (unless the reader is also a scholar) in light of the prehistory of its various bits. The interpretation of the text is determined, therefore, by textual clues which the reader gains progressively from the process of reading and not by knowledge of the origin of the text's component parts prior to their incorporation in the narrative.

> Reception theory...or reader-response criticism...expects the reader to form the text into a coherent whole...assumes that texts are open to more than one meaning and that readers may be more competent at construing some kinds of texts than others (M. Davies, 'Reader-Response Criticism', *DBI*, p. 579).

Reader-response approaches vary. Some purely literary-aesthetic forms are only interested in the 'ideal' reader 'in' the text ('the reader encoded by the text's strategies', Davies). Others, investigating how ancient readers actually read texts, focus on the reception of the text by its original readership, and hence retain a historical interest. Where Mark is concerned, reader-response criticism has been instrumental, as with both rhetorical and narrative criticism, in illuminating the literary strategies (e.g. opacity, intertextual allusion, ambiguity, verbal and dramatic irony, unanswered rhetorical questions, the use of 'reliable commentary', the use of the Old Testament, etc.) which the author uses to manipulate the reader (cf., e.g., R.M. Fowler). Some of these will be discussed below. It has also thrown much light recently on how the Gospel would have been interpreted by its first-century readers in light of their Graeco-Roman or Jewish educational background (cf. T.J. Weeden, M.A. Beavis, M.A. Tolbert).

Structuralism
Our final literary method, structuralism, is 'a mode of literary criticism [which]...focuses...on the relationship between the surface structure and the "deep" structures which lie implicitly or unconsciously beneath, around, or alongside of the text' (Patte, *Structural Exegesis*, p. iv). It is an abstract, synchronic, ahistorical investigation of the underlying mechanisms by which texts themselves come to express or achieve their meaning. It centres on the text itself rather than the author or the reader as the generator of meaning. Texts, it affirms, have a life of their own outside of their historical and cultural setting. Meaning resides in the structure of texts. Like the other holistic methods discussed, structuralism is opposed to fragmentation and focuses on the final form of the text without reference to its antecedents or pre-history. Unlike these other methods, however, with their emphasis on overall form, composition, arrangement, rhetoric, style, narrative, plot, etc. (the 'surface structure'), structuralism seeks to strip the text down to its essential elements (its 'deep structures') and to uncover its underlying 'grammar', its 'code' or conventions, the permanent rules by which it operates and through which it expresses universal human experience.

A broad and diverse movement, structuralism arose from the study of language, was inspired by the search for its permanent structures (which were seen as related to the essential categories of human perception) and is associated with the names of scholars such as F. de Saussure, R. Barthes, V. Propp, A.J. Greimas and C. Lévi-Strauss. The terminology of structuralists is daunting to the outsider (syntagmatic versus paradigmatic analysis, semiotics, signifier and signified, actants and functions, etc.) but repays study. Of special interest to biblical students are the theories of Propp and Greimas who, working on folktales, have produced models for reducing narrative texts to their essential roles and functions, and Lévi-Strauss who, investigating myth, has identified its operating system as a binary one (like that of computers!); that is, 'the tendency to think in oppositions [good/ evil; order/chaos; light/darkness; mortal/immortal, etc.] and the tendency to resolve such oppositions [mediation]' (M.W.G. Stibbe, 'Structuralism', *DBI*, p. 651). Of the various structuralist approaches to Mark, the series of Lévi-Straussian studies by E.S. Malbon are worth noting. Malbon has had some illuminating things to say about the mythic significance of Mark's spatial references, whether geopolitical (Galilee/Jerusalem), topographical (land/sea) or architectural (the house etc.).

The Genre of Mark

Mark as 'Gospel'

Let us now consider what these various literary methods have revealed about the Gospel of Mark and let us start with its genre. Genre criticism, as we have seen, raises questions concerning the literary antecedents or models by which the author may have been influenced in the overall conception of his work. In its attempt to identify the Gospel's literary type and environment and to place it within the history of ancient literature, it seeks parallels within the cultures of the Mediterranean world with which to compare it. Accepting that it is not an abridgment of Matthew, the following main issues are the ones which have led to debate among genre critics. Is the Gospel form the product of an evolutionary or revolutionary process? Is it unique or are there parallels? Are these parallels literary or non-literary? Are the closest parallels partial or complete, and are they Jewish or Hellenistic? Three main positions have been advanced. The first is that Mark's Gospel is a *nouveau genre* and would argue for its uniqueness. The second would claim that there are parallels and that these are to be found either in Jewish literature (e.g. in apocalyptic, wisdom literature or the Old Testament stories of the prophets) or in the wider Hellenistic world (e.g. Graeco-Roman biography, Greek tragedy, Hellenistic romance). A third, modified position would deny that exact parallels exist but that, since there is no such thing as a literary genre which has no roots in antecedent literary types, the most we can say is that Mark's Gospel represents a new type of 'evolved' literature for which numerous 'partial' antecedents in the ancient world can be suggested (e.g. 'sayings' collections, cycles of miracle stories, the martyrology, etc.). Two conflicting models for the emergence of the Gospel moreover are currently espoused, as previously mentioned. The first, the 'aggregate growth' model, based on form criticism, sees Mark as the product of an impersonal, collective, immanent process (e.g. cultic expansion of the kerygma), the other, based on redaction criticism and the newer literary methods, as the result of authorial creativity adopting or adapting existing genres.

The term 'Gospel' was first applied to texts like Mark by Christians in the second century, the earliest datable example of its use as a literary type occurring in the writings of Justin Martyr. The term was derived from the use of the term *euangelion* in the text of Mark for the 'good news' proclaimed by or about Jesus (cf. 1.1). This was not in itself a generic description but it came to be used subsequently as such for texts in which that 'good news' was to be found. If the term is a derivative one, therefore, the question is legitimately raised whether it is suitable (especially given the diversity which exists among the many texts which are now subsumed within this category) and whether other possibilities of description present themselves. Some scholars, as we have noted, would disagree, claiming that the 'Gospel' is a unique genre, the invention of early Christianity, that Mark was the originator of it, and that the term adequately describes its special features, namely, that it is 'kerygmatic in nature and evangelical in design' (Martin, *Mark*, p. 21). If it was developed out of partial antecedents, then the innovative feature of the Markan redactor was to provide an existing pre-Markan passion narrative (a martyrology) with an extended introduction (comprising, among other things, such collections of miracle stories as had circulated about Jesus, together with a series of his sayings set frequently in controversy settings). This view of the Gospel's basic structure was first suggested by M. Kähler, and has operated as a major premise for a number of subsequent studies. Another view, that it was an expansion by Mark of an existing apostolic 'framework' or summary (Dodd), has already been commented upon.

Mark as Graeco-Roman Biography

Let us now, however, consider some of the theories which suggest that complete and not partial ancient models were available to Mark in composing his work. His Gospel cannot be considered a biography in any modern sense but would it have been recognized as such in Mark's day? According to C.H. Talbert,

> Ancient biography is prose narration about a person's life, presenting supposedly historical facts which are selected to reveal the character or

essence of the individual, often with the purpose of affecting the behaviour of the reader ('Biographies of Philosophers and Rulers', *ANRW*, 2.16.2, p. 17).

In the words of C.W. Votaw, writing in 1915, the function of the 'popular' (as opposed to 'historical') biographies of the Graeco-Roman period was 'to eulogize and idealize their heroes...[to] select their best sayings and interpret them for practical use...[to] commend the message to the faith and practice of all' (*Contemporary Biographies*, p. 55; *gratia* Martin, *Mark*, p. 20). In this and in other respects, Graeco-Roman biography offers, in the opinion of a number of modern scholars (cf. D.E. Aune, H. Cancik, M. Hadas, M. Smith, C.H. Talbert), many close if not exact parallels to the Gospels.

Of the Graeco-Roman biographies, there were three main types: the 'Lives' or *Bioi* (*Vitae*) which give an account of the life of their subjects (cf. Lucian's 'Life' of the Cynic Demonax), the 'Acts' or *Praxeis* which record their heroic deeds (cf. the canonical 'Acts of the Apostles') and the 'Memorabilia' or *Apomnemoneumata* which collect anecdotes or sayings (cf. Xenophon's 'Memorabilia' of Socrates). The biography of the disciple-gathering teacher, which this latter text exemplifies, is taken by V.K. Robbins as an important influence upon Mark. The 'Lives' of the philosophers also provide striking parallels, as Talbert has pointed out. Certain didactic biographies of philosophers and rulers had cultic connections and exercised a role analogous, he claims, to that of the Gospel in the church.

One particular category, the 'aretalogy' (a list of virtues or accomplishments), is considered significant by Hadas and Smith. Developed perhaps out of collections of miracle stories, this presents the career of an impressive teacher, depicting him as a divine man with preternatural gifts, the gift of oratory, the power to work miracles, etc., and in some cases attributing to him a precocious childhood, a martyr's death and a subsequent apotheosis (cf. Philostratus, *Life of Apollonius of Tyana*; Porphyry, *Life of Pythagoras*; and Philo, *Life of Moses*). Critics, however (e.g. H.C. Kee), have expressed doubts regarding the legitimacy of the term 'aretalogy' for describing a definable literary type, and have pointed out that the extant 'aretalogies' with the strongest claim to similarity are of post-Markan date. In general, despite Talbert's arguments, there are still many who would hold that the Graeco-Roman biography hypothesis fails to account for certain major and special features of Gospels such as Mark, namely, their mythical structure, their cultic connections, their eschatological (or world-negating) orientation and their Jewish character.

Mark as Apocalyptic Drama

The Jewish character of the Gospel of Mark has been investigated in a number of ways, with attempts being made to find parallels in Jewish biographical literature. The stories of Moses or the miracle cycles associated with Elijah and Elisha have been suggested as paradigms. D. Lührmann has argued that Mark has conformed the Jesus tradition to the image of the suffering, righteous wise man/Son of God encountered both in the wisdom and prophetic tradition of Judaism (cf. Isa. 42.1; Wis. 2.12-20). Others (e.g. Kee) have looked to sectarian Judaism of an eschatological type, and especially apocalyptic, for the major influences.

Mark, as was earlier noted, can be construed as having an apocalyptic view of history. His Gospel (or at least the tradition on which it is based) presents Jesus not as a philosopher but as a Spirit-possessed prophet, teacher and exorcist who is engaged in eschatological battle with Satan and whose miracles (especially the exorcisms) are signs of the inbreaking of the kingdom. He suffers death at the hands of his enemies but is to return in glory as the triumphant Son of Man. These elements mirror the features of apocalyptic where the present world is under the domination of Satan, suffering is a prelude to vindication, and God will intervene, through intermediaries and with signs and wonders, to inaugurate his kingdom.

N. Perrin (*Introduction*, pp. 237-39) has suggested that Mark, therefore, is an 'apocalyptic drama' in three Acts; the forerunner, John the Baptist, has come and been 'delivered up' (*paradothenai*; cf. 1.14); God's messiah, Jesus, has come and will be 'delivered up' (cf. 9.31; 10.33) and his followers, the church, awaiting his parousia, will themselves also be 'delivered up' (cf. 13.9) prior to final vindication. Important as these ideological and structural elements are, the Gospel cannot be considered, in generic terms, an apocalypse (as can, for example, the Revelation of John). For this reason, scholars such as A.Y. Collins (*Beginning*, p. 27) would prefer to view it as 'an apocalyptic historical monograph' or as history 'in an apocalyptic mode'. In R. Guelich's view, therefore, 'Mark stands without a convincing generic parallel in Jewish literature' ('The Gospel Genre', p. 178).

Mark as Greek Tragedy

The dramatic aspects of the Markan Gospel touched upon here by Perrin have led some scholars (e.g. G.G. Bilezikian, and more recently M.A. Beavis) to investigate the links between Mark and the theatre, and to suggest that the evangelist may have been influenced by one of the most important contemporary forms of cultural expression, namely, Greek tragedy. Bilezikian claims that the plot of the Gospel reflects the structure which Aristotle established for tragedy in that it begins with an opening scene or prologue (*arche*; cf. 1.1-15 and esp. 1.1), proceeds to the complication (*desis*; cf. 1.16–8.26) and thence, after a climax or crisis (*anagnorisis*; cf. 8.27-30, here, as often, 'a recognition scene, the discovery of an identity previously concealed') to a change (*peripeteia*) in the hero's circumstances which leads to the dénouement (*lusis, katastrophe*; cf. 8.31–16.8). Other similarities to Greek drama are posited, for example, the presentation of Jesus as a typical hero with a 'tragic [but not necessarily immoral] flaw' (here his desire to carry out God's will). Mark was composed in Rome where, according to Bilezikian, such tragedies were being written and performed.

According to Beavis, 'by hellenistic times, the division of tragedies into five acts divided by choruses was well-accepted' (*Mark's Audience*, p. 128). She suggests, therefore, that Mark was a five-act drama, with scenes of private teaching taking the place of choral interludes according to the following scheme: Prologue (1.1-13); Act 1 (1.14–3.35); Teaching Scene 1 (4.1-34); Act 2 (4.35–6.56); Teaching Scene 2 (7.1-23); Act 3 (7.24–9.29); Teaching Scene 3 (9.30–10.45); Act 4 (10.46–12.44); Teaching Scene 4 (13.1-37); Act 5 (14.1–15.47); Epilogue (16.1-8). These theories are interesting but they assume, in Beavis's words, that 'the evangelist either read or saw plays, and that he composed his narrative according to the models provided by the tragic poets' (p. 34). This is disputed by critics although Beavis thinks that such scepticism ignores 'the wealth of data concerning the diffusion and influence of the theatre in antiquity' (p. 34).

Mark as Hellenistic Romance
Nevertheless, it has to be said that, in terms of form, content and style, Mark must be considered as popular literature, if not *Kleinliteratur*, as the classical form critics preferred to designate it. Because it appears less sophisticated, in comparison with the above Hellenistic works, but at the same time may be conscious literary creation, some scholars (e.g. M.A. Tolbert) have opted to locate the Gospel within the popular literary culture of the ancient Mediterranean world, and hence deem it more akin to the ancient novel (or romance), which often combined Greek drama and historiography. Tolbert has drawn parallels between Mark and such novels as Chariton's *Chaereas and Callirhoe* and Xenophon of Ephesus's *An Ephesian Tale*. One difficulty lies in the fact that all five extant novels from antiquity are erotic in nature which clearly Mark is not! Nevertheless, these popular works are written in a language and style which strikingly resembles that of the Gospel and

they offer us a glimpse of the level of literature which the evangelist produced.

Mark as Tragi-Comedy

From our discussion, it can be seen that the Gospel of Mark constitutes for many scholars a distinctive type of ancient biography combining Hellenistic form and function with Jewish content. All of the above studies seek to locate it within its contemporary context and are therefore literary-historical in orientation. One approach which differs from this, and indeed takes issue with this 'contextual' approach, is that of structuralism which maintains that genres derive from the deep structures of the human mind (our ways of ordering experience) and that instead of form and content dictating genre, the opposite is the case. This perspective is exemplified by D.O. Via, Jr, who claims that Mark can be seen in terms of both Greek tragedy and comedy, two classical genres emanating from the deep structures which control our perception of reality. Mark is a tragedy in terms of its theme (death) and the way that theme is executed in respect of plot, climax and dénouement but it is also a comedy (in generic terms) by consequence of its outcome, the reversal of the hero's fortunes in a final and joyous act of resurrection. It was the comic genre, then, as a category of the mind activated by early Christianity's death-resurrection kerygma, which generated the Gospel of Mark.

Structure and Arrangement

Outline

At the beginning of this book the contents of the Gospel were summarized, but it might now be useful to provide a general outline of its structure and arrangement. According to form and redaction critics Mark's material consists of linked pericopes which are found in certain main groupings (miracle stories, controversy stories, parables and teaching about discipleship combined with an apocalyptic discourse and a passion narrative) and presented within a loose overall geographical framework. The newer discipline of composition criticism, which attempts to investigate the structure of the Gospel and to ask what the overall arrangement of the material may tell us about the evangelist's literary and theological intent, has been noted. A number of interesting composition theories have been suggested, including the influential structural analysis of E. Schweizer which a number of scholars have followed, including N. Perrin.

Schweizer's main divisions are as follows ('Mark's Theological

Achievement', in Telford, *Interpretation of Mark*, pp. 57-58), with each division being marked off by summary passages or transitional sections: 1.14-15 (summary); 3.7-12 (summary); 6.6b (summary); 8.22-26 (opening blind eyes — *Bethsaida*); 10.45-52 (opening blind eyes and discipleship — *Jericho*).

I. 1.1-13 The beginning: time of salvation fulfilled (1-8) and prologue in heaven (9-13).

II. 1.14–3.6 Jesus' authority and the blindness of the Pharisees.

III. 3.7–6.6a Jesus' work in parables and signs, and the blindness of the world.

IV. 6.6b–8.21 Jesus' work extending to the Gentiles, and the blindness of the disciples.

V. 8.22–10.52 Jesus' revelation in uncoded speech and the discipleship of the disciples.

VI. 11.1–16.8 Suffering and Resurrection of the Son of Man.

Minor variations have been suggested to this scheme, of course, and there are some areas of dispute (e.g. does the prologue end at 1.8, 1.13 or 1.15?). Some would also prefer to divide the passion narrative further, for example 11.1–12.44 (Jesus in Jerusalem); ch. 13 (the apocalyptic discourse); 14.1–15.47 (the passion narrative proper); 16.1-8 (the resurrection). Schweizer's summary of the Gospel is made in the light of his understanding of Mark's theological and kerygmatic purposes but this raises the question of the organizing principle or principles behind the Gospel's composition. Were these historical, literary or theological? The general thrust of contemporary studies is to demonstrate that literary and theological factors were uppermost. Content, themes, summary and transitional passages, geographical and topographical indices and various patterns or cycles of recurrent or related material have all been invoked as clues to the literary and theological structure of the Gospel. Christology and discipleship are deemed to have played a major role, with some scholars seeing their sectional analysis reinforced by Mark's use of different christological titles and others, like Schweizer, emphasizing the recurring motif of the blindness of the disciples. Literary and structuralist studies have tended to highlight Mark's geographical (Galilee 1.14–8.26, Jerusalem 11.1–16.8) and topographical arrangement (e.g. wilderness 1.1-13; sea 3.7–8.21; way 8.26–10.52, temple 11.1–13.37; tomb 16.1-8) although such arrangement may not necessarily be in tension with a thematic one and may even reinforce it.

Chiasmus and Inclusio

An increasing number of scholars have lately been proposing concentric arrangement or ring composition as the key to the Markan structure. Chiasmus is a form of symmetrical organization in which materials are placed in a sandwich pattern (e.g. A-B-B´-A´) in such a way that inner and outer elements correspond to each other and the central unit, where it occurs, is highlighted (e.g. A-B-C-B´-A´). Inclusio is another framing device which 'refers to the practice of restating or paraphrasing the opening or leading idea or phrase at the conclusion in order to re-emphasize the point being made or the position being advocated' (Hayes and Holliday, *Biblical Exegesis*, p. 73). The use of such rhetorical devices was widespread in antiquity and they were employed and recognized both in oral teaching and in written discourse as structuring mechanisms.

Where Mark is concerned, a chiastic pattern has been detected not only in individual sections of the narrative (cf., e.g., J. Dewey) but also in the Gospel as a whole (cf., e.g., B. van Iersel), though as yet without unanimity. Dewey's *Markan Public Debate* (1980) was a landmark study in this field highlighting evidence of this rhetorical technique in 2.1–3.6. All five pericopes in this section (A 2.1-12; B 2.13-17; C 2.18-22; B´ 2.23-28; A´ 3.1-6) follow this pattern, their corresponding elements sharing a number of features in common. Van Iersel, employing a structuralist approach, divides the whole Gospel chiastically as follows, with the boundaries between the topographically distinct sections being marked by hinge or transition passages and the central section being the most important part of the Gospel:

> A1 In the desert (1.2-13)
> (y1) first hinge (1.14-15)
> B1 In Galilee (1.16–8.21)
> z1 blindness sight (8.22-26)
> C On the way (8.27–10.45)
> z2 blindness sight (10.46-52)
> B2 To Jerusalem (11.1–15.39)
> (y2) second hinge (15.40–41)
> A2 At the tomb (15.42–16.8)

Intercalation

Another 'sandwiching' device previously referred to is intercalation, the dovetailing or interlacing of one pericope with another in an A-B-A pattern. Nine of these sandwich units have been identified: 3.21, **22-30**, 31-35; 4.1-9, **10-12**, 13-20; 5.21-24, **25-34**, 35-43; 6.7-13, **14-29**, 30; 11.12-14, **15-19**, 20-25; 14.1-2, **3-9**, 10-11; 14.17-21, **22-26**, 27-31; 14.53-54,

55-65, 66-72; 15.40-41, **42-46**, 47–16.8. In each case, the evangelist begins to tell a story, interrupts it by inserting another, and then returns to the original in order to complete it. These intercalations, moreover, may not simply be a device, in the manner of the skilled raconteur, to fill up a space of time in the ongoing narrative or even to create suspense or tension in the narrative, but they may be intended to point the reader to a significant parallel between both pericopes. Both accounts, in other words, are mutually interpretative. According to J.R. Edwards ('Markan Sandwiches', p. 196), the Markan sandwiches 'emphasize the major motifs of the Gospel, especially the meaning of faith, discipleship, bearing witness, and the dangers of apostasy…the middle story nearly always provides the key to the theological purpose of the sandwich'.

Literary Techniques and Rhetorical Devices

The Narrator

The author of the Gospel of Mark employed a variety of literary techniques and rhetorical devices. Some of these have been commented upon already, such as the use of parenthetical statements which interrupt the Greek in various ways, whether as an afterthought, to provide explanation for the reader, to supply an Old Testament quotation or to offer translations of foreign words. Let us now focus on three of these techniques or devices which have been discussed in recent literary studies, namely the narrator, the use of irony and the use of the Old Testament (intertextuality). Where redaction criticism views the parenthetical statements just mentioned as the insertions of an editor (usually taken to be the evangelist himself) into his sources, a literary approach allocates these first and foremost to the narrator of the text who in this case is the implied author. That the 'narrator' is different from the actual author is clear when we consider the nature and 'point of view' of the narrator. According to N.R. Petersen (*Perspectives on Mark's Gospel*, pp. 97-121), Mark's narrator is an 'omniscient, intrusive, third-person narrator' with a definite and consistent 'point of view' (i.e. an ideology, standards of judgment, etc.) which he identifies with that of his central character, Jesus. The narrator is present in every scene, he is not bound by time and space and he is able to know and to say what his characters think and feel ('inside views') and hence establish them in the implied reader's mind as 'reliable' or 'unreliable' characters. Moreover, as we saw when examining the prologue, by divulging or withholding information, or by arranging the order of events (by prospective devices, foreshadowing what is to come [cf.

3.6], or retrospective devices, flashbacks [cf. 6.17-29]), he guides the reader throughout and suborns him or her into accepting his own ideological stance. This ideology we shall explore in Chapter 4 when we turn to Mark as a religious text.

The Use of Irony

The Gospel of Mark abounds with riddles, enigmas and unanswered questions, and with metaphor, mystery, and paradox (power and weakness, revelation and secrecy). It is characterized by allusiveness, ambiguity and ambivalence, by ellipsis and opacity, all terms used of it by contemporary literary critics. The subtlety of the Markan text has also been highlighted by recent studies on irony, such as that by J. Camery-Hoggatt (*Irony in Mark's Gospel*). To read Mark is to be aware that 'more is going on than meets the eye' (p. 179). Irony is 'saying one thing and meaning another' (Cicero) and it occurs, Camery-Hoggatt informs us, 'when the elements of the story-line provoke the reader to see beneath the surface of the text to deeper significances' (p. 1) and 'when the story-line itself plays upon the reader's own repertoire of knowledge and convictions to produce a distinctive subtext' (p. 2). Two examples from the passion narrative illustrate this. At the very moment when the Jewish authorities are mocking Jesus as a false prophet, the reader is aware that Peter is outside fulfilling Jesus' prophecy of his denial (cf. 14.30 and 14.65, 66-72). The claim that Jesus will destroy the Temple and build another 'not made with hands' (cf. 14.58; 15.29-30, 37-38) may be false in the eyes of Jesus' detractors but true for the implied reader in the light of the resurrection and the foundation of the Christian community. Such ironic contrasts, according to Rhoads and Michie, permeate the Markan story.

> The rule of God is hidden; the identity of the anointed one is secret; those disciples whom Jesus taught were on the inside turn out to be blind like those on the outside; Israel's leaders are blind to the rule of God; the rule of God overturns all worldly expectations; the most important are the least; the greatest become slaves; those losing their lives are saving them; and the king rules from a cross (p. 61).

The Use of the Old Testament

All texts, according to structuralists, reflect, absorb and transform other texts (intertextuality). Every reader, according to reader-response critics, brings to such texts certain competencies. Where Mark is concerned, the Old Testament has clearly been a formative influence both on the evangelist and on his tradition. One of the competencies expected of the implied reader, therefore, is intertextual competence, the ability to recognize, interpret and respond to the rich tapestry of Old Testament quotations and allusions which embroiders the text. Mark used the Old Testament to paint his portrait of Jesus and it acts as a lens through which his readers are encouraged to view him. A number of studies have examined this theme. H.C. Kee (*Community*, pp. 45-49), for example, has argued that Mark wished to present Jesus in terms of God's eschatological agent and drew, therefore, on the Psalms, the prophetic writings and Daniel to accomplish this. This theme has also been explored more recently by J. Marcus (*The Way of the Lord*). A number of test passages may serve to illustrate Mark's debt to the Old Testament.

Mark and the exodus motif (1.1-15). The phenomenon of intertextuality has already been touched upon in our examination of the Markan prologue. There we encountered the suggestion of J. Drury that the history of Israel in respect of its major foundation myths, namely, the story of Moses, the exodus from Egypt, the testing in the wilderness and so on, had constituted a formative 'text' or 'script' (other than the Jesus traditions) by means of which Mark, at a deeper level, had constructed his story. The Exodus story has also been cited as a more direct source for the Gospel of Mark by J.D.M. Derrett, though somewhat more fancifully. Derrett (*The Making of Mark*) argues that Mark used a considerable section of the Hexateuch together with Lamentations and related material as his grid, or model, for the story of Jesus. The Gospel proceeds, he claims, according to the following scheme: preparation for the trek (1.1–2.17), exodus (2.18–3.12), the crossing (3.13–5.20), facing a rebellion (5.21–6.29), invasion of the land (6.30–9.1), triumph (9.2–10.52), provocation (11.1–12.44), woe to Jerusalem! (13.1-37), martyrdom (14.1–15.47), and justification (16.1-8).

Mark and the Sinai motif (9.2-13). One prominent feature of the Exodus story was the revelation of God at Mount Sinai. Some (e.g. H.C. Kee, J. Ziesler) have drawn attention to the links between this story (cf. Exod. 24.1-18; 34.29) and the Markan transfiguration scene. The event, we are told, took place 'after six days' (cf. 9.1 and Exod. 24.16), Jesus is accompanied up the mountain by three named individuals (cf. 9.2 and Exod. 24.1), a cloud appears (cf. 9.7 and Exod. 24.15-18) and a voice issues from it (9.7 and Exod. 24.16), Jesus is transfigured, as was Moses (cf. 9.2-3 and Exod. 34.29), Moses himself is present, together with Elijah (9.4) and reference is made to 'booths' or 'tabernacles', the tents used by the Israelites on their wilderness journey.

Mark and the Psalms/Isaiah (14–15). Such intriguing correspondences are also to be observed in the Markan passion and resurrection narrative, so justifying the view of a number of scholars (e.g. F. Kermode) that these narratives, or parts thereof, have been generated by midrashic means from Old Testament texts. Chief among these have been the Psalms and the book of Isaiah. One need only refer to Psalm 22, for example, to find striking parallels to the details of the crucifixion account (cf., e.g., 22.1 for the cry from the cross, Mk 15.34; 22.7-8 for the mocking of the bystanders, Mk 15.29-30; 22.16 for the crucifixion itself; 22.18 for the division of garments and the casting of lots, Mk 15.24). Reference has already been made to D. Lührmann and his view that Mark conformed the Jesus tradition to the image of the suffering, righteous wise man found among other places in Deutero-Isaiah. Though Mark does not cite Isaiah 53, his narrative is suffused with motifs relating to it (cf., e.g., 53.7 'opened not his mouth' and Mk 14.61 and 15.5; 53.12 'numbered with the transgressors' and Mk 14.48 and 15.27; 53.9 'made his grave...with a rich man' and Mk 15.43-46).

Mark as Story

The Characters

Jesus. From the 'how' of the narrative, Mark's 'discourse', let us now turn to the 'what' and consider Mark as 'story'. I shall comment on the characters, the plot and the settings. The main characters in Mark's story are Jesus, the disciples and the Jewish authorities but there are also a number of minor characters who give cameo appearances. Our description will be a literary one since our interest will lie at this stage in the characters as they appear in Mark's narrative world rather than in the historical questions which Mark's presentation raises in connection with them. The literary critic employs certain terms to analyse characterization in a narrative. Characters may be 'round' (i.e. complex and unpredictable), 'flat' (i.e. predictable with a few, usually consistent traits) or 'stock' (i.e. with only one predictable and consistent trait). Characters may also be 'reliable' (i.e. enlisting the reader's sympathy or confidence and hence reinforcing the narrator's point of view; e.g., the voice of God from heaven, 1.11; the centurion at the cross, 15.39; the young man at the tomb, 16.5-7) or 'unreliable' (encouraging the reader's antipathy or serving to distance the reader from the values they represent; e.g., Judas, 3.19 or the scribes, 1.22; 2.6-8; 3.22).

Jesus is without doubt the central and dominant character in Mark's story. According to Rhoads and Michie (*Mark as Story*, p. 104), the

Markan Jesus is a 'round' character because of his many and varied traits (authority, integrity, faith, selflessness) and one towards whom the narrator maintains a consistently favourable point of view. It is often said that, of all the evangelists, Mark presents the most human Jesus (note his anger, 3.5; harshness, 8.33; impatience, 9.19; even vindictiveness, 11.13-14!). Mark was concerned, however, not so much with the human character of Jesus but with his status, that is, with what his words and deeds reveal about who he was. The Markan Jesus, as was noted in the opening summary of the Gospel, is a figure endowed with power (*dunamis*; cf., e.g., 5.30) and authority (*exousia*; cf., e.g., 1.22, 27). He wields this power over nature (cf., e.g., 4.35-41), he works miracles (cf., e.g., 4.35–5.43), he possesses supernatural knowledge (cf., e.g., 2.8) and he can be dramatically 'metamorphosed' before his disciples (9.2-8).

A key feature in Mark's presentation of Jesus is the aura of secrecy which surrounds his person and activity. He issues commands to silence in respect of his healing action and identity (cf., e.g., 1.44; 3.11-12; 5.43; 8.30; 9.9), gives private instruction to his disciples (cf., e.g., 4.11-12, 33-34; 7.17-23; 9.9-13), issues parabolic teaching meant to confuse (cf. 4.11-12), attempts to conceal himself (cf., e.g., 7.24; 9.30) and refuses to give a sign to establish his credentials (cf. 8.11-13). The mystery surrounding him is heightened by the various responses Jesus is described by the narrator as evoking from others (cf., e.g., 3.21 'mad!'; 3.22 'demon-possessed'; 6.14-16 'a reincarnated John the Baptist, Elijah or prophet'; 2.7 and 14.63-64 'blasphemer'; 3.11 and 15.39 'Son of God'). This range of reactions highlights the complex nature of the Markan Jesus. He provokes fear, offence, amazement, popularity and opposition from all who encounter him. It is in his interaction with two groups in particular, however, that the author achieves for his character this quality of striking enigma, namely the disciples and the Jewish leaders.

The disciples. Because of their conflicting traits, the disciples are to be regarded as 'round' characters, according to Rhoads and Michie, and the narrator characterizes them both favourably and unfavourably. 'On the one hand, they are loyal and courageous, with a capacity for sacrifice and enough fascination with Jesus to follow him. On the other hand, they are afraid, self-centered and dense, preoccupied with their own status and power' (*Mark as Story* p. 123). If anything, this even-handed description may underemphasize the negative aspects of the Markan portrayal (cf. M.R. Thompson, *The Role of Disbelief*) for, when filled out, it becomes almost damning: the disciples bar others

(9.38; 10.13-14); they are status conscious (9.33-37; 10.28-31, 35-45); they are fearful, afraid, cowardly (4.40-41; 6.50-51; 9.6, 32; 10.32; 14.50); they fail to take up their cross like true disciples (8.34-38); they are exhorted to have faith but admonished for the lack of it (4.40; 9.19; 11.22); they are unable to perform miracles (9.18, 19, 23); they are unable to keep watch but betray, forsake, and deny Jesus (ch. 14); they are unaware of the true identity of Jesus (namely the suffering Son of God); they fail to comprehend, in the first part of the Gospel, this secret, and positively misunderstand its implications in the second half.

I shall comment later on some of the historical explanations which have been offered for this harsh treatment but here one should mention the purely literary approach taken to this portrayal by R.C. Tannehill ('The Disciples in Mark', in Telford, *Interpretation of Mark*, pp. 169-95). In examining the narrative role of the disciples, Tannehill argues that the author first reinforces the positive view of the disciples as men called to follow Jesus and leads the reader to identify with them. Then he shows the inadequacy of their response to him, and their failure, so leading the implied (Christian) reader to self-criticism.

The Jewish leaders. Opposed to Jesus in the Markan story are the Jewish leaders. Although a number of different groups are named (the Pharisees, the Herodians, the Sadducees, the elders, the chief priests and the scribes), viewed from the perspective of the reader, they form a united front. According to literary critics (e.g. J.D. Kingsbury, E.S. Malbon), they hence stand forth as a single character. The authorities are 'flat' characters in Mark and their characterization is built upon their opposition to Jesus. They are viewed by the narrator almost consistently throughout in a negative light. According to Rhoads and Michie,

> the opponents have no faith, are blind to the rule of God, and are hardened against Jesus...They are self-serving, preoccupied with their own importance, afraid to lose their status and power, and willing to destroy to keep them (*Mark as Story*, p. 117).

Depicted as hypocrites (7.6-7), they are shown as guilty of an unforgivable sin in questioning the source of Jesus' power (3.28-30). For rejecting Jesus, they are implied to be wicked murderers (12.1-12), and their culpability in later plotting and executing his demise is also anticipated for the reader by the prospective device of the repeated passion prediction (8.31; 9.31; 10.33-34). Stealthy and devious in carrying out their design, according to the narrator (14.1-2), and acting out of envy in so doing, according to the 'reliable' Pilate (in an 'inside view', 15.10), they are shown at the end cruelly mocking Jesus on the cross (15.31-32), and oblivious to the dénouement which only the reader is in the privileged position to expect.

The minor characters. The narrative of the Gospel of Mark is also adorned by a number of minor characters, or 'the little people', as Rhoads and Michie describe them. They give as examples the men who bring a paralytic to Jesus, the leper, Jairus, the synagogue ruler, the Syrophoenician woman, the children Jesus embraces, the poor widow, and Joseph of Arimathea. 'They are "flat" characters with several consistent traits which they share in common: a childlike, often persistent, faith; a disregard for personal status and power; and a capacity for sacrificial service' (*Mark as Story*, p. 130).

Many of these are women, and, in line with contemporary interest, a number of studies in the 1980s (e.g. those of M.A. Beavis, E.S. Fiorenza, E.S. Malbon) have focused on them, investigating their narrative role and the literary image which they project. Women appear in Mark's healing stories (cf., e.g., 1.29-31; 5.24-34; 7.25-30), in isolated stories or incidents (cf., e.g., 3.31-35; 6.17-29; 12.41-44) and in connection with his passion and resurrection (14.3-9; 15.40-41; 16.1-8). Their portrayal is neither extensive nor uniformly positive (cf. 6.17-29), and the reader is only told explicitly as late as 15.40-41 that women were among those who followed Jesus and 'ministered to him'. Nevertheless, the thrust of these studies is the assertion that the women in Mark are exemplary figures embodying not only the ideals of female virtue (at least as these were espoused in antiquity) but also of faith, service and discipleship. The women are taken as models of those who recognize who Jesus is (cf., e.g., 14.3-9) and even as foils or positive counterparts for the faltering male disciples.

One further 'character' worth mentioning is the crowd (*ochlos*) which features frequently in the Markan narrative. 'Crowds with traits similar to those of the little people often respond to Jesus. They come to Jesus wherever he is…follow him, respond to his compassion and his power, and are "glad to hear him"' (Rhoads and Michie, *Mark as Story*, pp. 134-35). In the end, however, influenced by the Jewish leaders, they reject him (cf. 15.8, 11, 15), although this is partly, Rhoads and Michie claim, because they have failed to understood him. According to P.S. Minear, Mark assigned to the *ochlos* a very significant role in the events of the Gospel. They represent a continuing audience of committed believers (14.43; 15.8, 11, 15 are, he maintains, a different group), 'a primitive laity' with whom the laymen in the Markan community would have identified.

The Plot

The conflict between Jesus and his opponents. 'Our desire to impose maximum plot-coherence on a set of narrated events is an innate and powerful one; we pose as many connections as we can' (S.D. Moore, *Literary Criticism*, p. 14). Notwithstanding this fact, those who have recently taken a literary approach to Mark, as we have seen, have emphasized that Mark presents a single unified story with a consistent plot (cf. W.H. Kelber, *Mark's Story of Jesus*), a result that we should not expect if Mark were an edited collection of traditions. Kelber's book presents Mark as 'an interpretative retelling' of this story while that of J.D. Kingsbury (*Conflict in Mark*) analyses the plot, examining the principal story lines of the Gospel, and how they intertwine. According to Rhoads and Michie,

> [T]he narrator's point of view in telling the story is consistent through-
> out. The plot is coherent: events that are anticipated come to pass; con-
> flicts are resolved; predictions are fulfilled. The characters are consistent
> from one scene to the next...Thus, the unity of the gospel is apparent in
> the remarkable integrity of the story it tells (*Mark as Story*, p. 3).

The story which is recounted leads to a recognizable climax, namely, the death and resurrection of Jesus, and the narrator leads the implied reader to anticipate the course of events by dropping hints as to future developments early on (cf. 2.19-20; 3.6). There are two interrelated plot themes, the first of which concerns the conflict between Jesus and his opponents. This is built up successively section by section (cf. 2.1–3.6; 3.22-30; 7.1-23; 10.2-9; chs. 11–12; 14–15) culminating in Jesus' visit to Jerusalem, his besting of his opponents in argument, his arrest, trial and crucifixion. The plot appears to be resolved in the triumph of Jesus' enemies over him but in fact what appears to be a tragedy turns out to be (in literary terms) a comedy. The Jesus who cannot come down from the cross and save himself actually rises from the dead and is vindicated. This vindication is carried out beyond the text into the future (where the reader stands) by the apocalyptic discourse, a passage introduced before the passion narrative and pointing beyond it to Jesus' future return in triumph.

The conflict between Jesus and his family and disciples. The second and related plot theme is the conflict between Jesus and his family and disciples. The narrator chronicles Jesus' attempt to get them to under-stand who he is, and emphasizes their repeated failure to comprehend his divine nature and destiny. This theme, too, is built in stages. Before 8.30, they fail to recognize that he is the Son of God despite every invitation to do so (cf. 4.41; 6.52; 8.21). After 8.30, they positively misunderstand the true nature of Jesus' divine status and mission and the true nature of discipleship springing from it. By the end of the narrative, one has betrayed him, another has denied him, all have deserted him. The only ones to hear the claim that he is risen are the women at the tomb, and, although they are instructed to pass on the message, 'they said nothing to anyone', we are told, 'for they were afraid' (16.8). Any resolution of this second theme is left, therefore, to the implied reader who is invited, it appears, to supply his or her own ending.

The Settings

We come finally to Mark's settings. A good story, like a good film, must have not only stimulating characters and an exciting plot but, if it is to maintain our interest, attractive settings. If Mark were a film director, then we might award him high marks for his choice of locations. Mark's geographical and topographical settings are many and varied. The first part of the Gospel, as we have observed, is set in Galilee and its surrounding area, the second part in Jerusalem, with Jesus' journey from Galilee to Jerusalem forming the centrepiece. Within this overall framework, Mark's characters are encountered in a variety of places: in the wilderness (e.g. 1.4, 12, 35; 6.31; 8.4); at the sea (e.g. 1.16; 2.13; 3.7; 4.1; 5.21; 7.31); in the house (e.g. 2.1, 15; 3.20; 7.17, 24; 9.33; 10.10); in the synagogue (e.g. 1.21; 3.1); getting in/out of a boat (e.g. 3.9; 4.1, 36; 5.2, 21; 6.32, 45, 54; 8.10, 14); in the hills/on a mountain (e.g. 3.13; 6.46; 9.2; 13.3); on the way/road (e.g. 8.27; 9.33, 34; 10.17, 32, 46, 52); in the temple (e.g. 11.11, 15, 27); in the tomb (e.g. 5.2; 16.5).

Scholars have debated the significance of these settings. Some have obviously been taken over by the evangelist from his tradition and are integral to the stories themselves (e.g. John's appearance in the wilderness). Others seem artificial (e.g. the sudden appearances of 'the house'; e.g. 7.17; 10.10) and may be attributable to the evangelist himself. A number of the locations are pregnant with significance in relation to myth, history and tradition, both Jewish (e.g. 'the wilderness', 'the mountain', 'the synagogue', 'the temple') and Christian (e.g. 'the house', the early Christian meeting-place or 'the way', a metaphor for discipleship and the early Christian movement's self-designation, according to Acts 9.2; 19.9, 23 etc.). The narrative opposition between Galilee and Jerusalem or between the land and the sea (especially Jesus' frequent lake crossings) has received particular attention, with historical, symbolic or purely mythological significance being perceived in these dichotomies. For some, for example, the 'lake' symbolizes the fringes of Jewish society and the dividing line between Jew and Gentile. Galilee is the centre of order, Jerusalem of chaos. Reference has already been made in this respect to the work of E.S. Malbon and B. van Iersel in bringing out, from a structuralist perspective, the deeper meaning of these polarities.

In this chapter, to sum up, we have examined the Gospel of Mark as a literary composition. Having introduced six of the newer literary 'criticisms' and their respective presuppositions and methods, their contributions to questions concerning the Gospel's genre and its overall structure and arrangement were then summarized. I then went on to demonstrate the ways that these approaches have highlighted the literary techniques and rhetorical devices employed by the evangelist. In the concluding section the Gospel was considered as a story, with characters, a plot and settings. Examination of the settings, as with the other literary aspects we have considered, has revealed the extent to which the study of Mark as 'literature' is closely intertwined with the study of Mark as 'theology'. It is to the third and final of these aspects of the Gospel that we shall now turn, namely, to Mark as a religious text.

FURTHER READING

J.H. Hayes and C.R. Holliday, *Biblical Exegesis: A Beginner's Handbook* (London: SCM Press, 1982).

For literary approaches to Mark, see:

G. Aichele, *Jesus Framed* (Biblical Limits; London: Routledge, 1996).
J. Drury, 'Mark', in R. Alter and F. Kermode (eds.), *The Literary Guide to the Bible* (Cambridge, MA: Harvard University Press, 1987), pp. 402-17.
A.M. Farrer, *A Study in St Mark* (London: A. & C. Black, 1951).
F. Kermode, *The Genesis of Secrecy: On the Interpretation of Narrative* (Charles Eliot Norton Lectures, 1977–78; London: Harvard University Press, 1979).
N.R. Petersen (ed.), *Perspectives on Mark's Gospel* (Semeia, 16; Missoula, MT: Scholars Press, 1979).
—'"Literarkritik", the New Literary Criticism and the Gospel According to Mark', in F. van Segbroeck *et al.* (eds.), *The Four Gospels 1992* (Fs. F. Neirynck; Leuven: Leuven University Press/Peeters, 1992), pp. 935-48.
W.R. Telford, 'Mark, Gospel of', *DBI*, pp. 424-8.
—'Mark and the Historical-Critical Method: the Challenge of Recent Literary Approaches to the Gospel', in C. Focant (ed.), *The Synoptic Gospels: Source Criticism and the New Literary Criticism* (Leuven: Peeters/Leuven University Press, 1993), pp. 491-502.

On composition criticism:

J.R. Donahue, *Are You the Christ? The Trial Narrative in the Gospel of Mark* (SBLDS, 10; Missoula, MT: Scholars Press, 1973).

S.E. Dowd, *Prayer, Power and the Problem of Suffering: Mark 11.22-25 in the Context of Markan Theology* (SBLDS, 105; Atlanta, GA: Scholars Press, 1988).

N.R. Petersen, 'The Composition of Mark 4.1–8.26', *HTR*, 73 (1980), pp. 185-217.

P. Sellew, 'Composition of Didactic Scenes in Mark's Gospel', *JBL* 108 (1989), pp. 613-34.

On rhetorical criticism:

J. Dewey, *Markan Public Debate: Literary Technique, Concentric Structure, and Theology in Mark 2.1–3.6* (SBLDS, 48; Chico, CA: Scholars Press, 1980).

G.A. Kennedy, *New Testament Interpretation through Rhetorical Criticism* (Studies in Religion; Chapel Hill, NC: University of North Carolina Press, 1984).

B.L. Mack and V.K. Robbins, *Patterns of Persuasion in the Gospels* (Foundations and Facets: Literary Facets; Sonoma, CA; Polebridge Press, 1989).

J.I.H. McDonald, 'Rhetorical Criticism', *DBI*, pp. 599-600.

V.K. Robbins, *Jesus the Teacher: A Socio-Rhetorical Interpretation of Mark* (Philadelphia, PA: Fortress Press, 1984).

M.R. Thompson, *The Role of Disbelief in Mark: A New Approach to the Second Gospel* (New York: Paulist Press, 1989).

On narrative criticism:

J. Licht, *Storytelling in the Bible* (Jerusalem: Magnes Press, Hebrew University, 1978).

C.D. Marshall, *Faith as a Theme in Mark's Narrative* (SNTSMS, 64; Cambridge: Cambridge University Press, 1989).

M.A. Powell, *What Is Narrative Criticism?* (Minneapolis, MN: Augsburg Fortress, 1990).

D. Rhoads, 'Narrative Criticism and the Gospel of Mark', *JAAR* 50 (1982), pp. 411-34.

S.H. Smith, *A Lion with Wings: A Narrative-Critical Approach to Mark's Gospel* (Biblical Seminar, 38; Sheffield: Sheffield Academic Press, 1996).

W.S. Vorster, 'Literary Reflections on Mark 13.5-37, a Narrated Speech of Jesus', in Telford (ed.), *Interpretation of Mark*, pp. 269-88.

On reader-response criticism:

M.A. Beavis, *Mark's Audience: The Literary and Social History of Mark 4.11-12* (JSNTSup, 33; Sheffield: JSOT Press, 1989).

R.M. Fowler, *Loaves and Fishes: The Function of the Feeding Stories in the Gospel of Mark* (SBLDS, 54; Chico, CA: Scholars Press, 1981).

—*Let the Reader Understand: Reader-Response Criticism and the Gospel of Mark* (Minneapolis, MN: Fortress Press, 1991).

E.V. McKnight (ed.), *Reader Perspectives on the New Testament* (Semeia, 48; Atlanta, GA: Scholars Press, 1989).

N.R. Petersen, 'The Reader in the Gospel', *Neot* 18 (1984), pp. 38-51.

W.R. Tate, *Reading Mark from the Outside: Eco and Iser Leave their Marks* (Bethesda, MD: Christian Universities Press, 1995).

M.A. Tolbert, *Sowing the Gospel: Mark's World in Literary-Historical Perspective* (Minneapolis, MN: Fortress Press, 1989).

T.J. Weeden, *Mark: Traditions in Conflict* (Philadelphia, PA: Fortress Press, 1971).

On structuralism:

E.S. Malbon, *Narrative Space and Mythic Meaning in Mark* (New Voices in Biblical Studies; San Francisco: Harper & Row, 1986).

D. Patte, *What Is Structural Exegesis?* (Guides to Biblical Scholarship; Philadelphia, PA: Fortress Press, 1976).

D.O. Via, Jr, *Kerygma and Comedy in the New Testament: A Structuralist Approach to Hermeneutic* (Philadelphia, PA: Fortress Press, 1975).

For the genre of Mark, see:

D.E. Aune, 'The Problem of the Genre of the Gospels: A Critique of C.H. Talbert's *What is a Gospel?*', in R.T. France and D. Wenham (eds.), *Gospel Perspectives: Studies of History and Tradition in the Four Gospels* (Sheffield: JSOT Press, 1981), pp. 9-60.

—*The New Testament and its Literary Environment* (Philadelphia: Westminster Press, 1987).

M.A. Beavis, *Mark's Audience: The Literary and Social History of Mark 4.11-12* (JSNTSup, 33; Sheffield: JSOT Press, 1989).

G.G. Bilezikian, *The Liberated Gospel: A Comparison of the Gospel of Mark and Greek Tragedy* (Grand Rapids: Baker Book House, 1977).

A.Y. Collins, *The Beginning of the Gospel: Probings of Mark in Context* (Minneapolis, MN: Fortress Press, 1992).

R.A. Guelich, 'The Gospel Genre', in P. Stuhlmacher (ed.), *Das Evangelium und die Evangelien: Vorträge vom Tübinger Symposium 1982* (Tübingen: Mohr-Siebeck, 1983), pp. 173-208.

M. Hadas and M. Smith, *Heroes and Gods: Spiritual Biographies in Antiquity* (New York: Harper & Row, 1965).

H.C. Kee, 'Aretalogy and Gospel', *JBL* 92 (1973), pp. 402-22.

R.P. Martin, *Mark: Evangelist and Theologian* (Exeter: Paternoster Press, 1979), pp. 17-28.

N. Perrin, 'The Literary Gattung "Gospel": Some Observations', *ExpTim* 82 (1970–71), pp. 4-7.

—*The New Testament: An Introduction* (New York: Harcourt Brace Jovanovich, 1982).

V.K. Robbins, *Jesus the Teacher: A Socio-Rhetorical Interpretation of Mark* (Philadelphia, PA: Fortress Press, 1984).

M. Smith, 'Prolegomena to a Discussion of Aretalogies, Divine Men, the Gospels and Jesus', *JBL* 90 (1971), pp. 174-99.

A. Stock, *Call to Discipleship: A Literary Study of Mark's Gospel* (Good News Studies, 1; Dublin: Veritas; Wilmington, DE: Michael Glazier, 1982).

C.H. Talbert, *What Is a Gospel? The Genre of the Canonical Gospels* (London: SPCK; Philadelphia: Fortress Press, 1978).

—'Biographies of Philosophers and Rulers as Instruments of Religious Propagation in Mediterranean Antiquity', *ANRW*, 2.16.2, pp. 1619-51.

—'Once Again: Gospel Genre', *Semeia* 43 (1988), pp. 53-73.

M.A. Tolbert, *Sowing the Gospel: Mark's World in Literary-Historical Perspective* (Minneapolis, MN: Fortress Press, 1989).

D.O. Via, Jr, *Kerygma and Comedy in the New Testament: A Structuralist Approach to Hermeneutic* (Philadelphia, PA: Fortress Press, 1975).

C.W. Votaw, *The Gospels and Contemporary Biographies in the Greco-Roman World* (Philadelphia, PA: Fortress Press, 1970), pp. iii-viii, 1-29.

L.M. Wills, *The Quest of the Historical Gospel: Mark, John, and the Origins of the Gospel Genre* (London: Routledge, 1997).

For structure and arrangement, see the following:

D. Blatherwick, 'The Markan Silhouette', *NTS* 17 (1970–71), pp. 184-92.

J.G. Cook, *The Structure and Persuasive Power of Mark: A Linguistic Approach* (Society of Biblical Literature Semeia Series; Atlanta, GA: Scholars Press, 1996).

J. Dewey, 'The Literary Structure of the Controversy Stories in Mark 2.1–3.6', in Telford (ed.) *Interpretation of Mark*, pp. 141-51.

J.R. Edwards, 'Markan Sandwiches. The Significance of Interpolations in Markan Narratives', *NovT* 31 (1989), pp. 193-216.

E. Schweizer, 'Mark's Theological Achievement', in Telford (ed.), *Interpretation of Mark*, pp. 63-87.

A. Stock, 'Chiastic Awareness and Education in Antiquity', *BTB* 14 (1984), pp. 23-27.

G. van Oyen, 'Intercalation and Irony in the Gospel of Mark', in F. van Segbroeck *et al.* (eds.), *The Four Gospels 1992* (Fs. F. Neirynck; Leuven: Leuven University Press/Peeters, 1992), pp. 949-74.

For literary techniques and rhetorical devices, see:

H. Anderson, 'The Old Testament in Mark's Gospel', in J.M. Efird (ed.), *The Use of the Old Testament in the New and Other Essays: Studies in Honor of William Franklin Stinespring* (Durham, NC: Duke University Press, 1972), pp. 280-306.

E. Best, 'Mark's Narrative Technique', *JSNT* 37 (1989), pp. 43-58.

J. Camery-Hoggatt, *Irony in Mark's Gospel* (SNTSMS, 72; Cambridge: Cambridge University Press, 1992).

J.D.M. Derrett, *The Making of Mark: The Scriptural Bases of the Earliest Gospel* (Shipston-on-Stour, UK: P. Drinkwater, 1985).

J.H. Drury, 'Mark 1.1-15: an Interpretation', in A.E. Harvey (ed.), *Alternative Approaches to New Testament Study* (London: SPCK, 1985), pp. 25-36.

H.C. Kee, 'Scripture Quotations and Allusions in Mark 11–16', in *SBL 1971 Seminar Papers II* (Atlanta, GA: Scholars Press, 1971), pp. 475-502.

—'The Transfiguration in Mark: Epiphany or Apocalyptic Vision?', in J. Reumann (ed.), *Understanding the Sacred Text* (Fs. M.S. Enslin; Valley Forge, PA: Judson Press, 1972), pp. 135-52.

—*Community of the New Age: Studies in Mark's Gospel* (Philadelphia, PA: Westminster Press, 1977), pp. 45-49.

J. Marcus, *The Way of the Lord: Christological Exegesis of the Old Testament in the Gospel of Mark* (Louisville, KY: Westminster/John Knox Press, 1992).

N.R. Petersen, '"Point of View" in Mark's Narrative', *Semeia* 12 (1978), pp. 97-121.

V.K. Robbins, 'Psalm 22 in the Markan Crucifixion', in Segbroeck *et al.* (eds.), *The Four Gospels 1992*, pp. 1161-83.

J. Sergeant, *Lion Let Loose: The Structure and Meaning of St Mark's Gospel* (Exeter: Paternoster Press, 1988).

W.S. Vorster, 'The Function of the Use of the Old Testament in Mark', *Neot* 14 (1981), pp. 62-72.

J.A. Ziesler, 'The Transfiguration Story and the Markan Soteriology', *ExpTim* 81 (1969–70), pp. 263-68.

For Mark as story, see:

M.A. Beavis, 'Women as Models of Faith in Mark', *BTB* 18 (1988), pp. 3-9.

E.S. Fiorenza, *In Memory of Her* (New York: Crossroad, 1983).

W.H. Kelber, *Mark's Story of Jesus* (Philadelphia, PA: Fortress Press, 1979).

J.D. Kingsbury, *The Christology of Mark's Gospel* (Philadelphia, PA: Fortress Press, 1983).

—*Conflict in Mark: Jesus, Authorities, Disciples* (Philadelphia, PA: Fortress Press, 1989).

—'The Religious Authorities in the Gospel of Mark', *NTS* 36 (1990), pp. 42-65.

E.S. Malbon, 'Fallible Followers. Women and Men in the Gospel of Mark', *Semeia* 28 (1983), pp. 29-48.

—*Narrative Space and Mythic Meaning in Mark* (New Voices in Biblical Studies; San Francisco: Harper & Row, 1986).

—'Disciples, Crowds, Whoever: Markan Characters and Readers', *NovT* 28 (1986), pp. 104-30.

—'The Jewish Leaders in the Gospel of Mark: A Literary Study of Marcan Characterization', *JBL* 108 (1989), pp. 259-81.

P.S. Minear, 'Audience Criticism and Markan Ecclesiology', in H. Baltensweiler and B. Reicke (eds.), *Neues Testament und Geschichte: Historisches Geschehen und Deutung im Neuen Testament. Oscar Cullman zum 70. Geburtstag* (Tübingen: Mohr [Paul Siebeck], 1972), pp. 79-89.

D. Rhoads and D. Michie, *Mark as Story: An Introduction to the Narrative of a Gospel* (Philadelphia, PA: Fortress Press, 1982).

R.C. Tannehill, 'The Gospel of Mark as Narrative Christology', *Semeia* 16 (1979), pp. 57-95.

—'The Disciples in Mark: the Function of a Narrative Role', in Telford (ed.), *Interpretation of Mark*, pp. 169-95.

M.R. Thompson, *The Role of Disbelief in Mark: A New Approach to the Second Gospel* (New York: Paulist Press, 1989), pp. 104-35.

B. van Iersel, *Reading Mark* (Edinburgh: T. & T. Clark, 1988).

Chapter Four

MARK AS THEOLOGY: THE GOSPEL AS A RELIGIOUS TEXT

Mark and the Gentiles

The Use of the Word 'Gospel'
In considering Mark as a religious text, that is, as a text whose primary function was to convey a theological message, we need to return to the opening words of the Gospel where the evangelist announced his theme: 'The beginning of the gospel of Jesus Christ, the Son of God' (1.1). This verse has been the subject of endless debate. In employing the word 'gospel' or *euangelion*, it presents us with the first of the recurrent motifs, themes and interests of concern to the evangelist which are of importance in determining Mark's theological purpose. These were listed in Chapter 2 when discussing redaction criticism and they will occupy us in our remaining two chapters. In ordinary usage, the term *euangelion* meant 'good news', for example, the announcement or proclamation of 'victory in battle or the enthronement of a Roman ruler' (Martin, *Mark*, p. 22). Does it have its usual connotation here, or does it refer to the religious or doctrinal content of the message preached by (or perhaps about?) Jesus or even to the literary genre in which that proclamation is contained? To what, moreover, does the 'beginning' (*arche*) of the 'gospel' refer: to 1.1-8 (i.e. to John's activity as the forerunner of Jesus), to 1.1-11 or 1.1-15 (i.e. to Jesus' baptism, temptation and first preaching) or to the whole Markan composition as the beginning of what we might call 'Christian Origins'?

In the rest of the Gospel, the term *euangelion* is used to describe Jesus' teaching (cf. 1.14-15; 8.35; 10.29; 13.10; 14.9) but without specifying its precise content. According to W. Marxsen (*Mark*, pp. 117-50), Markan references to *euangelion* are redactional. The term is often avoided or reformulated by Matthew and Luke when following their source (cf., e.g., 8.38 or 10.29 par.) and is lacking in John. If it was a favourite expression of Mark, therefore, what meaning and significance did it carry for him? According to K. Kertelge, the word 'gospel' was taken up by Mark from early Christian missionary language (cf., e.g., Rom. 1.1-4) where it was used for the oral proclamation of Jesus Christ ('The Epiphany of Jesus', in Telford, *Interpretation of Mark*, p. 106). Hence, for R. Guelich, *euangelion* in Mk 1.1 means the gospel (preached by the church 13.10; 14.9) *about* Jesus Messiah, Son of God (objective genitive) and found in the literary work that follows. The beginning of the gospel was the fulfilment of Isaiah's prophecies about the forerunner (John) and his work in preparing the way for the one to follow, the Lord (Jesus) ('Beginning of the Gospel', pp. 5-15).

Galilee
The Markan Jesus first preaches his 'gospel' in Galilee (1.14). The special interest that the evangelist has in Galilee has been pointed out a number of times (cf. also, e.g., 1.16, 28, 39; 3.7; 7.31; 9.30; 14.28; 16.7), an interest not shared by Luke or John. Jesus conducts his ministry here, receiving an enthusiastic following, and it is the place to which he is to return after his resurrection (or parousia?). The interpretation of its significance for Mark, however, varies. Is Mark's frequent emphasis on Galilee a matter of purely historical import or does it carry symbolic significance? On the one hand, there are the purely historical evaluations, as we have seen. For W. Marxsen, who regarded the majority of the Galilee references as redactional and not traditional, Mark's preoccupation with Galilee reflects the historical fact that the Gospel was written in or near Galilee for a Jewish-Christian community which was awaiting the parousia. On the other hand, there are the structuralist assessments which eschew historical deductions and interpret the narrative opposition between Galilee and Jerusalem in symbolic and mythological terms. Some scholars opt for a symbolic interpretation of 'Galilee' but with historical significance. For N. Perrin, 'Galilee' is a paradigm for the Gentile mission (cf. Isa. 9.1; Mt. 4.15 'Galilee of the Gentiles') and reflects the author's interest in the Gentiles. For W.H. Kelber, the Galilee/Jerusalem polarity reflects an underlying tension in Mark between the traditions of Gentile and Jewish Christianity.

This point of view has been supported in a number of ways. The geographically implausible route ascribed to Jesus in 7.31 has been interpreted as serving a theological purpose for the evangelist, the places mentioned representing *in toto* the Gentile regions to the north and east of Galilee. All three stories in 7.24–8.10 are included in this journey, and have a theological unity in that they are concerned with Jew–Gentile relations and the mission to the Gentiles. Jesus is hence shown as blazing a trail in Gentile regions which the church was later to follow. This is perhaps especially the case with the feeding story of 8.1-10 which many have seen as the Gentile equivalent of the first feeding to Jews in 6.34-44. If 'Galilee' is to be taken as symbolic of the Gentile world, then the dramatic closing promise of the Gospel ('He goes before you to Galilee. There you will see him') is in effect a Gentile mission prediction, as C.F. Evans ('I will go before you', pp. 3-18) and others have long argued.

The Gentile Mission

That Mark's Gospel has a special interest in Gentiles and the Gentile mission can also be seen from other evidence supplied by the text. Attention has already been drawn to 7.24-30 where Mark has included a story depicting Jesus' (albeit reluctant) dealings with a Gentile woman. This is one of the very few instances of such contacts in the Jesus tradition. In the parable of the vineyard, the Markan Jesus is made to predict that the owner (God) will give the vineyard (interpreted by Matthew as the Kingdom of God; Mt. 21.43) 'to others' (12.9-11). This *vaticinium ex eventu* is made even more explicit in the apocalyptic discourse where a Gentile mission is prophesied as an important element of the apocalyptic scenario ('the gospel must first be preached to all the nations' or 'Gentiles' [*ta ethne*], 13.10; cf. also 13.27). That the evangelist has universal mission within his purview is confirmed by the words also placed on Jesus' lips in respect of the woman who anointed him at Bethany ('wherever the gospel is preached *in the whole world*, what she has done will be told in memory of her', 14.9). It is surely also significant that the only human character to confess Jesus as 'the Son of God' in the Markan text is a Roman centurion (15.39). For some, therefore (e.g. D. Senior), Mark's Gospel is not a mere collection of traditions but an intentional and thematic representation of the Christian mission initiated by Jesus. Whatever the merits of this position, the attitude shown to the Gentiles by the evangelist helps us to place him within the spectrum of early Christianity and to locate him in particular within a tradition representing or at least influenced by Gentile Christianity.

Mark and the Law

We shall explore shortly how Mark's 'Gentile perspective' is also reflected in his critique of the original disciples of Jesus as well as of the Jewish leaders but let us turn to a related theme, namely Mark's attitude to the Law. This is reflected primarily in the controversy discourses in which Jesus is found in conflict or debate with the Jewish leaders over a wide range of both legal and doctrinal matters. These occur, as we have seen, in major connected sections of the Gospel (cf. 2.1–3.6; 3.20-35; 7.1-23; 11.27–12.40; 14–15) as well as in isolated incidents (cf. 8.11-13; 9.11-13; 10.2-9) and are largely apophthegmatic in structure, taking the form of either controversy (e.g. 2.23-28; 7.1-8) or scholastic (didactic) dialogues (e.g. 12.28-34). In some cases, Jesus' own activity or attitude is in dispute (e.g. 2.1-12; 3.22-30; 11.27-33), in other cases, the actions of his disciples (e.g. 2.15-17; 2.18-22; 2.23-28; 3.1-6). A number embed legal sayings attributed to Jesus himself (e.g. 2.27; 7.15; 10.11-12). The specifically legal issues deal with such subjects as the forgiveness of sins (2.1-12), table fellowship (2.15-17), fasting (2.18-22), Sabbath observance (2.23-28; 3.1-6), the purity laws (7.1-23), divorce (10.2-12) and paying taxes (12.13-17).

Most scholarly work on these pericopes has concentrated on the question whether Mark used connected sources, on separating tradition from Markan redaction and on establishing what might go back to Jesus (cf., e.g., R. Booth, J.D.G. Dunn). In some places, Mark appears to be adding his own redactional comment to the tradition he has received by employing the 'private teaching in the house' device (cf. 7.17-23; 9.28-29; 10.10-12). In other places, it is not clear whether he was himself thoroughly conversant with the Law as it pertained in Jesus' day (cf., e.g., 7.3-4—was ritual lustration a practice of Jews other than priests before 70 CE?). Many of these stories, it is believed, reflect controversies between the early church and its opponents and they appear to have been redacted by the evangelist with the particular concerns of the Markan community in mind. They have been taken over by him to serve a christological function and to provide an introduction to and an explanation for the events leading up to the passion narrative and Jesus' crucifixion. By means of the controversy pericopes, a charismatic and predominantly Gentile-Christian Jesus is shown repudiating the authority and teaching of a legalistic Judaism. These stories exalt Jesus over the Jewish tradition and present him as the initiator ultimately of the community's break with its Jewish roots.

Mark and Paul

These considerations prompt the question of the relation between Mark and Paul, or between Mark's tradition and Pauline Christianity. The case that key themes from Paul's Epistles throw light on Mark was made some years ago by J.C. Fenton. Leaving aside the traditional link between Paul and the John Mark of the New Testament discussed in the first chapter, it may be significant that Mark's Gospel and the Pauline Epistles are the earliest extant writings of early Christianity that we possess, that both writers evince a similar attitude to the

Jewish Law (cf., e.g., Mk 7.1-23 and Rom. 10.4), that both present evidence of tension with the leaders of the Jerusalem church (cf., e.g., Mk 8.33 and Gal. 2.11), and that both demonstrate a concern for Gentiles (cf., e.g.; Mk 13.10 and Gal. 1.15-16), a sensitivity to issues of table fellowship (cf. Mk 2.15-17 and Gal. 2.11-21) and a regard for eucharistic symbolism (cf., e.g., Mk 8.14-21 and 1 Cor. 10.1-4, 17).

Alongside these similarities in praxis are correspondences in ideology. Both saw Jesus as 'Son of God' (cf., e.g., Mk 15.39 and Rom. 1.3) and 'Lord' (cf., e.g., Mk 11.3 and 1 Cor. 12.3), both emphasized faith in the context of discipleship (cf., e.g., Mk 9.20-24 and Rom. 1.16-17; Phil. 4.13) and it is only in Mark and Paul that we find, as we shall see later, a theology of the cross, a *theologia crucis*, placed in opposition to a triumphalist one, a *theologia gloriae* (Mk 15.31-32 and 1 Cor. 1.18-25). It is for this reason, among others, that a number of scholars would follow Bultmann in defining Mark's purpose as 'the union of the Hellenistic kerygma about Christ, whose essential content consists of the Christ myth as we learn of it in Paul (esp. Phil. 2.6ff.; Rom. 3.24) with the tradition of the story of Jesus' (*History*, pp. 347-48). Paul used the word 'gospel' (*euangelion*) to describe this kerygma but whether Mark's usage of the same term provides us with another link with Paul is a matter of dispute.

The classic case denying any direct influence between the two was made in 1923 by M. Werner, who argued that Mark's Gospel was representative of a type of Gentile Christianity which was independent of Paul. Comparing the Gospel with the Epistle, Werner noted that a number of specific Pauline concepts were on the whole lacking in Mark, while the resemblances between them were explicable as the product of beliefs which were common to and widespread in primitive Christianity. On the other hand, scholars such as W. Marxsen (*Mark*, p. 213) have claimed that insufficient allowance has been made for the different ways in which each writer has chosen to express his kerygma, Paul in abstract theological terms and in the direct form of an Epistle, Mark in the 'visual' and narrative form of a Gospel. If we see Mark as 'narrative Christology', then, it is possible to view it as a treatment of the Jesus tradition influenced by the Pauline emphasis on the salvific significance of the death and resurrection of Christ.

Mark and Jesus

The Jesus of the Tradition (Teacher, Prophet and Miracle Worker)

In Chapter 3, we discussed Mark's characterization of Jesus in literary terms. The significance of the Gospel as a literary composition is that it welded a number of prevailing traditions about Jesus into a more or less unified presentation and that the resultant product had thereafter an impact that was greater than the sum of its parts. Mark was also an interpreter of these Jesus traditions. Using literary-historical tools, let us now consider the nature of these traditions and what Mark has done with them. Three pre-Markan traditions in particular present themselves: the traditions of Jesus as a teacher, as a prophet and as a miracle-worker. Each of these is attested not only in Mark but also in Q and hence is almost certain to be pre-Markan.

One of the earliest impulses in the Jesus movement was the collection of Jesus' saying, as the 'Sayings' tradition underlying the Gospels indicates. In Q, attention focuses only on Jesus' sayings and there is little interest in his death or resurrection. In this early source, he is principally portrayed as a teacher, preacher or prophet of the coming Kingdom of God. Although some would qualify this (e.g. M. Smith), this aspect of Jesus' activity is also important for Mark. In a redactional passage, Jesus is described as a teacher (*didaskalos*) 'with authority [*exousia*] and not as the scribes' (1.22). The noun *didaskalos* is used 12 times in Mark (the Markan Jesus himself uses it as a self-designation in 14.14) and the verb *didaskein* 15 times (more often than in other New Testament writing). 'And he began to teach' is a favourite Markan expression, as we have seen.

The tradition of Jesus as a Jewish prophet is also deeply embedded in primitive Christianity as well as in Mark. Jesus is believed to have had close connections with John the Baptist whose disciple he may have been. Jesus' own consciousness appears to have been a prophetic one (cf., e.g., Mk 6.4; Lk. 13.31-35) and it is certain that he was regarded as such (cf., e.g., Mk 6.14-16; 8.27-28). A substantial number of the sayings attributed to him are prophetic or apocalyptic ones, with many regarded by form critics as authentic. Certain activities associated with him, it is suggested, may originally have been examples of dramatic prophetic action (e.g. the feeding in the wilderness, the triumphal entry, the cleansing of the temple, the cursing of the fig tree, the last supper). Traditions, furthermore, concerning his possession by the Spirit (cf., e.g., Mk. 1.9-11), ecstatic experience (cf., e.g., Lk. 10.21-22 = Mt. 11.25-27), clairvoyance (cf., e.g., Mk 2.8) and even celibacy would also fit the prophetic mould.

The Jesus of the pre-Markan tradition was also deemed a miracle-worker, and most notably a healer and an exorcist. Q preserves a saying which indicates that the significance of Jesus' miracle-working was eschatological, that is, it vindicated his claim to be an eschatological prophet and provided evidence that the Kingdom of God was imminent, as he proclaimed (cf., e.g., Mt. 12.28 = Lk. 11.20; Mt. 11.2-6 = Lk. 7.18-23). This tradition of Jesus as miracle-worker and particularly as healer and exorcist is also strongly emphasized in Mark (cf., e.g., Mk. 3.10-12), although his use of these stories, which we will consider shortly, together with the sayings, may indicate that he interpreted the tradition in a different light. According to some scholars (e.g. U. Luz), the Markan tradition (or the evangelist himself?) shows a strong tendency (when compared with Q) to de-eschatologize the life of Jesus and to present Jesus as fulfilling in his earthly life a kerygmatic function (rather than in his future appearance an eschatological function). Sayings which have strong eschatological emphasis in Q are less eschatological when paralleled in Mark, and a similar conclusion can be reached about the miracles.

The Person of Jesus in Mark: The Miracles and the Messianic Secret
The miracle pericopes are found mainly in the first half of the Gospel and are for the most part clustered into sections, as we have already observed (1.21–2.12; 4.35–5.43; 6.35-52; 7.24–8.10, 22-26; although compare also the single pericopes in 3.1-6; 9.14-27; 11.12-14, 20-25). The stories are of four types: exorcisms, other healings, raisings from the dead and nature miracles. As with the controversy pericopes, scholars have debated whether the evangelist took them over in connected form from sources and whether their origin or provenance was Palestinian (as has been argued, for example, for those in 1.21–2.12 or 10.46-52) or Hellenistic (e.g. 7.32-37; 8.22-26). Some have argued for the Jewish apocalyptic tradition as a background for the stories (e.g. Kee, *Community*, pp. 23-30, 32-38). Others have detected elements of the Hellenistic magic tradition, particularly in the last two examples (cf. J.M. Hull, *Magic*, ch. 5). Yet others have posited the influence of the Hellenistic 'divine man' concept (the 'aretalogical' tradition) upon the stories (e.g. H.D. Betz).

In selecting and incorporating these stories, Mark has edited them in various ways. For example, two of them, it appears, have been altered by him into controversy stories (2.1-12; 3.1-6), some have been deliberately placed on Gentile soil (cf. the second cycle of 7.24–8.26) and a number, it has been argued, have been used for symbolic purposes (e.g. the 'blind man' stories of 8.2-26 or 10.46-52; the cursing of the fig tree, 11.12-14, 20-23 or the feeding accounts of 6.35-44 and 8.1-10 with their Jew–Gentile implications and possible eucharistic overtones; cf. esp. 8.14-21). In his selection, the evangelist, it should be noted, has opted to include a number which easily lend themselves to symbolic, spiritual or theological interpretation, the cure of the blind, deaf or dumb, or the raising of the dead. How precisely did Mark interpret the significance of the miracles attributed to Jesus?

Three views have held the field until recently. In line with a Jewish and apocalyptic evaluation of the Gospel, the first would claim that Mark interpreted the miracles eschatologically; in other words, he saw Jesus (in continuity with the earlier Jewish-Christian tradition) as God's eschatological agent, 'the Strong One', the 'Son of God' (= Messiah) whose miracle-working signalled the rout of Satan and the coming of the Kingdom of God. Claiming a Hellenistic background for the miracle accounts, the second view would argue that Jesus is being portrayed by the evangelist in the colours of the divine man, the 'Son of God' in metaphysical terms. For Mark, Jesus' miracles were not eschatological 'signs or wonders' validating Jesus' role as a Jewish apocalyptic prophet or even as God's Messiah but the acts of one who betrays himself as an 'epiphany' of God in human form. The miracles have a positive function, therefore, in promoting a theology of glory (*theologia gloriae*) in connection with the figure of Jesus. They reveal him as a supernatural figure (cf., e.g., 4.35-41; 6.45-52; 9.1-8). A third view suggests that the miracles serve an opposite christological function, namely, to counter such a theology and, by suggesting that Jesus' true identity is to be discerned through his suffering rather than through his miracles, to emphasize instead a theology of the cross (*theologia crucis*). This is achieved in two ways; first, by juxtaposing the passion theme of the second part of the Gospel with the miracle accounts of the first, and, secondly, by means of the secrecy motif throughout.

In the description of Mark's literary presentation of Jesus above, a key feature was the aura of secrecy which surrounded his person and activity (puzzling commands to silence, private instruction to the disciples, parabolic teaching to the crowd, curious self-concealment, refusal to give a sign). This was first pointed out by W. Wrede in a book *The Messianic Secret in the Gospels* first published (in German) in 1901. Since Wrede, scholars have attempted to account for this feature in three main ways. Some have cast doubt on the existence of the motif as such, preferring to explain its various alleged components in different ways. Others have offered historical explanations, seeking to maintain that the motive of concealment was a feature of the historical Jesus' own behaviour and teaching, which is accurately reported upon by Mark. Others still opt for literary or theological explanations; in other words, the 'secrecy' motif was a literary or theological device whereby various traditions about the historical Jesus could be presented within the overall perspective of the Christology (and soteriology) adopted within the Markan community sometime after Jesus' death.

Wrede himself maintained that the origin of the secrecy motif lay in the fact that the early church had only claimed Jesus to be the Messiah after a belief arose that he had risen from the dead. There was hence a need to present originally non-Messianic traditions about Jesus as the action of a Messiah who in his lifetime has gone unrecognized or incognito. Since so much of Jesus' behaviour and that of his disciples is incomprehensive and contradictory, if viewed historically, the majority of scholars would now follow Wrede in preferring to see the so-called 'Messianic Secret' as Mark's way of representing Jesus to his readers as he was conceived to be in the light of subsequent post-Easter theological reflection. In modification of Wrede's thesis, however, it is now generally agreed that Mark has not imposed a Christology upon pre-Markan traditions that have no christological stamp, but rather that he sought to develop or counter, by means of his own, the Christology already implicit in these various traditions. Mark's main aim, then, by means of both the miracles and the secrecy motif, was christological—the desire to promote or advance a particular understanding of Jesus as 'Son of God', perhaps against contrary views.

The Message of Jesus in Mark: The Parables and the Sayings

Mark's secrecy motif, as we have already noted, extends also to the message of Jesus as it is expressed in his parables and sayings. 'To you has been given the secret of the Kingdom of God, but for those outside everything is in parables so that they may indeed see but not perceive, and may indeed hear and not understand; lest they should turn again, and be forgiven' (4.11-12). While the term 'parable' can bear the meaning of mysterious speech, of a riddle or enigma, it is normally understood as a brief narrative or saying which forcefully illustrates a single idea and that by means of vivid imagery drawn from everyday life. When employed originally by Jesus, parables were intended, it is usually assumed, to elucidate his message rather than to mystify his audience. By the time they came to be written down, however, they were frequently found to be puzzling or obscure, hence the tendency of the church or evangelist to invest them with allegorical meaning. Form critics have divided the parables into three categories, each of which can be found in Mark, namely, parabolic or figurative sayings or *Bildwörter* (cf., e.g., 2.17a, 19a, 21, 22; 3.23-27; 4.21, 24; 9.49-50; 10.25; 13.28), similitudes or *Gleichnisse* (cf., e.g., 4.26-29, 30-32; 13.34-36) and narrative parables or *Parabeln* (cf., e.g., 4.1-8; 12.1-9). The parables are frequently clustered (cf. 2.17-22; 3.23-27; 4.1-33), in some cases being

conflated as double parables (cf. 2.21-22; 3.24-25; 4.21-25) and allegorization is a common feature (cf. 2.19b, 20; 3.27; 4.13-20; 12.1-9; 13.34-36).

A number of Mark's parables are found in the important parable
discourse of 4.1-34 which, despite evidence of concentric arrangement,
a majority of scholars would still regard as dependent upon a pre-
Markan source. This source Mark has edited by adding an introduction (4.1-2), a secondary allegorical interpretation (4.13-20 – although
this application, while not original, may perhaps be pre-Markan) and
a conclusion (4.33-34). The evangelist was also perhaps responsible
not only for the insertion but even for the content of the awkward private scene describing the function of the parables (4.10-12), although
this is disputed. Whether due to Mark or the tradition before him, this
passage addresses the problem of Jewish unbelief by claiming, as Paul
had done (cf., e.g., 2 Cor. 4.3-4; Rom. 11.8), that such unbelief had been
predestined. The historical outcome of Jesus' teaching had been Jewish
rejection, and hence, to the theological mind, this must have been its
intended effect, since God's purposes could not be thwarted. Through
the medium of the parables, the secret or 'mystery' (*musterion*) of the
Kingdom of God had been given to 'those outside'. For Mark, therefore, the parables, as with the miracles, are not to be interpreted eschatologically but christologically. They are not the means by which Jesus
openly proclaims the coming Kingdom of God, but the means by
which he *secretly* intimates his true status and mission (cf., e.g., 12.1-
12).

The Mission of Jesus in Mark: The Kingdom of God and the Son of Man
How then did Mark conceive of 'the Kingdom of God' and how does
the evangelist's understanding relate to that of the historical Jesus for
whom it appears to have been a major tenet. 'Kingdom' sayings are
both numerous and multiply attested in the Synoptic tradition (Mark
13; Q 13; Special Matthew 25; Special Luke 6). The Jewish background
to the expression has been much investigated, particularly as it is
encountered in the literature of apocalyptic Judaism where it has been
found to have eschatological significance. Debate has ranged, therefore, not only over the authenticity of the sayings but also over the
question whether Jesus' conception of the Kingdom was an apocalyptic one or whether he envisaged the Kingdom's coming in essentially
non-apocalyptic (spiritual or existential) terms.

Various theories have been advanced. One view (thorough-going or
consistent eschatology) is that Jesus was an eschatological prophet
who (like his contemporaries) both expected and proclaimed the Kingdom as a future, imminent, apocalyptic event (cf. A. Schweitzer). The

sayings which claim that the Kingdom of God has already come in Jesus' person and mission are the product of the early church's 'theological accommodation' to the failure of apocalyptic expectations (especially the parousia). A second view (realized eschatology) claims that Jesus departed from the apocalyptic view of his contemporaries in that he saw the Kingdom rather as 'an order beyond space and time' (C.H. Dodd) already present in his person and ministry. The sayings which talk of the Kingdom's future coming in apocalyptic terms (together with the parousia) are the product of a subsequent 're-Judaization' of Christianity or 'a contamination of the authentically Christian stream' by Jewish apocalypticism. A third mediating position (inaugurated eschatology) states that a number of both 'present' and 'future' sayings originate with Jesus and must be kept in tension. Jesus was an eschatological prophet who proclaimed that the Kingdom of God had been inaugurated in his person and ministry, but who also looked for its consummation in the future, as did Jewish apocalyptic (J. Jeremias).

When we consider the Markan Kingdom sayings, we find evidence of all three emphases. In certain sayings, the 'apocalyptic' or 'future' element appears to be uppermost (cf., e.g., 9.1 — unless we translate 'see the kingdom of God come with power' as 'see *that* the kingdom of God *has* come with power'; 9.47; 10.23-25; 11.10; 14.25; 15.43), in others the 'realized', 'present' or 'spiritual' element is to the fore (cf., e.g., 4.11; 10.14-15; 12.34), in others still there is what can be construed perhaps as an 'inaugurated' accent (1.15; 4.26, 30). Mark's understanding of the Kingdom, therefore, is difficult to determine precisely but it is clear that for him it is bound up with Jesus' proclamation and presence, that it is hidden from those who fail to recognize him as 'Son of God', that it demands an ethical response now and that, while operating in secret, it is proceeding towards its future consummation (A.M. Ambrozic).

Mark's understanding of the Kingdom of God is also linked with his understanding of Jesus as 'the Son of Man'. The expression is a curious one. It is used in the Old Testament in a purely generic sense, that is, as a periphrasis or alternative expression for 'human(kind)' or 'human beings', especially as viewed in their humble creatureliness and mortality over against their transcendent Creator and God (cf., e.g., Pss. 8.4; 80.17; 146.3; Num. 23.19; Job 25.1-6; Isa. 51.12; 56.2). It is also used as a form of address to a prophet or apocalyptic visionary (cf., e.g., Ezek. 2.1; Dan. 8.17) and as a description of an apparently heavenly figure in the apocalypse of Daniel (7.13 'one like a son of man') to whom God would grant his 'kingdom'. Although in actuality a corporate personality representing Israel or 'the saints of the Most High', this Danielic figure came later to be interpreted by apocalyptic Judaism as an individual, transcendent, eschatological agent (cf. *1 En.* 48; 69.26-29; 71.14-17; *4 Ezra* 13.1-13).

Both of these usages of the expression 'son of man', the generic and the apocalyptic, are found in the New Testament, in the vast majority of cases in the Gospels (for the exceptions, cf. Acts 7.56; Rev. 1.13; 14.14) and, with the exception of the last two references, with the definite article. In most cases it appears on the lips of Jesus himself, and in many instances it occurs in a form that is tantamount to a title, '*the* Son of Man'. While Q, for example, gives us instances where the expression can be interpreted as a self-designation with no apparent apocalyptic significance (cf., e.g., Mt. 8.20 = Lk. 9.58; Mt. 11.19 = Lk. 7.34), other sayings indicate a belief in the coming of an apocalyptic Son of Man figure (cf., e.g., Mt. 24.27, 37-39 = Lk. 17.24, 26-30; Mt. 24.44 = Lk. 12.40).

Various theories seek to account for these observations. One school of thought holds that the non-titular, linguistic or generic usage goes back to the primary tradition and the apocalyptic usage is late and secondary. By a process of mistranslation coupled with misunderstanding the expression 'Son of Man' came to be viewed as a title for an apocalyptic redeemer (cf. G. Vermes). A second school maintains that the apocalyptic background is primary, Jesus as an eschatological prophet having shared the same kind of apocalyptic expectation entertained in Enoch circles. As part of his eschatological kerygma, he may have proclaimed the coming of the apocalyptic Son of Man. Either he thought of himself as this figure or the Jewish-Christian community (by virtue of a belief in his resurrection) claimed that he would return as this figure to judge the world (R. Bultmann; H.E. Tödt). He may also have used the term 'Son of Man' for himself but, departing from an apocalyptic conception, given it his own enigmatic content (E. Schweizer; F.H. Borsch; M. Hooker).

The 'Son of Man' sayings in the Gospel of Mark have traditionally been divided into three categories. A first group, in line with Q, depicts Jesus as a triumphant apocalyptic figure promising his future return (cf., e.g., 8.38; 13.26; 14.62); a second, as a charismatic figure proclaiming his present authority on earth (cf. 2.10, 28); and a third as a suffering, rejected figure predicting his death and resurrection (cf., e.g., 8.31; 9.31; 10.33-34). This third group, the passion predictions, has received particular attention. While some regard them as traditional, a case has been made that they are redactional (cf. N. Perrin) and that their creation by the evangelist reflects a special Markan emphasis.

While accepting what may have been a traditional Jewish-Christian identification of Jesus as the victorious apocalyptic Son of Man shortly to return to bring judgment and salvation, Mark may be claiming that Jesus as Son of Man had already begun to exercise his eschatological role on earth both in his teaching and activity (2.10, 28 – if these verses, too, are redactional) as well as in his pre-ordained suffering, death and resurrection (8.31; 10.45). The Gospel of Mark may represent, therefore, a stage in the process by which the apocalyptic Son of Man who judges or saves men at his parousia becomes the suffering Son of Man who judges or saves men by his redemptive death on the cross.

Mark and Israel

Eschatology and the Little Apocalypse

The conclusion here offered in respect of Mark's treatment of the Son of Man was also suggested in our study of the Parables and the Kingdom of God, namely, that the Gospel of Mark in its eschatology represents an early stage in the transformation of the apocalyptic hope of Israel, of Jesus and of primitive Jewish Christianity. Jesus 'the Proclaimer' of the coming eschatological Kingdom of God (to Israel and to fellow Jews) is in process of being seen as 'the Proclaimed' in whose person and ministry the Kingdom was (in another sense) already present ('the secret of the Kingdom'). Eschatology, to put it another way, is on the way to being eclipsed by Christology. With the coming of Jesus, there has been, for Mark, a judgment on Israel, and in his triumphant return as Son of Man this judgment will be consummated. To understand how the evangelist understands the apocalyptic hope, the future of Israel and the end of the world in light of his Christology, therefore, scholars have given a great deal of attention to Mark 13 where such ideas are encountered.

The 'little apocalypse', as it is called, is difficult to interpret and raises a great many questions and issues. Has the evangelist made use of a written source (or sources), and, if so, what was its origin? Does the discourse, or parts thereof, go back to Jesus? What debt does the discourse owe to the Old Testament? Is the eschatological discourse an alien body or an integral part of the Gospel? What is the nature and degree of redactional activity apparent in it? Does the evangelist entertain a positive or negative attitude towards apocalyptic?

Because of the numerous discrepancies and ambiguities which are apparent in it, particularly in the attitude expressed towards apocalyptic, a number of scholars believe that the discourse was based on an underlying written source or *Vorlage*. One prominent view is that it was built around the nucleus of an apocalypse (or apocalyptic 'fly-sheet', pamphlet or tract) of independent origin, which had originally circulated in Jewish, Jewish-Christian or early Christian circles, either in the reign of the Emperor Caligula (37–41 CE) or at the time of the Romano–Jewish War (66–70 CE). Because of parallels with other authentic dominical teaching, some think it unnecessary to postulate an extraneous origin for it and trace it back to Jesus himself therefore. Links, on the other hand, between Mark 13 and the prophetic and apocalyptic passages of the Old Testament (particularly Daniel, Micah, Joel and Zechariah) have led to the suggestion that it is, or developed from, an exposition, meditation or midrash on the book of Daniel. The advent of redaction criticism, moreover, has led to a growing awareness of the extent of Markan redactional activity within the discourse. A common view now is that the eschatological discourse, like that of the parables of Mark 4, is a redactional composition embodying certain traditional material (a written source, perhaps, or a combination of written sources, oral tradition, the Old Testament, scattered prophetic or apocalyptic sayings, some with links to Q) the extent and cohesiveness of which cannot be precisely determined. Some, following the newer literary emphases, are even abandoning the pursuit of sources and the recovery of the tradition history of the discourse in favour of treating it as a narrated speech with links, in terms of style, structure and content, with the rest of the Gospel.

What theological function, therefore, does the 'little apocalypse' play within the Gospel and what purpose was served in including it? An obvious answer is that the evangelist saw in the events of the 60s, and particularly in Israel's disastrous war with the Romans, signs that the world was coming to an end, and that the Christian community could take comfort from the fact that, despite suffering and persecution, these events had been foreseen by their founder, and that he himself would shortly be returning in triumph to punish his enemies and to reward the faithful. Using traditional apocalyptic sayings or even an existing apocalypse, he has, in the manner of the apocalypticist, updated his source material to make it relevant to a new situation. This construction makes Mark positive towards apocalyptic but a contrary view of his redactional emphasis would argue that he inserted the discourse into his Gospel in order to modify or tone down the apocalyptic fervour occasioned by the Romano–Jewish war, to disassociate these events from the end-time itself and to urge ethical 'watchfulness' as the appropriate response to the parousia expectation (cf. 13.32-37).

Mark and the Temple

Whether the apocalyptic events which would culminate in the parousia are connected, for Mark, *immediately* with the fall of Jerusalem or some time after that catastrophe, the fact that the discourse is occasioned by Jesus' prophesying the Temple's destruction (13.1-2) is surely instructive. Some have even argued (e.g. S.G.F. Brandon) that the fall of Jerusalem was the occasion for the Gospel itself. What was the attitude of Mark and his community to this event and in particular to the demise of Judaism's foremost institution? The reader is already given some indirect indication in 2.10 that the Markan Jesus, by forgiving sins, can fulfil one of the Temple's functions. In 2.25-26, moreover, he can cite with approval a scriptural example of what otherwise would have been regarded as an act of sacrilege against the Temple. In chs. 11–13, however, the Temple comes fully into focus with Jesus' climactic visit to Jerusalem. Here he is said, in popular parlance, to have 'cleansed' the Temple, although scholars are divided in their opinions concerning the significance attached to this tradition. As presented by the evangelist, the event could signify that Jesus acted merely to purify the Temple as a 'house of prayer for all the Gentiles' (11.17) by ridding it of commercial activity. Mark, however, could be further implying that Jesus intended to bring a halt to the sacrificial system itself (11.16), a more radical action. I myself have argued (*The Barren Temple*) that, by framing the Temple incident with the cursing of the fig tree story (11.12-14, 20-23), the evangelist is inviting his implied readers to view Jesus' words as pronouncing a sentence of judgment on the Temple, the withering of the tree acting as an eschatological sign prefiguring the destruction of a sterile Temple cultus. The Temple prophecy of 13.1-2 reinforces this impression as does the charge laid against Jesus at his trial (14.58) and mockingly repeated at his crucifixion (15.29-30). It is curious, nevertheless, that the charge is described by Mark as 'false witness'. Here perhaps Markan irony is at work. Some scholars (e.g. D. Juel) detect in the Gospel the influence of a 'new' or 'spiritual' Temple motif (cf. 1 Cor. 3.16-17). Hence it is possible that, while the evangelist may have wished to refute the charge literally, he intended notwithstanding to intimate to the discerning reader that a new temple 'not made with hands' (viz. the Christian community) had resulted from Jesus' salvific death and resurrection. Some support for this view can be garnered from Mark's last Temple reference, namely, the rending of the Temple veil at the moment of Jesus' demise (15.38).

Mark and the Jewish Leaders

Not everyone would adhere to the view that the cursed fig tree represents the Temple. Many would prefer to see it as standing for Israel,
either the Jews in general or the Jewish leaders in particular. In
Chapter 3, we discussed Mark's literary representation of the Jewish
leaders. Here let us consider some historical issues in connection with
them. What do we know about these leadership groups? Is Mark's
portrait of them historically accurate? How much did he himself know
about these groups? Does his negative portrait of them extend to the
Jewish people as a whole and is it fair to describe his attitude as anti-
Jewish?

The evangelist, as we have seen, treats a number of different groups
(the Pharisees, the Herodians, the Sadducees, the elders, the chief
priests and the scribes) as a united front in respect of their opposition
to Jesus. These groups, however, were anything but united in terms of
their religious and political affiliations. Although prominent in the
Gospels, the Pharisees were eclipsed in power and influence by their
sectarian opponents, the Sadducees, before the fall of Jerusalem, and
only came into the ascendancy thereafter. According to M. Smith,
there were practically no Pharisees in Galilee in Jesus' lifetime, nor do
we know of a Herodian party (an obscure group politically affiliated
to the Herodian dynasty) in existence at that time far less in alliance
with the Pharisees (3.6; 12.13). Our knowledge of the scribes is also
somewhat obscure (were they a sub-group of the Pharisees, a clerical
class common to both Pharisees and Sadducees or a separate group
influential before 70 CE?) In one study of the subject, M.J. Cook
(*Mark's Treatment*) claims that Mark himself knew very little about the
Jewish leadership groups he presumes were active in Jesus' time. The
evangelist was substantially dependent on three conflicting written
sources, and the portrait he offers of the Jewish authorities is hence
artificial and historically unreliable. One controversy pericope (cf.
10.2-12 'Is it lawful for a man to divorce his wife?') is a classic example
often cited in this regard. Would Pharisees have really asked this
question of Jesus when it was known that the Mosaic Law permitted
divorce (cf. Deut. 24.1-4)?

We have considered the controversy pericopes and their function
within the Gospel. Here these selfsame leadership groups, especially
the scribes and the Pharisees, are found in conflict or debate with
Jesus over a wide range of legal and doctrinal matters. By means of
these stories, a charismatic and predominantly Gentile-Christian Jesus
is shown repudiating the authority and teaching of a legalistic Judaism, and in consequence of this is tried and executed by the jealous

guardians of Israel's heritage. Does Mark's presentation, however, add up to a pronounced campaign of denigration against the Jewish people themselves? Various views have been expressed in regard to this. On the one hand, it has been argued that the evangelist's hostility is confined to the Jewish authorities and not to the nation as a whole. In his controversies with these leaders, his Jesus remains within the limits of intra-Jewish dispute (e.g. in Sabbath observance or divorce), and does not overstep the bounds of acceptable Jewish behaviour (e.g. by repudiating his people). As the feeding stories may indicate, Mark sees in the Christian community a place for Jew and Gentile alike. On the other hand, there are also hints that the evangelist's horizons extend to all Jews (cf., e.g., 7.3-4 'the Pharisees *and all the Jews*', as well as 7.6). Even accounting for their leaders' machinations, it is the Jewish crowd who in the end call for Jesus' crucifixion (15.13). For killing his heir, God will destroy the tenants and give the vineyard to others (12.9). The evangelist also links Jesus' family with his opponents (3.21, 22) and has Jesus repudiate, in effect, his blood ties with the former (3.31-35). The matter of Mark's attitude to the Jews is hard, therefore, to resolve.

The Way of the Cross

Discipleship, Persecution and Martyrdom

Mark is not only concerned with those who oppose Jesus but also with those who follow him. Christology and discipleship are interrelated themes in the Gospel. While the evangelist presents at various points aspects of discipleship such as faith (cf., e.g., 1.15; 4.20, 40; 5.34; 9.20-24; 10.52; 11.22-23) and prayer (cf., e.g., 1.35; 9.29; 11.24-25; 14.32-42), it is in the central section of the Gospel (8.27–10.45) that his teaching on the true nature of discipleship is concentrated. As noted in the summary of the Gospel's contents, various narratives and sayings linked ostensibly by this theme are here presented within the context of Jesus' journey or pilgrimage to Jerusalem, taking place 'on the way' or 'on the road' (cf. 8.27; 9.33, 34; 10.17, 32, 46, 52) to his appointment with death ('the way of the cross').

This 'way' motif, we have observed, has been seen as a metaphor for discipleship. While certain pericopes may appear out of place (e.g. 10.2-12), the climactic call to discipleship in 10.43-45 seems to reinforce the *Leitmotif* of the section as does the evidence of careful structuring. Two 'giving of sight' stories frame the section (8.22-26; 10.46-52), the second explicitly declaring that the blind man, whose 'faith' has 'saved' him, 'followed [Jesus] *on the way*' (10.52). The presence of three repeated passion predictions (8.31; 9.31; 10.33-34), each preceded by a geographical reference and each followed by the disciples' misunderstanding and Jesus' corrective teaching (N. Perrin), indicates that, for Mark, discipleship cannot be understood apart from the passion and resurrection of Jesus. Where following Jesus originally meant following an eschatological prophet proclaiming the imminent Kingdom of God, Mark presents discipleship as following Jesus on the road to the cross. Here, it is suggested, he may have been engaging with the 'real world' situation of his readers, a Gentile-Christian community suffering imminent or actual persecution, or even martyrdom, for the sake of the gospel (cf., e.g., 8.34–9.1; 10.29-30; 13.9-13) and one able to identify, therefore, with the fate of both John the Baptist (cf. 1.14; 6.17-29; 9.11-13) and Jesus (cf. 8.31; 9.31; 10.33-34, 45; 14.41).

The Disciples in Mark

If the true nature of discipleship is intimated in the central section, then what attitude does the evangelist harbour towards Jesus' original Jewish disciples? In Chapter 3, we considered Mark's literary representation of the disciples, outlining their narrative role and observing Mark's harsh treatment of them. In particular we noted the blindness motif which Mark associates with them as well as Jesus' opponents (cf., e.g., 6.52; 8.14-21). How is this phenomenon to be explained? We have already cited one literary explanation which claims that the disciples function as prototypical believers with whom the implied (Christian) reader is encouraged to identify and hence, through their weakness, be led to self-criticism. Here let us consider some historical explanations.

Mark's Gospel employs various expressions for the followers of Jesus. His principal terms are the 'twelve' (*dodeka*; cf. 3.14; 4.10; 6.7; 9.35; 10.32; [10.41-45]; 11.11; 14.10, 17, 20, 43), a number of whom are at intervals singled out, and the/his 'disciples' (*mathetai*; cf. 4.34; 6.35, 45; 7.17; 8.10, 34; 9.14, 28; 10.10, 13, 23, 46; 11.1, 14; 12.43; 13.1; 14.12, 13, 16, 32; 16.7). He also refers to those 'around him' or those 'who followed him' (cf. 3.34; 4.10; 10.32; 11.9), including frequently a crowd (cf. 3.32; 10.46) or on one occasion women (cf. 15.40-41). He generally avoids the term 'apostles' (*apostoloi*; although cf. 6.30 and the variant reading for 3.14). Most approaches to Mark and the disciples attempt to separate tradition from redaction. A number of issues occupy scholars. One issue is whether the term 'disciples' is synonymous with the 'twelve' or whether it indicates a wider circle. The use of two different terms has suggested to some the incorporation of separate sources. Discussion has revolved around the question whether the designation, the 'twelve', is traditional or redactional in Mark and to what extent the evangelist has a particular interest in this special group. Some would say that he wishes to single them out, others concluding, from his widening of the circle around Jesus, that he gives them no special place. A major question, however, is who the disciples represent for Mark and his actual readers and why are they shown in such a bad light.

Two main types of explanation have been offered. The first is what we may term variously the pedagogic, parenetic or pastoral theory (cf. E. Best). The 'misunderstanding' of the disciples, in other words, is a literary device with a pedagogic or didactic function, namely, to enable Mark to expand upon or clarify aspects of Jesus' teaching of importance to his community (e.g. 14.13-20; 7.17ff.; 9.28-29; 10.10-12; 13.3ff.; cf. also Jn 14.5, 8, 22ff.). The role of the disciples is hence to act as a foil to Jesus, reinforcing his stature in relation to their deficiencies. The disciples represent the church, therefore, or more accurately, the Markan community. In the conduct of the disciples, Mark sees reflected that of his own community whom he wishes to address, instruct, edify and exhort. Portraying the disciples in this way serves a parenetic function, to illustrate and develop the author's theme of discipleship, with all its demands, limitations and risks. This view sees Mark then as essentially a pastor writing primarily to offer encouragement to his community to remain steadfast in their discipleship despite the suffering it caused.

The second type of explanation is the polemical theory. While recognizing that the role of the disciples in Mark is not uniform, this hypothesis proceeds from the assumption that the harsh treatment of the original twelve is too often in excess of that demanded by the author's didactic or pastoral interests. There is, it is asserted, a polemical thrust to Mark's Gospel which eclipses its pastoral function. Two main forms of the theory have proved popular. The first seeks to identify heretics within the community whom the evangelist is in actuality addressing. In the view of T.J. Weeden, for example, Mark is attacking, in the person of the disciples, a 'divine-man' Christology which (in its blindness) emphasized the role of Jesus as a miracle-working Hellenistic divine man without recognizing the divine necessity of his redemptive suffering and death. However, if this is the Christology that the evangelist is really opposed to, is it a fitting one to be attributed to his original Jewish disciples? The second views the Gospel more appropriately as an attack, on behalf of Gentile Christianity, on the Jewish-Christian tradition represented by the disciples and Jesus' family. According to J.B. Tyson ('Blindness', pp. 261-68),

Mark is attacking, in the person of the twelve, the royal Messiah or Son of David Christology of the original Jerusalem church, which claimed authority over the nascent Gentile-Christian communities founded by Hellenistic Jews like Paul. Their hegemony was resented by communities such as Mark's and the conflict between the two traditions is reflected in the text.

The Suffering, Death and Resurrection of Jesus
What unites these two hypotheses is the notion that there are opposing Christologies, therefore, at work in the Markan text. In seeing Jesus primarily as a Hellenistic 'divine man' or as a messianic king (or even as the apocalyptic Son of Man shortly to return in glory), these Christologies share a triumphalist estimate of the person and role of Jesus, a *theologia gloriae*. Neither accords a significant place to the cross in its soteriological scheme, the latter in particular seeing Jesus as Messiah *despite*, and not *because of*, his death, and looking to Jesus' second return or parousia to effect humanity's salvation. In opposition to such a perspective is Mark's emphasis on the suffering, death and resurrection of Jesus, his *theologia crucis*. As with Paul, Mark appears to be claiming that Jesus discloses his true identity (as Son of God) and achieves his essential victory (as Son of Man) through his redemptive suffering on the cross. Unlike Paul's theology of the cross, however, the Markan soteriology is not spelled out (cf., e.g., 1 Cor. 1.18-25 with Mk 15.31-32). Apart from such passages as 10.45 or 14.24, the reader has to infer it from the prominence given to the three passion predictions (8.31; 9.31; 10.33-34) and, of course, to the passion narrative itself.

Although its parameters are in dispute, a majority of scholars, as we have seen, would still favour the view that the Gospel incorporates a pre-Markan passion narrative, and that this primitive account might even go back in some form to the Jerusalem church. The separate witness of the Johannine account (if John is indeed independent of Mark) would argue in favour of this. The presence of what appear to be discrete and self-contained units, however (e.g. the anointing at Bethany, 14.3-9; cf. Lk. 7.36-50; Jn 12.1-8), or passages which show signs of being redactional compositions (e.g. the Gethsemane pericope, 14.32-42; or the trial before the Sanhedrin, 14.53-72) have led others to claim that the passion narrative did not exist prior to Mark as a unified, coherent and consecutive whole but from beginning to end was composed of fragments of tradition. More recent studies still have highlighted the high degree of Markan redactional and even compositional activity in the narrative, and some (cf. W.H. Kelber [ed.], *The Passion in Mark*) have therefore concluded that the literary and theological achievement of Mark was to compose an entire Gospel, not just chs. 1–13, out of the multiplicity of disparate traditions available to him. Some of the kerygmatic or theological motivations which have coloured the passion narrative have already been commented upon, for example, the desire to show that Jesus died as Messiah or 'suffering righteous man', that his death had salvific significance, that his passion and resurrection were the fulfilment of Old Testament prophecies. These may be traceable either to Mark or to the tradition before him but a growing body of opinion (following Kelber *et al.*) would now recognize in chs. 14–16 a number of specifically Markan themes (cf., e.g., the private scene, the focus on three disciples, the prayer of Jesus, the disciples' failure in the Gethsemane passage, 14.32-42, or the 'Son of God' Christology in the trial or the crucifixion scene, 14.61; 15.39) and hence the recapitulation and climax of the paradoxical theology he has expressed in earlier chapters. One such theme is the secrecy motif which extends into Markan's sudden and enigmatic ending.

FURTHER READING

W.R. Telford, *The Theology of the Gospel of Mark* (New Testament Theology; Cambridge: Cambridge University Press, 1999).

For Mark and the Gentiles, see the following:

R.P. Booth, *Jesus and the Laws of Purity: Tradition History and Legal History in Mark 7* (JSNTSup, 13; Sheffield: JSOT Press, 1986).

J.D.G. Dunn, 'Mark 2.1–3.6: A Bridge between Jesus and Paul in the Question of Law', *NTS* 30 (1984), pp. 395-415.

C.F. Evans, '"I will go before you into Galilee"', *JTS* 5 (1954), pp. 3-18.

J.C. Fenton, 'Paul and Mark', in D.E. Nineham (ed.), *Studies in the Gospels* (Fs. R.H. Lightfoot: Oxford: Blackwell, 1957), pp. 89-112.

R.A. Guelich, '"The Beginning of the Gospel": Mark 1.1-15', *BibRes* 27 (1982), pp. 5-15.

R.P. Martin, *Mark – Evangelist and Theologian* (Exeter: Paternoster Press, 1979), pp. 24-28.

W. Marxsen, *Mark the Evangelist: Studies on the Redaction History of the Gospel* (Nashville: Abingdon Press; London: SPCK, 1969).

D. Senior, 'The Struggle to be Universal: Mission as Vantage Point for New Testament Investigation', *CBQ* 46 (1984), pp. 63-81.

M. Werner, *Der Einfluss paulinischer Theologie im Markusevangelium* (BZNW, 1; Giessen: Alfred Töpelmann, 1923).

For Mark and Jesus, see the following:

A.M. Ambrozic, *The Hidden Kingdom: A Redaction-critical Study of the References to the Kingdom of God in Mark's Gospel* (CBQMS, 2; Washington, DC: Catholic Biblical Association of America, 1972).

H.D. Betz, 'Jesus as Divine Man', in F.T. Trotter (ed.), *Jesus and the Historian* (Fs. E.C. Colwell; Philadelphia: Westminster Press, 1968), pp. 114-33.

J.L. Blevins, *The Messianic Secret in Markan Research 1901–1976* (Washington, DC: University Press of America, 1981).

M. Boucher, *The Mysterious Parable* (Washington, DC: Catholic Biblical Association, 1977).

E.K. Broadhead, *Naming Jesus: Titular Christology in the Gospel of Mark* (JSNTSup, 175; Sheffield: Sheffield Academic Press, 1999).

B. Chilton, *The Kingdom of God in the Teaching of Jesus* (Issues in Religion and Theology, 5; London: SPCK; Philadelphia: Fortress Press, 1984).

M.D. Hooker, *The Son of Man in Mark* (London: SPCK, 1967).

J.M. Hull, *Hellenistic Magic and the Synoptic Tradition* (Studia biblica et theologica, 28; London: SCM Press, 1974).

W.H. Kelber, *The Kingdom in Mark: A New Place and a New Time* (Philadelphia: Fortress Press, 1974).

K. Kertelge, 'The Epiphany of Jesus in the Gospel (Mark)', in Telford (ed.), *Interpretation of Mark*, pp. 105-23.

N. Perrin, 'The Christology of Mark: A Study in Methodology', in Telford (ed.), *Interpretation of Mark*, pp. 125-40.

H. Räisänen, *The 'Messianic Secret' in Mark* (Studies of the New Testament and its World; Edinburgh: T. & T. Clark, 1990).

M. Smith, 'Forms, Motives and Omissions in Mark's Account of the Teaching of Jesus', in J. Reumann (ed.), *Understanding the Sacred Text* (Fs. M.S. Enslin; Valley Forge, PA: Judson Press, 1972), pp. 153-64.

C.M. Tuckett, 'The Present Son of Man', *JSNT* 14 (1982), pp. 58-81.

—*The Messianic Secret* (Issues in Religion and Theology, 1; London: SPCK; Philadelphia: Fortress Press, 1983).

W. Wrede, *The Messianic Secret* (The Library of Theological Translations; Cambridge: James Clarke, 1971).

For Mark and Israel, see the following.

A.Y. Collins, *The Beginning of the Gospel: Probings of Mark in Context* (Minneapolis, MN: Fortress Press, 1992).

M.J. Cook, *Mark's Treatment of the Jewish Leaders* (NovTSup, 51; Leiden: Brill, 1978).

T.J. Geddert, *Watchwords: Mark 13 in Markan Eschatology* (JSNTSup, 26; Sheffield: JSOT Press, 1989).

D. Juel, *Messiah and Temple* (Missoula, MT: Scholars Press, 1977).

E. Schweizer, 'Eschatology in Mark's Gospel', in E.E. Ellis and M. Wilcox (eds.), *Neotestamentica et Semitica* (Fs. M. Black; Edinburgh: T. & T. Clark, 1969), pp. 114-18.

W.R. Telford, *The Barren Temple and the Withered Tree: A Redaction-Critical Analysis of the Cursing of the Fig-tree Pericope in Mark's Gospel and its Relation to the*

Cleansing of the Temple Tradition (JSNTSup, 1; Sheffield: JSOT Press, 1980).

W.S. Vorster, 'Literary Reflections on Mark 13.5-37, a narrated speech of Jesus', in Telford (ed.), *Interpretation of Mark*, pp. 269-88.

D. Wenham, *The Rediscovery of Jesus' Eschatological Discourse* (Gospel Perspectives, 4; Sheffield: JSOT Press, 1984).

For the Way of the Cross, see the following:

E. Best, *The Temptation and the Passion: The Markan Soteriology* (SNTSMS, 2; Cambridge: Cambridge University Press, 1965).

—*Following Jesus: Discipleship in the Gospel of Mark* (JSNTSup, 4; Sheffield: JSOT Press, 1981).

—*Disciples and Discipleship: Studies in the Gospel According to Mark* (Edinburgh: T. & T. Clark, 1986).

C.C. Black, *The Disciples According to Mark: Markan Redaction in Current Debate* (JSNTSup, 27; Sheffield: JSOT Press, 1989).

J.R. Donahue, *The Theology and Setting of Discipleship in the Gospel of Mark* (Milwaukee; Marquette University Press, 1983).

J.R. Green, *The Death of Jesus: Tradition and Interpretation in the Passion Narrative* (WUNT, 2.33: Tübingen: Mohr-Siebeck, 1988).

W.H. Kelber (ed.), *The Passion in Mark: Studies on Mark 14–16* (Philadelphia, PA, Fortress Press, 1976).

F.J. Matera, *Passion Narratives and Gospel Theologies: Interpreting the Synoptics through their Passion Stories* (New York: Paulist Press, 1986).

R.C. Tannehill, 'The Disciples in Mark: The Function of a Narrative Role', in Telford (ed.), *Interpretation of Mark*, pp. 169-95.

J.B. Tyson, 'The Blindness of the Disciples in Mark', *JBL* 80 (1961), pp. 261-68.

T.J. Weeden, *Mark: Traditions in Conflict* (Philadelphia, PA: Fortress Press, 1971).

Chapter Five

CONCLUSION

The Significance of the Markan Ending

Describing the visit of the women to the empty tomb, the young man's announcement that Jesus had risen, the reiterated promise that he would be seen in Galilee (16.7; cf. 14.28) and the women's consequent silence, the ending of Mark's Gospel is not only distinctive but also puzzling. No post-resurrection appearances or apostolic commission are recounted such as are found in the later Gospels. A number of different endings after 16.8 are given in the manuscript tradition (some supplying a short one-verse ending recounting the women's report to the disciples and their subsequent commission; some a longer ending, detailing appearances, apostolic commission and Jesus' ascension, 16.9-20; and a few inserting additional material after v. 14). There is a widespread agreement, however, that these endings are secondary and that none of them (even in part) belonged to the original Gospel. Was Mark's Gospel intended to end at 16.8, therefore? Why then did the evangelist omit, if he knew them, the appearances given by later writers but also known (though not in identical form) to Paul (cf. 1 Cor. 15.3-11)? Was the original ending lost, damaged or suppressed? The account itself raises a host of other questions and issues, at least one of which we have touched upon already. Is the promise of 16.7 to be interpreted as a resurrection appearance, Jesus' parousia or a Gentile mission prediction? What was the origin of this empty tomb tradition, a story apparently unknown to Paul? Was it part of a pre-Markan passion narrative, an isolated tradition edited by the evangelist and brought into connection with it, or Mark's own free composition? All three positions have been argued, the triple mention of the women (15.40, 47; 16.1) and the repetition of the Galilee prediction (16.7; cf. 14.28) being appealed to as evidence of a combination of source and redaction.

While a number of scholars would still maintain that the Gospel originally extended beyond 16.8, a growing majority now accepts that it was intended to end there, the content of the verse itself allowing of no continuation ('and they said nothing to anybody, for they were afraid'). A number of the themes of importance to the evangelist converge in this final pericope, and are expressed by means of characteristic stylistic devices. The brief parenthetical statement ('for they were afraid'), here offering an 'inside view' of the characters' motivation, is something we have observed already (cf., e.g., 3.21b, 30; 9.6). Such explanations, often, as here, introduced by the preposition 'for' or *gar* (cf., e.g., 1.16; 5.42; 10.22, 11.13; 16.4), can also be noted at the end of some sections of narrative (cf., e.g., 6.52; 14.2). The stylistic possibility, moreover, of a book, as well as a sentence or paragraph ending with 'for' (*gar*) has also now been established. The 'fear' motif is a prominent one in Mark, and is an appropriate note, therefore, on which to end (cf. 4.40-41; 6.50-52; 9.6, 32; 10.32-34). The dramatic juxtaposition of divine promise and human failure in these last two climactic verses (16.7-8) also coheres with the rest of Mark's narrative (cf., e.g., 8.27-33), as A.T. Lincoln has pointed out. Indeed, according to literary critics like F. Kermode, N. Peterson or J.L. Magness, textually generated plot patterns or expectations are satisfied when the narrative ending is considered in terms of the literary category of 'closure'.

What then is the significance of the Markan ending if it in some sense 'completes' the Gospel as it stands? Recent literary approaches have tended to treat 16.8 ironically rather than literally, claiming that the implied reader, informed perhaps by ch. 13 and its prediction of events beyond the ending (especially 13.9-13), is expected to supply an ending which assumes the women's obedience, the meeting of the disciples in Galilee with Jesus and their subsequent commissioning. If 16.8 is taken literally, however, it clearly frustrates the expectation generated by 14.28 and 16.7, and hence may lend support to a historical explanation of a polemical kind. Mark's Gospel ends, in other words, quite appropriately and consistently, by proclaiming to the (Gentile-Christian) reader that the risen Jesus is to be found in the Gentile world (in 'Galilee of the Gentiles') but that, as in all else, his original Jewish disciples didn't get the message!

The Purpose and Setting of Mark's Gospel

The Gospel of Mark ends, characteristically, on a note of secrecy, and one of the secrets that it still withholds from us is its overall purpose and setting. By ending where it began, namely, with Jesus' appearance in Galilee, it invites the reader to return to the beginning and to review its many puzzling features. This, by way of conclusion, we shall now do. In the opening chapter, I offered some suggestions which had been made concerning the Gospel's date, audience and provenance. Any valid theory of the Gospel's overall purpose must take into account all of its distinctive features and assess them accordingly. These features, to repeat, were the secrecy motif in respect of Jesus' identity, the emphasis on Jesus' death and resurrection, the special treatment of the Kingdom of God and the Son of Man, the focus on Galilee, the use of the term 'gospel', the interest in Gentiles and the Gentile mission, the accent given to persecution, suffering and martyrdom and the true nature of discipleship, and finally the harsh treatment accorded to the Jewish leadership groups, Jesus' family and his original disciples. With these features in mind, let us then review some of the theories which have been advanced.

Only a minority of scholars would nowadays hold that Mark's primary purpose in creating his 'Gospel' was a historical one, the desire to write a life of Jesus, to preserve the reminiscences of Peter or to record past events or traditions without subordinating them to the needs of the present. Even if, in terms of genre, the Gospel is to be placed within the category of Graeco-Roman biography, the edificatory purpose of these works should be borne in mind. Nor would most scholars, given the speculative nature of the evidence, opt for a liturgical purpose, as B. Standaert has suggested, with the work created as a drama for catechetical instruction, perhaps in a baptismal context. Current theories are inclined to view the evangelist's main purpose as parenetic (cf. E. Best), kerygmatic (cf. E. Schweizer) or christological (cf. N. Perrin).

According to Best, the evangelist wrote with a suffering church in mind, to deepen their faith with his theology of the cross and to equip them to face persecution as well as resist the temptation presented by their culture. For Schweizer, this desire on the part of Mark to communicate the kerygma of the cross is paramount, the Gospel being about 'the unbelievable condescension and love of God who, in Jesus, seeks the world. This, however, is so blind that it is unable to recognize him despite all his efforts to encounter it' ('Mark's Contribution', p. 431). A major aspect of Mark's purpose, in the view of N. Perrin, and indeed of most Markan commentators, is christological, the desire to promote a particular view of Jesus. We have already encountered the notion that the evangelist wrote in order to oppose what was, in his view, a false Christology, whether a 'divine man' Christology of a Hellenistic kind (cf. T.J. Weeden), a royal messiah Christology of a Jewish-Christian kind (cf. J.B. Tyson) or even, as some have suggested, a Gnostic or Docetic Christology which offered a divine Christ divorced from the 'historical' Jesus (cf. E. Schweizer, R.P. Martin).

If the purpose of the Gospel cannot be accurately determined, what about its socio-historical setting and the community for which it was created? Opinions on the Gospel's provenance have already been discussed, the major ones being Rome, Galilee or Syria (Antioch or rural, small-town southern Syria). Three suggestions for its date have also been given (the mid-60s, the second half of the 60s or post-70 CE) as well as corresponding occasions for its composition, namely the Neronian persecution at Rome, the Romano–Jewish War in Palestine and the destruction of Jerusalem and its Temple (which precipitated a belief in Jesus' imminent parousia). The internal evidence of the Gospel would now offer support for the view that Mark's audience consisted of Greek-speaking Christians of Gentile origin who were in tension with their Jewish inheritance, but can the Markan community be more precisely delineated? Some scholars with a literary approach (e.g. M.A. Tolbert) would have us speak of a 'readership' rather than a 'community', but most scholars, influenced by form criticism, would prefer to see the work as directed to the needs of a particular audience with an organization, activities, beliefs and traditions of a specifically religious kind. Urban Gentile Christians in Rome suffering persecution (cf. V. Taylor, S.G.F. Brandon), Jewish Christians in Galilee awaiting the parousia (W. Marxsen) and rural lower-class Gentile peasants enduring military occupation in southern Syria (H.C. Waetjen) have all been suggested. Employing sources whose ideologies reflect a plurality of Jesus movements, Mark, according to B.L. Mack, created a foundation myth for a reform-minded community which needed to be distinct from the synagogue. The quest for the Markan community is unresolved to date, and may never indeed be resolved, given the difficulties of working back to it from the textual evidence.

If the socio-historical setting of the Gospel defies resolution, what about the Gospel's literary setting, its place in the theological history of early Christianity? Here the relation of Mark to the traditions represented by or incorporated in comparable literature (e.g. the Pauline letters, Q, Matthew, Luke, the *Gospel of Thomas*, etc.) has offered a fruitful but neglected field of study. An issue arising in so many aspects of Markan study is whether the Gospel in its tradition and/or redaction lies closer to Judaism or to Hellenism, or rather to the Palestinian Jewish-Christian tradition or that of Gentile Christianity (especially as represented by Paul). Is the evangelist dominated by apocalyptic or does he wish to qualify it? Are the miracles eschatological signs or pointers to Jesus' divinity ('epiphanic')? Is Jesus the suffering, righteous man of the Jewish tradition or the transcendent 'Son of God' in

Hellenistic terms? Does Mark's use of the term 'gospel' show influence from Paul or does it mean simply the 'good news' of the coming Kingdom as proclaimed by Jesus? Perhaps in the end the answer lies somewhere in between. The creative genius of Mark may reside in the fact that, in producing his Gospel, he has successfully combined disparate Jesus traditions under the influence of a Christology and soteriology closer to Paul than to Jesus' original disciples, and that he has done this in the service of a Gentile-Christian community struggling to make sense of its Jewish-Christian heritage within a Hellenistic world which is henceforth to be its mission field.

FURTHER READING

For the significance of the Markan ending, see the following:

A.T. Lincoln, 'The Promise and the Failure: Mark 16.7, 8', in Telford (ed.), *Interpretation of Mark*, pp. 229-51.

J.L. Magness, *Sense and Absence: Structure and Suspension in the Ending of Mark's Gospel* (SBL Semeia Series; Atlanta, GA: Scholars Press, 1986).

N.R. Petersen, 'When is the End not the End? Literary Reflections on the Ending of Mark's Narrative', *Int 34* (1980), pp. 151-66.

For the purpose and setting of Mark's Gospel, see the following:

E. Best, 'The Purpose of Mark', *Proceedings of the Irish Biblical Association* 6 (1982), pp. 19-35.

S.G.F. Brandon, 'The Date of the Markan Gospel', *NTS* 7 (1960–61), pp. 126-41.

J.R. Donahue, 'The Quest for the Community of Mark's Gospel', in F. van Segbroeck *et al.* (eds.), *The Four Gospels 1992* (Fs. F. Neirynck; Leuven: Leuven University Press/Peeters, 1992), pp. 817-38.

H.C. Kee, *Community of the New Age: Studies in Mark's Gospel* (Philadelphia: Westminster Press, 1977).

B.L. Mack, *A Myth of Innocence: Mark and Christian Origins* (Philadelphia: Fortress Press, 1988).

R.P. Martin, *Mark: Evangelist and Theologian* (Exeter: Paternoster Press, 1979), ch. 6.

J.M. Robinson, 'The Literary Composition of Mark', in M. Sabbe (ed.), *L'évangile selon Marc: Tradition et rédaction* (Leuven: Leuven University Press, 1974), pp. 11-19.

S. Schulz, 'Mark's Significance for the Theology of Early Christianity', in Telford (ed.), *Interpretation of Mark*, pp. 197-206.

E. Schweizer, 'Mark's Contribution to the Quest of the Historical Jesus', *NTS* 10 (1963–64), pp. 421-32.

—'Mark's Theological Achievement', in Telford (ed.), *Interpretation of Mark,* pp. 63-87.

B. Standaert, *L'évangile selon Marc: Composition et genre littéraire* (Nijmegen: Stichting Studentenpers, 1978).

G. Theissen, *The First Followers of Jesus/Sociology of Early Palestinian Christianity* (London: SCM Press; Philadelphia: Fortress Press, 1978).

H.C. Waetjen, *A Reordering of Power: A Socio-political Reading of Mark's Gospel* (Minneapolis: Fortress Press, 1989).

T.J. Weeden, 'The Heresy that Necessitated Mark's Gospel', in Telford (ed.), *Interpretation of Mark*, pp. 89-104.

Part III

LUKE

Christopher M. Tuckett

COMMENTARIES AND GENERAL WORKS ON LUKE'S GOSPEL

Commentaries on the text of Luke's Gospel are many and varied. Some of the following are specifically based on the English text, some on the Greek; however, most of the latter can be studied profitably by those without a knowledge of Greek, while several of those ostensibly based on the English text refer to Greek at times. No attempt has therefore been made in what follows to divide the commentaries into two lists. All the secondary literature cited here is restricted to works written in English.

G.B. Caird, *The Gospel of St Luke* (Pelican New Testament Commentaries; Harmondsworth: Penguin Books, 1963).

J.M. Creed, *The Gospel According to St Luke* (Macmillan: London, 1930). A classic study based on the Greek text.

E.E. Ellis, *The Gospel of Luke* (New Century Bible; London: Marshall, Morgan & Scott, 1974). Based on the English text and of medium length. Careful and thorough exegesis.

C.F. Evans, *Saint Luke* (TPI New Testament Commentaries; London: SCM Press, 1990). Based on the English text. Very long and detailed.

J.A. Fitzmyer, *The Gospel According to Luke* (AB; 2 vols.; Doubleday: New York, 1981, 1985). An extremely thorough and invaluable treatment, with a monograph-length introduction on Luke. A standard work.

M.D. Goulder, *Luke: A New Paradigm* (JSNTSup, 20; Sheffield: JSOT Press, 1989). In the form of a commentary, but focusing primarily on the question of Luke's sources, and advocating the theory that Luke is dependent on Matthew.

J.B. Green, *The Gospel of Luke* (NICNT; Grand Rapids: Eerdmans, 1997). Full coverage with a more 'literary' slant.

I.H. Marshall, *The Gospel of Luke* (NIGTC; Exeter: Paternoster Press, 1979). Very full and clear, though with a tendency to concentrate on questions of historicity.

J. Nolland, *The Gospel of Luke* (3 vols.; WBC; Dallas: Word Books, 1990–94). Very full coverage.

R.C. Tannehill, *The Narrative Unity of Luke–Acts: A Literary Interpretation*. I. *The Gospel According to Luke* (Philadelphia: Fortress Press, 1986). A fine literary analysis of the Gospel.

Other works on Luke dealing with a range of critical issues:

C.K. Barrett, *Luke the Historian in Recent Study* (London: Epworth Press, 1961). An excellent, concise survey.

F. Bovon, *Luke the Theologian: Thirty-three Years of Research (1950–83)* (trans. A.

Park; Pittsburgh: Pickwick Press, 1987). The French original covers up to 1975; the appendix, covering more recent material, is very cryptic. The quality of the English translation is also not easy at times.

H.J. Cadbury, *The Making of Luke–Acts* (Macmillan: New York, 1927; repr. London: SPCK, 1968). A classic study.

H. Conzelmann, *The Theology of Saint Luke* (ET; London: Faber, 1960). Again a classic, in many ways inaugurating modern Lukan studies.

F.W. Danker, *Luke* (Proclamation Commentaries; Philadelphia: Fortress Press, 1976). Concise treatment of a range of issues in the study of Luke.

P.F. Esler, *Community and Gospel in Luke–Acts* (SNTSMS, 57; Cambridge: Cambridge University Press, 1987). A powerful analysis, useful too for showing the ways in which sociological insights can assist exegesis.

J.A. Fitzmyer, *Luke the Theologian: Aspects of his Teaching* (New York: Paulist Press, 1989). Effectively a supplement to his commentary.

E. Franklin, *Christ the Lord: A Study in the Purpose and Theology of Luke–Acts* (London: SPCK, 1975). A general study of many aspects of Lukan theology.

J.B. Green, *The Theology of the Gospel of Luke* (Cambridge: Cambridge University Press, 1995). Covers many key aspects of Lukan theology.

D. Juel, *Luke–Acts: The Promise of History* (Atlanta: John Knox, 1983). A brief and clear study of key Lukan themes.

R. Maddox, *The Purpose of Luke–Acts* (Edinburgh: T. & T. Clark, 1982). An excellent treatment of many of the topics discussed in this book.

I.H. Marshall, *Luke: Historian and Theologian* (Exeter: Paternoster Press, 1970). Clear and incisive discussion of all the main themes in contemporary Lukan study by a renowned Lukan specialist.

—*The Acts of the Apostles* (New Testament Guides; Sheffield: JSOT Press, 1992). A companion to the present volume in the same series, covering a range of topics in the study of Acts.

E. Schweizer, *Luke: A Challenge to Present Theology* (London: SPCK, 1982). A brief survey of Luke with an eye to contemporary theology.

The following collections of essays are also important:

L.E. Keck and J.L. Martyn (eds.), *Studies in Luke–Acts* (Nashville: Abingdon Press, 1966; repr. London: SPCK, 1968). A classic set of essays.

C.H. Talbert (ed.), *Perspectives on Luke–Acts* (Edinburgh: T. & T. Clark, 1978).

J.B. Tyson (ed.), *Luke–Acts and the Jewish People: Eight Critical Perspectives* (Minneapolis: Augsburg, 1988). Showing the variety of different views on this topic.

J.H. Neyrey (ed.), *The Social World of Luke–Acts* (Peabody, MA: Hendrickson, 1991). An important collection showing some of the ways in which application of the social sciences can aid interpretation of the text.

Other works related to the topics covered in the individual chapters are listed at the end of each chapter.

Chapter One

INTRODUCTION

The Gospel of Luke raises many problems for any contemporary interpreter. In one sense such a claim is of course trite: any ancient text written almost two thousand years ago raises problems for anyone who wants to try to understand it. There are, for example, problems of language: Luke's Gospel is written in Greek, a language which for many of us is not our own. We need therefore to be able to translate Luke's Greek into a language which we can understand. Yet even that process is by no means simple or straightforward. Even if we can work out what the individual words, or perhaps sentences, mean at one level, we often have to undergo a potentially complex and prolonged process of seeking to understand the background, the social and cultural conventions within which the text operates, if we are to understand it in more than the most superficial of senses. We can, for example, understand the meaning of the words of parables such as the Good Samaritan (Lk. 10.30-35) or the Pharisee and the tax-collector (Lk. 18.10-14) by translating them into English or by reading the parables in a modern English translation. But unless we know something about Samaritans, Pharisees or tax-collectors, we shall probably miss large parts of the meaning. Similarly, we can read the parable of the Great Supper (Lk. 14.16-24) at one level in English translation; but without some idea of the social conventions of the first century—about the nature of meals, the conventions of invitations, the possible background of the excuses made by the original guests etc.—we shall miss parts of the meaning, or, worse, misinterpret the parable by reading in anachronistically our own twentieth-century presuppositions and conventions into the story. Thus in order to understand any text we need to know something of its literary, cultural and historical context to be able to understand it more than just superficially.

In relation to biblical texts, many of the broader issues of general cultural and historical background are dealt with in other textbooks. However, with any text, we also need to know something of the particular circumstances of its composition and indeed of its very nature: Who wrote it? For whom? Why was it written? And what kind of a text is it trying to be? Many of these questions in biblical study come under the broad rubric of 'Introduction', and it is with some of these introductory problems that we shall be concerned in this first chapter.

The interpretation of one of the New Testament Gospels does, however, raise even more complex issues than is the case with some other texts from antiquity, or even from the New Testament. The Gospels all purport to be historical (at least in a loose sense) accounts of events that have taken place prior to the time of the writer: they are all accounts of some parts of the life, passion and death of Jesus, with at least some kind of sequel, however small, of what was claimed to follow his death. There are then at least two possible ways of approaching a text like a Gospel: do we use it to try to understand something about the history being described? Or do we use it to try to discover something about the person who wrote it? Such a distinction is, of course, far too simplistic since there are many shades of grey between the two extremes I have just mentioned, as there are also other possibilities. Yet the two can perhaps serve to focus the discussion here: do we seek to use a text like the Gospel of Luke to tell us something about Jesus, or about Luke?

It is probably fair to say that the vast bulk of contemporary study of the Gospel of Luke today, if faced with such a choice, opts for the latter and not the former. If we want to discover information about Jesus, Luke's Gospel may be one of our sources, but it will certainly not be our only one, and some might argue not our main one. As we shall see shortly, Luke's Gospel is almost certainly not the first Gospel to be written and hence is not closest in time to the events being described. That is not to say that Luke's Gospel does not have any contribution to make to our knowledge about Jesus: many of the best-known parables of Jesus are found in Luke's Gospel, and it is the parabolic teaching of Jesus that has often been thought most characteristic of Jesus. Nevertheless, the dominant trend in modern study of the Gospels has been to focus on the particularity of each Gospel and to see what that might tell us about its writer and the circumstances in which and for which it was written, quite as much as seeking to unravel the history it describes.

This is something of a change from the past, certainly in relation to the so-called Synoptic Gospels (i.e. Matthew, Mark and Luke, as opposed to John). A tradition as early as Clement of Alexandria (early third century CE) contrasted John with the other Gospels, saying that whilst the latter presented the 'bodily things' (probably meaning a reasonably straight factual history), John 'wrote a spiritual Gospel'. And in the nineteenth and early twentieth centuries, scholars expended much energy on sorting out the relationships between the three Synoptic Gospels, primarily with a view to rediscovering the history which they described. In the early part of the twentieth century, attention shifted to the traditions which the evangelists had used, and scholars focused on the ways in which these smaller units of tradition had been handed on and used in the early church. (This discipline was known as form criticism.) In this, the evangelists were often regarded as simply editors, people who stitched together the individual stories or units of the tradition in a fairly mechanical way.

However, in the second half of the twentieth century, this view of the matter changed significantly. The evangelists are now seen no longer as mechanical editors, cutting and pasting material without too much thought. Rather, they have come to be seen as theologians (at least in some sense) in their own right, with their own particular theological agendas and their own distinctive ideas which have significantly influenced the ways in which they have told their story about Jesus. No longer is there such a qualitative line implicitly drawn between John and the Synoptics: rather, all have written in some sense 'spiritual' Gospels, that is, accounts which are not *just* dry recitals of physical facts (though what ever is?!), but accounts which are deeply impregnated by the concerns and beliefs of their authors. Further, in recent years it has been increasingly recognized that just as important as any theological ideas of a writer are the *social* factors in any situation which may significantly affect the way in which an author writes. Anyway, it is the attempt to find out what these concerns and factors are that dominates so much of Gospel studies today. (The technical term for this is redaction criticism, which we shall discuss in a little more detail later.) Such an approach is the one which will be adopted here. Thus in what follows, I shall be trying to consider primarily what we can discover about Luke, his concerns and his ideas, and not so much about Jesus and the events which Luke describes.

However, in the case of Luke's Gospel, there is a further complicating factor, one which is in one way a great advantage, but also one which makes life more complex. This is the fact that, by almost universal consent today, the Gospel which we now call the Gospel of Luke is part of a two-volume work: the author of Luke's Gospel also wrote a sequel to his Gospel, namely the Acts of the Apostles. As far as we know Luke was unique in this. No one else thought that his Gospel account should be continued with an extended history of the early church. All this means that if we are to try to discover something about the special features of Luke's Gospel with a view to discovering Luke's own concerns, we simply cannot ignore Acts. Acts itself sometimes gives us insight into specific features of Luke's special concerns and situation; but even its very existence is significant.

This creates a slight tension in the present context. On the one hand, we have to take full account of Acts in assessing Luke and his concerns. On the other hand, this present section is intended as an introduction to Luke's Gospel, and many of the features of Acts are discussed in Professor Marshall's excellent treatment of that book (I.H. Marshall, *The Acts of the Apostles*). The discussion here thus has to try to strike a balance between seeking to do justice to Luke and his work, which must include Acts as well as the Gospel, and seeking to focus primarily on the Gospel.

No doubt each reader of Luke's Gospel would strike that balance differently. For better or worse, I have decided to try to take significant account of the evidence provided by Acts at relevant points in the discussion of the various topics considered here. Nevertheless, the fact that the primary focus is on the Gospel does mean that the evidence of Acts will generally not be treated as fully as the evidence from the Gospel, and that some topics, of prime significance in the interpretation of Acts rather than the Gospel, will be discussed only briefly here. For example, the question of authorship, which I shall consider shortly, is probably of far less significance in relation to the Gospel than it is in relation to Acts. Nevertheless, we cannot ignore Acts in any assessment of what Luke's concerns were, and so inevitably we shall have to draw the evidence of Acts into the discussion at times.

In the present chapter I shall look at some of the so-called introductory problems of Luke's Gospel before going on to look at some of the most characteristic features of his ideas, as well as some of the problems of contemporary Lukan studies, in subsequent chapters. A small book like this cannot hope to provide a comprehensive coverage of Luke's leading ideas or of the social factors influencing Luke. Thus I have chosen to focus on a smaller number of key areas to try to illustrate important aspects of Luke's Gospel. Those who are interested can find more extended treatments of Lukan theology, and wider coverage, in the further reading suggested in the bibliographies.

Author

One 'introductory' problem frequently raised in relation to many ancient texts is that of authorship. By tradition, we always call the third Gospel the 'Gospel of Luke'. But both the Gospel itself and Acts are anonymous. Nowhere does the author explicitly say who he is. (However, the Lukan writings are significantly different from some other texts in that the author does explicitly refer to himself and his work in the prologues in Lk. 1.1-4 and Acts 1.1. The problem of the so-called 'we-passages' in Acts, where the narrative slips into the first person plural, is more debated and complex.) What then can we say about the author of our Gospel?

In one way the question is probably not very important in the interpretation of the Gospel, and the issue is probably more pressing in relation to Acts. It is universally agreed that the tradition naming the author of this two-volume work as 'Luke' is identifying him with the person mentioned occasionally in the Pauline corpus as a member of Paul's entourage (Phlm. 24; Col. 4.14; 2 Tim. 4.11. The social set-up of the time makes it almost certain that the author was a man: I shall therefore refer to him as male, rather than use 'him/her'). There has been fierce debate about the accuracy of this identification. If correct, it would make the author a companion of Paul and hence (presumably) an eye-witness of at least some (though only some) of the events described in Acts. The interpretation of the we-passages is clearly relevant here: is the author here indicating that he was an active participant in the events described? The debate is so fierce partly because there are a number of discrepancies, or inconsistencies, at many levels between the picture of Paul in Acts and the picture of Paul which emerges from his letters. Hence the question arises of how accurate the account of Paul in the second half of Acts really is.

There is, however, more than one issue involved here. Whether the author was an eyewitness of (some) events of Paul's career, and whether he reported Paul accurately, are two rather different matters. We could quite happily answer yes or no to either question quite independently of the other: the author could have been an inaccurate eyewitness, or a highly accurate non-eyewitness!

But whatever we decide, the issues are probably of little relevance to the study of the Gospel itself. The author of the Gospel seems to distinguish himself in his prologue from eyewitnesses of the events he describes (Lk. 1.2). He may even be indicating too that he belongs to a third generation of Christianity: it is unclear how the 'servants of the word' of 1.2 relate to the 'eyewitnesses'; but it seems clear that Luke is not a direct participant in the events about to be described in his Gospel.

In part too this also depends on the precise interpretation of another much disputed word in the Lukan prologue, namely the assertion by Luke that he has 'investigated' (so NRSV, Greek *parēkolouthēkoti*) everything 'carefully' (Greek *akribōs*). The verb has sometimes been interpreted as implying that Luke actually participated in the events concerned (so H.J. Cadbury, 'Commentary on the Preface of Luke', p. 502). However, such a meaning seems unlikely in view of the claim that Luke had done this to 'everything'; moreover, 'carefully' is a very odd adverb to use in this context if a claim of active participation is being made. Hence most would interpret the verb as the NRSV translates, that is, as 'investigate', or 'make oneself familiar' (cf. L.C.A. Alexander, *The Preface to Luke's Gospel*, pp. 128-30).

I shall therefore continue to call our author Luke simply for convenience sake if nothing else, without prejudging one way or the other the issue of whether this Luke is the same Luke as the person mentioned in the Pauline corpus.

Date

Partly connected with the authorship question is the problem of the date of Luke–Acts. This issue is also potentially connected with the problem of the purpose of Acts, and hence insofar as Acts is part of the whole of Luke–Acts, with the purpose of Luke's Gospel as well. As is well known, the second half of Acts is dominated by the activity of Paul, with the last quarter of the book taken up with Paul's journey to Rome as a prisoner facing trial. Acts ends, however, without ever telling the reader the outcome of Paul's trial. This has led some to argue that Paul's trial may not yet have taken place by the time Acts was written: hence Acts, and perhaps Luke–Acts, is to be dated in the early 60s.

This seems implausible. It is possible, but not likely, that Luke's Gospel was written after Acts: the present form of the prologues certainly suggests that the two books are conceived of as a unity right from the start. In fact most scholars would wish to date Luke–Acts after the fall of Jerusalem in 70 CE. Luke himself states that he has had predecessors in writing a Gospel account (Lk. 1.1), and one such predecessor is almost certainly the author of the Gospel we call Mark (cf. below). Mark's Gospel is probably to be dated in the late 60s or early 70s, and hence Luke's Gospel must be after this. Other evidence would also seem to point to a date after 70 CE. For example, at one point Luke rewrites the prediction of Mark's Jesus of a terrible calamity to arise: in Mk 13.14 Mark's Jesus speaks of 'the desolating sacrilege set up where it ought not to be', using language applied to the desecration of the temple in the book of Daniel (cf. Dan. 9.27). Luke rewrites this to read 'When you see Jerusalem surrounded by armies...' (Lk. 21.20), and seems clearly to interpret the enigmatic Markan verse in terms of the fall of Jerusalem in 70 CE. Similarly, the prediction of

Jesus in Lk. 19.43 of Jerusalem ('The days will come upon you, when your enemies will set up ramparts around you and surround you, and hem you in on every side') looks very much as if it is written after the siege of Jerusalem, with moderately precise knowledge of exactly what happened then (even if some more general prophecy of the destruction of the city may be traced back to Jesus). Hence a date after 70 seems most plausible. (Further, whatever one makes of the ending of Acts, it seems unlikely that Acts is written before Paul's trial has happened: the prediction of Luke's Paul to the Ephesian elders in Acts 20.25, that 'none of you...will ever see my face again', is widely regarded as a clear hint that Luke does know that Paul was executed and is now dead.)

How much after 70 Luke–Acts is to be dated is more uncertain and a wide variety of possible dates has been proposed. O'Neill (*The Theology of Acts*) suggests quite a late date, that is, into the second century, on the basis of affinities between Luke and apologists like Justin. This, however, seems difficult to maintain. As we shall see, Luke has a relatively positive attitude to the state authorities; and such an attitude is difficult to conceive by c. 125 CE when, as far as we can tell, profession of the Christian faith became an offence automatically punishable by death. (Cf. the correspondence between Pliny, governor of Bithynia, and the Emperor Trajan.) Luke's positive and irenic view of the state authorities seems to be more at home in the first century than in the second. Thus a date at some period in the last quarter of the first century seems most likely, though it is probably impossible to be more precise.

Text

A brief word needs perhaps to be said here about the text of Luke's Gospel. We do not, of course, have Luke's own autograph copy of the text he wrote. We only have copies of copies of the text, made at a later date. The earliest manuscripts of the text of Luke–Acts come on papyrus from the early third century, and the text in full Bibles from the fourth century onwards.

For the most part, the lack of an autograph of any New Testament book is rarely felt to be problematic. There will always be debates about some details, but the text is generally thought to be reasonably well established so that we can in practice be fairly confident that our modern text in a critical edition of the Greek New Testament is not so far removed from the 'original'.

The Lukan writings do, however, pose a number of peculiar text-critical problems. There is not enough space to do more than scratch the surface of the discipline of textual criticism here. But, very broadly speaking, the earliest manuscripts of the New Testament can be divided into two groups, one usually called Alexandrian, and the other Western. Again, very broadly speaking, the Alexandrian tradition has often been felt to be more reliable and a better witness to the original text; the Western text tends to embellish and add details for a variety of reasons.

Now the difference between these two major textual traditions is often relatively small, though, for some reason, there is a far greater difference between the two textual traditions in the text of Acts. In itself that is a problem for the study of Acts and will therefore be left on one side here. However, the textual tradition of Luke's Gospel also shows a number of significant differences between the two main textual traditions. In particular there are a number of places where the Western text (represented above all by the manuscript Codex Bezae, usually known as D) is shorter than the Alexandrian text. Since the tendency of the Western text is usually to amplify and add elements to the text, it has been thought by some in the past that these Western readings could be original (since the Western text's tendency is to expand, not to contract). These texts, sometimes called (sadly and somewhat tendentiously) 'Western non-interpolations', have aroused much discussion.

For a reason which is by no means clear, these Western non-interpolations seem to cluster in the Lukan passion narrative. To mention three of the most famous, there is the reference to Jesus' ascension, apparently on the first Easter day, in Lk. 24.51 (omitted by D, though also with some support from one major Alexandrian manuscript, codex Sinaiticus), the note about Peter running to the tomb and finding it empty in Lk. 24.12, and, perhaps the most perplexing of all the textual variants, almost (but not quite) all of Jesus' words of institution at the Last Supper in Lk. 22.19b-20, so that codex D has Jesus just take bread and say 'This is my body', with no more interpretation of the bread and also no reference to taking the cup and interpreting it/its contents. One other notable textual variant comes in Lk. 23.34 where several manuscripts (not just Western ones) omit Jesus' words praying for forgiveness for his executioners.

There is no space to discuss the issue in detail here. The tendency in recent years has probably been to discount these Western readings as having no value. Thus while in older editions of the Greek New Testament, and in older English translations (e.g. the Revised Version), the shorter (Western) reading was often taken as the text, and the longer (Alexandrian) reading either bracketed in the text or consigned to a footnote, the trend more recently has been to read the fuller, longer reading as the genuine text of the Gospel, and to mention the variant shorter reading only in a footnote (if indeed at all).

Perhaps each case has to be considered on its own merits; but the texts are potentially significant in a number of ways. For example, Lk. 24.12, if part of the text of Luke, provides a notable feature paralleling Luke and John. Luke 22.19b-20 raises the question of whether Jesus' death is the inauguration of a *new* covenant relationship (the reference is precisely in the disputed v. 20). One should therefore be at least aware of the text-critical problems associated with Luke's Gospel.

Sources

If we are concerned above all to discover something of Luke's own concerns, how should we proceed? One way which has been very much in vogue in the past has been to look at the way in which Luke uses and changes his sources. If that is the case, then it is vital to know what sources Luke used in his Gospel. (The problem of the possible sources used in Acts will not be discussed here.)

The whole question of Luke's sources is a complex one for which there is again not space enough to discuss in detail here. (For fuller treatments, see Fitzmyer, 'The Priority of Mark', and Tuckett, 'Synoptic Problem'.) Luke's Gospel is one of the Synoptic Gospels (Matthew, Mark and Luke), so-called because they are so similar to each other in many ways, in wording and in order, that they can usefully be viewed together. (The Greek preposition *syn* means together, 'optic' means looking at.) When one does this, it becomes apparent that the similarity between all three is too close to be coincidental. (If one needs any counter example to show that not every Gospel must have been written this way, one has only to glance at the fourth Gospel.) Hence it seems most likely that the three are in some kind of literary relationship with each other: one Gospel writer has used one or more of the others, or the evangelists have had access to common sources. Trying to sort out the nature of these dependencies is known as the Synoptic Problem.

We may perhaps distinguish two aspects of the problem: broadly the agreements between the Gospels may be divided into material where all three are parallel to each other, and material where only two are, and in the latter case this is almost always Matthew and Luke.

Mark

In the case of material which is in Mark as well as the others, the standard solution today is that Mark's Gospel was the source used by both Matthew and Luke independently. The detailed reasons can be found elsewhere (see Streeter, *The Four Gospels*; Fitzmyer, 'The Priority of Mark'), but it should also be noted that this is by no means a universally held view: a small but powerful minority of scholars (e.g. Farmer, *The Synoptic Problem*) would hold that the agreements between Mark and Matthew/Luke are better explained if Mark came last, combining both Matthew and Luke (the so-called 'Griesbach hypothesis'). However, the majority have remained unconvinced, not least because it is hard to see any very good reason why Mark would have been produced if Matthew and Luke were already in existence: virtually everything in Mark is in either Matthew or Luke or both. On the other hand, the reverse situation seems very much more plausible. Mark's Gospel is shorter; and Matthew and Luke, if written later, may have wanted to supplement Mark with extra material they had available. Similarly, many of the detailed changes in both wording and order are relatively easy to envisage if Mark came first, and much harder to envisage happening in reverse if Mark came last. Thus I shall assume here the theory that Luke used Mark as one of his sources.

Q

Luke also shares a lot of material with Matthew alone. The solution to this aspect of the Synoptic Problem is more disputed. The standard solution today is that Matthew and Luke do not depend on each other, but both have used a common source, now lost, called Q. However, the nature of Q, and the fact that Q (if it existed) is now lost, has always caused difficulty for many. Thus some have argued that Q was never a single source but only a collection of possibly disparate material which never existed together before being used by Matthew and Luke; others have argued that Q never existed at all and that the agreements between Matthew and Luke are to be explained by Luke's direct dependence on Matthew (so above all Goulder, *Luke: A New Paradigm*, as well as advocates of the Griesbach hypothesis).

Again there is no space for a detailed discussion here. Suffice it to say that, despite the arguments of Goulder and others, the theory of Luke's dependence on Matthew has not carried the day. Above all, such a theory would have to account for a radically greater freedom by Luke in relation to Matthew's ordering of events than is the case in relation to Luke's use of Markan material (where Luke very rarely changes the Markan order); further, Luke must have studiously ignored all of Matthew's additions to Mark in Markan material (cf. Mt. 16.16-19, added by Matthew to Mark, but Luke shows no awareness of it). Further, most have argued that neither Matthew nor Luke has any monopoly on the more original form of the tradition in the material they share in common: sometimes Matthew seems to be more original; but equally often, if not more so, Luke seems to be more original (cf. Lk. 6.20-21; 11.2-4; 11.49; 12.8 etc. For detailed discussion of individual texts, see Catchpole, *The Quest for Q*, ch. 1.; more generally Tuckett, 'The Existence of Q'). This combination of part-negative, part-positive arguments has convinced many that Luke did not know Matthew, and hence both depend on common source material(s), usually known as Q. The precise nature of Q is perhaps then a further question which need not concern us here.

The position taken in the rest of this book will be then the so-called Two Source Theory, the two main sources (of Matthew and Luke) being Mark and Q.

Proto-Luke

It is clear that Markan and Q material does not cover the whole of Luke's Gospel. Luke contains a substantial body of material which is peculiar to his Gospel. This includes the birth stories (Lk. 1–2) as well as many of the best-known parables in the Gospels (the Good Samaritan, the Prodigal Son, the Rich Man and Lazarus etc.), and this material is usually known as L. Whether L ever existed in written form prior to Luke's Gospel is very uncertain. The L material may simply consist of isolated sayings and traditions which Luke had at his disposal but which may have come to him from a variety of different origins.

There is, however, one theory concerning L which has been fashionable in the past, though less popular today, and which should perhaps be mentioned briefly here. This is the so-called Proto-Luke theory. This argues that, although L alone may never have existed in written form, the material Q + L together may have done. Luke may have written a first draft of his Gospel using the Q + L material; subsequently he came across Mark's Gospel, and added the material from this to his existing draft, adding too at this stage perhaps the birth narratives. It is this earlier version of Luke, a Proto-Luke, which may lie behind our present Gospel (so Streeter, *The Four Gospels*; Taylor, *Behind the Third Gospel*; Caird, *The Gospel of St Luke*).

The theory is possible, but scarcely provable. It is true that the birth narratives may have been added at a slightly later stage: Lk. 3.1 looks

as if it could have been an original opening of a book, and the genealogy in Lk. 3.23-28 would then come immediately after the first mention of Jesus. (In the present form of the Gospel the genealogy seems
to come very late.) So too Luke's Gospel is notable for the way in
which Markan and non-Markan material seems to come in large,
alternating blocks.

Yet while the evidence can be explained by a Proto-Luke theory, it
by no means demands such a theory. The birth narratives do play a
key role in Luke's presentation and can scarcely be relegated to the
status of an afterthought. The block phenomenon could be adequately
explained just as well if Luke were inserting Q + L material into Mark,
rather than vice versa. And in any case, some at least of the present Q
+ L material seems to show vestiges of Markan influence (e.g. Lk. 4.23;
12.10; 17.31); at the very least one would then have to allow for Luke
having touched up his Proto-Luke here and there. In the end the
theory is probably untestable and ultimately not very useful. The Q +
L material clearly comes from a variety of sources and it is not clear
how much is gained by positing an earlier form of Luke's Gospel as
having combined them.

Passion Narrative
There is, however, one part of the source problem that is more uncertain, and this concerns the passion narrative in Luke. It is widely
agreed that Q did not contain a passion narrative: Matthew seems to
show no knowledge of any major source other than Mark in his version of the passion. Luke's relationship to Mark here, however, is very
unclear. Certainly it is doubtful how far Luke used Mark as his source
for the passion narrative. The verbal agreement between Luke and
Mark drops quite sharply (from over 50 per cent in the rest of the
Gospel to under 30 per cent in the passion narrative); and whereas in
the rest of the Gospel Luke hardly ever changes the Markan order,
there are suddenly about 12 (albeit small) differences in order between
Luke and Mark in the passion narrative. All this has led a number of
scholars to suggest that Luke may have used another source for the
passion. And in view of the supreme importance for many of the
accounts of Jesus' death, the source-critical question here is of considerable significance (see Streeter, *The Four Gospels*; Taylor, *The
Passion Narrative of St Luke*, and others; the issue is reviewed in Brown,
The Death of the Messiah, pp. 64-75.)

The historical issue is undoubtedly extremely important. However,
in the present context, I shall not pursue the matter further. How
much all this may tell us about Luke himself is not quite so clear. But

to consider this we need to look at the question of methodology in so-called redaction criticism.

Redaction Criticism: Methods and Approaches

The broad aim of redaction criticism (at least as I defined it earlier) is to discover something about the author's own concerns and ideas. How then does one proceed in this?

One of the classic ways in which this has been done in the past has been by considering the ways in which an author has *changed* his sources. (Indeed that is where the phrase 'redaction criticism' comes from: the technical word for 'changing' is 'redacting'.) By looking at the changes Luke has made to Mark, and perhaps to Q if we can recover the Q wording with sufficient certainty, we may be able to see something of Luke's own concerns and interests. Thus, for example, in the next chapter, we shall be looking at some of the changes Luke has made to Mark as revealing perhaps something about his eschatological views.

Such an approach is valid in principle. It is, however, open to one or two cautionary qualifications. Clearly such an approach is heavily dependent on the correct identification of Luke's sources. As we have seen, there is some debate about all aspects of the source theory adopted here, namely the Two Source Theory. Hence, if Luke in fact used Matthew, his changes to Matthew would look rather different from the changes he made to the supposed Q source (unless of course Q was identical with Matthew at every point!); correspondingly the picture that emerges of Luke's redactional activity, and hence of his major interests and concerns, would look rather different. All of this may, however, simply indicate the provisional nature of any conclusions we can draw in a discipline such as biblical studies.

There are, however, more serious problems in relation to the method of redaction criticism as defined just now. First, the actual changes Luke makes to the wording of his sources may not be the only way he imposes his ideas on his material. The way in which the material is arranged and structured within the present narrative may also be revealing. Sometimes this may be by changing the order of one of his sources; but it might equally be by the way in which different sources are combined to create a wider literary unity.

Secondly, there is the phenomenon of the material which Luke may have taken over from his sources without any change at all. If we only focus on the positive changes Luke has made to his sources, such material will be ignored. However, a moment's thought should reveal the inappropriateness of this. If Luke decided to include something from one of his sources in his Gospel, this may well have been precisely because he liked it and agreed with it wholeheartedly. Indeed the presumption must surely be that this is the case, unless we have compelling reason for thinking otherwise: if he did not like it, he could presumably simply have omitted it.

In the light of these difficulties, many scholars today would therefore argue that seeking to discover Luke's concerns only via his redaction in the strict sense, that is, by focusing on the changes he has made to his tradition, would give us a potentially lop-sided view of Luke. Rather, we should combine this with a more literary approach, taking seriously *all* the material Luke has included as potentially giving us insight into his ideas. Thus we should look at the structure of the whole of Luke's work, and the totality of his finished literary product, quite as much as comparing Luke with his sources via a synopsis. Further, if we consider Luke's readers, rather than Luke, such an approach makes much more sense. Luke's initial readers presumably did not have the luxury of a Greek Synopsis available to them. They *may* have known Mark's Gospel, but it seems highly unlikely that they knew it in sufficient detail to have been aware of the instances where Luke was actively changing his Markan source, at least in some of the small ways which redaction critics have noted in the past. They will have been aware primarily of the finished product of Luke's Gospel itself, whether heard or read. Thus any message they may have got will have been that produced by the present form of the literary work as it now stands.

Some would even go so far as to argue that a literary approach is the only legitimate approach, and that we should bracket off the question of sources completely. Certainly one Lukan specialist has written a two-volume analysis—virtually a commentary—on Luke–Acts from this perspective, emphasizing the narrative unity of the whole in its present form and the ways in which the different parts of the narrative cohere with each other (Tannehill, *The Narrative Unity of Luke–Acts*).

Perhaps a balanced approach can be maintained, seeking in one way to use the insights provided by source criticism so that Luke's changes to his traditions can be taken into account; but this needs to be balanced by a literary, holistic approach, considering Luke's narrative as a literary whole in its own right, irrespective of where it has come from. Indeed hopefully the two approaches should support each other and produce similar results. Conversely, if a literary approach produces a radically different picture from that of a redactional (i.e.

changes-based) approach, then this may indicate that there is some-thing amiss.

As one illustration of a more holistic approach, we may glance briefly at the so-called 'Travel Narrative' in Luke. For whatever reason, Luke has a long section in his Gospel (Lk. 9.51–18.14) of mostly non-Markan material to do with Jesus' teaching which Luke clearly places in the context of a journey to Jerusalem (cf. the very heavy stylized language introducing this in 9.51, and the reminders of the journey context in 13.22; 17.11). It is of course a moot point whether this comes under the rubric of a change to Mark (Luke interrupting the Markan sequence to insert such a lot of material) or a structural feature of Luke's narrative unity. But either way it is an important feature of Luke's Gospel.

Quite what its significance is for Luke is not certain. It could just be a convenient literary device for Luke to include a lot of teaching mate-rial which he has available and has to put in somewhere in his outline. This is possible, though this does not easily explain why the journey motif itself is stressed so much. Some have sought to explain the detailed structure of the Travel Narrative, for example, by (at times quite complex) chiastic structures, or by seeing parallels between Luke's narrative and the book of Deuteronomy, so that Jesus is per-haps being presented as a new prophet like Moses. The fact then that the Travel Narrative may have christological significance for Luke means that we shall consider it again when we look at the question of Luke's Christology (see Chapter 4 below). But it is perhaps enough to note here that a concentration on the detailed changes in wording alone that Luke makes to his sources may leave important pieces of data untouched in any search for Luke's own concerns and ideas.

Purpose

Why then did Luke write? The question of purpose is often one of the questions brought up in any introductory discussion. In relation to a text like Luke's Gospel it is, however, not really answerable in either abstract or concrete terms at the start of a discussion of the Gospel. Luke's particular purpose is only likely to emerge once we have dis-covered something of his particular concerns. For those concerns are almost certainly in part a reflection of his purpose in writing.

On the other hand, we do have a statement (albeit brief) of Luke's purpose from Luke himself: in his prologue to the Gospel (Lk. 1.1-4) Luke states something of his purpose in writing, in part reiterated in his prologue to Acts (Acts 1.1).

This prologue to the Gospel has been analysed in great detail on many occasions. It is written in relatively high-class Greek and seems to indicate both Luke's actual credentials and what Luke would like others to think of his credentials. (The two are not necessarily identical!) The standard critical opinion today is that Luke is here laying claim to be a *historian*. Parallels have been drawn between Luke's prologues in the Gospel and in Acts and similar prologues in the works of historians such as Herodotus, Thucydides, Josephus and others. The prologues of the two volumes of Josephus's *Contra Apionem* are often thought to be particularly close to Luke's two prologues in his own two-volume work. With this in mind, many have argued that Luke is laying claim, via his prologues, to have his work considered as that of a historian.

This conclusion has been questioned to some extent recently by Loveday Alexander's detailed study of the Lukan prologues (*The Preface to Luke's Gospel*). She rightly draws attention to a number of differences between the Lukan prologues and those of other contemporary historians. For example, Luke's prologues are much shorter, their style is not really comparable to that of the Hellenistic historians, Luke does not give us his own name, as do most of the historians (using the third person), and the dedication to Theophilus is unlike the normal practice of historians. By contrast, Alexander finds far closer parallels between Luke's prologues and those of so-called scientific treatises so that Luke's books belong within a rather more 'middle-brow' literature within which biography was possible.

All this is well said. On the other hand, as Marshall has pointed out, whatever the formal similarities may imply, the *contents* of Luke–Acts surely place the work more closely in the realm of a history than anything else (*The Acts of the Apostles*, pp. 21-22). We should also remember the firm attempt to anchor the events being described within the broad sweep of world history in Lk. 2.1 and 3.1. Alexander's analysis shows that Luke may not have been considered by others at the time to have been quite so comparable to other great Hellenistic historians of the period; and indeed the modern high evaluation of Luke's rhetorical and literary ability may need considerable revision. Nevertheless, it still remains the case that Luke may be staking a claim to be writing some kind of history and to be accepted as a historian.

We must, however, be careful how much we deduce from this, and we should remember that Luke was a first-century writer, not a twentieth-century one. Hence we should not judge Luke's worth as a historian by anachronistic criteria. Some have in the past perhaps tried to do this. For example, taken up with issues of historical factual accuracy, many have sought to judge Luke on this basis, and on this basis different conclusions have been reached. Especially in relation to Acts, it has been shown that Luke is at times remarkably accurate in some of the details he records of the cities of the Empire visited by the Christian mission. (For example, the civic leaders in Thessalonica are called *politarchs* in Acts 17.6, a term which would have been applicable to only a very few cities of the time, but would have been correct in Thessalonica.) On the other hand, several details of Luke's account of Paul's mission do not tally with the evidence of Paul's own letters. Sometimes too Luke's chronology is suspect (cf. the well-known crux in Lk. 2.1 where Luke apparently dates the census to the time when Quirinius was governor of Syria, i.e. c. 6 CE, well after the time of Herod [cf. Lk. 1.5 and Mt. 1–2] who died in 4 BCE).

Yet accuracy of this nature and at this level is probably not the best criterion by which to judge Luke or any historian. Almost certainly Luke was striving for accuracy at this level; and almost certainly he may not have achieved perfection. After all, if he were writing 30-40 years after the events of the Pauline mission, it is scarcely surprising that one or two details have been accidentally confused; and despite having excellent knowledge about some aspects of the Roman Empire (e.g. the *politarchs* in Thessalonica), he may have had a slightly less than perfect grasp of the relative chronology of people like Herod, Quirinius *et al.*

But that is perhaps not so important. Luke as a historian is not interested *just* in dates and places, the dry facts and nothing more. No historians worth their salt ever have been, and ancient historians are no exception. Ancient historians (like modern ones!) write not only to present facts but also to get across a message. A historian like Livy writes his history to commend his national cause and to present ideals for moral conduct through his characters. In the Old Testament, the deuteronomistic historian presents his account of Jewish history in such a way as to illustrate his theology that virtue is rewarded and sin punished by God in this-worldly terms; the Chronicler in turn rewrites the deuteronomistic history to be even more deuteronomic than the Deuteronomists themselves: hence the stories are changed so that, for example, good kings who die young must have been bad, and bad kings who lived long must have been good. Thus Manasseh repents in 2 Chron. 33.12-13; Josiah, a good king who died young, disobeys in 2 Chron. 35.21. So too Josephus writes his histories to defend the status of the Jewish people in the eyes of non-Jewish detractors. All this suggests that, if Luke is a historian, then he is doing far more than just trying to get his dates and places correct. He is writing with a purpose, and presenting his story to further that purpose. What then might that purpose be?

One possibility, which has been very influential in the past, has been that Luke is in part writing to counter worries about eschatological beliefs: in particular he is writing to apologize for the delay in the parousia. In the next chapter we shall therefore consider the question of Luke's eschatology.

FURTHER READING

L.C.A. Alexander, *The Preface to Luke's Gospel* (SNTSMS, 78; Cambridge: Cambridge University Press, 1993).

R.E. Brown, *The Death of the Messiah* (New York: Doubleday, 1994).

H.J. Cadbury, 'Commentary on the Preface of Luke', in F.J. Foakes Jackson and K. Lake (eds.), *The Beginnings of Christianity* (London: Macmillan, 1922), II, pp. 489-510.

D.R. Catchpole, *The Quest for Q* (Edinburgh: T. & T. Clark, 1993).

W.R. Farmer, *The Synoptic Problem* (Dillsboro' NC: Western North Carolina Press, repr. 1976 [1964]).

J.A. Fitzmyer, 'The Priority of Mark and the "Q" Source in Luke', in D.G. Miller (ed.), *Jesus and Man's Hope* (Pittsburgh: Pittsburgh Theological Seminary, 1970), I, pp. 131-70; repr. in *To Advance the Gospel* (New York: Crossroad, 1981), pp. 3-40.

M.D. Goulder, *Luke: A New Paradigm* (JSNTSup, 20; Sheffield: JSOT Press, 1989).

J.C. O'Neill, *The Theology of Acts in its Historical Setting* (London: SPCK, 1970).

B.H. Streeter, *The Four Gospels* (London: Macmillan, 1924).

V. Taylor, *Behind the Third Gospel* (London: Macmillan, 1926).

—*The Passion Narrative of St Luke* (SNTSMS, 19; Cambridge: Cambridge University Press, 1972).

C.M. Tuckett, 'Synoptic Problem', *ABD* (1992), pp. 263-70.

—'The Existence of Q', in R.A. Piper (ed.), *The Gospel behind the Gospels: Current Studies on Q* (NovTSup, 75; Leiden: Brill, 1995), pp. 19-47.

Chapter Two

ESCHATOLOGY

One of the classic studies of Luke's redactional activity was that of H. Conzelmann's 1953 book *Die Mitte der Zeit (The Middle of Time)*, translated into English with the blander title *The Theology of St Luke*. A key part of Conzelmann's discussion concerned Luke's eschatology, and ever since, eschatology has been regarded as a key area in any study of Luke's concerns.

Conzelmann's basic theory is that Luke's church was faced with a crisis at the end of the first century, due to the fact that the parousia, the return of Jesus in glory and the end of the present world order, had failed to materialize as predicted. Faced with this situation, Luke undertook a radical revision of his Christian tradition to eliminate expectation of an imminent End from his sources. Thus for Luke, the parousia was no longer to be expected soon, but only at the end of an almost indefinite future. And in place of the stock early Christian belief in eschatology, Luke substituted a belief in *Heilsgeschichte*, salvation history. In this the history of the world was seen as the sphere of God's saving activity, through the ministry of Jesus, and in the life of the church, which would carry on for a considerable time as far as Luke was concerned. In this scheme, salvation history was conceived of as divided into three clear, mutually exclusive epochs: the era of the Old Testament which reached up to and including John the Baptist (Lk. 16.16 is often appealed to by Conzelmann in this context), the era of Jesus (the 'middle of time' of Conzelmann's original title) which Conzelmann thought was free from influence of Satan (cf. Lk. 4.13; 22.3) and the era of the church. In this too the history of the church was no longer regarded as eschatological in any sense, and the gift of the Holy Spirit to the church was no longer regarded as the eschatological gift, but rather as a substitute for the *eschaton*.

Such, in very brief outline, is Conzelmann's theory about eschatology in Luke. The theory has been enormously influential, convincing many and provoking others to criticize in detail parts or all of the total schema. We should, however, note that the schema is a very complex one with many aspects, some of which do tend to become rather jumbled in the discussion if one is not careful.

Salvation History

It is probably fully justified to say that Luke has a strong and powerful idea of salvation history. We have already seen that Luke probably wishes to present his work self-consciously as that of a historian, that is, he writes a history. Luke alone of the evangelists takes care to situate the story he relates into the wider context of world history (cf. the attempted synchronization with broader world history in Lk. 2.1 and 3.1, despite the problems of detailed accuracy which these verses engender), and it is clearly important for him that Paul can say to Festus of the life and history of the church: 'These things were not done in a corner' (Acts 26.26). Further, this history is one in which Luke believes God is active, and acting purposefully, to bring salvation to humankind. The idea that the whole of history is under the control and guidance of God is reflected in a number of references throughout Luke–Acts to God's plan (Lk. 7.30; Acts 2.23; 4.28; 5.38-39; 13.26; 20.27), or will (Lk. 22.42; Acts 21.14), as well as references to the necessity of what is happening (the Greek word *dei*, 'it is necessary', is used 18 times in Luke, 24 times in Acts: cf Lk. 2.49; 4.43; 9.22; 13.33 etc.), and the foreknowledge and predetermination of God in planning all that happens (perhaps more common in Acts: cf. Acts 2.23; 3.20; 4.28; 10.41 etc., but also Lk. 22.22). (For the whole theme, see Squires, *The Plan of God*.)

So too Luke, perhaps more than other New Testament writers, shows a greater awareness that the events of Jesus lie in the *past*. For writers like Mark and Paul, a case can be made that they have to some extent collapsed the time between past and present (though of course not entirely!). Thus for Mark, the gospel of Jesus and preached by Jesus (Mk 1.1, 14) is also the present gospel for which Christians suffer, which is so closely parallel to Jesus (Mk 8.35; 10.29) that there is almost a sense in which Jesus is present in the Gospel and the two come together. For Paul, the 'day of salvation' is the 'now' of Paul's own preaching and proclamation (2 Cor. 6.2, a verse often adduced to compare with Luke's view). By contrast, the 'now' salvation for Luke is the *past* event of Jesus in the synagogue in Nazareth (Lk. 4.21: '*today* this Scripture has been fulfilled in your hearing').

However, it would probably be quite wrong to drive too much of a wedge between Luke and other early Christian writers in this respect.

Paul almost certainly has just as much of an idea of God being active in history, and hence salvation history in this sense, as Luke does (cf. Rom. 4; 9–11; 1 Cor. 10.1-11; Gal. 4.4-6); and it is very unlikely that Mark has abolished the distinction between the ministry of Jesus in the past and his own present preaching of the gospel entirely.

Conzelmann's detailed theory of a very specific threefold schema of salvation history has been much discussed and much criticized: for example it is not at all clear that John the Baptist belongs to the old era of the Old Testament and not to the new Christian dispensation for Luke; the description of Jesus' ministry as 'Satan free' is questionable (cf. Lk. 10.18; 11.14-20; 13.16); and it is often unclear in Conzelmann's theory exactly where the dividing line between the epoch of Jesus and that of the church lies: is it at 22.3 with the arrival on Satan on the scene? Or at 22.36 where Jesus apparently rescinds the previous instructions about money and possessions? Or at Jesus' death? Or at the ascension? Or at Pentecost?

However, these criticisms do not necessarily affect the basic schema. John the Baptist could quite happily be shifted from the Old Testament era to the era of Jesus (and probably should be) without altering the underlying theory significantly. So too, despite some ambiguity and unclarity about the precise dividing line between the era of Jesus and the era of the church, there are clear differences between the two. For example, the most obvious is that Jesus is present in his ministry, but mainly absent in the era of the church: the ascension serves in Luke to remove Jesus from the sphere of activity of Christians, and the prime medium of God's saving activity is now the Holy Spirit, who/ which in turn has been mostly—and remarkably—absent during the time of the ministry of Jesus himself.

It is one of the peculiar features of Luke's Gospel that Luke seems to want to generate an enormous expectation of activity by the Spirit in the ministry of Jesus in the first four chapters of the Gospel, but then this never seems to materialize. The birth narratives witness to a great upsurge of activity by the Spirit in prophetic outbursts by various figures. Jesus himself is baptized with the Spirit in ch. 3, led by the Spirit into the desert for the temptations in ch. 4, and then, in a scene in which Luke clearly invests an enormous amount of narrative significance, announces that the prophecy of Isaiah of being anointed by the Spirit has been fulfilled in himself (4.16-21). Yet after this, the Spirit is barely mentioned in relation to Jesus' activity. Rather, the sphere of the Spirit's activity seems to be that of the church in the period *after* Jesus has departed. Why Luke is so silent about any activity of the Spirit in Jesus' ministry after ch. 4 is something of an enigma.

Overall then, despite possible differences of opinion in some details, it seems clear that Luke does work with an idea of salvation history. Moreover, there is also some idea of significantly different periods in this history, although the dividing lines may be placed in a slightly different way than Conzelmann suggested, and the lines themselves may be at times slightly blurred. Whether we should think of a *three-fold* division as the governing one in Luke's schema will be considered shortly.

Delay of the Parousia?

Did Luke believe that the parousia had been delayed? And did he then radically rewrite his sources in the light of this to eradicate such an expectation entirely? The two questions are in fact rather different and should probably be separated. As we shall see shortly, Luke is probably aware of a delay in the Parousia. However, to claim that this was due to a crisis which only hit the church in Luke's day would go beyond the evidence. It may of course be that Luke's community had never bothered about the non-appearance of the parousia until Luke's day. But this seems unlikely. Certainly we know of other Christians in the first century adjusting in various ways to the fact that history was going on without interruption. For example, Paul, writing perhaps 30–40 years before Luke, seems to have moved from a position of expecting the parousia in his own lifetime (1 Thess. 4.15; 1 Cor. 15.51) to a position where he seems to anticipate that he will himself die before any parousia event (Phil. 1.23; perhaps 2 Cor. 5.2-4). So too Mark's apocalyptic chapter in Mark 13 probably shows some awareness that history has gone on rather longer than some at least were anticipating. In any case, any problems of a delay in the parousia would presumably have arisen well before the 80s or 90s of the first century. By this stage almost all the first generation of Christians and contemporaries of Jesus must have died. It is hardly likely then that Luke was the first to face any problem caused by the delay of the parousia.

Nevertheless, even if Luke may not have been unique, and Christians had faced the problem of the delay of the parousia before Luke's day, this does not mean that Luke was *not* concerned with this issue! There is certainly quite a lot of evidence to suggest that Luke was aware of the delay of the parousia and he adjusted some his traditions accordingly. This can be seen in a number of places.

Awareness of Delay

The most famous example is Luke's rewriting of Mk 14.62 in Lk. 22.69. Here, in the reply of Jesus to the High Priest at the Sanhedrin trial, Mark has Jesus predict 'You will see the Son of Man seated at the right hand of the Power, and coming with the clouds of heaven'. Luke has instead simply 'From now on the Son of Man will be seated at the right hand of the power of God'. By omitting the words 'coming with the clouds of heaven', and replacing 'you will see' by 'from now on', Luke has changed a prediction of a universally visible coming (presumably to earth) by Jesus as Son of Man to a statement about his position (presumably in heaven) which will take place immediately. Thus a prediction of a future parousia has been replaced by a statement about Jesus' present status (present, that is, for the author and the reader). It may be that embarrassment about the failure of the parousia to materialize has led to the change being made.

A similar concern may lie behind the introduction which Luke (and Luke alone) gives to his version of the parable of the pounds in Lk. 19.11: here Luke says that Jesus told this parable to the disciples 'because he was near Jerusalem and they thought that the kingdom of God was about to appear immediately'. The parable of the man going away and entrusting his servants with money seems to have been interpreted in terms of Jesus' going away and returning at the parousia with the explicit warning that any return is not going to take place immediately. It looks then as if Luke is aware that Jesus' return has been delayed.

It is possible (though not certain) that the same concern lies behind Luke's apparent change to Mk 9.1 in Lk. 9.27. In Mark, Jesus predicts that 'There are some standing here who will not taste death until they see the kingdom of God come with power'. Luke, in reproducing this verse, omits the final words 'come with power'. In Mark the prediction is clearly of a cosmic event to take place in the lifetime of the audience. In Luke the saying is at least open to a rather different interpretation: the 'kingdom' might be more of a spiritual reality, or the 'seeing' might be not related to quite such a visual event. However, the precise interpretation of Luke's version here is much disputed.

The initial summary of Jesus' preaching in Mark is 'The kingdom of God has come near' (Mk 1.15). Luke replaces this initial summary with his grand scene of the rejection of Jesus at Nazareth (Lk. 4.16-30), and the summary statement of Jesus' message is no longer about the imminence of the kingdom, but the claim that Scripture has now been fulfilled in the 'today' of Jesus' presence (Lk. 4.21).

An awareness of some delay in the parousia seems to be evident in a number of other small changes Luke makes to Mark, especially in the apocalyptic discourse of Mark 13, which Luke rewrites in Luke 21. For example, in Lk. 21.8, Luke adds to Mark a warning of what false claimants might say. In Mark they will come and make some claim by saying 'I am he!' (Mk 13.5: the precise interpretation of this is disputed); Luke adds to this a warning about people who will say 'The time is near!' Warnings of an imminent End seem to be rejected by Luke's Jesus as those of false claimants.

We have already noted in another context that Luke rewrites the apocalyptic and enigmatic language of Mk 13.14, which refers to the desolating sacrilege, by making a clear allusion to the fall of Jerusalem: 'When you see Jerusalem surrounded by armies' (Lk. 21.20). It looks as if Luke then has interpreted the enigmatic Markan verse as a clear reference to the fall of Jerusalem which for Luke is now past and hence *not* a prelude to the End.

In line with this too, Luke makes a small change to the beginning of the paragraph containing this verse. In Mk 13.9 Mark has Jesus predict persecution for the disciples which appears to follow the wars and earthquakes and famines of Mk 13.8. Luke adds here 'But before all this occurs…' (Lk. 21.12), so that the persecution etc. of the disciples is predicted to take place before the natural disasters etc. Perhaps then again Luke knows that persecutions have taken place and have not heralded the End.

Above all we should note here what is a remarkable silence in Acts about the any idea of an imminent End. At the start of Acts, the disciples ask the risen Jesus whether he is going to restore the kingdom to Israel 'at this time' (Acts 1.6). Jesus brushes aside the question, telling them 'it is not for you to known the times or periods that the Father has set by his own authority' (1.7). Thus any temporal concerns about the End are swept away and the disciples are told to go and be witnesses 'in Jerusalem, in all Judea and Samaria, and to the ends of the earth' (1.8). Thereafter, there is hardly any reference to an imminent End event in the preaching of the church's mission. Occasionally it is referred to in general terms (Acts 3.21; 10.42; 17.31), but with no indication that such an event might be imminent.

Individual Eschatology?

There is a further small body of evidence in Luke–Acts which may be relevant here. This concerns a few verses which may suggest that Luke had moved away from the view, widespread as far as we can tell in early Christianity, whereby men and women expected a great irruption into the world which would bring about the end of the present world order and the final judgment of humankind; instead Luke may have adopted a more 'individual eschatology', whereby the decisive moment of judgment took place at each individual's death.

In support of this one can refer to the parable of the Rich Man and Lazarus (Lk. 16.19-31), where both parties seem to receive their final reward or punishment immediately after death. So too Jesus' words to the dying thief on the cross, 'Today you will be with me in Paradise' (Lk. 23.43) may point in the same way. Similar too is the account of the death of Stephen who says that he sees the Son of Man standing (Acts 7.56), language which is more normally associated with the parousia and the final judgment at the end of time (cf. Lk. 12.8 etc.), and perhaps then indicating an individualized parousia for Stephen at the time of his own physical death.

The evidence is not entirely clear and it is uncertain precisely how it should be interpreted. The evidence is certainly not extensive, and in any case could be interpreted along slightly different lines, for example, the position of individuals who have just died could be thought of as in some kind of intermediate waiting stage, prior to final judgment itself. (Such an idea can be well attested in Jewish thought of the time.) Perhaps it may show too that Luke is not entirely consistent in his thinking.

The net result of all the evidence considered so far, whether about the delay of the parousia or about the possible reinterpretation of eschatological hopes in an individualized direction, has suggested to many that Luke is conscious of the delay in the parousia and has adjusted his source material in quite a major way to reflect that concern. The trouble is that there is a significant amount of evidence in Luke's Gospel that gives a very different picture, suggesting that an imminent End should be taken very seriously. We need therefore to glance briefly at this evidence.

Imminent End?

In Lk. 3.9, Luke repeats (from Q) the preaching of John the Baptist, warning of an imminent destructive power: 'Even now the axe is lying at the root of the trees'. In Luke's account of the mission of the 70, the 70 are told to greet both receptive and unreceptive cities with the greeting/warning 'the kingdom of God has come near' (Lk. 10.9, 11). (The first of these may be from Q: cf. Mt. 10.7; the second has no parallel in Matthew and hence may be Luke's own addition to what is basically Q material.) The parables of the thief at night and the waiting servants (Lk. 12.39-40, 42-46) both warn of an event which may come at any moment and catch out those who are unprepared with disastrous consequences. The same message comes out of the apocalyptic material Luke takes from Q in Lk. 17.23-37: for example, vv. 26-30 have Jesus warn that the day of the Son of Man will catch people unawares just as the flood in the days of Noah, or the fire and brimstone in the days of Lot. So too, at the end of the parable of the widow and the unjust judge in Lk. 18.1-8, Luke's Jesus claims that God will vindicate his elect 'quickly'.

Finally, Luke retains from Mark 13 the clear statement that everything predicted in the preceding discourse will happen before 'this generation' passes away (Lk. 21.32, cf. Mk 13.30). It is true that there is a slight change in that Luke omits the word for 'these' in Mark, so that in Luke Jesus says that this generation will not pass away until 'all things', rather than 'all these things', happen. However, it is difficult to see how this really affects the problem in relation to the prediction of an end of the world within the lifetime of the present generation. There have been attempts too to reinterpret the word for 'generation' here, as if it might refer to the whole human race (cf. commentaries on this verse); but this does not seem entirely convincing.

There is then a substantial body of material in Luke's Gospel which seems to be not the slightest bit embarrassed about affirming a hope of an eschatological climax which is about to come, and warning of the dire consequences which will fall on those who are not prepared.

How then can one resolve this apparent tension? On the one hand Luke seems to be at pains to play down predictions by Jesus of an imminent End; on the other, he has elements which vigorously and positively urge such a belief.

Possible Solutions

A number of possible solutions have been proposed. Conzelmann, who argued that Luke's dominant concern was to apologize for the delay in the parousia, claimed that the elements in Luke stressing an imminent End were simply vestiges from Luke's sources. For example, John the Baptist's warning in Lk. 3.9, the parables in Luke 12 and the eschatological warnings in Luke 17 are all from Q; the saying about this generation not passing away before everything happens is from Mark. This is, however, not very satisfactory. As we saw when considering the proper method of redaction criticism, we cannot ignore material which a writer has taken from a source without altering it. Such material is potentially just as significant for determining an author's concerns as any positive changes to a source which can be identified (see p. 267 above). Hence we have to take seriously the fact of both strands in Luke.

Some have suggested that Luke may have been faced with a dual situation in his community, and the two strands of Luke's eschatology meet each half of this dual situation: in the face of a delay in the parousia, some may have given up hope altogether—hence the stress on the imminence. Others may have developed a fanatical belief that the End was very near, and even already present—and hence Luke stresses the delay motif (see Wilson, *The Gentiles*).

Again this is not entirely convincing. The duality in the situation is never explicit, and such a theory makes for a somewhat schizoid community; presumably too the situation would be open to some abuse since, if each party in the community read the wrong bit of the Gospel, they would be confirmed in their (for Luke) dangerous views, rather than being corrected; and there is no indication that the Gospel is to be read selectively by different people.

No solution is entirely satisfactory, but perhaps the one that explains most of the evidence is related to the view I have already referred to that Luke is a historian. Luke is conscious of the fact that the events of Jesus' life and death are now past. He is also aware of the delay in the parousia, at least insofar as quite a lot of water has flowed under the metaphorical bridge since Jesus' day and the parousia has not materialized. In this sense Conzelmann is right: Luke is concerned about the delay of the parousia. But Luke may *not* have yet given up the hope and expectation of the End for his own day. Thus Conzelmann may be wrong to suggest that Luke has postponed the parousia into the indefinite future. Rather, Luke may still want to reaffirm the eschatological hope in his own time and hence preserves some of the elements in his tradition which warn of a sudden End that may arrive at any moment. Thus for Luke, Jesus predicts delay, and Luke tones down some of the predictions of the parousia that Jesus makes; but this is not because Luke himself has surrendered all such hope completely. Rather it may be precisely in order to reaffirm such hope in his own day that Luke rewrites his sources in this way (see Hiers, 'The Problem of the Delay'; Carroll, *Responses*).

In due course, Christians did have to make considerable adjustments to their eschatological timetables and beliefs. The parousia did not happen as expected, and Christians eventually had to come to terms with the fact that the era of the church was going to last for some considerable time. Within the New Testament, such an adjustment may already have taken place with the writer of Ephesians (probably not Paul) who evidently thinks of the church as the place where God's glory is displayed 'to all generations, forever and ever' (Eph. 3.21). But it seems unlikely that Luke himself had yet taken that step.

Significance of the Present

A final plank of Conzelmann's overall theory was that Luke attributed little eschatological significance to the present: the *eschaton* had shifted to the distant future, and the gift of the Spirit to the church in the present was just a substitute for the *eschaton*.

This is, however, not fully persuasive. Indeed it may be shown to be misleading by some of the evidence we have considered already. The most famous example of Luke's alleged concern to apologize for the delay of the parousia is often held to be his rewriting of Mk 14.62 in Lk. 22.69 (see above). However, we also need to bear in mind not only what Luke does not say (by omitting or changing elements from Mark), but also what he does say. As noted already in general terms, no reader of Luke's present text without the benefit of a Synopsis (or perhaps very detailed knowledge of Mark's text) would pick up that this is apologizing for a delay in the parousia. Rather, what the verse is doing is stressing the immense significance and importance of Jesus' *present* position (i.e. present for Luke): Jesus is now at God's right hand in glory and that is what is of paramount concern for Luke. In Luke's story, Jesus takes his place in this position by virtue of his ascension, and it is the ascension of Jesus to the position of glory that all scholars agree is of central significance for Luke (cf. especially Franklin, *Christ the Lord*).

But for Luke the importance of the present applies not only to the situation in the post-ascension era. For Luke it is of central significance that the whole era of Jesus *and* the church is one of the *fulfilment* of Jewish hopes and expectations. To this we now turn.

Prophecy and Fulfilment

As far as the era of the church is concerned, this is perhaps clearest in the Pentecost story of Acts 2. Here, in Acts 2.17-21, the gift of the Spirit is explicitly portrayed as the fulfilment of the prophecy of the Old Testament in Joel 2.23-27 (LXX 3.1-5). Further, it is significant that Luke almost certainly alters the text of the LXX of Joel from 'after these things' to 'in the last days' (v. 17). (This reading in Acts 2.17 is, however, slightly uncertain in view of a textual variant in a few manuscripts of Acts which read 'after these things', agreeing with the LXX. This may well be due to assimilation to the LXX and hence is probably not original.) Luke's version (which actually now agrees with the Hebrew text of Joel 2) indicates clearly (*pace* Conzelmann) that the gift of the Spirit is not a replacement or a substitute for the *eschaton*. Rather, the presence of the Spirit implies the *fulfilment* of eschatological hopes and indicates that the last days have in a real sense already arrived. Far from pushing the *eschaton* into the indefinite future, Luke brings it firmly into the present.

This note of fulfilment, especially the fulfilment of Scripture, runs through many parts of Luke–Acts. We shall leave aside any detailed discussion of Acts, though we may note in passing the way in which key events in the story in Acts are presented as fulfilling Scripture: for example, Judas's defection fulfils Ps. 69.26 (Acts 1.20); the Gentile mission is said by James in Acts 15.16-17 to be in fulfilment of the Scripture of Amos 9.11-12 (though 'James' needs the LXX of Amos to show this!), and the final rejection (if that is what it is) by Paul of the Jews in Rome is portrayed as the fulfilment of Isa. 6.9-10 in Acts 28.26-27.

Such a note of prophetic fulfilment—explicitly of Scripture, or more generally—is a prominent feature of Luke's Gospel as well. We have already noted the importance of the inaugural scene in Nazareth in Luke's narrative (Lk. 4.16-30), with the focal point of Jesus' speech in his claim that 'Today this Scripture [Isa. 61.1-2] has been fulfilled in your hearing' (v. 21). Such explicit references to a specific proof text are perhaps less common in Luke and more characteristic of Matthew in the Gospels. But Luke has no less firm an idea than Matthew that the Gospel events fulfil Scripture, even if the picture is sometimes painted with broader strokes of the brush.

Luke is, for example, convinced that Jesus' sufferings and death are in fulfilment of Scripture (though he rarely says which particular texts he has in mind). This is of course explicit in relation to the specific text of Isaiah 53 in the story of the Ethiopian eunuch in Acts 8. But in more general terms, Luke rewrites Mark's third passion prediction in Mk 10.33 completely, changing Mark's 'The Son of Man will be handed over to the chief priests and the scribes' to read instead 'Everything that is written about the Son of Man by the prophets will be accomplished' (Lk. 18.31). Thus the whole of the passion is brought under the rubric of Scripture fulfilled.

This comes out very strongly indeed in the scenes Luke records of the teaching given by the risen Jesus to the disciples at the end of the Gospel in Luke 24. Here Jesus tells the disciples on the road to Emmaus that everything that has happened to him, including his passion, was foretold in Scripture (Lk. 24.26-27), a claim that is then repeated when Jesus meets the eleven in the upper room (Lk. 24.44-46). Similarly, Luke has characters in Acts say three times that the suffering of the Messiah is foretold in Scripture (Acts 3.18; 17.3; 26.22-23).

The same general idea of the time of Jesus as the era of fulfilment is provided by the birth narratives. As already indicated (p. 265 above), these are probably no afterthought, added as an optional extra to the rest of the story. Rather, they incorporate many key Lukan themes. Here we may note simply the way in which they portray in general terms the outburst of prophetic activity and the work of the Spirit. As we have already seen, the Spirit for Luke (as indeed for many parts of Judaism) was thought of as the gift of the End-time. The sudden outburst of activity of the Spirit, as portrayed in Luke's account of the birth narratives, is therefore extremely significant. Not only is the Holy Spirit the power which engenders the birth of Jesus himself (Lk. 1.35), the Spirit also inspires a series of individuals in various ways. Thus it is predicted that John the Baptist will be 'filled with the Holy Spirit' (1.15), Elizabeth is filled with the Spirit to sing her praise of Mary (1.41); perhaps there is too a hint of the activity of the Spirit in Mary's own song of praise, the Magnificat (1.47: 'My spirit rejoices in God my Saviour'). Zachariah is filled with the Spirit as he utters the Benedictus (1.67), just as the Spirit 'rested on' Simeon as he comes to the temple (2.25) to utter the Nunc Dimittis (2.29-32). This outburst of prophetic activity by the Spirit thus clearly marks the era of Jesus as one of eschatological fulfilment of Jewish hopes.

The same may also be indicated by one of the words in Luke's prologue. In Lk. 1.1 Luke refers to the events he is going to cover in his work as 'the events that have been fulfilled among us' (NRSV). The verb translated here 'fulfilled' is in Greek *peplērophorēmenōn*. Its precise meaning is a little uncertain, and it may simply be a rather flowery way of saying 'the events that have happened'. However the Greek root *plēro-*, from which this verb comes, is a highly significant one for Christian terminology referring to the 'fulfilment' which is claimed for the Christ-event. It is therefore quite likely that Luke has this deeper meaning in mind so that the events he is about to describe have not merely 'happened' in his view, but have happened by way of 'fulfilling' ancient hopes and expectations. (On this general theme, see Dahl, 'The Story of Abraham'; Schubert, 'Structure'; Tiede, *Prophecy and History*.)

Salvation

Perhaps relevant too is the stress Luke places on the 'salvation' which is now available through the preaching of Jesus and the missionary activity of the early church. Luke is famous for using the vocabulary of 'salvation', or being 'saved', or speaking of Jesus as 'Saviour', more frequently than other New Testament writers. It is part of Luke's characteristic vocabulary to describe the benefits which the Christian gospel brings to men and women.

Yet for the New Testament generally, 'salvation' is an eschatological gift. For example, salvation for Paul is entirely future and the part of the eschatological blessings which has yet to come (cf. Rom. 5.9-10). For Luke it is implied that it is available in the present. Jesus himself is the 'Saviour' (Lk. 2.11), and 'salvation' is announced by Zachariah in the Benedictus (Lk. 1.71, 77). Zacchaeus is told by Jesus, when he responds positively, that 'Today *salvation* has come to this house' (Lk. 19.9). The sinful woman in Luke 7 and the leper who returns to Jesus to thank him are both told 'your faith has *saved* you' (Lk. 7.50; 17.19), and Jesus summarizes his work by saying that 'the Son of Man came to seek out and to save the lost' (Lk. 19.10). So too in Acts the 'salvation' available in Jesus, and in Jesus alone, is a strong motif in the church's preaching (Acts 4.12; 13.26, 47; 16.17).

It is, of course, not absolutely certain that Luke was aware of such eschatological significance in the word, but it seems not improbable that in his stress on the 'salvation' that is available in the Christian message, Luke is again stressing the present as the era of the fulfilment of old hopes and expectations.

Conclusion

We have looked at various aspects of Luke's eschatology in this chapter, especially in the light of Conzelmann's work on Luke–Acts which has done so much to shape contemporary Lukan scholarship. I have tried to argue that while some aspects of his overall theory are valid, other parts may perhaps need modification. Luke does write with an idea of salvation history; and there is a real sense in which he has a threefold division of such history in mind. But there is a deeper sense in which perhaps this threefold division is better seen as a twofold division. Despite real differences between the time of Jesus and the time of the church (cf. p. 274 above), both are together the era of fulfilment of the prophetic hopes and expectations of Judaism. Moreover, rather than postponing the *eschaton* into the indefinite future, Luke still has a firm hope for an imminent eschatological event, while at the same time affirming a belief in the present as in a very real sense a realization of some of these eschatological events (e.g. the activity of the Holy Spirit).

Yet this raises a serious question. If the events of Jesus and the Christian church fulfil Jewish Scripture, why have the Jews themselves not responded positively? Luke–Acts is famous for showing how the Christian gospel has gone to the Gentiles. Indeed Luke's Gospel is sometimes known as the Gospel for the Gentiles; and Luke's story ends in Acts with Paul uttering what have appeared to many as words expressing a final and definitive rejection of the Jewish people (Acts 28.26-27, citing Isa. 6.9-10). What then is Luke's attitude to the Jewish people and/or Judaism? This will be the topic of the next chapter.

FURTHER READING

J.T. Carroll, *Responses to the End of History: Eschatology and Situation in Luke–Acts* (SBLDS, 92; Atlanta: Scholars Press, 1988).

H. Conzelmann, *The Theology of Saint Luke* (ET; London: Faber, 1960).

N.A. Dahl, 'The Story of Abraham in Luke–Acts', in Keck & Martin (eds.), *Studies in Luke–Acts*, pp. 139-58.

R.H. Hiers, 'The Problem of the Delay in the Parousia in Luke–Acts', *NTS* 20 (1974) pp. 145-55.

R. Maddox, *The Purpose of Luke–Acts* (Edinburgh: T. & T. Clark, 1982), esp. ch. 5, 'The Lucan Eschatology', pp. 100-57.

P. Schubert, 'The Structure and Significance of Luke 24', in W. Eltester (ed.), *Neutestamentliche Studien für Rudolf Bultmann* (Berlin: Töpelmann, 1954), pp. 165-86.

J.T. Squires, *The Plan of God in Luke–Acts* (SNTSMS, 76; Cambridge: Cambridge University Press, 1993).

D.L. Tiede, *Prophecy and History in Luke–Acts* (Philadelphia: Fortress Press, 1980).

S.G. Wilson, *The Gentiles and the Gentile Mission in Luke–Acts* (SNTSMS, 23; Cambridge: Cambridge University Press, 1973), esp. ch. 3, 'Lukan Eschatology', pp. 59-87 (= *NTS* 16 [1970], pp. 330-47).

Chapter Three

JEWS, GENTILES AND JUDAISM

The subject of Luke's attitude to Jews and/or Judaism is perhaps one of the most controversial in contemporary Lukan studies. That the question is an important one for Luke is scarcely to be doubted; and of course the whole issue is given added significance for all who have to live and work as biblical exegetes in a post-Holocaust era. There is no doubt that some parts of the New Testament can be read in a way that some describe as anti-Semitic. Luke's writings are no exception in this regard, and hence this aspect of Luke's work has increasingly come under critical scrutiny in recent years. Two preliminary points should be made first.

1. In one way it might be thought that the whole topic is more to do with the interpretation of Acts, rather than of Luke's Gospel. It is certainly true that a great deal of the relevant evidence comes from Acts. But we cannot say that the issue has no relevance for the interpretation of the Gospel as well. Key parts of the Gospel, including the birth narratives, the rejection scene in Nazareth (Lk. 4.16-30), the passion narrative, as well as the denunciations of the Jewish audience in the Gospel, are all clearly also relevant, and their interpretation depends significantly on the overall interpretation one adopts in relation to this wider issue. In any case, I have already tried to show that, in general terms, one cannot interpret Luke's Gospel in isolation from Acts. Thus, although the prime focus of this book is Luke's Gospel, we shall have to take the evidence from Acts fully into account here.

2. The interpretation of the evidence is also crucially connected with one's understanding of more so-called introductory problems of who Luke was, whom he was writing for, and why he was writing. Further, it is really impossible to separate these issues from the broader questions of Luke's attitude to Judaism. As we shall see, one's decisions on the latter question may not only be informed by, but also to a certain extent determine, one's answers to the more introductory questions. At the very least there is an inevitable element of circularity here.

The whole question is, as I said, a controversial one in current Lukan studies. This is due in no small measure to the fact that the evidence in Luke seems to point in different ways simultaneously. This has led one recent writer to say that 'Luke–Acts is one of the most pro-Jewish and one of the most anti-Jewish writings in the New Testament' (Gaston, 'Anti-Judaism', p. 153). But perhaps before we consider Luke and Judaism, we should consider Luke's attitude to Gentiles.

Gentiles

Traditionally Luke has been considered the most pro-Gentile of all the evangelists. Above all, the evidence of Acts, and the account of the success of the Gentile mission there, is often adduced. Thus many have taken the command in Acts 1.8 by the risen Jesus to the disciples, that they are to be 'witnesses in Jerusalem, in all Judea and Samaria, and to the ends of the earth', as a programmatic summary of the book of Acts itself, which shows how the gospel does spread out from Jerusalem and Judaea (chs. 1–7) to Samaria (ch. 8) and on to the ends of the world (symbolically represented by Rome) in the ensuing spread of the Gentile mission (chs. 9–28). Whether this is an appropriate interpretation of Acts we shall leave on one side here, but it is clearly a matter of considerable importance of Acts to show the spread of the mission to reach beyond the national boundaries of Judaism.

When we turn to Luke's Gospel, it is perhaps surprising that there is relatively little to do with this theme. It is certainly true that there are hints of what is to come, but these are mostly by way of a preview of the future. Thus Simeon in the temple says of the infant Jesus that he will be 'a light to lighten the Gentiles', and provide 'salvation which you have prepared in the presence of all peoples' (Lk. 2.32, 31). In the introduction to the preaching of John the Baptist, Luke takes over from Mark the citation of Isa. 40.3 ('a voice crying in the wilderness…'), but extends it as far as Isa. 40.5, to include the words 'All flesh shall see the salvation of God' (Lk. 3.5), showing not only Luke's interest in the vocabulary of salvation, but also his concern to bring out the universal nature of that salvation.

In the rejection scene in Nazareth (Lk. 4.16-30), Luke's Jesus refers to the examples of Elijah and Elisha as prophets sent to those *out*side their own *patris* (Lk. 4.25-27), to illustrate the claim that 'no prophet is accepted in his own *patris*' (v. 24). It is clear in the context that the Greek word *patris* in v. 23 means home *town* ('Whatever we have heard done in Capernaum, do here in your own *patris*'), but in v. 24 may shift its meaning to become home *country*, and is illustrated by the stories of Elijah and Elisha going outside the limits of Israel (to the widow of Zarephthah and Naaman the Syrian respectively). Thus the story as a whole, which is widely regarded as a programmatic summary of the whole of Luke's story to come, probably here points forward to the way in which the gospel will be taken to non-Jews.

In the ministry of Jesus itself as recorded in the Gospel, there is, however, little on this directly. Unlike the Jesus of the other Gospels, Luke's Jesus does not really have any direct contact with a Gentile. The story of Jesus and the Syro-Phoenician woman in Mk. 7.24-30 is part of a whole section of Mark (6.45–8.26) omitted by Luke. The reasons for this omission are not entirely clear. In part it may be because the material is somewhat repetitive (e.g. the feeding of the 4000 after the feeding of the 5000), in part because some parts may have been felt to be offensive (e.g. the stories in Mk 7.32-37; 8.22-26, where Jesus uses what could have been regarded as magical techniques), but also in part because Luke knew that Jesus did not go into Gentile territory (as Mark records him doing in this section). Alternatively, Luke may have wished to avoid such an impression quite deliberately, because in his somewhat schematic version of history, the Gospel only goes to the Gentiles in the era of the church under the guidance of the Spirit and (to a certain extent) only when the Jews have rejected its offer.

As part of the same phenomenon, it may be quite deliberate on Luke's part that the healing of the centurion's servant in Lk. 7.1-10 takes place without the centurion ever meeting Jesus (unlike Matthew, Luke has the centurion send messengers to Jesus, and Luke may have added this detail himself, precisely in order to keep any contact between Jesus and Gentiles as at most indirect).

Luke duplicates the story of the mission of the disciples, so that alongside a mission of the 12 (Lk. 9.1-6) there is a mission of the 70 (Lk. 10.1-16). It is possible that the latter prefigures the Gentile mission, with the number 70 perhaps intended to correspond to the total number of the nations of the world. However, this is at best implicit, and the story itself in Luke 10 does not indicate that the 70 themselves visit Gentiles.

In the parable of the Great Supper (Lk. 14.16-24), Luke seems to have expanded the end of the story so that the servants, who are sent out to find replacement guests for those who refused to come originally, cannot fill all the places at the first attempt and are sent out again. This detail (which is possibly superfluous in the parable as it stands) is lacking in Matthew's version of the parable, and may well be Luke's own addition to the story, the double mission of the servants now prefiguring the dual mission of the later church, to Jews and then to Gentiles.

Finally (at least in the Gospel's terms), in Lk. 24.47 the risen Jesus makes explicit what has so far been only adumbrated: the disciples are to go out in Jesus' name and proclaim repentance and the forgiveness of sins 'to all the nations, beginning from Jerusalem'. And this command is then taken up again at the beginning of Acts with the charge of the risen Jesus in Acts 1.8, which then leads on to the development of the story in the rest of Acts, as we have seen.

We may therefore say that the theme of the Gentiles' reception of the gospel is an important one for Luke. It is, however, one which shows Luke's sensitivity as a historian. He is either aware of the fact that, or wants positively to maintain that, Jesus himself did not have any extensive contacts with Gentiles. For Luke then the Gentile mission is prefigured in the Gospel; but it is not written back into the pre-Easter story. Luke is conscious of the distinctions between the different eras of history.

Jews and Judaism

What then of the other side of the coin? What is Luke's attitude to Jews and/or 'Judaism'? It is here that enormous debate arises, in part simply because there is so much conflicting evidence. For on the one hand, there are elements of Luke–Acts that seem extremely positive about Jews and Judaism; on the other hand, there are elements that seem to betray an intense, almost unrelieved, hostility.

As already noted, much of the relevant evidence is from Acts; but, as I have said, we cannot ignore Acts if we wish to come to some assessment of Luke's own attitudes and concerns. In what follows I shall therefore allude to the Acts evidence, but, as this is meant to be a study of Luke's Gospel, not in such detail as if this were a study of the whole of the Lukan writings equally. I consider the negative elements first.

Anti-Judaism?

The negative attitude to Jews and Judaism does not dominate Luke's Gospel in a way that is necessarily qualitatively different from the other Gospels, and such an attitude comes much more to the fore in Acts. Nevertheless it is not lacking in the Gospel.

The rejection scene in Nazareth (Lk. 4.16-30) acts, as we have already noted, as a programmatic summary of the whole story that is to follow in Luke's two-volume work, and here the motif of the rejection of Jesus by the Jews is sounded clearly. Further, if, as I argued above, the references to Elijah and Elisha are rightly to be interpreted as prefiguring the Gentile mission, then the division here portrayed is clearly set in national or ethnic terms right from the start.

In the rest of the Gospel, Luke preserves many of the polemical, and at times extremely bitter, tirades by Jesus against his Jewish contemporaries. Some of these are, it is true, already present in Luke's sources; but at the very least, Luke has evidently decided to include them in his Gospel and shows little inclination to modify them significantly. Thus the Q tirade against 'this generation' culminates in the doom oracle of Lk. 11.49-51, concluding the series of woes against the scribes/ lawyers and Pharisees; here 'this generation' is accused of sharing (in some way) in the murderous activity of their predecessors by killing the prophets and other sent to them, 'so that this generation may be charged with the blood of all the prophets shed from the foundation of the world' (v. 50).

So too Jesus' contemporaries who have eaten and drunk with him and in whose streets he has taught (Lk. 13.26) are rejected harshly by Jesus: 'I never knew you: Depart from me all you workers of iniquity' (13.27); and the sequel in vv. 28-30, which speaks of many coming from the east and the west, the north and the south, and replacing the addressees, seems quite clearly to have in mind the latter as Jews being replaced by Gentiles. Similarly, we have seen that the parable of the Great Supper in Lk. 14.16-24 in Luke's version becomes a clear statement of Gentiles replacing Jews as the guests in the banquet (whatever may have been the meaning of the original parable).

The destruction of Jerusalem is predicted by Luke's Jesus in vivid terms in Lk. 19.34-35 (a passage peculiar to Luke), though whether this, set in the context of Jesus' weeping over the city (v. 41), is intended as implying sorrowful regret or righteous anger, is not so clear.

Perhaps more to the point is the way in which Luke seems to present at least some details of the account of Jesus' trial as if it is the Jews who are responsible for Jesus' death, perhaps even that it is the Jews who are directly instrumental in executing Jesus. In general terms it is notable that, in the passion narrative, the opposition to Jesus seems no longer to come from the Jewish leaders with the crowds being generally sympathetic (as is mostly the case earlier in the Gospel): rather, the crowds too are now hostile (cf. Lk. 23.13-25). Pilate, on the other hand, is almost friendly, and certainly portrayed as desperately anxious to release Jesus, three times declaring him innocent (Lk. 23.4, 14, 22). And in the end Pilate hands Jesus over to 'their' (= the Jews') will (v. 25), so that the decision to crucify is apparently a Jewish, not a Roman, one. Moreover, the sequel (in Lk. 23.26-33) uses general third person plurals ('they led him away...when they came...there they crucified him'), which, if one interprets the syntax strictly, refer to the 'they' of v. 25, that is, the Jews.

Yet it is perhaps the story as told in Acts which contributes most to this picture of hostility to Judaism by Luke. We shall not go into many details here, but the general outline is often stereotyped and, for many, crystal clear. Stephen's speech in Acts 7 accuses the Jews of continual disobedience to God, resulting in a constant pattern of rejection and violence inflicted on God's messengers, including (by implication) Stephen himself. As the Christian mission goes into the wider world, a set pattern seems to be established as the story progresses. Regularly, the Christian missionaries start by preaching to the Jews; equally regularly the Jews reject the Christian message and stir up trouble against the Christians. As a result, the Christians are as often as not in trouble with the civic authorities, and are driven out of one city; they go to the next where the same pattern is repeated. Three times, in what appear to many as programmatic statements, Paul responds to the situation almost in exasperation, by saying that if the Jews will not listen, then the Christian mission will go to the Gentiles. This happens in Pisidian Antioch (Acts 13.46), in Corinth (Acts 18.6) and finally in the dramatic final scene in Rome, where Luke seems to save up the full quotation of Isa. 6.9-10 from Mk 4.11-12 to illustrate the apparently divinely intended Jewish refusal to respond and the apparently equally final decision now to desert the Jewish people for good: 'Let it be known to you that this salvation of God has been sent to the Gentiles: *they* will hear' (Acts 28.28).

Yet this is by no means the whole story in Luke–Acts, for balancing this apparently highly negative picture of Judaism are some equally powerful positive elements.

Pro-Judaism?
Luke is clearly steeped in Jewish Scriptures. We have already noted the way in which the theme of prophecy and fulfilment dominates the Lukan narrative. The events of Luke's story are thus the fulfilment of Jewish Scripture. Jewish Scripture is thus part of the Christian heritage and to be regarded thoroughly positively.

Luke's Gospel starts with the portrayal in the birth narratives of a series of figures who are presented as models of Jewish piety, with no hint of any critique of such piety. Further, their actions closely involve the person of Jesus. Zachariah, the father of John the Baptist, is a priest serving in the temple. Simeon and Anna are also based in the temple. Jesus' parents circumcise him on the eighth day and bring the baby to Jerusalem to offer what is apparently the appropriate sacrifice (Lk.

2.23). So too, in the various 'prophetic' speeches/hymns (i.e. the canticles of later Christian tradition) which are put on the lips of the characters in these birth narratives, the hope is expressed that the arrival of John and Jesus will be the fulfilment of so many long-standing hopes for Israel (cf. Lk. 1.54-55, 68-69; 2.30-32).

The centrality of Jerusalem and the Jerusalem temple continue to dominate other parts of the story. Jesus' journey to Jerusalem is given central importance in Luke's structure of his Gospel by his development of the travel narrative, structured around the journey motif to which Luke gives solemn significance at the start (9.51), with its goal as Jerusalem, the place where a prophet 'must' meet his final destiny (13.33). When Jesus arrives in Jerusalem, he is again found in the temple, just as he was in the temple in the one story Luke records of Jesus' childhood (see 2.41-51 and the story of the 12-year-old Jesus in the temple). Thus after the story of the 'cleansing' of the temple (which Luke drastically abbreviates from Mark: cf. 19.45-46 par. Mk 11.15-17), Luke says that Jesus was 'teaching *daily* in the temple' (19.47): presence in the temple is a regular pattern for the Lukan Jesus in Jerusalem.

So too Luke rewrites parts of his tradition to ensure that the risen Jesus appears in Jerusalem. Luke says nothing of an appearance of Jesus in Galilee (possibly implicit in Mk 16.7, certainly explicit in Mt. 28.16-20); and he carefully rewrites any hint of this (cf. Lk. 24.6-7, where a prophecy of a future event in Galilee [Mk 16.7] becomes a statement about Jesus' past teachings in Galilee). Thus for Luke, the resurrection appearances are all located and focused in Jerusalem, the centre of the Jewish faith. It is then thoroughly characteristic of Luke that his final word in the Gospel has the disciples in the temple in Jerusalem continually, praising God (Lk. 24.53). The focus is entirely on the Jewish matrix of faith, with no hint of any critique.

This picture continues on in Acts (though, as before, I shall be briefer here). The early Christian community in Acts continues to worship in the temple, and carries on doing so for as long as it is allowed. Further, any critique of Jewish responsibility for inflicting violence and death on (at least some of) the Christian figures, including Jesus, is ameliorated in part by the concession that the Jews acted in ignorance. (Acts 3.17; 13.27. Cf. too the prayer of Jesus on the cross in Lk. 23.34 for his executioners, who are excused because of their ignorance: 'Father, forgive them, for they do not know what they are doing'. The verse is textually uncertain, but the close parallel in the prayer of the dying Stephen in Acts 7.60 makes it likely, in view of the number of close parallels between the accounts of the deaths of Jesus and

Stephen, that Lk. 23.34 is indeed a genuine part of the text of Luke's Gospel.) So too, Luke's general picture in Acts seems to be that it was only the Jewish leaders in Jerusalem who were responsible for the death of Jesus, not the Jewish people as a whole (see Matera, 'Responsibility'; Weatherly, *Jewish Responsibility*).

Above all, the positive picture of Judaism emerges from Luke's portrait of Paul in Acts. Throughout his account of Paul's career, Luke presents Paul as a law-abiding Jew, always anxious to keep the feasts in Jerusalem, concerned to have the backing of the Jewish-Christian church in Jerusalem for all his endeavours, and adhering throughout to Torah observance, performing, if necessary, acts of supererogation to convince others of his attitude in this respect (cf. his paying the expenses of those who had a vow in Acts 21.23-26). In the account of the various trials and hearings which Paul undergoes in the last quarter of Acts, it is a constant motif that Paul is a law-abiding Pharisee (Acts 23.6), and that he has done nothing wrong by breaking either Jewish or civil law (Acts 25.8). Paul is presented as agreeing with one major strand of Judaism, namely Pharisaism, in the one point that is portrayed as the reason for his being arrested and tried, that is, in his affirmation of a belief in resurrection which is a hope that God has given to the Jewish people as a whole. 'I stand here to be judged for the hope of the promise made by God to our fathers [i.e. resurrection]' (Acts 26.6).

Finally we may note the occasions in Acts when Luke records considerable success in the Christian mission among Jews. After Peter's initial sermon at Pentecost, 'about three thousand' Jews join the Christian ranks (Acts 2.41), 'about five thousand' join a little later (Acts 4.4), 'great numbers of both men and women' converts are mentioned in Acts 5.14 etc., so that when Paul arrives back in Jerusalem after his travels, James tells him 'how many thousands of believers there are among the Jews' (Acts 21.20). Even in the final scene in Acts 28, there is a mixed picture: although some Jews reject Paul's message, 'some believed' (Acts 28.24).

How then should one resolve these apparently contradictory elements in Luke's writings? Is Luke incorrigibly opposed to the Jews to the extent of being virtually 'anti-Semitic'? Or is Luke thoroughly positive about the Jews and Judaism?

Possible Solutions

The theory that Luke is thoroughly opposed to Jews, if not Judaism, has certainly had many defenders in the past, from Overbeck to scholars such as Haenchen in his monumental and highly influential commentary on Acts, and in the work of J.T. Sanders today (Sanders, *The Jews in Luke–Acts*). Thus Sanders is not afraid to accuse Luke effectively of anti-Semitism. Any positive elements in Luke's writings are simply designed as part of the narrative development leading up to the final scene in Acts 28, which expresses the final and definitive rejection of the Jewish people. The Jewish people have been found guilty of the death of Jesus, and have not taken the opportunity to repent at the offer of forgiveness in the Gospel. In Haenchen's words, 'Luke has written the Jews off' (Haenchen, 'The Book of Acts', p. 278).

A rather different overall view has been presented vigorously in recent years by J. Jervell in a number of essays and articles. Jervell argues that the view of Haenchen and others does not do justice to the note of *success* among at least some Jews of the Christian mission (cf. above). The people of God is now for Luke a divided people, some having accepted the Christian message, some having rejected it. The Gentile mission is then the result of (part of) Israel having been saved. There is thus no rejection of the Jewish people in principle: rather, only those who have refused to repent are rejected. Thus the people of Israel are regarded in principle positively, and Gentiles join this repentant Israel.

Jervell is surely right to draw attention to notes of success by Christians among Jews. Yet his overall theory has a number of weaknesses. It is certainly hard to interpret verses such as Acts 13.46 and 18.6 as implying that the Gentile mission results from a successful mission among Jews. The very opposite seems to be the case. So too it is not so clear that in the end, Jervell's interpretation is very different from that of the older view. Jervell too acknowledges that the scene of Acts 28 implies that the days of an appeal to Jews by Christians are for Luke past and gone: the unrepentant Jews are indeed written off as far as Luke is concerned. Thus while Jervell's Luke may have a slightly different theoretical/theological slant to Haenchen's or Sanders's Luke, as far as contemporary non-Christians Jews are concerned, there is not much difference: non-Christian Jews are no longer envisaged as likely to come into the church, and are rejected finally.

A very different interpretation has been offered by R. Tannehill, in a highly sensitive literary reading of Luke's two-volume work. Tannehill refers to the way in which the birth narratives set up hopes and expectations for the reader for things to come, much of which fails to materialize in the story Luke actually recounts. Many of these hopes and expectations are associated with those of the Jewish people for their own destiny. The angel Gabriel tells Mary that the child to be born will be given (by God!) 'the throne of David his father, and he will reign over the house of Jacob for ever' (Lk. 1.32-33). Zachariah tells of the 'redemption' of God's people and 'a horn of salvation for us in the house of his servant David' (1.68-69), and this salvation is specified later as 'salvation from our enemies' (1.71, cf. v. 74 too). Anna too speaks of the 'redemption of Jerusalem'. Moreover, all these are clearly 'reliable characters' in the story of Luke–Acts. The way they are presented suggests that the reader should take seriously — and positively — what they say and predict.

Yet as it develops, the story indicates that these hopes fail to materialize: indeed not only in the story but in the parts of later history (future for the story, past for Luke) which are hinted at, above all the fall of Jerusalem. Luke's readers surely know that Anna's hopes of the redemption of Jerusalem have not materialized. Above all the Jewish people have rejected the salvation offered to them. Tannehill thus suggests that the work is presented by Luke as a tragic story, a story filled with pathos as it tells of hopes that are *not* fulfilled. And yet, as the hopes are of *God's* promises, the implication must be that the story is still open as far as the Jews are concerned, even by the end of Luke's actual story line in Acts 28. The fact that these promises are still 'on the table', still waiting to be fulfilled, and that in Luke's day there is still no sign of their being fulfilled, is what gives the story its tragic quality.

Tannehill produces many fine insights in his study; and his work shows the importance and the value of taking seriously the whole of Luke's two-volume work as a literary unity. Nevertheless, it is not entirely persuasive. Whatever the element of tragedy in Luke's work, it seems that Luke in no way intends to evoke the readers' sympathy for non-Christian Jews. On a reasonably straightforward reading of Luke–Acts (if such is possible!), the sympathies of the reader seem to be drawn quite self-consciously by Luke to Jesus or the Christians who suffer at the hands of (at least some of) the Jews. Any sympathy for Jews has to be read out of quite a complex reading of Luke's work. Further, it is clear that Luke does go in for a quiet, but nevertheless quite radical, redefinition of many of the hopes expressed in the birth narratives. This comes out perhaps most clearly in some of the speeches in Acts (cf., e.g., Acts 13). Here it is clear that the hopes for a new king who will produce salvation for his people *have* been fulfilled in the person of Jesus who *is* the new heir to the Davidic promises (by virtue of his resurrection) and who has brought salvation through the offer of repentance and the forgiveness of sins (see Räisänen, 'Redemption'). One may wish to accuse Luke of some sleight of hand here: such fulfilment has redefined the national and political Jewish expec-

tations in a radically individualistic way; and it could be regarded as
somewhat tongue-in-cheek to say that an offer of forgiveness of sins is
a radical fulfilment of Jewish eschatological expectations! (After all, is
not forgiveness available anyway in Judaism?!) Nevertheless, it does
seem to be the case that, for Luke, these hopes of pious people at the
start of the story *are* fulfilled (at least in his eyes) in the story he does
recount. For Luke there is not much idea that these hopes are still
waiting to be fulfilled.

It seems hard to avoid the impression that, at least for many Jews if
not for Judaism, the scene in Acts 28 is drawing a fairly firm line. Luke
does not seem to hold out much more hope of any success for any
Jewish mission after this time.

Is then Luke to be regarded as anti-Semitic? In trying to answer
such a question, much depends on where Luke himself is to be sited
in relation to Judaism: is Luke himself an insider or an outsider? (See
Salmon, 'Insider or Outsider?') For if Luke is writing from outside the
fold of Judaism completely, then the negative parts of his picture of
the Jews come close to being an attack on, and rejection of, Judaism as
such, so that the charge of anti-Semitism is not completely absurd.
(Though one must also remember that any negative portrait of the
Jews in Luke–Acts gives no encouragement at all to any policy of
direct physical persecution of Jews by Christians.)

If, however, Luke is writing as an insider, from inside the fold of
Judaism, then the negative elements in his story are on a par with
prophetic indictments of Israel's people which have been a constant
feature of Israel's history since the time of the classical prophets. Accu-
sations of sin, apostasy or whatever issued by Jews against other Jews
by no means imply that the accusers are anti-Semitic. An Amos or an
Isaiah is not anti-Semitic simply by virtue of the harsh invective used!

Yet putting the authorship question in such a way probably makes
things too clear-cut and black-and-white. It seems unlikely that Luke
is a total outsider in relation to Judaism. The positive picture of Judaism and the Jewish roots of the Christian story seem to show that the
author is one who is deeply in sympathy with the Jewish heritage of
Christianity. Similarly, the portrait of Paul in Acts shows Luke anxious to defend his hero against any charge that he has deserted ('true')
Judaism. On the other hand, it seems unlikely that Luke is a complete
insider in relation to Judaism. There is a well-known catalogue of
instances in the Lukan writings where Luke seems to show more than
a little ignorance about some features of Jewish life. For example,
Luke seems to be unclear, or inaccurate, about the legal requirements
apparently being fulfilled by Mary and Joseph in 'presenting' Jesus in

the temple (Lk. 2.22-24); he seems to assume that there were two high priests when Jesus' ministry begins (Lk. 3.2); and his accounts of Paul's cutting his hair because of a vow in Cenchreae (Acts 18.18), or of Paul paying the expenses of four men in Jerusalem who had a vow (Acts 21.24-26), raise well-known problems of historicity because of their lack of correspondence with what we know of Jewish practice (see the commentaries).

Perhaps the category which might fit all the evidence best is that of a 'godfearer', that is, a Gentile who is attracted by, and closely attached to Judaism by participating in synagogue worship, though without undertaking the full commitment of circumcision. (There is some debate about whether such people existed in a formal category. However, it seems likely that such people existed in general terms, even if the formal 'title', or description, of 'godfearer' is harder to establish.)

But on any showing it is clearly of vital importance for Luke to show that Christianity is in a line of almost unbroken continuity with Judaism. This is shown in the Gospel above all by the birth narratives, as we have seen; the motif of prophecy and fulfilment, emphasized above all in the programmatic scene in Nazareth (Lk. 4.21), supports it; and the picture is reinforced at the end of the Gospel by the emphasis given in the teaching of the risen Jesus to the effect that everything that has happened has been ordained by God and fulfils Scripture. So too the story in Acts as told by Luke continues in the same vein, above all in the portrait of Paul which emerges, as we have seen.

There is thus a real sense in which, for Luke, the Christian church is the true Israel. The pattern of prophecy and fulfilment shows the true roots of the Christian church. The opposition to the Christian movement shown by other Jews is portrayed as part of a continuous and continuing pattern of disobedience by some Jews to God's will, which has characterized Jewish history from the very start. (This is very much the burden of Stephen's speech in Acts 7: the long survey of Israelite history is to show that [some] Jews have always disobeyed and rebelled against God's messengers.) As far as 'Judaism' is concerned, therefore, there is certainly no suggestion at all that Christianity is in antithesis to Judaism. Quite the contrary!

Indeed it is not that clear that Christianity is so very new in relation to Judaism. Certainly Christianity fulfils Jewish hopes and prophecies. But there is equally as great a stress on the *continuity* between the Christian church and Israel, as Stephen's speech makes clear. It would thus not be entirely un-Lukan if the reference to the *new* covenant established by Jesus' death (Lk. 22.20) were *not* part of the Lukan text. (As we saw earlier, the verse is one of the notorious 'Western non-interpolations' in Luke's Gospel and textually uncertain; see p. 261 above.) Whatever the merits of the manuscript evidence here, the fact remains that the overall picture presented by Luke is of the one covenant, made by God with the Jewish people at Sinai; and if the Jews have disobeyed, then the Christians are the true heirs of this heritage. Luke's Paul reiterates, almost *ad nauseam*, that it is *Israel's* hope which is the cause of his trial, and that hope is one that is *shared* by Christians and ('true') Jews (i.e. Pharisees) alike. Given this, it is hard to accuse Luke of anti-Semitism.

Luke's Purpose

Nevertheless, there is still the further question of why Luke presents his story in this way. Certainly it is hard to deny that Luke has something of an axe to grind here. His picture of Paul, which is notoriously so unlike the Paul of the letters, seems to be skewed, and perhaps deliberately so. Several answers to this problem have been suggested, though all involve an element of circularity in the argument.

Political Apologetic?

One answer given by some in the past is that the picture of the relationship between Christianity and Judaism is part of an apologetic ploy on Luke's part in relation to the Roman authorities, or to non-Jewish society in general. Thus some have argued that the picture Luke paints of almost unbroken continuity between Christianity and Judaism is aimed at a Hellenistic audience to convince them that Christianity is really true Judaism. The aim of this may then be to give the Christian religion more respectability, and perhaps legitimacy, in the eyes of a sceptical non-Jewish audience. Two slightly different underlying reasons have been suggested.

First, it may be that Christianity is claiming the same status as Judaism, as a *religio licita*: Judaism was an accepted religion and Jews were given a number of rights to be able to practise their religion. Christianity, if shown to be nothing other than true Judaism, could therefore claim the same status.

Secondly, it may be that the picture here meets a problem faced by Christians, namely, how to explain the novelty of their faith. Religions in the ancient world were many and varied, and mostly tolerated; but what was suspect was anything new. Luke's picture, by presenting Christianity as essentially Judaism, makes the implicit claim that Christianity is not new at all: it has all the antiquity of Judaism and should therefore be accorded equal respect.

Further, the picture Luke paints of consistent Jewish opposition to the Christians has the effect of showing the Roman authorities in a good light. The civic authorities are generally shown to be tolerant, or at worst indifferent, to the Christian movement. Thus the story Luke tells may have been intended to mount a powerful piece of apologetic on behalf of the Christian church to make it acceptable to Roman, or Hellenistic, society (cf. Conzelmann, *Theology*, pp. 137-44).

This overall explanation may have some truth in it, though some details are unpersuasive. In particular, the notion of a *religio licita* is rather improbable, since it has been shown that such a formal category probably did not exist in the ancient world (see Maddox, *Purpose*, pp. 91-93). The theory that Luke is presenting a piece of political apologetic in more general terms may have an element of truth in it. Certainly the portrait of some of the civic authorities in Acts is often painted in more positive terms than is at times probable; and in the Gospel, as we have seen, Pilate is almost exonerated from any involvement in the execution of Jesus by declaring him innocent three times (see p. 290 above).

On the other hand, such a theory is hard pushed to explain the whole of Luke–Acts. There is so much in the two-volume work that does not seem to be addressed to a non-Christian, Roman audience. So much of the Gospel is taken up with teaching by Jesus which is clearly addressed explicitly to the Christians of Luke's own day. Teaching on prayer (Lk. 11.2-13), on ethics (Lk. 6.20-49) or on eschatology (cf. Chapter 2 above) and so on is really not related to the theme of political apologetic. Hence the relevance and appropriateness of an often-quoted remark of C.K. Barrett: 'No Roman official would ever have filtered out so much of what to him would be theological and ecclesiastical rubbish to reach so tiny a grain of relevant apology' (*Luke the Historian*, p. 63). We do not know for certain who Theophilus, the person directly addressed in Luke's two-volume work, was. But it seems much more likely that Luke is primarily addressing his work to a Christian audience.

Legitimation

With this in mind, a number of scholars have suggested that Luke is primarily addressing problems faced by Christians in his own situation via his picture of Judaism. Again the nature of the solution proposed depends critically on the alleged problem, or situation, being addressed. Thus some have argued that Luke's story serves to provide some kind of legitimation for the Christian community in a context of external threats. In the face perhaps of criticisms by non-Christian

Jews creating a hostile environment, Luke's story serves to give assurance to the Christian church of its legitimacy (cf. Maddox, *Purpose*).

Esler (*Community and Gospel*) has adduced a more sociological approach to argue a broadly similar case. Analogies in other situations suggest that splinter groups within larger organizations can have a variety of relationships with their parent bodies. However, at some stage the relationship can become so strained that the splinter group is almost forced to separate socially so that it becomes, in sociological terms, a sect. In response to this, and facing a situation of powerful hostility from the parent body, members of the sect may feel intense worry about the validity and self-identity of the new movement. It is precisely such a situation that Esler postulates for Luke's community: he argues that the references to powerful Jewish hostility to Jesus and the new Christian movement (cf. Lk. 4.28-30; 6.22; also the evidence of Acts) indicates that the Christians of Luke's day were facing direct antagonism from their Jewish contemporaries. Most too had originally been closely attached to Judaism, whether directly as Jews or indirectly as 'godfearers' (or the like). In this situation creating uncertainty and worry, the members of the new community needed reassurance that their decision to leave the old fold and join the new was correct. Luke's story thus provides just such legitimation for the Christian community, creating a symbolic universe, a total worldview, to explain and defend the origins of the movement and its separation from its parent body (*Community and Gospel*, esp. pp. 46-70). So too the presentation of Christianity as an ancestral religion may have a powerful legitimating function for Gentile Christians of Luke's day (pp. 201-19).

Esler's study certainly shows the fruitfulness of adopting a less overtly theological approach and using the insights afforded by sociological analyses to throw light on a text such as Luke–Acts. However, in any such overall interpretation, seeking to explain the text in relation to its setting and vice versa, much depends on the situation of Luke's community that is proposed. Esler's model would fit very well *if* we knew for certain that the Christian community and the Jewish community had separated finally, and that the former were experiencing hostility and threat from the latter (though his persuasive arguments about the legitimating function of Luke's implied stress on the ancestral nature of Christianity does not depend on such a reconstruction in quite the same way, and hence can stand independently).

I argued above that the first of these assumptions is likely (though by no means unanimously agreed by Lukan scholars today!). I interpreted the scene in Acts 28 as implying that the era of any success among a Jewish mission seems here to be signalled as a matter of past history by Luke. Yet what of the second assumption? Is the threat faced by Luke from Jewish opponents? Such a theory is possible, and many have argued for such a situation precisely on the basis of the constant motif of *Jewish* opposition in Luke's story world. The difficulty is to know whether Luke's story world and Luke's real world match each other so precisely.

The one point at which virtually all scholars agree that Luke allows his real world to be glimpsed is the prediction by Luke's Paul in his farewell speech to the Ephesian elders in Acts 20. Here Paul looks ahead to his future, but almost certainly to what is for Luke present reality. Paul predicts that 'savage wolves' will come in and harry the flock (v. 29) and that 'men will arise out of your midst who speak perversely in order to lead disciples astray after them' (v. 30). The trouble is that the language is rather elliptical and not at all clear. It is not certain, for example, whether the savage wolves are Christians or non-Christians, though the language is often used of 'heretics', rather than complete outsiders, and hence it may be that Christians, or at least people claiming to be Christians, are in view (cf. Mt. 7.15). Certainly the reference in v. 30 seems to be to Christians (cf. 'men will rise *out of your midst*').

Are these then Jewish-Christian heretics? Or are they so-called Gnostics? (We know that later, in the middle to late second century, the church was deeply divided by the presence of Gnostics.) Certainty is simply not possible, but the language here does seem to read more easily if the threat is being conceived of as involving a quite different set of ideas/people than has been the case in the story hitherto. This might then tell against the theory that Luke is trying to defend Christianity (or perhaps just his hero Paul) against hostile attacks from non-Christian Jews.

Some have argued that Luke is facing threats from Gnostics, and, for example, Paul's insistence in his farewell speech in Acts on his openness and frankness in all his preaching (Acts 20.20-21) is a quiet dig at Gnostics who are claiming secret, esoteric teaching, allegedly from Paul, as their own. Similarly, the motif of Jesus' full bodily resurrection in Luke 24 (cf. especially 24.39 and the command of Jesus to handle him and to see that he is not a ghost; also 24.43 showing Jesus physically eating) may reflect some critique of possible Gnostic claims of some kind of a spiritual, non-physical resurrection of Jesus (see Talbert, *Luke and the Gnostics*).

Again this seems to focus on a small part of Luke–Acts at the expense of an enormous amount elsewhere. As in the case of the theory of political apologetic on the part of Luke, such a stress on openness and so on scarcely affects large sections of Luke's work.

Anti-'Marcionite' Tendencies?

In a short article, Houlden ('The Purpose of Luke') has argued that much of the evidence of Luke's story might fit together if Luke were writing in a situation of what he regarded as dangerous tendencies among some Christians to cut themselves off from their Jewish roots entirely. We know of at least one Christian who did precisely this, namely Marcion. Marcion is almost certainly later than Luke, but it may well have been that Marcionite tendencies were present in the church at an earlier period.

In such a setting, Luke's account might make a lot of sense. If Luke's community were predominantly Gentile, and were seeking to cut their links with Judaism entirely, Luke's narrative would provide a powerful corrective. Christianity is shown to be inextricably tied to Judaism. Luke's own situation may be one in which Jewish presence is no longer a reality in his community; but the narrative then shows that the Gentile mission is a result solely of Jewish refusal to accept the gospel. It is not a result of any definitive rejection of the Jews by the Christians.

If this reconstruction is correct, then it may draw on many previous, and different, analyses of Luke–Acts. Luke may indeed be indicating in Acts the de facto break between the Christian and Jewish communities of his own day. But this is *not* in the sense of any anti-Semitism. Luke does not want to jettison the Jewish roots of the Christian faith, nor does he necessarily want to damn all contemporary Jews to oblivion, or to eternal punishment. If there is a split between the communities, it is because the Jews have rejected the gospel, not vice versa. But Luke's aim may be more pastoral, in the sense of being directed to his own community, rather than theologizing about the fate of those outside his community. Luke above all wants to show that Christians do come from a Jewish stock. Thus to quote one conclusion of one scholar (who nevertheless offers a rather different overall interpretation of Luke–Acts in other respects to the one suggested here): 'Rather than setting gentile Christianity free, Luke ties it to Judaism' (Brawley, *Luke–Acts and the Jews*, p. 159). Certainly this effort to tie the Christian story to its Jewish roots pervades a large part of Luke's two-volume work, as we have seen. As such, Houlden's theory may then perhaps explain more adequately than some why Luke presents the whole story in the way he has.

FURTHER READING

R.L. Brawley, *Luke–Acts and the Jews: Conflict, Apology, and Conciliation* (SBLMS, 33; Atlanta: Scholars Press, 1987).

P.F. Esler, *Community and Gospel in Luke–Acts* (SNTSMS, 57; Cambridge: Cambridge University Press, 1987).

L. Gaston, 'Anti-Judaism and the Passion Narrative in Luke and Acts', in P. Richardson and D. Granskou (eds.), *Anti-Judaism in Early Christianity* (Waterloo, Ontario: Wilfrid Laurier University Press, 1986), pp. 127-53.

E. Haenchen, 'The Book of Acts as Source Material for the History of Early Christianity', in Keck and Martyn (eds.), *Studies in Luke–Acts*, pp. 258-78.

J.L. Houlden, 'The Purpose of Luke', *JSNT* 21 (1984), pp. 53-65.

J. Jervell, *Luke and the Divided People of God: A New Look at Luke–Acts* (Minneapolis: Augsburg, 1972), esp. ch. 2 'The Divided People of God', pp. 41-74.

R. Maddox, *The Purpose of Luke–Acts* (Edinburgh: T. & T. Clark, 1982).

F.J. Matera, 'Responsibility for the Death of Jesus According to the Acts of the Apostles', *JSNT* 39 (1990), pp. 77-93.

H. Räisänen, 'The Redemption of Israel. A Salvation-Historical Perspective in Luke–Acts', in P. Luomanen (ed.), *Luke–Acts: Scandinavian Perspectives* (Helsinki: Finnish Exegetical Society, 1991), pp. 94-114.

M. Salmon, 'Insider or Outsider? Luke's Relationship with Judaism', in Tyson (ed.), *Images of Judaism in Luke–Acts*, pp. 76-82.

J.T. Sanders, *The Jews in Luke–Acts* (London: SCM Press, 1987).

C.H. Talbert, *Luke and the Gnostics* (New York: Abingdon Press, 1966).

R.C. Tannehill, 'Israel in Luke–Acts: A Tragic Story', *JBL* 104 (1984), pp. 69-85.

J.B. Tyson (ed.), *Images of Judaism in Luke–Acts* (Columbia: University of South Carolina Press, 1992).

—*Luke–Acts and the Jewish People: Eight Critical Perspectives* (Minneapolis: Augsburg, 1988). (All the essays here are relevant to this chapter and provide a good representation of the variety of scholarly opinions on the issue.)

J.A. Weatherly, *Jewish Responsibility for the Death of Jesus in Luke–Acts* (JSNTSup, 106; Sheffield: JSOT Press, 1994).

S.G. Wilson, *The Gentiles and the Gentile Mission in Luke–Acts* (SNTSMS, 23; Cambridge: Cambridge University Press, 1973).

Chapter Four

THE PERSON AND WORK OF JESUS

In thinking and writing about Luke, Luke's view on this, his theology of that, or whatever, we must not lose sight of the fact that our access to any such view or theology is at best indirect and derivative. Luke does not explicitly set out to tell us what *his* views or theology as such are. Rather, the medium he chooses is that of a story. He chooses to tell the story in Acts of aspects of the life and history of the early church; and in his Gospel he gives us a record of the life and ministry of Jesus. In discussing his Gospel, therefore, we must remember that the prime focus of attention is the person of Jesus. (This is in one sense a comment which is trite to the point of being absurdly obvious, but in the light of some discussions of Luke's theology on this or that topic, needs occasionally to be spelt out explicitly.) If then our prime focus is on Luke's Gospel, one key question must be: what does Luke think about Jesus? How does he think that Jesus is important? And perhaps a related question: why is Jesus' life (and death) important? What is it that Jesus' life and/or death have achieved? In the words of later theologizing, therefore, we need to consider Luke's Christology and, perhaps related, his soteriology. Before embarking on this, however, we must consider some methodological problems.

Methodology

How do we study the Christology of a Christian writer or thinker? One traditional answer has been to consider the use of christological titles used by the writer to refer to Jesus. Does the writer prefer one or more particular titles: Son of God, messiah or whatever? An analysis of the meaning of such titles in the background thought of the time may then give us significant insight into the christological ideas of the writer.

Such an approach has come under attack in recent years (cf. Keck, 'Renewal'). On the one hand, an exclusive concentration on the use of titles may miss other, less direct ways in which an author may wish to signal the significance of Jesus. On the other hand, a titular approach is in danger of assuming that titles applied to Jesus are, if not univocal, at least unchanging in their potential meanings; if one is not careful, one may assume that a title carries with it a constant and unchanging range of meaning whereby, when the title is applied to Jesus, it is assumed that this meaning is being ascribed to him.

Such an approach is, of course, misleading. Some titles are, of course, multivalent (though that in itself would not matter: it would just be a question of sorting out which, among a discrete and limited range of options, the relevant meaning was in each case.) More importantly, it is almost certainly the case that many titles, or descriptions, when applied by Christians to Jesus, significantly changed their meaning. Hence sometimes it would seem that Jesus' own life and person determine the meaning of the Christian use of a significant term quite as much as any usage in the background.

All these problems are particularly relevant in the case of the Lukan writings. A vital part of the significance of Jesus for Luke is the fact that Jesus has been raised from the dead. And although, as we shall see, this is integrally related in Luke's writings to a number of christological titles, it is not exhausted by any one title and indeed is in part determinative of the meaning of some of the titles.

So too it is not always clear how much Luke is aware of the background meaning of some of the titles used of Jesus. In at least one case, it seems that it is the story of Jesus which determines what is said of the titles, quite as much as the reverse (cf. below on the link between messiahship and suffering). So too Luke may at times run some of the titles together. All of them are, of course, predicated of Jesus, but it is not always clear that Luke has necessarily compartmentalized the meaning and significance of the various terms and categories used by characters in his story with the same precision as all his modern interpreters.

Above all we must remember that Luke is not writing a doctrinal treatise on Christology, nor does he write a book, or a doctoral thesis, on his theology with a neat summary chapter on Christology. What he does write is a story, a narrative, and anything he wishes to say has to be communicated via that medium. This means that, as often as not, Luke's views emerge only indirectly, by more subtle hints and allusions, and by narrative structures and plot development, rather than by a neatly structured model student essay with clear subheadings and numbered, bulleted points.

Yet despite all these caveats, we must also remember that Luke's chosen medium of narrative, even if not a doctrinal treatise, still uses words, and it conveys its meaning verbally. Moreover, it is clear that very often the significance of Jesus is articulated in Luke's story by means of the use of key titles applied to Jesus. Thus, while being fully aware of the difficulties and dangers inherent in a titular approach to the Christology of a writer such as Luke, we cannot ignore titles completely. Not only does Luke use them, but they also can serve as a very useful way of categorizing our own ideas, and providing us with a reference grid, to enable us to distinguish different ideas and concepts. Thus, as a way of getting into the subject, I shall adopt a titular approach here, simply as a useful reference point, though one must be fully alive to the limitations of such an approach and also be wary of assuming that any one title has a fixed meaning.

Luke's writings also present considerable further difficulties in this context for other reasons as well. In one way Luke is similar to the other evangelists in that they all communicate their message via the medium of an account of the life of Jesus. It is something of a commonplace now to say that the evangelists are theologians of some sort, and have influenced the story they tell to get their own particular message across. The question though is: How much has this happened? How far has Luke allowed his own ideas to colour his presentation? Conversely, how far can we take the presentation in Luke's own story as a full treatment of Luke's own Christology?

Such questions arise in the case of all the four evangelists. But with Luke there is the added complication due to the existence of Acts. I have said repeatedly that Acts cannot be ignored in assessing Luke's ideas and concerns. Now Acts is rich in material to do with Christology, both in general terms (i.e. concerning the significance of Jesus' life and death) as well as the more specific christological material contained there, especially in the speeches. Yet the Acts material presents particular problems here, since it is not always clear how much Luke's own theology is reflected and how much is due to Luke's tradition. There need be no dichotomy between the two, and we have already noted that Luke's willingness to include traditional material may be just as significant in any assessment of his concerns as any positive changes he makes (see pp. 266-67 above). Nevertheless, the fact that the Gospel and Acts together present such a variety of views, especially over the question of Christology, should at least alert us to the possibility that we cannot simply read Luke's Christology from an amalgam of the whole material in Luke–Acts.

Again, Luke, and Luke's Gospel, cannot be interpreted in isolation from Acts, and the area of Christology is no exception. But on the question of the differences and agreements of Luke's Gospel and Acts it is striking how much Luke seems at times to be sensitive (to say the least) to the context of the story world he is narrating at any one point. Jesus' preaching in the Gospel is frequently about the kingdom of God; in Acts references to the kingdom are far less frequent. In the Gospel Jesus refers to himself as Son of Man on more than 20 occasions; in Acts, there is just one reference to Jesus as Son of Man (Acts 7.56). Conversely, the speeches in Acts are full of exhortations to repent so that people may receive the forgiveness of sins; such language is not lacking in the Gospel, but it is far less prominent. Luke thus seems to show that he is aware of the different categories used by various people in his story and he seeks not to confuse them.

Even within Acts, Luke may show some considerable sensitivity, or literary skill (whatever one decides to call it). The speeches in Acts are often regarded as Lukan compositions through and through; yet it is still the case that Luke seems to show sensitivity about what his characters can or should appropriately say. Significantly it is Paul, and only Paul, in Acts who is made to say something about justification and faith (Acts 13.42), even if what is said is in the end rather un-Pauline; still Luke seems to know something of the characteristic vocabulary of his characters and he does not confuse them.

Such a view has been developed in an important essay by Moule ('Christology') on the Christology of Acts. As we shall see, some details of his argument are perhaps questionable (cf. below on 'Lord'), but in general terms his thesis is persuasive: Luke writes a life-like narrative (which is not necessarily the same as a historically accurate narrative); thus when we read the words of a character in the story, we hear as much what Luke thinks the character would have said as what Luke himself might have said.

Luke's Christology

With these methodological caveats, we may turn to the topic of this chapter, that is, the significance of Jesus for Luke, and as already said, despite the methodological dangers outlined above, I shall approach the topic via the use of key terms, or titles, applied to Jesus in Luke's story. I start with the term 'Lord'.

Lord

One of the most frequently used titles to refer to Jesus in Luke–Acts is 'Lord' (Greek *Kyrios*). This occurs very often in both of Luke's books and may be regarded as one of his most characteristic christological terms. To be sure, it is not very distinctive within early Christianity: the term is very common in Pauline Christianity as well. Nevertheless, this cannot hide the importance of the term for Luke.

Moule ('Christology', pp. 160-61) has sought to discern a significant distinction in Luke's use of the term between the Gospel and Acts. Recognizing that *Kyrios* almost certainly represents Luke's own Christology from a post-resurrection perspective, Moule nevertheless argues that the usage in the Gospel is different. Distinguishing between a use in the vocative ('O Lord'), which in Greek need only be a polite form of address (equivalent roughly to our English 'Sir!'), and the use in other cases (e.g. 'The Lord said'), Moule points to the fact that virtually no human characters in the story refer to Jesus as Lord in an obviously christologically significant way: they only use the vocative; the nominative and other cases are used by the narrator (though Elizabeth in Lk. 1.43 may be an exception to this rule). Hence, it is argued, Luke is clearly distinguishing his own perspective from the pre-Easter situation, and Luke does not seem to be reading back his own viewpoint into the pre-Easter story.

In general terms this might be persuasive, but some instances in the Gospel suggest that the picture is more complex. On at least two occasions, a vocative usage is placed just next to a non-vocative. Thus in Lk. 19.8, Zacchaeus says 'to the Lord', 'Look half of my possessions, Lord, I will give to the poor' (cf. also Lk. 12.41-42). The vocative usage gains considerably by virtue of its juxtaposition with the non-vocative usage. The one who is addressed as Lord is precisely *the* Lord. Hence we probably cannot distinguish the Gospel from Acts quite so easily.

What though does the word signify for Luke? The Greek word *Kyrios* has an enormous breadth of possible meaning, ranging from a polite form of address, through a reference to the master of a slave, to the gods of Hellenistic cults, right up to the point where it was (almost certainly) used by Greek-speaking Jews to refer to Yahweh himself. Where within this spectrum—from very human to absolutely divine—does Luke's use of *Kyrios* to refer to Jesus lie?

The answer is probably somewhere in the middle (cf. Tuckett, 'Christology', pp. 149-57, discussing Buckwalter, *Character*). Luke's usage in Acts is in fact notoriously imprecise, so that it is often uncertain whether a reference to *Kyrios* is intended to refer to God or Jesus. But the very existence of such confusion suggests that, for Luke, at least some of the attributes or functions of God are now conceived as being exercised by Jesus. Thus, for example, the Spirit, which is regarded in Acts 2.17 as a gift of God, is said to be the gift of Jesus in Lk. 24.49.

On the other hand, it would probably be quite wrong to see this as necessarily ascribing divinity as such to Jesus. Such categories would probably be quite alien to Luke. Much more significant is probably the fact of the resurrection in establishing Jesus' Lordship. The logic is spelt out in Peter's speech in Acts 2 and its reference to Ps. 110.1 ('The Lord said to my Lord, Sit at my right hand...'). According to Luke's Peter, the resurrection shows that Jesus has fulfilled this text since he is now at God's right hand—hence he is appropriately called 'Lord'; or in the words of v. 36: 'God has made him Lord...' Thus it is primarily by virtue of the resurrection, and the fulfilment of Scripture, that Jesus is shown to be Lord. Again we see the crucial significance of the fulfilment motif for Luke.

This does, however, create something of a tension with the picture in the Gospel where frequently Luke presents Jesus as Lord already, prior to the resurrection. For example, Elizabeth speaks of Mary as 'the mother of my Lord' (Lk. 1.43), the angel proclaims the birth of Jesus as that of 'Christ, the Lord' (2.11), and Luke, as we have seen, in his role as the narrator frequently refers to Jesus as Lord in his Gospel.

The use of 'the Lord' by the narrator need be no problem and is no more anachronistic than saying 'Mrs Thatcher left school at the age of 18' (when of course she was not yet married and hence was not called Mrs Thatcher). Texts like Lk. 1.43 and 2.11 are, however, more difficult, and there is no easy answer to what is a standing problem for all studies of Lukan Christology. The resurrection is of crucial significance for Luke in establishing Jesus' position and status for the post-Easter church, and yet that status seems to be already attained prior to Easter. (It is, of course, not so different from many other parts of the New Testament: cf. the Philippian hymn of Phil. 2.5-11). Nor is it confined to Luke's use of *Kyrios*: it is there too in the next term we shall consider, 'messiah'.

Messiah

Again this is a very common term in Luke–Acts: Jesus is the *Christos*, the anointed messiah of Judaism (cf. Strauss, *Davidic Messiah*). ('Messiah' is the transliteration of the Hebrew word *mashiah*, meaning an anointed figure, the Greek equivalent being *Christos*, from where we get our English usage 'Christ'.) As with *Kyrios*, Luke shares this description of Jesus as *Christos* with a wide range of other early Christians: there is no doubt that the term was applied to Jesus at a very early date and became so firmly attached to him that, also at a very early date, it often lost virtually all of its original connotation and became just a proper name (as in 'Jesus Christ', 'Christ Jesus', or even just 'Christ', as in the very early pre-Pauline formula in 1 Cor. 15.3).

Luke's own slant on the term comes in at least two ways. First, as with *Kyrios*, the resurrection and the fulfilment of Scripture are vital keys in the ascription of the term 'Christ' to Jesus. Again the Pentecost speech of Acts 2 is crucial, this time in relation to Ps. 16.10, cited in vv. 27 and 31 ('You will not abandon my soul to Hades, or let your Holy One experience corruption'). This is assumed to refer to the messiah (since it manifestly cannot apply to David himself since David died and was buried: cf. v. 29). Since Jesus by his resurrection has not been allowed to 'experience corruption', he must be the messiah of the psalm. Hence the other half of the conclusion in Acts 2.36: 'God has made him both Lord *and messiah*'. Thus once again we see the importance of the fulfilment motif for Luke.

But secondly, Luke adds another significant twist to his talk of Jesus as messiah by insisting that Jesus' suffering and death are necessary functions of the messiah as foretold in Scripture. This is said by the risen Jesus to the disciples on the road to Emmaus (Lk. 24.26-27), and is repeated again by Peter and Paul in Acts (Acts 3.18; 17.3; 26.23). It is, in fact, universally agreed that there are no instances in the Old Testament of a messiah figure having to suffer, let alone die. (Figures such as the suffering servant of Isa. 53 are not messiah figures.) What has almost certainly happened is that Luke has brought together his beliefs (a) that Jesus is the messiah and (b) that Jesus fulfils Scripture with (c) the brute fact of Jesus' suffering and death to produce the somewhat artificial scheme that 'the messiah must suffer'. Thus once again we see Luke's concern for the motif of fulfilment; but we also see a good illustration of the way in which titles may well change their significance when applied to Jesus. The events of Jesus' life and death may themselves determine the meaning of the description, quite as much as vice versa.

What else Luke may have understood by the term is not certain. Messianic expectations in the first century were in a state of considerable flux, and it was by no means the case that Jews of the period had a monolithic expectation of a single figure called 'the messiah'. As we have seen, a messianic figure is simply one who is anointed, and anointing could take place in a variety of contexts. One such context was certainly that of a royal figure: a new king was anointed, and so a messianic figure could be a royal person, in Judaism then a descendant of David and a new king who would restore the political fortunes of the people.

There is a little of such expectation reflected in Luke, though not a great deal. The idea of Jesus as Son of David, which occurs elsewhere in the New Testament, surfaces only occasionally here, mostly in the birth narratives. Thus the angel Gabriel tells Mary that the son to be born will be given 'the throne of his ancestor David', and 'he will reign over the house of Jacob for ever' (Lk. 1.33-34). Zachariah proclaims that God 'has raised up a mighty saviour for us, in the house of his servant David' (1.69); and Joseph is said to be of Davidic descent (1.27; 2.4; cf. 3.23ff.). Luke also takes over from Mark the cry to Jesus by blind Bartimaeus 'Jesus, Son of David, have mercy on me' (Lk. 18.38 = Mk 10.48). But elsewhere not a lot is made of any Davidic descent of Jesus by Luke.

The royal idea is also not absent from Luke, though it is not very prominent. Royal/political hopes are clearly raised in the birth narratives (Lk. 1.33, 69). But it is equally clear through the rest of the story that whatever benefits and blessings Jesus brings, they are not in the form of political involvement, let alone any military or political victory, for Israel. The explicit idea of Jesus as a king rarely surfaces — though it does come once (redactionally) in Luke's account of the triumphal entry, where Luke rewrites Mark's 'Blessed is the one who comes in the name of the Lord' (Mk 11.9) to become 'Blessed is the king who comes in the name of the Lord' (Lk. 19.38). But the context in which the saying is placed — Jesus riding into Jerusalem on a donkey — makes it crystal clear that any kingship of Jesus is not that of a politically powerful ruler.

Similarly, in the passion narrative, Jesus is accused of being a king before Pilate (Lk. 23.2), but alongside two other charges that are (for Luke) clearly false (perverting the nation, and forbidding the payment of taxes); hence Jesus' kingship is at the very least quite unlike the kingship that would threaten Pilate's political power directly. On the cross, Jesus is mocked as king (Lk. 23.36-37 in dependence on Mark), but, as before, the context indicates that, insofar as the taunt is true, Jesus' kingship is not that of this-worldly political power. So too the suggestion that Jesus is a king and thereby a threat to the political status quo is raised in Acts 17.7, but in a context which suggests that this is a wrong assessment of the situation.

Luke thus seems to be aware of royal language being ascribed to Jesus, and in part he adopts it, but only by also playing down any political associations linked with such language (see Tuckett, 'Christology', pp. 158-63).

In Judaism, priests were also anointed, but there is nothing in Luke similar to the argument of Hebrews that Jesus is a priestly figure (and in Hebrews Jesus is not explicitly presented a 'Christ' figure, i.e. an anointed person, by virtue of his [high-]priesthood).

The third class of anointed figures in Judaism is that of prophets (cf.

Ps. 105.15; 2 Kgs 1.9), and it is this which in part Luke seems to have adopted positively. We turn therefore to the idea of Jesus as a prophetic figure in Luke

Prophet
Luke is the one New Testament writer to explain in a little more detail just how he conceives of Jesus being anointed. Kings and priests are of course anointed with oil. Luke conceives of Jesus as anointed with the Spirit. This is announced by Jesus himself in the opening scene in Nazareth where he quotes the words from Isa. 61.1-2: 'The Spirit of the Lord is upon me, because he has anointed me…', and then asserts they have been fulfilled in the today of his presence (Lk. 4.17, 21). This claim is echoed by Peter later in Acts 10.38: 'God anointed Jesus of Nazareth with the Holy Spirit and with power'. Further, the fact that these words from Isaiah 61 are in the Old Testament the words of a prophet, and the evidence we now have from some Qumran texts about the way in which this verse from Isaiah 61 was being used by other Jews of this period to refer to a prophetic figure, suggests very strongly that what is in mind here is a *prophetic* anointing. Jesus is presented as the one anointed by the Spirit to be a *prophet*. It is thus the prophetic, rather than royal, overtones which therefore come to the fore in the specific anointing experienced by Jesus, according to Luke's telling of the story.

The category of prophet certainly comes out elsewhere in the Gospel strongly. Later on in the scene in Nazareth, Jesus uses the examples of Elijah and Elisha working outside the confines of Israel to illustrate the proverb that 'no prophet is accepted in the prophet's own *patris*' (Lk. 4.24), which is evidently regarded as applicable to his own situation. Clearly then Jesus is seen as a prophet and, as such, finds no welcome in his own home place.

In the story of the raising of the widow of Nain's son (Lk. 7.10-17), a story peculiar to Luke and with many echoes of the story of Elijah raising the widow of Zarephthah's son (1 Kgs 17.17-24), the crowd acknowledge Jesus at the end with the words 'A great prophet has risen among us' (v. 16). Jesus in his ministry is thus seen by others, and almost certainly by Luke, as a prophet, recapitulating the work of the prophets of the past.

Similarly in the story of the sinful woman (Lk. 7.36-50), which comes shortly afterwards, the prophetic aspect comes out once again. The Pharisee, in whose house Jesus is, says 'If this man were a prophet, he would have known what kind of woman that is who is touching him—that she is a sinner' (v. 39). But the rest of the story makes it very clear that Jesus knows perfectly well exactly what kind of a woman this is, and hence by implication he really is a prophet.

In the middle of the long journey to Jerusalem, solemnly announced at Lk. 9.51, Jesus claims that he *must* reach his goal in the city of Jerusalem 'because it is impossible for a prophet to be killed outside of Jerusalem' (Lk. 13.33): again this is a tradition which occurs in Luke alone.

Luke also takes over from Mark the notes of the speculations by Herod and the crowds about whether John or Jesus might be a prophet. It may be significant that Luke slightly alters Mark in the second case. In Mark, the disciples echo the speculations of the crowds about Jesus that he might be a prophet. By implication, the structure of the story suggests that such views are wrong, and Peter articulates the better (i.e. for the evangelist) view that Jesus is the messiah. Luke has the same structure of the pericope as Mark, but he has the disciples say that the crowds think that 'one of the ancient prophets has arisen'. Thus what is implicitly denied is not so much that Jesus is a prophet per se, but that he is one of the ancient prophets returning. The latter then leaves open the possibility that Jesus himself *is* a prophet, a term which in Luke's understanding is not then necessarily antithetical to the view that Jesus is God's messiah (Lk. 9.20) or anointed one since he is anointed with the Spirit.

Finally in the Gospel, we may note the words placed on the lips of the disciples on the road to Emmaus, who say that Jesus 'was a prophet mighty in deed and word before God and all the people' (Lk. 24.19). They also note that he has been crucified and that they had hoped that he would 'redeem Israel' (v. 21). Jesus' reply is in terms of the necessity of the messiah to suffer (v. 26). But the stress is on the necessity of the suffering: it is not on the fact that Jesus is messiah and not prophet. Thus the christological category of prophet is not questioned by the story, even if the role and activity of the person concerned is quietly corrected.

In Acts the prophetic category for Jesus comes at two critical points, in Acts 3.22-23 and 7.37, where the prediction by Moses of 'a prophet like me' who is to come in the future (Deut. 18.15) is quoted and clearly by implication applied to Jesus. Jesus is thus presented not just as any old prophet, but specifically as the prophet like Moses, expected on the basis of the verse in Deuteronomy 18. (We now know from a Qumran text, 4QTest, that this verse from Deuteronomy had led to expectations by some Jews of a prophet like Moses who would come in the future.)

Luke's portrayal of Jesus as a prophet in the Gospel may thus be significantly influenced by the idea of Jesus as the prophet like Moses.

Such influence may also be seen in a few details of Luke's account apart from the explicit references to Jesus as prophet we have noted already. For example, in Luke's account of the transfiguration story, Luke adds to Mark the note that Moses and Elijah were speaking with Jesus 'of his departure which he was about to accomplish in Jerusalem' (Lk. 9.31). The Greek word for 'departure' here is *exodos*, with clear echoes of the Moses story: Jesus' 'journey' to Jerusalem is thus portrayed as a new 'exodus' journey, recapitulating the first 'exodus' by the first Moses. So too the command of the voice from heaven 'Listen to him!' (Lk. 9.35) is aligned by Luke more closely to the command of Deut. 18.15 itself.

The importance of the 'prophet like Moses' theme for Luke has been strongly stressed by a number of scholars in recent studies. Johnson (*Literary Function*) has argued that the pattern of Moses as set out in Stephen's speech has heavily influenced Luke's presentation and provides the key pattern to the whole of the structure of Luke–Acts. Moses is sent by God, rejected by the people, and then raised up again, but rejected a second time. So too Jesus, the prophet like Moses, is sent by God, rejected by his people, but raised up by God (i.e. in the resurrection); the mission goes out a second time to the people, this time in the form of the mission of the disciples sent out by Jesus, but is again rejected. This pattern of double mission and double rejection finds its logic in the Mosaic typology.

The theory is attractive, though not fully persuasive in all its details. The parallel in the second mission becomes less close, since Jesus himself is no longer a direct participant in the mission: it is rather the disciples who go out in Jesus' name. Nevertheless the pattern of prophecy, and prophecy rejected, is clearly one which has heavily influenced Luke's presentation in his Gospel, with the Mosaic category providing an important greater precision.

A similar thesis has been propounded by Moessner (*Lord of the Banquet*) who has argued that at least the model of a single prophetic ministry and prophetic rejection can find its origin in the Mosaic pattern. Moessner has also argued that the great Central Section, or Travel Narrative, in Luke (Lk. 9.51–18.14) may be based on the book of Deuteronomy, so that Jesus is here presented on a grand scale as the prophet like Moses.

The parallels between Deuteronomy and the Central Section in Luke have been noted by others before Moessner (cf. Evans, 'Central Section'), though Moessner's book is probably the most detailed and fullest working out of the theory. One wonders if at times the theory becomes almost too specific. The parallels are at times rather general, and it is not clear how far an ancient reader would have picked them up. Nevertheless, whatever one makes of the detailed structure of the Travel Narrative, the general theory seems justified that, for Luke, Jesus is a prophet, and the prophet like Moses. Like Moses (though also like many other prophets) Jesus experiences rejection. Thus Luke uses the Q traditions in Lk. 11.49-51 and 13.34-35 which express the idea that all God's prophets have suffered rejection, violence and even death. Luke (and Q) is probably echoing a very widespread tradition in Judaism which had developed such an idea within a deuterono-mistic view of history, referring to the violence suffered by the proph-ets as illustrating the continuing disobedience of the people, but using this as the basis for an appeal to repent and change their ways.

Luke's view of Jesus as a prophet is thus a very important theme for him. It surfaces explicitly on a number of occasions and may also be related, as we have seen, to a number of other details in Luke's story, as well as to the use of the messianic category. It is, however, by no means the only category used by Luke, and some of these other themes we shall consider briefly here.

Son of God

Perhaps one of the most perplexing problems of Luke's Christology is his use of the term Son of God to refer to Jesus. The term is not used very frequently—certainly in Acts it is far less common than *Kyrios* or *Christos*. Many of the uses in the Gospel are already present in Luke's sources. Certainly it is very hard to find any clear consistency in Luke's use of the phrase.

For example, in some instances the phrase is used in a messianic way, to refer to Jesus as messiah. Perhaps what is in mind is a royal idea of messiahship (though we have seen that a prophetic idea of messiahship in Luke is equally strong if not stronger), with the idea of the Davidic king as son of God (cf. Ps. 2.7; 2 Sam. 7.14). Thus in Lk. 4.41, Luke adds a clarification to Mark's account of Jesus' rebuking the demons who cried out that he was the Son of God 'because they knew him' (Mk 1.39) so that it is now 'because they knew that he was the messiah' (Lk. 4.41). 'Son of God' and 'messiah' seem here to be virtu-ally equated. Similarly, the angel's words to Mary in Lk. 1.32 seem to equate divine sonship with a royal Davidic position: 'He will be called the Son of the Most High, and the Lord God will give him the throne of his ancestor David'.

On the other hand, in Luke's account of the Sanhedrin trial, what is in Mark a single question to Jesus 'Are you the messiah, the Son of the Blessed One?' (Mk 14.61) becomes in Luke two separate questions, asking what appear to be thought of as two different things: 'If you are the messiah, tell us' (Lk. 22.67), and 'Are you then the Son of God?' (Lk. 22.69). In Mark, the parallelism in the single question seems to imply that the two terms are regarded as virtually synonymous. The separation of the two into different questions in Luke seems to imply that 'messiah' and 'Son of God' are distinct titles with different connotations.

Luke also takes over from Q the temptation story with the Devil addressing Jesus as Son of God (Lk. 4.1-13), and the cry of exaltation (Lk. 10.21-22) where Jesus addresses God as Father and refers to himself as Son as the mediator of exclusive revelation.

When exactly Jesus becomes Son is not clear either. In one of the speeches in Acts, Luke has Paul cite Ps. 2.7 ('You are my son, today I have begotten you'), applied apparently to the moment of Jesus' resurrection (Acts 13.32). This would suggest that Jesus becomes Son of God at and by virtue of his resurrection. On the other hand, Luke has God's voice from heaven declare Jesus as his Son at Jesus' baptism (Lk. 3.22 *possibly* with the words 'today I have begotten you': this is the reading of the Western text, though the Alexandrian texts read 'with you I am well pleased', as in Mark). And the angel tells Mary in the birth narratives that because of her conception by the Holy Spirit, the child to be born will be holy and 'will be called Son of God' (Lk. 1.35). Both these latter passages suggest that Jesus is already Son of God in his pre-Easter existence. We have thus the same ambiguity that we noticed when looking at the use of *kyrios* as applied to Jesus.

The background of the term 'Son of God' is enormously varied. Certainly the phrase on its own does not imply necessarily any divinity as such (although it became the vehicle for expressing Jesus' divinity in later Christian language). A son of God in Judaism could be a royal human figure (cf. Ps. 2.7; 2 Sam. 7.14), or even a faithful, obedient human being (Sir. 4.11; Wis. 2.15). Luke too knows this kind of language, since followers of Jesus can be sons of God (cf. Lk. 6.35), and they too can address God as Father (Lk. 11.2).

Some of Luke's confused picture here might be explained on source-critical grounds: many of the references to Jesus as Son of God clearly come from his sources Mark and Q; others may come from other sources he has available (e.g. his account of the Sanhedrin trial). But one cannot drive too much of a wedge between Luke and his sources: after all, he did decide to include them in his Gospel (cf. pp. 266-67 above)! Perhaps consistency is unattainable; but clearly Luke knows of the tradition that Jesus is thought of as Son of God, and he does develop it in different ways.

Son of Man

There is no space here to discuss the vexed question of what the term Son of Man meant on the lips of Jesus, and Luke's use of the term can be dealt with only briefly (see further Tuckett, 'The Lukan Son of Man').

Luke knows and uses almost all his sources' (Mark's and Q's) uses of the term. He adds quite a number of his own (Lk. 17.22; 18.8; 19.10; 21.36; 22.22, 48; Acts 7.56), many (if not all) of which may well be his own redactional creations. Yet, with the exception of Acts 7.56, these are all in the Gospel: Luke perhaps knows that 'Son of Man' was not a widely used term in the church's preaching, and he uses his literary/ historical sensitivity by not writing the term into the story in Acts. Similarly, all his additional (i.e. to Mark and Q) uses of the term occur in contexts that are very similar to those of his sources, namely to refer to the suffering of Jesus and his vindication/exaltation, as well as his mission to save (Lk. 19.10 cf. Mk 10.45). Luke thus has developed and expanded the range of Son of Man sayings; but he has not significantly altered the basic slant of his source material.

Servant

Finally, in this list of categories, we may consider the application in Luke–Acts to Jesus of language associated with the suffering servant passage of Isaiah 53 (this is scarcely a title).

It is perhaps one of the surprising features of the New Testament that Isaiah 53 is used so rarely to interpret Jesus' life and death. Luke does have a few references to the servant passages. For example, in the Nunc Dimittis, Simeon echoes the words of the third servant song in predicting that Jesus will be 'a light to lighten the Gentiles' (Lk. 2.32; cf. Isa. 49.6), although it is not certain if Luke, or his readers, would have associated together what modern scholarship has identified as *the* four servant songs.

In a passage peculiar to Luke in his passion narrative, Luke has Jesus say that the saying of Scripture 'He was counted among the lawless' must be fulfilled in his case (Lk. 22.37), and this Scripture is Isa. 53.12, that is, part of the fourth servant song.

A few passages in Acts carry on the theme. Thus Peter in Acts 3.13 claims that God 'glorified his servant', language that is reminiscent of Isa. 52.13. (However, the references to Jesus as 'servant' in Acts 4.27 seem to be in a context of Jesus as a Davidic figure and may reflect the language of David as God's servant.) In Acts 8.32-33, Isa. 53.7-8 is cited *in extenso* as the words being read by the Ethiopian eunuch, who subsequently has the passage explained to him by Philip as being a reference to the person of Jesus.

References to Jesus as the servant are thus present in Luke–Acts, and indeed are more numerous than in the other Gospels, but are still not extensive. It is perhaps part of Luke's general fulfilment motif: Jesus fulfils the role of many Old Testament figures. But it is by no means the only, and certainly not the most dominant, example of this in Luke–Acts.

The significance of the Servant idea does, however, raise by implication a more wide-ranging question, namely, what does Luke think that the life and/or death of Jesus have achieved? The issue is raised by the possible Servant Christology, because Isaiah 53 is about the only passage in the Old Testament where the suffering of a person is said to be vicarious, benefiting others by in some sense suffering instead of them. Now it is of course a well-known feature of early Christianity, especially Pauline Christianity, that it too claimed that Jesus' death was vicarious: it was 'for us', or 'for our sins'. In itself this makes it all the more surprising in many ways that Isaiah 53 was not explicitly used more often by early Christians in their talk about Jesus' death. What then of Luke?

The Significance of Jesus' Death

Luke is notorious for having so little to say at one level about the significance of Jesus' death. All the Synoptic evangelists are somewhat reticent, to say the least, about any positive significance in Jesus' death. Luke is even more so. Mark has two sayings which seem to attribute saving significance to Jesus' death: Mk 10.45 ('the Son of Man came… to give his life a ransom for many'), and the saying over the cup at the Eucharist in Mk 14.24 ('This is my blood of the covenant, which is poured out for many'). Luke famously (or infamously) has no direct parallel to the ransom saying in Mk 10.45b: he either rewrites, or has an independent tradition of, the verse in Lk. 22.27 which focuses on the substance of only the first half of Mk 10.45 and speaks of the importance of serving; and Luke's parallel to Mk 14.24 in Lk. 22.20 is a famous Western non-interpolation: hence it is not certain if this is part of the genuine text of Luke's Gospel (see pp. 261-62 above). There are no other texts in the Gospel which ascribe positive, saving significance to Jesus' death.

Nor is there much, if any, evidence of this in Acts. Only one verse really seems relevant: in Paul's speech to the Ephesian elders he speaks of 'the church of God which he obtained with the blood of his own Son' (Acts 20.28), which might suggest ideas of purchasing or redemption. But this is about the only verse where the topic is mentioned explicitly. The use of Isaiah 53 in Acts 8 is famous for the fact that the actual verses cited from Isaiah 53 (vv. 7-8 cited in Acts 8.32-33) are not those which actually mention the specifically vicarious nature of the servant's suffering. (It is though unclear whether they are implied: is the citation of one extract from the chapter intended to evoke the whole of the rest of the chapter in the reader's mind? The issue is a debated one, and not easily resolvable.)

Luke then would seem to imply that Jesus' death in itself is not of the same central significance as it is given by Paul (or John or Mark for that matter). Now one can argue that, just as Luke does not present us with a treatise on Christology, he does not give us an essay on soteriology either. Instead he writes a story, and, as we have seen, it is in literary or historical terms often a very sensitively written story. Luke makes his characters say what he thinks that it is appropriate for them to say in the contexts in which he places them in his story world. Thus, in relation to soteriology, it may be that teaching about the significance of Jesus' death did not characterize early Christian missionary preaching to outsiders, but was more a feature of in-house teaching to those already converted. Could it then be no coincidence that the only reference to Jesus' death in Acts is in the one speech made to those already converted, while it is missing from the other speeches which are addressed to outsiders?

This is certainly possible, and many have argued in this way, though the relative silence in the Gospel, where much of the teaching is evidently directed to those who are already Christian disciples, is still surprising. The silence has given rise to a number of claims by scholars that in Luke 'there is indeed no *theologia crucis* beyond the affirmation that the Christ must suffer, since so the prophetic Scriptures foretold' (Creed, *St Luke*, p. lxxii). This is perhaps not entirely fair, and probably expects more from Luke and his chosen genre than may be appropriate. Luke is not Paul; nor is Luke's medium of story the same as Paul's medium of doctrinal letter. Nevertheless, one must say that the relative silence of such ideas, in the Acts material especially, does suggest that Luke does have a rather different slant on things.

If one asks of the Lukan writings what has been achieved by Jesus' death, the answer is very often in relatively general terms. As far as vocabulary is concerned, it is clear that the language of salvation is extremely important for Luke. It is a constant feature of the speeches in Acts that people may be 'saved', or receive 'salvation', as we have already seen; and Jesus is explicitly called a 'saviour' on a few occasions. Thus the angel tells the shepherds that 'to you is born this day in the city of David a Saviour' (Lk. 2.11), a term echoed twice in Acts (Acts 5.31; 13.23). Yet precisely how this salvation is achieved, or how (if at all) it directly relates to Jesus' death, is not spelt out.

The second main benefit resulting from the Christ-event is the forgiveness of sins, again a motif which concludes many of the speeches of Acts. The fact that the Christ-event somehow deals with sin/sins and its/their effects is, of course, common to Luke, Paul and many others in early Christianity. But again one has to say that any specific theory about how such forgiveness is made available though what Jesus has done, either in his life or his death, is left open. Indeed, as already noted, it could be seen as somewhat tongue-in-cheek to suggest that Jews almost need to be converted to another religion (or a special event associated with Jesus) to receive forgiveness of their sins! (However, the extent to which Christianity is another religion for Luke is of course debatable: see Chapter 3 above.)

Perhaps though, if Luke is rather vague here, he is by no means unique. Even Paul's more explicit statements about the meaning of the death of Jesus defy logic when examined closely. They represent rather a rich variety of an almost riotous mixture of metaphors and images (Jesus' death as a sin offering, a covenant sacrifice, a ransom price paid [to whom?!], a victory over the Devil etc.). No doubt what was primary was the experience of early Christians of the new life they claimed was theirs, made possible, they believed, in and through the death and resurrection of Jesus. The means by which this happened came from later attempts at rationalization (see Tuckett, 'Atonement'). If Luke's rationalizing goes on a different track from Paul's then that maybe simply shows that Luke is not Paul, and we cannot blame him for that!

The third result of the death of Jesus was, of course, in Luke's eyes the gift of the Spirit. In one sense we can leave a full discussion of this on one side here, since it is above all the material in Acts that is relevant; in any case, we have already considered some aspects of this already (see too Marshall, *The Acts of the Apostles*, pp. 66-69).

We may note once again that, insofar as this is a study of Luke's Gospel, the Spirit is mentioned in a surprisingly uneven way. In part this is due to Luke's salvation-historical scheme whereby the Spirit is a feature of the post-Easter situation, the Spirit being the gift of the risen Jesus to the church (Lk. 24.49). Yet as we have seen, this is not the whole story at all, since Jesus' own birth is preceded by an outburst of prophetic activity inspired by the Spirit; Jesus himself is baptized with the Spirit in Luke 3, he is led by the Spirit into the desert and then proclaims in Nazareth that he is anointed by the Spirit for his task as set by God. The gift of the Spirit is thus a feature of Jesus' ministry quite as much as of the post-Easter church. Yet, as we have already noted, references to the Spirit suddenly become very sparse in Luke's Gospel after ch. 4.

Is it perhaps that Luke assumes that, after his build-up in chs. 1–4, it is self-evident that everything else in Jesus' ministry is done in the power of the Spirit? This is possible, although why Luke should have proceeded so differently in Acts where the narrative is positively saturated with references to the working of the Spirit, is not clear.

Conclusion

Luke thus has a rich variety of ways in which to express both the significance of the person of Jesus and also the relevance and significance of Jesus' death. Not all of this can be tied down into neat formulae. In part this may be due to Luke's own lack of clarity. In part too it is due to the medium of story, or history, which Luke has chosen as his literary tool to get his message across. Moreover, Luke, as we have seen, is a skilful writer and is sensitive to the story world he is narrating, so that his characters say *appropriate* things: they are not simply transparent windows letting us see Luke and his concerns directly. We must then also be equally sensitive in reading Luke's narrative.

As much, if not more, sensitivity is demanded if we ask how Luke thinks that the Christian life should be conducted in practice and what Luke thought of the significance of Jesus' life and teaching (as opposed to his death). One part of this broad question will form the focus of our next chapter.

FURTHER READING

C.K. Barrett, 'Theologia Crucis—in Acts?', in C. Andresen and G. Klein (eds.), *Theologia Crucis – Signum Crucis* (FS E. Dinkler; Tübingen: Mohr, 1979), pp. 73-84.

H.D. Buckwalter, *The Character and Purpose of Luke's Christology* (SNTSMS, 89; Cambridge: Cambridge University Press, 1996).

M. de Jonge, 'The Christology of Luke–Acts', in *Christology in Context: The Earliest Christian Responses to Jesus* (Philadelphia: Westminster Press, 1988), pp. 97-111.

C.F. Evans, 'The Central Section of Luke's Gospel', in D.E. Nineham (ed.), *Studies in the Gospels: Essays in Memory of R.H. Lightfoot* (Oxford: Basil Blackwell, 1955), pp. 37-53.

L.T. Johnson, *The Literary Function of Possessions in Luke–Acts* (SBLDS, 39; Missoula, MT: Scholars Press, 1977).

L.E. Keck, 'Toward the Renewal of New Testament Christology', *NTS* 32 (1986), pp. 362-77, repr. in M.C. de Boer (ed.), *From Jesus to John: Essays on Jesus and New Testament Christology in Honour of Marinus de Jonge* (JSNTSup, 84; Sheffield: JSOT Press, 1993), pp. 321-40.

G.W.H. Lampe, 'The Lucan Portrait of Christ', *NTS* 2 (1956), pp. 160-75.

D.P. Moessner, *Lord of the Banquet: The Literary and Theological Significance of the Lukan Travel Narrative* (Minneapolis: Fortress Press, 1989).

C.F.D. Moule, 'The Christology of Acts', in Keck and Martyn (eds.), *Studies in Luke–Acts*, pp. 159-85.

M.L. Strauss, *The Davidic Messiah in Luke–Acts: The Promise and its Fulfillment in Lukan Christology* (JSNTSup, 110; Sheffield: Sheffield Academic Press, 1995).

D.D. Sylva (ed.), *Reimagining the Death of the Lukan Jesus* (BBB, 73; Frankfurt: Anton Hain, 1990). A collection of essays offering a variety of views.

C.M. Tuckett, 'Atonement in the New Testament', *ABD*, 1, pp. 518-22.

—'The Lukan Son of Man', in Tuckett (ed.), *Luke's Literary Achievement: Collected Essays* (JSNTSup, 116; Sheffield: JSOT Press, 1995), pp. 198-217.

—'The Christology of Luke–Acts', in J. Verheyden (ed.), *The Unity of Luke–Acts* (BETL, 142; Leuven: Leuven University Press/Peeters, 1999), pp. 133-64.

Chapter Five

LUKE AND THE CHRISTIAN LIFE: POVERTY AND POSSESSIONS

So far we have looked at Luke's ideas — on eschatology, on the place of Israel and the Gentiles, and on the significance of the person of Jesus. In very broad terms, this might be called part of Luke's theology. But what of his more concrete, and less abstract, ideas about the implications of the Christian faith? What of his so-called ethics? How is the Christian life to be lived out in practice? And what does the Christian gospel mean for the world? What too is the value of Jesus' teaching given in the Gospel for the present?

Some of these issues might be expected to be answered, if at all, in the book of Acts rather than the Gospel, since Acts does present a picture of Christians actually living out their faith in concrete situations. Certainly some aspects of that living out are clearly emphasized there: the importance of the guidance of the Holy Spirit, evangelism, preaching, prayer and so on.

There is, however, one theme which is fairly prominent in (at least some parts of) Acts and is also a major feature of Luke's Gospel. This is the theme of poverty and riches, and possessions or lack of possessions. This theme has often been noted in modern Lukan studies. Indeed it is not just academic studies which have focused on Luke's work in this respect. Luke's Gospel is renowned for having a large amount to say on the topic of riches and poverty. As we shall see, there is a lot of material in Luke that seems to privilege the poor and castigate the rich. Hence for many today who would advocate some kind of a social gospel, with concern to advance the interests of the poor, the persecuted, the exploited and the socially marginalized, the material in Luke has been the part of the New Testament to which they most often appeal. Luke is seen very much as the social gospel, with a bias towards the poor.

Moreover, other aspects of Luke's Gospel are often allied with this concern for the poor. Luke is well known in having a positive attitude to Gentiles (see Chapter 3 above), to women (Lk. 7.11-17, 36-50; 8.2-3; 10.38-42; 23.27-31), to tax-collectors and sinners (Lk. 3.12; 5.27-30; 7.29-30, 34, 36-50; 15.1-32; 18.9-14; 19.1-10) and to Samaritans (Lk. 9.52;

10.29-36; 17.10-17). Many have in the past seen all these concerns as simply part of an overall concern on Luke's part for the poor. As we shall see this may in part be the case, but it is by no means self-evident: tax-collectors, for example, were not at all impoverished, nor are all of Luke's women!

The general theme of the poor is prominent in many passages in Luke's Gospel. However, the various traditions recorded by Luke do not all necessarily speak with one voice; nor is it easy to unite Luke and Acts together in this respect, as we shall see. I take first some of the evidence from the Gospel.

The Poor

The poor are clearly stated as the prime objects of Jesus' preaching in the programmatic scene in the synagogue in Nazareth, a story I have referred to already on several occasions: here Jesus proclaims the ful-filment in himself of the text from Isa. 61.1, thereby taking up the announced task to 'bring good news to *the poor*' (Lk. 4.18). Similarly, the teaching of Jesus in Luke's Sermon on the Plain opens with the proclamation in the first beatitude, 'Blessed are you who are poor, for yours is the kingdom of God' (Lk. 6.20); and the messengers of John the Baptist are told by Jesus to go and tell John all the things they have seen and heard: Jesus is performing miracles of healing blindness, deafness, leprosy, even raising the dead, but the climax is the asser-tion that 'the poor have good news brought to them' (Lk. 7.22 NRSV; perhaps a better translation would be 'the poor are being evangel-ized'). Similarly, in the Magnificat Mary praises God as the one who 'has brought down the powerful from their thrones, and lifted up the lowly; he has filled the hungry with good things, and sent the rich away empty' (Lk. 1.52-53).

These programmatic statements about the nature of God, and the nature of Jesus' own mission, make it clear that, for Luke, the gospel is indeed primarily one that is for the benefit of the poor.

Critique of the Rich

Coupled with this is a powerful critique of the rich at a number of points. We have already noted the verse from the Magnificat, saying that God is the God who has 'sent the rich away empty' (Lk. 1.53). The beatitude on the poor (6.20) is of course part of a series of beatitudes, probably derived from Q (cf. Mt. 5.3-11). But in Luke, and in Luke alone, the beatitudes are matched by a parallel series of woes (Lk. 6.24-26) so that the blessing on the poor is matched by a corresponding woe: 'Woe to you who are rich, for you have received your consolation' (Lk. 6.24). What is good news for the poor is clearly not good news for those who are not poor.

So too some of the parables in Luke's Gospel are notable for their apparently highly negative attitude to riches: the parable of the rich fool (12.16-21) and the parable of the rich man and Lazarus (16.19-31) are particularly relevant in this context. Especially in the latter case, the prime reason for the fate of the rich man, in torment in Hades, seems to be solely that in his earthly life he was rich, and in a postmortem existence earthly roles will be reversed (cf. Lk. 16.25).

Discipleship and Possessions

A notable feature of Luke's Gospel is the way in which he seems to emphasize the fact that Jesus' disciples gave up *everything* they had when they became disciples. Often Luke seems to go out of his way to stress this. Thus the story of the call of Peter in Luke ends with the note that Peter and his companions 'left *everything* and followed him' (Lk. 5.11; the parallel in Mk 1.20 simply has them leaving their homes and following Jesus). Similarly, in the story of the call of Levi, Luke adds to Mark the note that Levi 'left everything' and followed Jesus. (Lk. 5.28 cf. Mk 2.17). The rich young ruler is told in Luke's version of the story to 'sell *all* that you own' (Lk. 18.22: Luke has added the word for 'all' to Mark here: cf. Mk 10.21). Luke records the traditions (from both Mark and Q) of the disciples being sent out on mission by Jesus with virtually no possessions at all (Lk. 9.1-6; 10.1-16: the former is mostly Markan, the latter Q). Finally, Luke concludes his double parable of the tower builder and the king going to war with the saying 'None of you can become my disciple if you do not give up all your possessions' (Lk. 14.33). Discipleship in Luke's Gospel seems to involve an even more radical break with one's possessions than is the case in Luke's sources.

Charitable Giving

Coupled with the negative attitude to riches is the strong theme in Luke's writings on the importance of generosity in giving and sharing. Right at the start, Luke (alone of the evangelists) gives the teaching of John the Baptist, advocating generous sharing or giving of goods by those who have plenty to benefit those who have few or none: 'Whoever has two coats must share with anyone who has none; and whoever has food must do likewise' (Lk. 3.11). Similarly, one of the parables peculiar to Luke is the story of the friend at midnight (Lk. 11.5-8) which can be taken, at least on one reading, as a parable encouraging generosity to those in need and a willingness to share one's possessions.

A similar picture emerges from Luke's parable of the Good Samaritan (Lk. 10.29-36, again a parable which appears only in Luke). Whatever the parable may have meant in the pre-Lukan tradition (and one wonders if the fact that the hero of the story is a Samaritan originally had more significance), for Luke it is a clear example of practical charitable action which serves as an example for the listener to imitate. The framework in which the parable is now set is a series of questions or statements about positive action: 'What must I *do*?' asks the lawyer in 10.25; after the exchange about the law including the command to love one's neighbour, Jesus says '*Do* this and you will live' (v. 28); the man then counters with a further question (about the identity of the neighbour), to which the parable responds, and Jesus' final comment is 'Go and *do* likewise' (v. 37). Whatever the significance of the fact that the hero of the story was a Samaritan may have been originally, Luke sees the story as a clear illustration of the importance of direct involvement by helping those in need, if necessary by giving or sharing one's material resources.

This is coupled with a powerful stress on the importance of 'giving alms', or charitable giving, in Luke's Gospel. In Lk. 6.30 Jesus says 'Give to everyone who begs from you'. The word for 'everyone' is absent from Matthew's parallel and may be Luke's addition to Q here. Thus charitable giving is encouraged, and extended to potentially universal scope. In Lk. 11.41 Luke probably rewrites the conclusion of the woe from about purity and cleaning the outside and inside of cups to have Jesus say, 'So *give for alms* those things that are within'. (The quite extraneous nature of the reference to almsgiving makes it likely that Luke has changed Q which is more closely represented by Matthew's 'First clean the inside of the cup' [Mt. 23.26], though the Q version is hard to recover with any certainty.) Similarly, in Lk. 12.33 Luke probably changes Q again by having Jesus exhort the listeners to 'Sell your possessions and *give alms*'. (Again, Matthew's parallel [Mt. 6.19] has no reference to giving alms.) Finally, the story of Zacchaeus (Lk. 19.1-10), a story again peculiar to Luke, ends up with Zacchaeus giving half his possessions to the poor (19.8) in what is in some sense clearly an exemplary act from Luke's point of view.

There is thus a large amount of material in Luke's Gospel indicating a positive attitude to the poor, a rather negative attitude to the rich, an apparently negative attitude at times to possessions, and a strong stress on the importance of giving and sharing on the part of those who are relatively well-off. Moreover, much of this material is either in material peculiar to Luke among the evangelists, or is due to Luke's own redaction of his sources. All this strongly suggests that this concern with the issue is Luke's own at least as much as reflecting any concern from his source materials.

The fact that much of this material, especially the critiques of the rich, appear predominantly in L material has led at least one modern critic (Mealand, *Poverty and Expectation*) to argue that Luke himself may have been not so concerned with this, since it is less easy to document from Luke's redaction of his sources; hence it may be a reflection of a pre-Lukan 'L' stratum of the tradition alone. This is possible, though one must remember that (a) Luke's redaction has not been inactive in stressing the importance of lack of possessions, especially by disciples (cf. above), and (b) we cannot drive too much of a wedge between Luke and his traditions (see pp. 266-67 above): hence even if some of the L material on poverty is not a redactional creation *de novo* by Luke, the fact that Luke has decided to include it in his Gospel is still of significance in telling us something about Luke's own interests. Thus in what follows I shall assume that this theme is an important one for Luke, not just for a pre-Lukan stratum of the tradition.

It is apparent, however, that not all of the material considered is quite of the same nature, nor does it all point the same way in relation to wealth, poverty, possessions or asceticism. Some parts seem to indicate an almost absolute rejection of the value and importance of money and material possessions; other parts seem only to encourage a willingness to share some of the excesses one may enjoy. For example, in relation to possessions and money, the disciples of Jesus are apparently expected to—and do—give up everything; and yet some of the teaching on almsgiving and sharing presupposes that people do still have possessions over which they retain control.

The situation becomes even more confusing if we ask the question how far all this is considered by Luke to be still applicable to the Christians of his own day, or even if we try to bring in the evidence of Acts to supplement the evidence of the Gospel.

The Evidence of Acts

The evidence of Acts is certainly rather confusing and not clear. The early chapters of Acts (Acts 1–5) present a picture of the primitive church in Jerusalem in one sense obeying the radical calls for renunciation by the Lukan Jesus: the disciples have nothing they can call their own individual property and they hold everything in common, used for the common good (2.44-45; 4.32-35).

However, even within these chapters, there is some inconsistency as to whether this was a universally practised phenomenon within the Christian community (as the summaries just cited seem to imply), or whether people only sold some of their surplus, and moreover did so on a voluntary basis (as seems to be implied by the note about Barnabas selling his field in Acts 4.36, and the story about Ananias and Sapphira in Acts 5.1-11: the sin of the latter is not that they have kept some of their possessions for themselves, but that they have not been honest in telling others what they have done).

What is perhaps more surprising is that, after the first five chapters in Acts, the situation seems to change. The economic set-up of the primitive Jerusalem church is not replicated in other communities founded by the Christian mission; the Christians themselves do not give up all their possessions, and in fact the story presupposes that the Christians have quite a lot of material means at their disposal to finance all the various comings and goings that take place. The church seems to include various people who may have had considerable means (cf. the proconsul Sergius Paulus in Acts 13.1, Lydia who was 'a dealer in purple cloth' in 16.14, or the reference to 'not a few Greek women and men of high standing' in Beroea in 17.12 etc., none of whom appear to give up their possessions). Further, there is absolutely nothing in the way Luke tells the story in Acts to suggest that the economic arrangements in the later churches represent a disastrous come-down from the glorious golden days of the first community.

Yet despite this discrepancy within Luke–Acts as a whole, which is very real, it should also be noted that some themes remain important throughout Luke's story. This applies especially to the evident importance for Luke of charitable giving. On a number of occasions in Acts, individuals who are evidently regarded as paradigms of virtue in the story are described in terms of their activity in giving generously. For example, Cornelius was a devout man who feared God with all his household; *he gave alms generously* to the people and prayed constantly to God' (Acts 10.2). Tabitha in Joppa 'was devoted to good works and *acts of charity*' (9.36). Paul defends himself before Felix by saying that he came to Jerusalem '*to bring alms* to my nation and to offer sacrifices' (24.17: this is Luke's only — and very oblique — reference to the great collection organized by Paul among the Gentile churches for the Jerusalem church).

Finally we should note that, although (perhaps strangely) the Christians in the story in Acts hardly ever refer to the teaching of Jesus in their own preaching, the one exception is when Paul cites a saying of Jesus (*not* recorded in Luke's, or any other, Gospel) that 'It is more blessed to give than to receive' (Acts 20.35). Thus at least the theme of charitable giving is one that retains its importance throughout Luke's two-volume work.

Yet even here we can see some differences between the Gospel and Acts. In the Gospel, giving seems to be encouraged for the benefit of the poor in general. In Acts it is predominantly the Christian poor who receive bounty from more well-to-do Christians. Christians in Acts do not go around helping the poor and needy outside their own ranks. Christian charity seems to be rather strictly 'in-house'.

What though are we to make of the more radical elements in Luke's Gospel, the parts which seem to imply and demand a total renunciation of all goods and possessions of any would-be follower of Jesus, and the stinging attacks on the rich simply apparently because they are rich?

It seems hard to deny that Luke does not regard the elements of his Gospel, apparently insisting on radical and total renunciation of all property and possessions, as essential for Christian discipleship after the time of Jesus. The story in Acts seems quite clear on this: the deafening silence of a total absence of any critique of Christians' still having money and property throughout so much of Acts makes this fairly clear. Indeed it may be explicitly signalled by Luke in his Gospel. In a passage peculiar to Luke, Jesus speaks to the twelve, and refers to the mission instructions given earlier in the Gospel (in fact the instruction given to the 70!), asking them 'When I sent you out without a purse, bag or sandals, did you lack anything?' (Lk. 22.35). When they reply 'No, not a thing', Jesus says 'But now, the one who has a purse must take it, and likewise a bag. And the one who has no sword must sell his cloak and buy one' (v. 36). It looks as if Luke's Jesus is consciously signalling a change in the circumstances of Christian disciples: the model of radical renunciation applies during the time of Jesus, but in Luke's day the situation is different: Christians will have possessions, even if they are expected to use them circumspectly and generously.

Who Are the Poor?

Before we go further, we need to ask perhaps what Luke actually understands by 'poverty'. Who are 'the poor' in Luke's eyes?

The situation is complicated by different meanings of the word for 'poor' (Greek *ptōchos*) in different contexts. Very broadly speaking, the Hellenistic world used the word 'poor' to refer to those in social and economic poverty, indeed usually in situations of very extreme poverty. The 'poor' are thus the materially deprived, the financially destitute. In Judaism, this language is also used; but alongside it there develops a slightly different usage. The materially poor and destitute are of course the object of God's concern and care in the Old Testament; this then leads to the idea that the poor are those who rely totally on God in utter dependence for their existence. The poor are thus the humble, the pious. Hence in Judaism the language develops whereby the 'poor' are equally those who are spiritually poor, those who are humble before God, the pious, and in some contexts this idea supplanted the reference to the 'poor' as the materially destitute. 'Poverty' can then be seen as a term denoting religious attitude, as much as, or at times instead of, material destitution.

We may see such vocabulary being used in Isa. 61.1, where the prophet announces good news to the 'poor', perhaps meaning the humble and pious. Matthew seems to have taken some of the language about poverty in this way, so that, for example, his version of the first beatitude is 'Blessed are the poor *in spirit*' (Mt. 5.3), meaning the humble and pious, those who are poor before God.

What though of Luke? Certainly the material and economic side of 'poverty' is never lost in Luke's understanding. The contrasts set up between the 'poor' and the 'rich' (Lk. 6.20, 24), or the beatitude in Lk. 6.21 which speaks of the 'hungry' (Matthew has those who 'hunger and thirst after righteousness', Mt. 5.6), and contrasts them with those who are physically full in the corresponding woe (Lk. 6.25), make it clear that material situations are in mind. The illustrations of the poor in the parables such as the rich man and Lazarus (16.19-31) also indicate that in many respects poverty is material, economic and financial poverty, not spiritual poverty. Even the quotation of Isaiah 61 in Luke 4 makes it fairly clear that, for Luke at least (and perhaps unlike the author of Isa. 61 itself), the recipients of the good news are the materially poor.

On the other hand, the idea of a less material kind of poverty is not absent from Luke. The diatribe of the Magnificat against the 'rich' and the promise to the 'hungry' (1.53) is set in parallel to the claim that God has exalted not the 'poor' but the 'lowly' (1.52 NRSV) or 'humble'. Those who are 'hungry' and suffering are also for Luke the 'humble' and pious.

Conversely, the attacks on the rich in Luke need to be read carefully. The parable of the rich fool (12.16-21) is very revealing. The fool is portrayed as the one who has wealth and makes provision for the future. But the punch line at the end does not just condemn the possession of riches as such. Jesus says, 'So it is with those who store up treasures for themselves *but are not rich towards God*' (v. 21). It is thus not so much, or not only, riches and possessions as such that is crucial: it is the attitude of the person towards God.

One modern writer has even gone so far as to suggest that possessions and money in Luke's story operate almost as a cipher for one's attitude to God and/or Jesus: 'the expressions rich and poor function within the story as metaphorical expressions for those rejected and accepted because of their response to the prophet' (Johnson, *Literary Function*, p. 140). In its most literal form this is probably too extreme, since Luke does not lose sight of the idea of economic and material poverty as well (as Johnson himself fully acknowledges in his study). Nevertheless, it is an important aspect of Luke's overall presentation of the theme of poverty in his writings.

Luke: The Rich and the Poor

What though of the material side of things? As was the case when we considered Luke and Judaism, quite a lot depends on how one envisages Luke's situation. To put it crudely, is Luke addressing a community that is rich or a community that is poor? Are the tirades against the rich meant as a cry of frustration from a poverty-stricken community, produced in a way similar to the way in which many have argued apocalyptic traditions are used by disadvantaged and/or persecuted groups to try to come to terms with their present situation and give hope for the future? Or are the exhortations to poverty directed at people who are reasonably affluent as a critique of their present lifestyle? Or is it a matter of both?

The trend in recent Lukan studies has been to argue that Luke is addressing a community that is certainly partly, maybe dominantly and perhaps even exclusively, quite well-to-do in material terms. Certainly there is quite a lot of material suggesting this. For example, Luke mentions the women who helped Jesus in his ministry (one of whom comes from Herod's household) and who evidently have sufficient material resources to support Jesus and his followers (Lk. 8.3). In Acts, as we have seen, Christian followers and sympathizers often appear as reasonably well-to-do: the Ethiopian eunuch (Acts 8.26-40), Manaen who is a member of Herod's court (13.1), the pro-consul Sergius Paulus (13.7), the people of 'high standing' in Beroea (17.12) and so on.

Moreover, much of the material in Luke's Gospel on the topic of money and the like is clearly directed at those who have possessions, for example, the exhortations to give generously (Lk. 6.30, 35; 11.41; 12.33-34) which we have already noted and which would be somewhat precious if addressed to those who are destitute. So too the parable of the rich fool is addressed to those with riches. The parable of the rich man and Lazarus gives the lion's share of attention in the story to the rich man and his fate: Lazarus, despite his having a name, is a very minor character and in many ways simply a foil to drive home the lesson of the story about the rich man. The context in which the parable of the Great Supper is placed by Luke is one of teaching about who should be invited to meals (Lk. 14.12-14); again this would be at best precious if addressed to the destitute who cannot feed themselves, let alone provide dinner parties. Similarly, the exhortation at the end of the parable of the unjust steward (Lk. 16.1-8), to 'make friends for yourselves by means of mammon [i.e. wealth]' (v. 9) clearly has in view those with money, not those without.

It seems very likely that Luke is, at least in part, addressing Christians who are certainly not materially destitute, but reasonably affluent. As such then, Luke's picture presents demands on the rich to use their money wisely and properly, and to give generously to those in need (see Karris, 'Poor and Rich'; Stegemann, 'The Following of Christ').

Nevertheless, the other side of things cannot be ignored. Esler has argued that the general social mix found in any Hellenistic city of the time would indicate that the poor, that is, the destitute, were also a part of the Christian community, and that a mixture of the extremes of financial and social situations may be reflected in the stories of Elijah and Elisha helping the impoverished widow and the relatively well-to-do Naaman respectively (Lk. 4.25-27). Hence the Lukan community may have been socially very mixed. The same may be shown by the parable of the Great Supper, told by Jesus, according to Luke, to exhort the hearers to invite not only their social equals who could respond in kind, but also their social (and financial) inferiors who could never respond in kind (Lk. 14.12-14). According to Esler, this may also then reflect the situation of Luke's community, with table fellowship at the *same* table being strongly urged on all members of the community, especially on those whose social position was such that they would not normally engage in such practice.

This is possible, though one must also note that much of the conversation seems to be rather one-sided: the exhortations are constantly to the rich, the influential and those with possessions. In one sense this is inevitable since the poor, precisely by virtue of their poverty, are in a position of total powerlessness and cannot do anything either for themselves or for others. Nevertheless, the powerful arguments and exhortations directed to the rich do suggest that Luke's community may have been predominantly reasonably well-to-do.

It may be too in this light that Luke's portrait of the disciples should be read. As we have seen, Jesus' disciples during his lifetime adopt a lifestyle of material and financial renunciation that is far more radical than that reflected in Acts. Perhaps though, in part, this picture—which is not peculiar to Luke since it is there in his sources, but is certainly developed by him—is intended as a challenge and a critique for richer Christians of Luke's own day. The disciples are not necessarily role models to be imitated precisely. As we have seen, Luke is aware that the era of Jesus now lies in the past; perhaps too then the same applies to the model of discipleship as seen in the Gospel stories. Yet the picture painted by Luke can still serve as a powerful image of the total commitment, and the potential renunciation, which Christians in his own day may have been called to make.

We should also note that for Luke, poverty as such is not an ideal. The poor and the needy in Luke are not told that their life of freedom from property and material goods is itself true happiness. Luke then is no Cynic philosopher, preaching the value of detachment from the cares of this world. The hungry and the needy are promised that their needs will be satisfied (Lk. 6.21). Even when the disciples practise their radical lifestyle, we are told that they in fact did not suffer materially (22.35), presumably because others gave them what they needed. Luke's positive picture of renunciation by the disciples during Jesus' lifetime is thus in no way promoting an ascetic ideal. The poor are promised that a better future lies ahead. Similarly, in Acts, any ideal in the model of the economic set-up of the primitive Jerusalem church does not lead to a life of asceticism: any money that is available is pooled and used, not given away to third parties.

Moreover, for Luke the good news which is promised to the poor is by no means simply an other-worldly hope for a better time that will come in a future life. Such an idea is not lacking (cf. Lk. 16.19-31), but Luke also has a firm idea that the Gospel has—or should have—real concrete implications for the poor in this world. (The point is strongly emphasized by Esler, *Community and Gospel*, pp. 193-97.) The blessings announced in the Nazareth sermon, including sight for the blind and release of the captives, are enacted by Luke's Jesus (cf. Lk. 13.10-17; 18.35-43). The feeding of the hungry takes place in Jesus' feeding of the 5000 (Lk. 9.10-17). The good news for the poor is shown to have

practical consequences for the really poor in the picture of the early
church in Acts where no one is in need and everything is shared (Acts
2.44-46; 4.32-37, cf. especially v. 34: 'There was not a needy person
among them'). Thus, despite an undoubted other-worldly element in
the promises for the poor, Luke's story shows that the gospel can, and
should, lead to a changed reality in this world. Luke's Gospel is thus a
promise to the poor of a change in their fortunes, as well as a challenge to the rich to bring that change about.

Reversal

The whole matter of poverty or riches may be part of a still wider and
more inclusive theme in Luke–Acts. This is the thesis of the recent
study of York (*The Last Shall Be First*): the theme of riches/poverty is
part of a more all-embracing scheme of *reversal* in Luke, covering not
only money but more importantly status, worth and value, or, to use
the language adopted by some social anthropologists in relation to
biblical texts seen in the context of the Mediterranean world, honour
and shame.

   If we look once again at the parable of the Great Supper and its context in Luke, the poor are coupled with 'the crippled, the lame, and
the blind' as the people whom one should invite and share a table
with (Lk. 14.13, cf. also v. 21 and 7.22). But these are not only the
people who are financially destitute; they are also those who are
excluded from participating in the Jewish cult (cf. Lev. 21.18): they are
thus the *social* outcasts, the people who have no honour in the eyes of
the respectable and well-to-do. They are unable to repay any hospi-
tality (and so bring any return of honour to the host); and being in
positions of shame themselves, they provide no honour to a
benefactor who would seek to become a patron for them. What is rec-
ommended is thus the exact antithesis of any seeking of honour for
oneself in such an honour–shame society. What is demanded is not
only an ending of financial and economic hardship (though this *is* part
of things), but also a deeper re-evaluation of what is to count as
honour, as worthy of recognition, and what is not. As often as not, the
gospel brings about a *reversal* of previously held human values, and
certainly a strong condemnation of any attempt to establish or to
enhance one's own honour in the sight of others.

   York seeks to show that this theme of reversal pervades the whole
of Luke's narrative at a very deep level. It not only surfaces in the
riches/poverty theme, but also in the sayings about being humbled
and exalted (Lk. 14.11; 18.14), and in parables such as the Pharisee and

the tax-collector (18.9-13). Here the issue is not clearly one of rich against poor: the Pharisee is not necessarily rich, and the tax-collector is almost certainly the very opposite of poor in material terms. Yet like the rich/poor antithesis, we see here a not unrelated total reversal of the value systems of other human beings, so that what counts as honour and worth in the eyes of men and women is shown to be reversed in God's eyes. Thus, to return to one of the points with which we started this chapter, the poor and the tax-collectors *may* be on a par in Luke's story, not necessarily because tax-collectors were destitute (they were not!), but because both lack honour in a culture dominated by the categories of honour and shame. The gospel is then not only good news for the economically poor, but also good news for those without any honour in society, in proclaiming the reversal of such human values in the sight of God.

York's study raises some very interesting ideas. Not all of his argument is equally persuasive. It is, for example, not always clear how far Luke is advocating a reversal of the whole value system, the whole set of criteria for attributing honour/shame (as for example in the parable of the Pharisee and the tax-collector) and how far Luke's Jesus is simply adopting the current criteria to critique just selfishness. For example, neither the rich fool who does not use his money and wealth to benefit others, nor the rich man in relation to Lazarus, would be accorded honour in the honour–shame culture as outlined by York (in dependence on the work of Malina and others) simply because they refused to share their wealth with others. Benefaction in such a society was highly regarded; self-interested hoarding was not. Any reversal here is perhaps not as fundamental as in Lk. 18.9-13 or 14.12-14. Nevertheless, York's work shows the value—and the importance—of extending the parameters of the discussion to include insights from social anthropology and sociology, as well as the more limited, traditional categories used by biblical exegetes to throw light upon the text.

Conclusion

We have focused in this chapter on just one aspect of the Christian life, and of the teaching of Jesus in Luke's Gospel, as shown in the Lukan writings. As we have seen, the picture is a complex one. In part, no doubt, this is due once again to Luke's sensitivity as a storyteller, or as a history-teller. Luke writes as a historian and he is thus aware that the events he narrates are in the past. He knows too that not everything said in the past can be transferred to a later time without alteration. Thus the model of discipleship which Luke develops in his Gospel is, in at least one respect anyway, not a model which is repeated after the time of Jesus: disciples no longer give up *everything* when they become believers. Luke is thus aware of the distance between his own day and the time of Jesus. The story world he creates cannot simply be applied without thought to the real world of his own day.

Luke thus shows himself to be perhaps surprisingly modern in this. In dealing with traditions from the past, which Luke no doubt thinks are of great importance for his present, one cannot just ignore the difference between past and present and pretend that the past speaks to the present simply by repeating the same words which can then be understood in the present's terms without more ado. It is to some of these hermeneutical reflections that we shall turn in the final chapter.

FURTHER READING

P.F. Esler, *Community and Gospel in Luke–Acts* (SNTSMS, 57; Cambridge: Cambridge University Press, 1987).

L.T. Johnson, *The Literary Function of Possessions in Luke–Acts* (SBLDS, 39; Missoula, MT: Scholars Press, 1977).

R.J. Karris, 'Poor and Rich: The Lukan *Sitz im Leben*', in Talbert (ed.), *Perspectives on Luke–Acts*, pp. 112-25.

D.L. Mealand, *Poverty and Expectation in the Gospels* (London: SPCK, 1980).

T.E. Schmidt, *Hostility to Wealth in the Synoptic Gospels* (JSNTSup, 15; Sheffield: JSOT Press, 1987), esp. ch. 7, 'Hostility to Wealth in the Gospel of Luke', pp. 135-62.

W. Stegemann, 'The Following of Christ as Solidarity between Rich, Respected Christians and Poor, Despised Christians (Gospel of Luke)', in L. Schottroff and W. Stegemann, *Jesus and the Hope of the Poor* (ET; Maryknoll, NY: Orbis Books, 1986), pp. 67-120.

J.O. York, *The Last Shall Be First: The Rhetoric of Reversal in Luke* (JSNTSup, 46; Sheffield: JSOT Press, 1991).

Chapter Six

CONCLUDING HERMENEUTICAL REFLECTIONS

In the previous chapters, I have tried to look at some of the problems surrounding the interpretation of the Gospel of Luke, viewed as an ancient text. The approach has been, broadly speaking, a historical-critical one: by this I mean that the attempt has been made to view the text in, and as part of, its original setting in history. With regard to a text which is giving an account of events prior to its time of writing, there are of course peculiar problems. Does original refer to the time of the story, or to the time of the writing of the text? How far should one focus on the events of the story, and how far on the author and his/her situation? Nevertheless, the historical nature of the text is important, even if we begin to bracket off some of these historical questions and begin to analyse the text as a literary whole in its own right.

Few would want to go so far as to ignore historical questions completely. We have to understand the language of the text—and that involves placing the text in a historical linguistic context (in this case the Greek-speaking world of the late first century CE). We have to know something of the background against which we can and should appropriately understand key words and phrases. (It would, I suggest, be quite wrong to take Luke's language of Jesus as 'Son of God' as meaning exactly what the Council of Chalcedon meant by the same words without ever worrying about the issue of possible anachronism.) We also need to know something about the social realities of the context of the text. Often in our quest, the insights from other academic disciplines, such as sociology or social anthropology, can help to throw important light on the text (as we saw in relation to legitimation, or in relation to Luke's ideas on reversal). Often too we would like to know more than we in fact do about key aspects of the context of the text which would affect the interpretation significantly: for example, the author's Jewishness, or non-Jewishness, might affect our assessment of what the text says about Jews and Judaism very significantly, as we saw. But all these historical issues are vitally important in our understanding of Luke's Gospel, just as in the case of any text from antiquity.

However, Luke's text is not quite like any other text from antiquity. Whether we like it or not, the fact is that this text we have been studying is a *Gospel*, a book which has its place in a Christian Bible, and as such is part of the sacred Scripture of the Christian church. For many people, therefore, and indeed for many people studying this text within an academic context, the text has religious significance for their own contemporary religious faith. Luke's Gospel is to be seen not only as an ancient text but also as a text which it is believed is still relevant (in some way) for the present and still speaks to the present.

The previous paragraph could of course have been written about any book of the New Testament. In the case of Luke's Gospel, the situation is even more acute, since a Gospel gives an account of the life and teaching of Jesus, and for the Christian faith, the person of Jesus is of absolutely central significance. The interpretation of a Gospel thus raises vital hermeneutical issues for many people. Such issues raise profound questions, though these can only be discussed here in a very superficial way — partly for reasons of space, partly for reasons of expertise. So what is offered here is only a very brief, and naive, set of suggestions.

For many people, the teaching of Jesus is central to contemporary Christian faith and morality. In relation to the interpretation of Luke's Gospel, one must say that, *if* one's concern is to recover the teaching of the historical Jesus on this or that topic, then Luke's Gospel may be a means to that end, but it is not that end in itself. It is certainly a means to that end. Some of the L material, especially the parables, may give us very important aspects of Jesus' teaching which would otherwise not be available to us. But Luke's Gospel certainly does not give us a pure, unadulterated account of the teaching of Jesus. We have seen a number of occasions where Luke has almost certainly *changed* his tradition (whether Mark or Q, or perhaps even one of his other sources). Luke adds things to Mark here, changes Q there, alters a saying here, omits a story there and so on. If we want the pure, unadulterated teaching of Jesus (if such an aim could ever be realized!), then we shall have to make full allowances for the things Luke has done to his traditions. We certainly cannot simply read Luke's Gospel as if it were an exact transcript of the life or teaching of Jesus. In reading Luke's Gospel, therefore, we see *Luke's* Jesus, not the pure unvarnished Jesus.

Although many starting critical studies of the Gospel find this a little difficult to accept at first, there are real questions to ask about whether this should be regarded as all loss. There are immense problems about ever succeeding in recovering the pure unvarnished Jesus of history. But even if we could, some would argue that this is not necessarily as central for Christian faith as others would claim. Certainly the early Christians might have argued in this way. What was important for them was not so much a voice from the past as rigid and unchanging, giving timeless, fixed and unalterable dogmas or ethical instructions which would never change to all eternity. The early Christians believed, rightly or wrongly, that the Jesus of history, the Jesus who had come from Nazareth and had been crucified, had been in some profound sense raised by God in a unique way and was now alive and present with his people, enabling them to be guided and inspired in their lives in ways they had never experienced before. It was, they believed, the same Jesus who had lived among them (or their predecessors) in Palestine; and that in part was no doubt one of the reasons why traditions found now in our Gospels were preserved. But this same Jesus was now the source and inspiration which was leading them into new areas and in new ways.

In all this Luke seems to have been no exception. Luke was, of course, unlike many other Christians of his time. Very few wrote books; even fewer wrote Gospels; and no one else wrote an equivalent of Acts. So too Luke's idea of the guiding presence of Jesus in the post-Easter church is far more of an indirect presence than, say, Paul's: for Luke, Jesus is alive in heaven, and the guiding action on earth is more the work of the Holy Spirit than of Jesus directly. Yet Luke shows us, perhaps more so than some other New Testament writers, that the Christian gospel can be, and perhaps should be, adapted to changing circumstances.

We have already noted on a number of occasions what I have called Luke's sensitivity or literary skill: Luke takes some care at times not to write back too much of his own ideas into his story. He lets the characters of his story say their thing in their own way, and this may apply to Jesus in the Gospel quite as much as to characters like Peter or Paul in Acts. Luke has his own agenda—that is clear. But he does not always write it back into his story world. All this means in one way that we can perhaps have greater confidence in Luke as a reliable historian: he certainly tries to report many things accurately (even if his level of success may have been variable!).

But the other side of the coin is perhaps equally significant in the present context. Luke realizes that there is a difference between past and present. We saw this, for example, in relation to eschatology. Thus, as I have said, the present is not read into the past without more ado. But then the past cannot simply be translated into the present without ado either. Luke's agenda, and Luke's vocabulary, are no doubt very real for him: but they are not necessarily the same as the agenda and the vocabulary of the past. We have seen this at more than one level and in relation to more than one issue. In relation to Judaism, the battles and disputes which take place in Luke's story are not necessarily the battles and disputes in which he himself is engaged. The ethical stance of the Gospel in relation, say, to discipleship and possessions is not quite the same as that of his own day, or even as that of Acts: the instructions of the Gospel are *not* timeless unchanging words which can be repeated ever anew in changed situations. The words, if they are to be applied in the present, may have to be changed. Indeed, Luke's Jesus does this quite explicitly in relation to the question of possessions and discipleship (cf. Lk. 22.35).

Luke does little explicitly to show how this change takes place. He shows himself to be surprisingly modern in his awareness of the gap between his own time and the past—a gap which is certainly historical, perhaps cultural as well, perhaps hermeneutical. Yet he does not do so much to tell us how he bridges that gap, let alone how others might bridge it. Nevertheless, it is clear that a real amount of bridging is going on. Luke does not tell his story just for fun. He does not write for his own amusement. Writing in the ancient world was a time-consuming and expensive business. Luke writes because he believes that his history will have a relevance to his own situation—but perhaps in a less direct way than others have envisaged. His Gospel story of Jesus, privileging the poor, castigating the rich, and having disciples who give up everything, does *not* necessarily set up a blueprint for his own day. Rather, it seeks to challenge a status quo that is perhaps becoming too complacent. So too his picture of Judaism may serve a number of aims, one of which is to unite the Christian church firmly to its Jewish roots.

For a modern Christian reader of Luke's work, one can perhaps pay him the greatest compliment if one is prepared to follow in his footsteps of *not* simply transferring the words of his Gospel to quite different situations and expecting them to have an unchanging, eternal significance and meaning. An elementary understanding of semantics should have warned us against this anyway: words change their meaning when placed in different contexts, and can never have the eternal, immutable meaning for which some would vainly hope.

There is no doubt that Luke's picture of Jesus can, and does, challenge many today. The Jesus who challenges the rich and affluent of his day also challenges a world such as our own, with glaring social and economic inequalities. Few who go to church in the Western world can hear the parable of the rich man and Lazarus with any comfort today. The Jesus whose story is so profoundly rooted in the

Jewish faith and the Jewish community must surely challenge a Christian church which bears his name but which is so separated from contemporary Judaism. The Jesus of Luke's story, whose ethic is so practical and down-to-earth in helping those in need, must surely challenge any would-be followers to be equally practical and down-to-earth in the practice of their religion.

Yet how all this might work out in practice is never spelt out—and perhaps wisely so—by Luke. Luke does not even carry over the words of the teaching of the Gospel into his story in Acts: as we noted in passing earlier, Jesus' words of the Gospel are never cited in Acts. (There is only one saying of Jesus cited [Acts 20.35] and that is not a saying recorded in Luke's Gospel.)

There is not a little justification for Luke's silence in not spelling out the hermeneutical moves he might have made, or at least not recording them for posterity. The hermeneutical task, of reappropriating the tradition and applying it to ever-new situations, is a task which can only be undertaken by the individuals and groups themselves in their own situations. Luke's economic model (if that is what it is) of the set-up in the primitive Jerusalem church would not necessarily apply in a post-industrial modern city. Nor would it really address the deeper societal problems which create, and perpetuate, inequality, deprivation and poverty in the first place. Someone else's solution, in a different social situation, cannot simply be transformed to a new social context and remain unchanged. A corollary must be that what is a solution in one context will not necessarily succeed in another. For example, Luke's solution to the problem posed by the eschatological teaching in his traditions, seeking to reassert the teaching of an imminent End in the face of delay, can scarcely be ours, living nearly 2000 years later. Similarly, however powerful in general terms the teaching of the Lukan Jesus on poverty may be for a situation of the gross inequalities that characterize our world today, few would probably feel happy with Luke's own apparent interpretation of that teaching in his story in Acts which seems to envisage practical action for the relief of poverty being restricted to benefit poor Christians only.

Luke's Jesus is a challenging Jesus for those who live in relative affluence. But Luke himself is a challenging writer too. His implied hermeneutic means that he hands nothing to his readers on a plate. Or rather, what he hands on is his account of the past in a history. He, in his day, struggles to make that history relevant to his own situation. Those for whom Luke's writings now form part of a canon of Scripture have an obligation to make the same struggle; but the easy option of a biblical fundamentalism which simply repeats the words from the past is not, one suspects, Luke's preferred option. For Luke, the church goes forward in the power of the Holy Spirit, ever conscious of its past and tied irrevocably to his roots, but seeking too to change and adapt to the new situations in which it finds itself. The struggle to maintain the balance between the past and the future is part of the challenge which Luke's writings pose for every generation of Christians.

FURTHER READING

N. Lash, 'What Might Martyrdom Mean?', in W. Horbury and B McNeil (eds.), *Suffering and Martyrdom in the New Testament* (Cambridge: Cambridge University Press, 1981), pp. 183-98.

R. Morgan and J. Barton, *Biblical Interpretation* (Oxford: Oxford University Press, 1988).

C.M. Tuckett, *Reading the New Testament* (London: SPCK, 1987).

INDEXES

INDEX OF REFERENCES

OLD TESTAMENT

Genesis
1.1-2   153
1.1   115

Exodus
1.15   117
3   119
4.19   116
18   119
23.20   151
24.1-18   209
24.1   209
24.15-18   209
24.16   209
34.29   209

Leviticus
19.2   97
19.18   97
20.26   97
21.18   334

Numbers
23.19   231

Deuteronomy
18   313
18.15   313, 314
19.15   99
24.1-4   236

Joshua
10.12-14   96

2 Samuel
7.14   315, 316

1 Kings
17.16   312
17.17-24   312
19   115

2 Kings
1.8   115, 151
1.9   312
4.42-44   115

2 Chronicles
33.12-13   270
35.21   270

Job
25.1-6   231

Psalms
2.7   315, 316
8.4   231
16.10   310
22   122, 210, 220
22.1   210
22.16   210
22.18   210
69.26   282
80.17   231
105.15   312
110.1   309

137.9   96
146.3   231

Isaiah
6.9-10   282, 285, 291
9.1   222
29.3   140
29.13   91
40.3   151, 287
40.5   287
42   114
42.1-4   113
42.1   202
49.6   317
51.12   231
52.13   317
53   113, 210, 282, 310, 317, 319
53.7-8   317, 319
53.7   210
53.12   210, 317
53.19   210
56.2   231
61   312, 330
61.1-2   282, 312
61.1   324, 330
61.24   140

Ezekiel
1   142
2.1   231

Daniel		2.23-27	281	Malachi	
7.13	231	3.1-5 (LXX)	281	3.1	151
8.17	231				
9.27	259	Amos		Wisdom of Solomon	
		2.16	136	2.12-20	202
Hosea		9.11-12	282	2.15	316
11.1	114, 116			2.18	122
		Zechariah			
Joel		9.9	169	Sirach	
2	281	13.4	151	4.11	316

NEW TESTAMENT

Matthew		3.16-17	113	5.10	94, 104
1–7	40, 42,	3.17	111, 112,	5.11-12	103
	71, 82,		114, 122	5.12	82
	85, 87,	4.1-34	166	5.13	57
	90, 94,	4.1-13	154	5.17-20	48
	95, 101,	4.1-11	154	5.17	80, 93,
	103-105,	4.3	111		118
	117	4.6	111	5.18	48, 80
1–2	47, 66,	4.8	111	5.19-20	80
	164, 270	4.12	67	5.19	173
1.1–4.17	112	4.14-16	89	5.20	24, 75,
1.1–4.16	70, 112	4.14ff.	48		94
1.1-15	165	4.15	222	5.21-26	96
1.14-16	111	4.17–10.42	111	5.21-24	80
1.21–2.12	166	4.17	66	5.21-22	48, 173
1.21-39	166	4.18–16.20	112	5.23-24	173
1.22-23	48, 89	4.23–11.30	122	5.27-32	80
1.23	83, 90,	4.23	25, 58,	5.27-30	96
	111, 119,		75	5.27-28	48, 173
	120	4.26-29	164	5.29-30	173
1.40-49	165	4.35–5.43	166	5.31-32	48, 96,
2.1–3.6	166	4.35–5.13	166		173
2.6	90	5–8	65	5.33-37	80, 96,
2.11	116	5–7	47, 67,		173
2.15	48, 89,		164	5.33-34	48
	90, 114	5	95	5.38-42	80, 96
2.17-18	48, 89	5.1	111	5.38-39	48
2.19-21	116	5.3-12	172	5.39-42	80
2.23	48, 89	5.3-11	325	5.43-48	96
3–4	47	5.3	330	5.43-44	48
3.7-12	166	5.5	103	5.44-48	80
3.7-10	162, 164	5.6	94, 104,	5.45	94
3.7	24		330	5.48	94, 97,
3.8	71	5.7-9	103		100
3.15	71	5.9	97	6.1-18	24

6.1	94	8.27	117	12.28	174, 227
6.2-4	173	8.29	111	12.32	100
6.5-13	173	8.31–14.62	122	12.34	172
6.9-13	94	9.6	117	12.38-42	91
6.10	94, 100	9.9-17	24	12.38	75
6.16-18	173	9.13	90	12.39	166
6.19	326	9.14-29	164	13	26, 39,
6.25-33	79	9.18-26	58		47, 65
6.25ff.	77, 82	9.27	120	13.13	68
6.30–7.23	166	9.32-34	24	13.14-15	59
6.31-52	166	9.34	59	13.16-17	172
6.33	94, 95	9.35	75	13.24-30	57
6.34-44	166	10	47, 65	13.35	48, 89
6.34	172	10.1-4	58	13.36-43	80
6.45-51	166	10.1ff.	77	13.41	121
6.45	94	10.1	117	13.47-50	80
6.53-56	166	10.7-16	79	13.52	82
6.53	166	10.9-14	58	13.53	64, 65
7.1-23	166	10.17-23	172	13.54	48, 75
7.12	80, 94,	10.17	75	14–17	47
	106, 118	10.26-40	79	14.27	111
7.13	107	10.33	166	14.28-33	174
7.15-23	82, 97	10.34-36	173	14.33	11, 21
7.15	77, 301	10.39	159	15.1-20	91, 93
7.20-21	95	10.41	77, 82	15.1	75
7.24-30	166	10.46-52	120	15.12-14	75, 91
7.28-29	58	11–12	47, 166	15.13	86
7.28	64, 65	11	65	15.15	169
7.29	75, 82,	11.1	64, 65,	15.29	18, 111
	117		75	16.1	169
7.32-37	164, 166	11.2-6	171, 227	16.2-3	59
8–9	47, 65,	11.7-30	66	16.13	121
	67, 72	11.19	232	16.16-19	264
8.1-21	166	11.20	166	16.16	20, 111
8.1-10	166	11.25-30	118, 122	16.17-19	80
8.4	118	11.25-27	80, 173,	16.18-19	173
8.5-13	33, 46,		226	16.18	48, 75
	86	11.27	46	16.19	100
8.11-12	172	11.28-30	122	16.20	121
8.14-17	58	12	114	16.21–28.20	112
8.17	48, 89,	12.1-8	24	16.21	66, 67
	113	12.9	48, 75	16.22	169
8.18-22	79	12.17-21	89, 113	16.28	121
8.18ff.	77	12.17ff.	48	17.1	111
8.19	82	12.18-21	114, 122	17.3-4	118
8.20	111, 232	12.23	120	17.5	111-13,
8.22-26	164, 166	12.24-30	80		119
8.23-24	58	12.24	75	17.9	121

Matthew (cont.)					Mark	
17.24-27	85, 171	23.1-39	66		1–13	241
18	47, 65,	23.2-3	85, 118		1–8	128
	97, 98	23.2	75		1.1–8.28	128
18.1-5	98	23.3	95		1.1–2.17	209
18.11-14	99	23.8-12	98		1.1-15	151, 166,
18.12	99	23.8-11	80			189, 203,
18.14	99	23.8-10	173			209, 219,
18.15-22	80, 173	23.8	82			221, 241
18.15-20	99	23.13	75		1.1-13	131, 151,
18.15-17	99	23.14	75			203, 205
18.15ff.	98	23.15	75		1.1-11	159, 221
18.17	48, 75	23.16-26	120		1.1-8	151, 205,
18.18	82	23.23	75			221
18.19-20	100	23.27	75		1.1	132, 151,
18.20	111, 119	23.29	75			154, 200,
18.23-35	100	23.34	77, 82			203, 221,
18.34	100	23.36	326			222, 273
19–22	47	23.37	82		1.2-13	206
19.1	64, 65	24–25	47, 65		1.2-3	183
19.21	97	24.10-12	82		1.4	215
19.28	121	24.26-28	80		1.7	115
20.28	114	24.27	232		1.8	205
20.30-31	120	24.30	121		1.9-13	205
21.2ff.	169	24.37-41	80		1.9-11	175, 226
21.4-5	48, 89,	24.37-39	232		1.9	182
	164	24.44	232		1.10-13	154
21.14-16	120	25	102		1.11	132, 154,
21.18-19	58	25.1-13	80			210
21.27	117	25.31-46	80		1.12-13	175
21.29-31	59	25.31	121		1.12	215
21.33-41	87	26–28	47, 66		1.13	155, 205
21.41	86	26.1	64, 67		1.14–8.26	205
21.43	48, 86,	26.63	111		1.14–5.43	181
	126, 223	26.64	121		1.14–3.35	203
21.44	59	27.9-10	48, 90		1.14–3.6	205
21.45	75	27.25	48		1.14-15	131, 183,
22.1-46	121	27.40	111			205, 206,
22.1-14	48	27.54	111			221
22.11-13	173	27.62	75		1.14	138, 140,
22.34-40	91	28.15	86			157, 182,
22.34-35	75	28.16-20	117, 119,			202, 222,
22.41-46	91		122, 292			238, 273
22.41	75	28.16	111, 164		1.15	205, 231,
23–25	65	28.18-20	48			237, 276
23	20, 32,	28.18	117		1.16–8.26	203
	47, 75,	28.20	83, 111,		1.16–8.21	206
	93, 126		120		1.16-29	135

1.16-20	115, 131, 170	2.1-10	224, 227 162	3.7–8.21 3.7–6.6	205 205
1.16	140, 181, 182, 215, 222, 245	2.1 2.3	181, 182, 215 183	3.7-12 3.7-8 3.7	131, 205 58 140, 182, 215, 222
1.20	325	2.6-12	156		
1.21–2.12	181, 227	2.6-8	210	3.9	215
1.21-45	131	2.7	211	3.10-12	227
1.21-22	182	2.8	211, 226	3.11-12	132, 156, 211
1.21	75, 182, 183, 215	2.10	160, 232, 235	3.11	211
1.22	58, 183, 210, 211, 226	2.13-17 2.13	206 181, 182, 215	3.13–5.20 3.13-19	209 58, 131, 135, 160
1.23-28	57	2.14	131, 159, 160	3.13-15 3.13ff.	157 239
1.23-27	156				
1.23	75, 181, 183	2.15-17 2.15	224, 225 181, 183, 215	3.13 3.14	182, 215 238
1.24	183			3.17	136, 183
1.25	183	2.17-22	229	3.19	182, 210
1.26	183	2.17	175, 229, 325	3.20-35 3.20-21	131, 224 57
1.27	79, 183, 211	2.18–3.12	209	3.20	215
1.28	140, 183, 222	2.18-22 2.18-19	206, 224 175	3.21	183, 206, 211, 237, 245
1.29-39	166	2.18	183		
1.29-34	58	2.19-20	214	3.22-30	156, 166, 206, 214, 224
1.29-31	175, 213	2.19	175, 229, 230		
1.29-30	210				
1.29	181, 182	2.20	175, 230	3.22	210, 211, 237
1.32	163, 181, 315	2.21-22 2.21	175, 330 229	3.23-27	229
1.34	156	2.22	229	3.24-25	330
1.35-38	57	2.23-28	206, 224	3.27	230
1.35	181, 182, 215, 237	2.23-27 2.25-26	229 235	3.28-30 3.30	212 183, 245
1.36	135	2.27	175, 224	3.31-35	58, 175, 206, 213, 237
1.39	58, 140, 182, 222, 315	2.28	160, 175, 232	3.34	238
		3.1-6	156, 175, 181, 206, 224, 227	4	166
1.40-54	162			4.1-34	131, 159, 175, 181, 203, 230
1.40	181, 182	3.1	48, 169, 182, 215		
1.44	183, 211	3.5	211	4.1-33	229
2.1–3.6	131, 166, 195, 214, 217, 224	3.6	136, 160, 208, 214, 236	4.1-9 4.1-8	206 229
2.1-14	135			4.1-2	230
2.1-12	175, 206,				

Mark (cont.)

4.1	160, 182, 215	5.24-34	213
4.2	182	5.25-34	182, 206
4.10-20	173	5.30	211
4.10-12	206, 230	5.34	237
4.10ff.	160	5.35-43	182, 206
4.10	238	5.37	135
4.11-12	160, 211, 217, 229, 291	5.41	136, 183
		5.42	245
4.11	182, 231	5.43	211
4.13-20	206, 230	6	77
4.20	237	6.1–9.50	181
4.21-25	330	6.1-6	131
4.21-22	175	6.1	182
4.21	182, 229	6.2	48
4.24	182, 229	6.4	226
4.25–5.43	135	6.6–8.21	205
4.26-29	57, 229	6.6	182, 205
4.26	231	6.7-13	131, 135, 206
4.30-32	229	6.7	58, 238
4.30	231	6.8-11	58
4.33-34	211, 230	6.14-29	206
4.34	238	6.14-16	159, 211, 226
4.35–6.56	203		
4.35–6.54	131	6.14-15	183
4.35–5.43	131, 159, 181, 211, 227	6.17-29	57, 138, 208, 213, 238
4.35–5.17	58	6.17	136
4.35-41	159, 211, 228	6.27	139
4.35-36	160	6.30–9.1	209
4.35ff.	166	6.30–7.23	159
4.36	215	6.30-56	135
4.40-41	212, 245	6.30-52	131
4.40	212, 237	6.30-44	159, 187
4.41	131, 215	6.30-34	182
5.1	136	6.30	206, 238
5.2	215	6.31	215
5.4-5	57	6.32	215
5.9	139	6.34-44	223
5.20	58	6.34	170
5.21–6.29	209	6.35-52	181, 227
5.21-43	58	6.35-44	227
5.21-24	182, 206	6.35	238
5.21	215	6.37	139
		6.45–8.26	159, 288
		6.45–8.21	57
		6.45-53	159

6.45-52	159, 228
6.45	136, 160, 215, 238
6.46	215
6.48	140
6.50-52	245
6.50-51	212
6.51-52	21
6.52	215, 238, 245
6.53-56	131
6.53	160, 182
6.54	215
7	91
7.1-23	131, 166, 203, 224, 225
7.1-8	171, 224
7.2-4	136, 139
7.3-4	159, 183, 224, 237
7.6-7	183, 212
7.6	140, 237
7.11	136, 183
7.15	136, 173, 224
7.17-23	211, 224
7.17	169, 215, 238
7.17ff.	239
7.17	160
7.19	79, 92, 183
7.24–9.29	203
7.24–8.26	131, 159, 227
7.24–8.10	181, 222, 227
7.24-30	223, 288
7.24	160, 182, 211, 215
7.25-30	213
7.31-37	175
7.31	18, 136, 140, 182, 215, 222
7.32-37	227, 288
7.34	136, 183

8.1-21	159	8.34–9.1	22, 132,
8.1-10	159, 187,		159, 166,
	223, 227		238
8.1-9	170	8.34-38	22, 212
8.1	182	8.34	22, 238
8.2-26	227	8.35-37	175
8.4	215	8.35	159, 182,
8.10	182, 215,		221, 273
	238	8.36	182
8.11-13	211, 224	8.37	182
8.11	169	8.38	166, 175,
8.12	166		182, 221,
8.14–9.48	135		232
8.14-21	131, 225,	9.1-8	228
	227, 238	9.1	160, 175,
8.14	215		209, 231,
8.21	215		276
8.22–10.51	205	9.2–10.52	209
8.22-26	57, 175,	9.2-13	209
	181, 205,	9.2-8	132, 175,
	206, 227,		211
	237, 288	9.2-3	209
8.22	136, 182,	9.2	135, 209,
	183		215
8.26–10.52	205	9.4	209
8.27–10.51	132	9.5-6	136
8.27–10.45	181, 206,	9.6	212, 245
	237	9.7	209
8.27-33	132, 245	9.9-13	57, 132,
8.27-30	203		211
8.27-28	226	9.9	211
8.27	182, 215,	9.11-13	138, 224,
	237		238
8.28	159	9.14-27	175, 227
8.29	20, 135	9.14	238
8.30-33	160	9.15-16	57
8.30	211, 215	9.16-27	181
8.31–16.8	203	9.17	169
8.31–9.1	138	9.18	212
8.31	21, 22,	9.19	211, 212
	132, 159,	9.20–10.45	203
	173, 212,	9.20-24	225, 237
	232, 233,	9.21-24	57
	238, 240	9.23	212
8.32-33	57	9.28-29	57, 224,
8.32	169		239
8.33	136, 183,	9.28	238
	211, 225	9.29	237

9.30-32	132, 138		
9.30	182, 211,		
	222		
9.31	132, 159,		
	202, 212,		
	232, 238,		
	240		
9.32	212, 245		
9.33-50	132, 159,		
	166		
9.33-37	98, 212		
9.33	160, 215,		
	237		
9.34	215, 237		
9.35	238		
9.36-37	159, 187		
9.38-40	57		
9.38	212		
9.40	182		
9.41	182		
9.42-48	99		
9.42	175		
9.47	231		
9.48	140		
9.49-50	57, 159,		
	229		
9.49	182		
9.50	182		
10	166		
10.1-52	181		
10.1-31	132		
10.1-12	57		
10.1	136, 182		
10.2-12	224, 236,		
	237		
10.2-9	181, 214,		
	224		
10.2	136		
10.5	79		
10.10-12	224, 237,		
	239		
10.10	160, 215,		
	238		
10.11-12	175, 224		
10.12	245		
10.13-16	159, 171,		
	187		
10.13-14	212		

Mark (cont.)

10.13	238	11.1-10	132, 160, 175	12.13ff.	160
10.14-15	231	11.1	136, 238	12.13	136, 236
10.17	215, 237	11.2ff.	169	12.14-17	175
10.21	325	11.3	225	12.28-34	224
10.23-25	231	11.9	238, 311	12.29-30	175
10.23	238	11.10	231	12.34	231
10.25	229	11.11	215, 238	12.38-40	175
10.28-31	212	11.12-14	57, 58, 181, 206, 227, 235	12.40-44	57
10.29-30	172, 238			12.41-44	213
10.29	221, 273			12.42	139, 183
10.30	138	11.12	182	12.43	238
10.31	175	11.13-14	211	13	102, 138, 139, 141, 156, 166, 175, 181, 230, 233, 234, 242, 245, 277
10.32-52	135	11.13	140, 159, 245		
10.32-34	132, 138, 245				
10.32	212, 215, 237, 238	11.14	238		
		11.15-19	132, 206		
10.33-34	132, 159, 212, 232, 238, 240	11.15-18	159		
		11.15-17	292	13.1-37	132, 203, 209
		11.15	215	13.1-2	138, 139, 235
10.33	202, 282	11.16	235		
10.35-45	132, 212	11.17	235	13.1	238
10.35-40	57	11.20-25	57, 227	13.3-37	159
10.41-45	238	11.20-23	227, 235	13.3-4	135
10.42-44	175	11.20ff.	181	13.3	135, 215, 239
10.43-45	237	11.21	135		
10.45-52	205	11.22-25	159, 166, 217	13.5-37	242
10.45	138, 175, 233, 238, 240, 317, 318	11.22-23	237	13.5	277
		11.22	212	13.6-8	138
		11.23	166	13.8	138, 277
		11.24-25	237	13.9-13	238, 245
10.46–12.44	203	11.24	182	13.9	138, 202, 277
10.46-52	206, 227, 237	11.25	175, 182		
		11.27–12.40	132, 181, 224	13.10	79, 138, 160, 221-23, 225
10.46	160, 182, 215, 237, 238	11.27-33	162, 172, 224		
				13.11-13	138
10.48	311	11.27	215	13.14	137, 139, 183, 259, 277
10.52	215, 237	11.32	183		
11–16	181, 219	12.1-12	173, 212, 230		
11–13	235			13.17-23	138
11–12	166, 214	12.1-11	181	13.24-31	138
11.1–16.8	205	12.1-9	229, 230	13.24	139
11.1–15.39	206	12.9-11	223	13.26	232
11.1–13.37	205	12.9	139, 237	13.27	223
11.1–12.44	205, 209	12.12	160	13.28-29	175
11.1-33	135	12.13-17	224		

13.28	229			238	15.40-41	206, 207,
13.30	139, 160,	14.46	169			213, 238
	279	14.47	169		15.40	159, 244
13.32-37	135, 138,	14.48	210		15.42–16.8	206
	234	14.49	90		15.42-46	207
13.32ff.	160	14.50	212		15.42	139
13.34-37	175	14.51-52	135, 136,		15.43-46	210
13.34-36	229, 230		160		15.43	231
13.35	140			241	15.47–16.8	207
14–16	160, 241	14.53-72	135, 206		15.47	159, 244
14–15	166, 210,	14.53-54	135		15.51-52	57
	214, 224	14.54	207		15.66-72	208
14	212	14.55-65	208, 235		16.1-8	132, 154,
14.1–15.47	132, 203,	14.58	183, 210,			203, 205,
	205, 209	14.61	241, 315			209, 213
14.1-2	206, 212		232, 276,		16.1	159, 244
14.1	136	14.62	281		16.2-8	169
14.2	245			211	16.4	183, 245
14.3-9	206, 213,	14.63-64	136		16.5	160, 215
	240	14.64	208		16.6-7	210
14.9	221-23	14.65	58, 135,		16.7-8	245
14.10-11	206	14.66-72	207		16.7	135, 140,
14.10	159, 238		136			222, 238,
14.12-16	175	14.66ff.	210			244, 245,
14.12	139, 238	15.5	213			248, 292
14.13-20	239	15.8	213		16.8	21, 183,
14.13	238	15.10	213			215, 244,
14.14	226	15.11	237			245, 248
14.16	238	15.13	139, 213		16.9-20	244
14.17-50	135	15.15	139, 183		16.14	244
14.17-21	206	15.16	206		2.223-38	224
14.17	238	15.20-25	140, 141		22.7-8	210
14.20	159, 238	15.21	136		27.3-10	174
14.22-26	206	15.22	210		27.51-53	169
14.24	240, 318	15.24	210		33.32	238
14.25	231	15.27	208, 235			
14.27-31	206	15.29-30	225		*Luke*	
14.27	183	15.29	213, 225,		1–7	287
14.28	140, 222,	15.31-32	240		1–4	321
	244, 245	15.32	169		1–2	164, 264
14.30-31	136	15.34	136, 183,		1.1-4	68, 258,
14.30	208		210			268
14.32-42	237, 240,	15.37-38	208		1.1	259, 283
	241	15.38	139, 169,		1.2	258
14.32	238		235		1.5	270
14.36	136, 183	15.39	136, 139,		1.15	283
14.41	138, 238		210, 211,		1.27	311
14.43	159, 213,		223, 241		1.32-33	295

Luke (cont.)

1.32	315
1.33-34	311
1.33	311
1.35	283, 316
1.41	283
1.43	308, 309
1.52-53	324
1.52	330
1.53	324, 330
1.54-55	292
1.67	283
1.68-69	292, 295
1.69	311
1.71	284, 295
1.74	295
1.77	284
2.1	269, 270, 273
2.3	272
2.4	311
2.11	284, 309, 320
2.22-24	297
2.23	292
2.25	283
2.29-32	283
2.30-32	292
2.31	287
2.32	287, 317
2.41-51	292
2.49	273
3	274, 320
3.1	264, 269, 273
3.2	297
3.5	287
3.7-9	162, 164
3.7	24
3.9	278, 279
3.11	325
3.12	323
3.22	316
3.23-28	265
3.23ff.	311
4	274, 321, 330
4.1-13	316
4.13	272
4.16-30	276, 282, 286, 287, 289
4.16-21	274
4.17	312
4.18	324
4.21	273, 276, 282, 297, 312
4.23	265, 287
4.24	287, 312
4.25-27	287, 332
4.28-30	300
4.41	315
4.43	273
5.1-11	170
5.11	325
5.27-30	323
5.28	325
6.6	169
6.12-16	58
6.19-31	333
6.20-49	93, 299
6.20-26	172
6.20-21	264
6.20	324, 330
6.21	330, 333
6.22	300
6.24-26	324
6.24	325, 330
6.25	330
6.30	326, 332
6.31	172
6.35	316, 332
7.1-10	33, 46, 288
7.10-17	312
7.11-17	321, 323
7.18-23	227
7.22	324, 334
7.29-30	323
7.30	273
7.34	232, 323
7.36-58	312
7.36-50	240, 323
7.39	312
7.50	284
8	287
8.2-3	323
8.3	331
8.19-21	58
9–28	287
9.1-6	288, 325
9.10-17	333
9.20	20, 313
9.22	273
9.27	276
9.31	137, 314
9.35	314
9.38	169
9.51–18.14	268, 314
9.51	292, 313
9.52	323
9.58	232
10.1-16	288, 325
10.7	278
10.9	278
10.11	278
10.18	274
10.21-22	173, 226, 316
10.23-24	172
10.25	326
10.28	326
10.29-36	324, 326
10.30-35	254
10.37	326
10.38-42	323
11.1	316
11.2-13	299
11.2-4	264
11.5-8	325
11.14-20	274
11.16	169
11.20	174, 227
11.29	166
11.41	326, 332
11.49-51	290, 315
11.49	264
11.50	290
12	279
12.8-9	173
12.8	264, 278
12.9	166
12.10	265

12.13-14	171	17.19	284	22.48	317		
12.16-31	325	17.20-21	172	22.50	169		
12.16-21	330	17.22	317	22.56-62	58		
12.21	331	17.23-37	279	22.67	316		
12.33-34	332	17.24	232	22.69	276, 281,		
12.33	326	17.26-30	232, 279		316		
12.39-40	278	17.31	265	23.2	311		
12.40	232	17.33	159	23.4	290		
12.41-42	308	18.1-8	279	23.13-25	290		
12.42-46	278	18.8	317	23.14	290		
12.51-53	173	18.9-14	323	23.22	290		
13	279	18.9-13	335	23.25	290		
13.1-5	171	18.10-14	254	23.26-33	290		
13.10-17	333	18.14	334	23.27-31	323		
13.16	274	18.22	325	23.34	292, 293		
13.22	268	18.31	282	23.36-37	311		
13.26	290	18.35-43	333	23.39-43	169		
13.27	290	18.38	311	23.42	277		
13.28-30	290	19	34	24	282, 285,		
13.28-29	172	19.1-10	323, 326		301		
13.30	173	19.8	308, 326	24.6-7	292		
13.31-35	226	19.9	284	24.12	261, 262		
13.33	273, 292,	19.10	173, 284,	24.19	313		
	313		317	24.21	313		
13.34-35	315	19.11	276	24.26-27	282, 310		
14.11	334	19.34-35	290	24.26	313		
14.12-14	235, 332	19.38	311	24.34	261		
14.13	334	19.41	290	24.39	301		
14.15	172	19.43	260	24.44-46	282		
14.16-24	254, 288,	19.45-46	292	24.47	288		
	290	19.47	292	24.49	308, 320		
14.21	334	21.8-31	23	24.51	261		
14.33	325	21.8	277	24.53	292		
14.34-35	57	21.12	277				
15.1-32	323	21.20	260, 277	*John*			
15.4	99	21.32	279	1.1	115		
15.7	99	21.36	317	1.19-34	159		
16.1-8	332	22.3	274	2.13-22	159		
16.9	332	22.19-20	261, 262	3.14	115		
16.16	272	22.20	262, 297,	4.46-53	46		
16.18	96		318	6	159, 166		
16.19-31	277, 330	22.22	273, 317	6.1-14	170		
16.25	325	22.27	318	9.22	74		
17	279	22.35	329, 333,	12.1-8	240		
17.3-4	99		340	12.42	74		
17.6	166	22.36	274, 329	14.5	239		
17.10-17	324	22.37	317	14.8	239		
17.11	268	22.42	273	14.22ff.	239		

John (cont.)

16.2	74
18.10	169
19.35	156
21.1-14	170
21.24	156

Acts

1–5	327
1	77
1.1	258, 268
1.6	277
1.7	277
1.8	277, 289
1.15-20	174
1.20	282
1.21-22	156
2	281, 309, 310
2.17-21	281
2.17	281, 308
2.23	273
2.27	310
2.29	310
2.31	310
2.36	310
2.41	293
2.44-46	334
2.44-45	328
3.13	317
3.17	292
3.18	282, 310
3.20	273
3.21	277
3.22-23	313
4.4	293
4.12	284
4.27	317
4.28	273
4.32-37	334
4.32-35	328
4.34	334
4.36	328
5.1-11	328
5.14	293
5.31	320
5.38-39	273
6	76

6.13	76
7	291, 297
7.37	313
7.56	232, 278, 307, 317
7.60	292
8	319
8.1	77
8.26-40	331
8.32-33	317, 319
9.2	215
9.36	328
10.2	328
10.39-41	156
10.41	273
10.42	277
11.19-30	141
11.20	141
11.22-26	141
12.12	134
12.25	134
13	295
13.1	78, 328, 331
13.5	134
13.7	331
13.13	134
13.23	320
13.26	273, 284
13.27	292
13.32	316
13.42	307
13.46	291, 294
15.16-17	282
15.37	134
15.39	134
16.14	328
16.17	284
17.3	282, 310
17.6	270
17.7	311
17.12	328, 331
17.31	277
18.6	291, 294
18.18	297
19.9	215
19.23	215
20.20-21	301

20.25	260
20.27	273
20.28	318
20.29	301
20.30	301
20.35	329, 341
21.14	273
21.20	293
21.23-26	293
21.24-26	297
23.6	293
24.17	328
25.8	293
26.6	293
26.22-23	282
26.23	310
26.26	273
28	293-96, 300
28.24	293
28.26-27	282, 285
28.28	291

Romans

1.1-4	222
1.3	225
3.24	225
4	274
4.3-4	230
5.9-10	284
9–11	274
10.4	225
11.8	230
15.30-31	78
16.13	140

1 Corinthians

1.18-25	225, 240
3.16-17	235
9	78
9.1-2	78
9.1	78
10.1-11	274
10.1-4	225
10.17	225
12.3	225
15.1ff.	156
15.3-11	244

15.3	309	*Ephesians*		*1 Peter*	
15.51	275	3.21	280	5.1	156
				5.13	134, 140
2 Corinthians		*Philippians*			
3	78	1.23	275	*2 Peter*	
3.6	78	2.5-11	309	1.12	156
4.3-4	230	2.6ff.	225	1.15	137
5.2-4	275	4.13	225		
5.16	78			*1 John*	
6.2	273	*Colossians*		1.1-3	156
		4.14	258		
Galatians				*Revelation*	
1.12	78	*1 Thessalonians*		1.13	232
1.15-16	225	4.15	275	1.17-18	173
1.18-19	77			3.20	173
2.11-21	225	*2 Timothy*		4	142
2.11	77, 141,	4.11	134, 258	14.14	232
	225			16.15	173
4.4-6	274	*Philemon*			
4.10	134	24	134, 258		

OTHER ANCIENT REFERENCES

Pseudepigrapha		Josephus		*2 Clement*	
1 Enoch		*Ant.*		7.6	140
48	232	2.205-209	117		
69.26-29	232	2.205	117	*Didache*	
71.14-17	232	2.206	117	11.4	77
		2.210-16	116		
4 Ezra		2.228	116	Eusebius	
13.1-13	232	2.234	117	*Ecclesiastical History*	
		13.171-73	83	3.5.3	138
Qumran		18.11-25	83	3.39.14-16	133
1QS					
1.10-11	96	*War*		Classical Authors	
9.21-22	96	1.5-111-16	100	Cicero	
10.17-18	96	2.58-65	138	*Orator*	
		2.119-66	83	34.120	12
CD		2.184-87	137		
1.9	92	2.192-203	137	Tacitus,	
		6.316	138	*Annals*	
Mishnah		6.392-408	138	14.28	138
Git.				15.13-17	138
9.10	96	Christian Authors		15.44	138
		1 Clement			
		15.2	140		

INDEX OF AUTHORS

Aichele, G. 216
Alexander, L.C.A. 259, 269, 271
Allison, D.C., Jr 42, 114-18, 124
Alter, R. 39
Ambrozic, A.M. 242
Anderson, H. 128, 219
Anderson, J.C. 149
Augustine, St 38
Aune, D.E. 63, 72, 218

Bacon, B.S. 65, 72
Bacon, B.W. 150
Barbour, R. 129
Barclay, J. 93, 108
Barclay, W. 149
Barr, A. 57, 72
Barrett, C.K. 252, 299, 321
Barton, J. 342
Beavis, M.A. 203, 217, 218, 220
Bellinzoni, A.J. 164, 189
Belo, F. 150
Berger, P. 108
Best, E. 63, 72, 79, 149, 186, 191, 219, 243, 248
Betz, H.D. 242
Bilezikian, G.G. 218
Black, C.C. 186, 191, 243
Blatherwick, D. 219
Blevins, J.L. 242
Booth, R.P. 241
Borg, M. 37
Bornkamm, G. 39, 94, 108
Boucher, M. 242
Bovon, F. 252
Boyce, J. 191
Brandon, S.G.F. 150, 248
Brawley, R.L. 302, 303

Broadhead, E.K. 242
Brown, R.E. 90, 114, 124, 129, 265, 271
Buckwalter, H.D. 321
Bultmann, R. 178, 190, 225
Burridge, R.A. 40

Cadbury, H.J. 253, 259, 271
Cadoux, A.T. 189
Caird, G.B. 37, 252, 264
Camery-Hoggart, J. 208, 219
Carroll, J.T. 280, 285
Casey, P.M. 189
Catchpole, D.R. 264, 271
Chatman, S. 197
Chilton, B. 242
Collins, A.Y. 129, 202, 218, 242
Conzelmann, H. 39, 253, 272, 285, 299
Cook, J.G. 219
Cook, M.J. 236, 242
Corner, M.A. 150
Cranfield, C.E.B. 129
Creed, J.M. 252, 319
Crossan, J.D. 37, 190

Dahl, N.A. 283, 285
Danker, F.W. 253
Davey, N. 37
Davies, M. 197
Davies, W.D. 42, 108, 114
Delbanco, A. 37
Denck, H. 106
Derrett, J.D.M. 209, 219
Dewey, J. 39, 191, 195, 206, 217, 219
Dibelius, M. 63, 72, 168, 170, 172, 174, 190

Dodd, C.H. 189
Donahue, J.R. 217, 243, 248
Doudna, J.C. 191
Dowd, S.E. 217
Drury, J.H. 72, 189, 216, 219
Duling, D.C. 149
Dungan, D. 38
Dunn, J.D.G. 39, 241

Edwards, J.R. 207, 219
Edwards, R.A. 69, 72
Elliott, J.H. 150
Ellis, E.E. 252
Ernst, J. 129
Esler, P.F. 253, 300, 303, 333, 336
Evans, C.F. 223, 241, 252, 314, 321

Farmer, W.R. 19, 38, 72, 263, 271
Farrer, A.M. 72, 216
Fenton, J.C. 241
Fiorenza, E.S. 150, 220
Fitzmyer, J.A. 129, 252, 253, 262, 271
Fortna, R.T. 179
Fowler, R.M. 217
Franklin, E. 253, 281
Fuller, R.H. 149
Funk, R.W. 37

Gaston, L. 287, 303
Geddert, T.J. 242
Gnilka, J. 129
Goulder, M.D. 72, 252, 263, 271
Green, J.B. 39, 252, 253
Green, J.R. 243
Griesbach, J.J. 38
Guelich, R.A. 128, 189, 202, 218, 222, 241
Gundry, R.H. 40, 42, 129
Güttgemanns, E. 190

Hadas, M. 218
Haenchen, E. 39, 294, 303
Hagner, D.A. 11, 37
Harrington, D.J. 129
Hawkins, J.C. 38, 191
Hayes, J.H. 206, 216
Hengel, M. 76, 104, 108, 149
Hiers, R.H. 280, 285

Hill, D. 42, 114, 124
Holliday, C.R. 206, 216
Hooker, M.D. 128, 242
Hoover, R.W. 37, 90
Horsley, R.A. 38
Hoskyns, E. 37
Houlden, J.L. 302, 303
Howell, D.B. 69-71, 73
Hull, J.M. 227, 242
Humphrey, H.M. 149
Hurst, L.D. 37
Hurtado, L.W. 40

Iersel, B.M.F. van 129, 220

Jeremias, J. 37, 38
Jervell, J. 303
Johnson, L.T. 314, 321, 331, 336
Jonge, M. de 321
Juel, D. 242, 253

Karris, R.J. 332, 336
Keck, L.E. 253, 322
Kee, H.C. 141, 147, 149, 150, 189, 209, 218, 219, 227, 248
Kelber, W.H. 190, 214, 220, 240, 242, 243
Kennedy, G.A. 194, 195, 217
Kermode, F. 216
Kertelge, K. 221, 242
Kingsbury, J.D. 26, 39, 66, 69, 73, 111-14, 124, 214, 220
Kloppenborg, J.S. 38, 64, 73
Knox, W.L. 189
Koester, H. 40, 190
Kümmel, W.G. 149, 166, 167

Lagrange, M.-J. 130
Lampe, G.W.H. 322
Lane, W.L. 128
Lash, N. 342
Lemcio, E. 37, 40
Levine, A.-J. 32, 40
Licht, J. 217
Lincoln, A.T. 248
Lohmeyer, E. 130
Lührmann, D. 130
Luz, U. 30, 40, 42, 71, 82, 85, 87, 90,

94, 95, 101, 103-106, 108, 120-22, 124

Mack, B.L. 153, 217, 248
Maddox, R. 253, 285, 299, 303
Magness, J.L. 248
Malbon, E.S. 218, 220
Malina, B.J. 150
Maloney, E.C. 191
Mann, C.S. 128
Manson, T.W. 149
Marcus, J. 128, 129, 209, 220
Marshall, C.D. 196, 217
Marshall, I.H. 252, 253, 257, 269, 320
Martin, R.P. 149, 200, 201, 218, 221, 241, 248
Martyn, J.L. 108, 253
Marxsen, W. 39, 149, 190, 221, 225, 241
Matera, F.J. 189, 243, 293, 303
McDonald, J.I.H. 195, 217
McKnight, E.V. 218
McKnight, S. 32, 37-40
Meagher, J.C. 190
Mealand, D.L. 327, 336
Meier, J.P. 38
Meyer, B.F. 37
Michie, D. 39, 196, 210-14, 220
Minear, P.S. 220
Moessner, D.P. 314, 322
Moore, S.D. 149, 214
Morgan, R. 342
Moule, C.F.D. 308, 322
Muilenburg, J. 195
Murphy, R.E. 129
Myers, C. 150

Neirynck, F. 149, 190, 191
Neyrey, J.H. 253
Nineham, D.E. 128, 150, 157, 189
Nolland, J. 252

O'Neill, J.C. 260, 271
Osburn, C.D. 191
Overman, J.A. 84, 89, 91, 92, 100-102, 108
Oyen, G. van 219

Parker, P. 150
Patte, D. 198, 218
Peabody, D.B. 38, 191
Perrin, N. 38, 39, 129, 149, 179, 181, 191, 202, 218, 242
Pesch, R. 130
Petersen, N.R. 39, 207, 216-18, 220, 248
Powell, M.A. 217
Pryke, E.J. 191

Räisänen, H. 242, 303
Reiser, M. 191
Rhoads, D. 39, 196, 197, 210-14, 217, 220
Robbins, V.K. 217, 218, 220
Robinson, J.A.T. 150
Robinson, J.M. 189, 248
Rohde, J. 39
Rowland, C.R. 150

Saldarini, A.J. 39, 108
Salmon, M. 296, 303
Sanday, W. 38
Sanders, E.P. 38, 108, 190, 294, 303
Schmidt, K.L. 63, 73, 190
Schmidt, T.E. 336
Schmithals, W. 130
Schubert, P. 283, 285
Schuler, P.L. 40
Schulz, S. 248
Schweizer, E. 42, 129, 189, 191, 204, 205, 219, 242, 246, 248, 253
Sellew, P. 217
Senior, D. 43, 241
Sergeant, J. 220
Sim, D.C. 108
Smith, M. 190, 218, 242
Smith, S.H. 217
Squires, J.T. 273, 285
Standaert, B. 249
Stanton, G.N. 24, 37, 39, 42, 59, 64, 65, 67, 71, 73, 81, 86, 87, 89, 90, 92
Stegemann, W. 332, 336
Stein, R.H. 39, 178, 191
Stendahl, K. 88, 108
Sterling, G.E. 40

Sternberg, M. 39
Stibbe, M.W.G. 199
Stock, A. 219
Strauss, M.L. 309, 322
Strecker, G. 40
Streeter, B.H. 38, 56, 73, 263-65, 271
Styler, G.M. 164
Sylva, D.D. 322

Talbert, C.H. 40, 200, 219, 253, 301,
    303
Tannehill, R.C. 40, 196, 212, 220, 243,
    252, 267, 303
Tate, W.R. 218
Taylor, V. 129, 264, 265, 271
Telford, W.R. 129, 149, 186, 212, 216,
    222, 235, 241, 242
Theissen, G. 77, 108, 150, 249
Thompson, M.R. 211, 217, 220
Tiede, D.L. 283, 285
Tolbert, M.A. 218, 219
Trilling, W. 98, 108
Trocmé, E. 189
Tuckett, C.M. 38, 242, 262, 264, 271,
    308, 311, 317, 322, 342
Turner, C.H. 191

Turner, H.E.W. 150
Tyson, J.B. 239, 243, 253, 303

Vermes, G. 11, 37, 38
Via, D.O., Jr 218, 219
Vorster, W.S. 217, 220, 243
Votaw, C.W. 40, 201, 219

Waetjen, H.C. 147, 249
Watson, F. 16, 39
Weatherly, J.A. 293, 303
Weeden, T.J. 218, 243, 249
Wellhausen, J. 130
Wenham, D. 243
Werner, M. 241
White, E.B. 20
Williams, M.C. 40
Wills, L.M. 219
Wilson, S.G. 280, 285, 303
Wrede, W. 124, 228, 242
Wright, N.T. 12, 37, 38

York, J.O. 334, 336

Ziesler, J.A. 220

EASTERN SEMINARY LIBRARY

3 9900 1001 3027 3